THE PELICAN HISTORY OF ART
Founding Editor: Nikolaus Pevsner
Joint Editors: Peter Lasko and Judy Nairn

Axel Boëthius
ETRUSCAN AND EARLY ROMAN ARCHITECTURE
Revised by Roger Ling and Tom Rasmussen

Axel Boëthius, born in 1889, in 1921–4 worked on the excavations at Mycenae.
In 1925 he became the first Director of the Swedish Institute in Rome. Thereafter Rome
was to be his second home and Roman topography and architecture the main
interests of a busy working life. After serving as Professor and subsequently as Rector
Magnificus of the University of Göteborg, he retired to Rome to settle. He died
in 1969, soon after passing the page proofs of the present volume which, taken in con-
junction with the published version of his Jerome Lectures (*The Golden House of
Nero*, 1960), is the culmination of, and an enduring memorial to, a lifetime's interest
and research.

Axel Boëthius

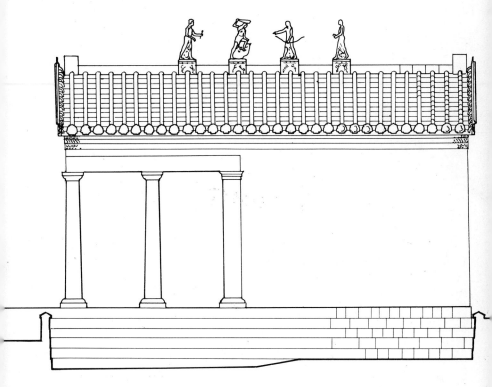

Etruscan and Early Roman Architecture

Penguin Books

Penguin Books Ltd, Harmondsworth, Middlesex, England
Penguin Books, 625 Madison Avenue, New York, New York 10022, U.S.A.
Penguin Books Australia Ltd, Ringwood, Victoria, Australia
Penguin Books Canada Limited, 2801 John Street, Markham, Ontario, Canada L3R 1B4
Penguin Books (N.Z.) Ltd, 182–190 Wairau Road, Auckland 10, New Zealand

First published as Part One of *Etruscan and Roman Architecture* 1970
Second integrated edition published under the title
Etruscan and Early Roman Architecture 1978

Library of Congress Cataloging in Publication Data
Boëthius, Axel, 1889–1969.
    Etruscan and early Roman architecture.
    (The Pelican history of art)
    Earlier ed. published in 1970 under title:
Etruscan and Roman architecture.
    Bibliography: p. 247.
    Includes index.
    1. Architecture—Italy—Etruria. 2. Architecture—Rome.
I. Ling, Roger. II. Rasmussen, Tom. III. Title. IV. Series.
NA300.B63   1978   722'.7   78–1875
ISBN 0 14 0561.44 7 (paperback)

Phototypeset in Monophoto Ehrhardt
Printed in Great Britain by
Fletcher & Son Ltd, Norwich
Bound by Richard Clay (The Chaucer Press) Ltd,
Bungay, Suffolk

Designed by Gerald Cinamon

CONTENTS

FOREWORD TO THE SECOND EDITION

This work appeared originally in 1970 as Part One of a combined volume on Etruscan and Roman architecture. For various reasons – among them ease of handling – it has been decided that for the second edition the volume should be split into two, one on the Etruscan and Republican period, the other on the Imperial. The latter, revised by its author, John Ward-Perkins, will appear in due course.

For the first edition, Professor Boëthius received invaluable help from a circle of friends and helpers far too wide to name individually, though Professor Arvid Andrén, who undertook the laborious task of seeing the book through the press in its final stages, and for the illustrations, Dr Ernest Nash in Rome, and Miss Sheila Gibson who executed the drawings with such enthusiasm, insight, and skill, must be singled out for special thanks.

For the second edition the book has been fortunate in the meticulous care of its revisers, Tom Rasmussen and Roger Ling. Dr Rasmussen was responsible for Chapters 1-4 and Dr Ling for Chapters 5-6 (though each suggested emendations in the other's section). Their prime concern has been to attempt to bring the Notes and Bibliography up to date. Most of the revision has been carried out through the Notes, where square brackets indicate the more important additions; of necessity only minor alterations could be made to the text. Warm thanks are extended to Professor C. E. Östenberg for supplying illustration 52.

NIKOLAUS PEVSNER

The dimensions throughout are expressed both in feet and inches and in metres and centimetres. In all cases it is the latter figure which is that of the original text.

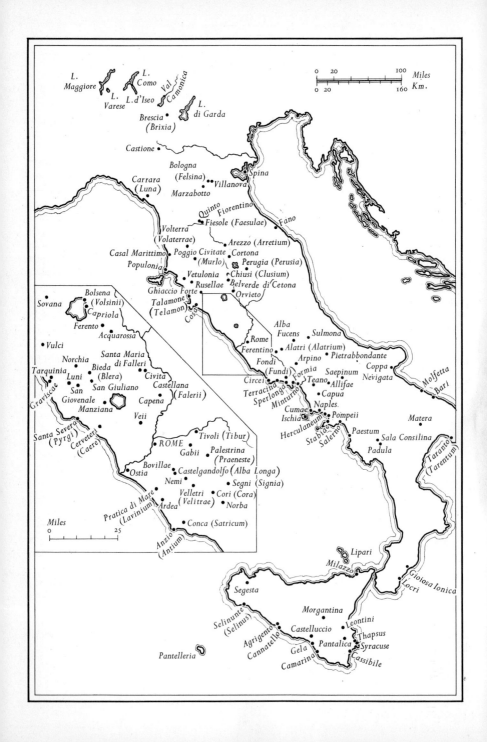

CHAPTER I

THE STONE AND BRONZE AGES

Dociles vires are the splendid words with which Pliny in his *Historia Naturalis* (XXXVI, 101) characterizes the achievements of the Romans as architects and town-planners. The words emphasize on the one hand their capacity to learn from others, and on the other their strength in adapting and reshaping their borrowings according to the traditions and demands of their own life and society. The process was not one of using undigested elements from the Greeks and the Orient, nor of retaining the petrified remains of old Italic lore; all indigenous traditions as well as foreign loans were gradually transmuted into a new unity with its own capabilities for development.

The final result of these eight hundred years of endeavour (as Pliny puts it) was the Late Republican and Augustan architecture of Rome, the hellenized Italic architecture which Vitruvius in the fifth book of his *De architectura* styles *consuetudo italica*. It was destined to be of the greatest importance for the common Mediterranean architecture of the Roman Empire when, after Sulla and Caesar, the old world became a mighty cultural unity, a Roman κοινή, with contributions from all its lands. For a full understanding of this Roman architecture as it appears in remains from the Augustan Age and the first centuries A.D., and as it will be found described in the fifth and sixth chapters of this book, it seems necessary to study its background in oldest Italy, and in the Orient, Greece, and the Etruscan city-states of the eighth and following centuries.

The history of ancient Italy differs fundamentally from that of Greece. Italy inherited no higher culture, no great memories and legends from the Bronze Age. Further, Italy had no Early Iron Age comparable with the Greece of the Geometric Period and of Homer; indeed, Roman authors very often delight in describing the primitive simplicity of Old Latium with its shapeless wooden gods and their simple dwellings (καλιάδες) – if, indeed, they had any huts and images at all[1] – its pastoral life in green valleys, its poor pottery or wooden cups.

Typical, for instance, are Vergil's descriptions in the *Aeneid* (VIII, 359–69) of the poor home of Evander on the Palatine, and of the couch of leaves covered by a Libyan bearskin upon which 'big Aeneas' slept. Equally suggestive is Propertius's picture of the Rome of Romulus and Remus in the first elegy of his fourth book. Modern archaeological research proves that this rustic, albeit romantic, conception of prehistoric life in Italy was substantially correct. But occasionally poets and historians also tried to recast the early history of their country in a heroic Greek mould. Undisturbed by the current rustic conception, they describe great palaces – like that of Latinus in Vergil's description of Laurentum (*Aeneid*, VII, 170 ff.) – and attribute to them impregnable walls and mighty gates. The descriptions of this and other palaces of the *Aeneid* are based on hellenistic models, however, and have no true archaic basis whatever. Moreover, again and again it becomes clear that their heroic wars fought by mighty armies were really nothing more than quarrels about damaged crops and stolen cattle which disturbed the peace between petty city-states and villages of the Campagna. The real background to the history of Roman architecture is the millennial cultural twilight and rude primitivism of Western Europe before the Phoenicians, Etruscans, and Greeks brought eastern culture to the far and barbaric Hesperian coasts of the eighth century B.C.

It has to be remembered that trade from the glorious Minoan and Mycenaean Bronze Age of Greece reached south Italy. The northernmost outposts in Italy of this trade with the great eastern cultural world, as far as we know at present, are Ischia and Luni (Monte Fortino), in a central position on the River Mignone south-west of Viterbo, but recent research has shown that influence from the Mycenaean world reached even as far as Stonehenge. A real problem which remains to be explained is why only superficial influence from this high eastern culture can be traced even in the south of Italy. It is true that the south of the peninsula enjoyed somewhat less barbarous conditions than central and northern Italy, even in the Stone Age, and that it had more contact with the civilized world; but barbarous it was and barbarous it remained all the same, right down to the later Iron Age.

The influences from the Near East and Greece towards the end of the eighth century made a clear break with the past and marked the arrival of a new era, in total and evident contrast to the Bronze Age. As we see it, the pioneers were Phoenician traders and also – as Geometric vases show and Homer describes – Greek adventurers like Odysseus. After them came Greek colonists. Thus the high culture from the east attained a strong position in the distant barbaric land and at the same time met with a people prepared to receive it – the Etruscans. From the seventh century the art and architecture of the Etruscan and archaic Greek city-states conquered central Italy, and provided Rome and the Latin towns with new means of expressing the spirit of their commonwealth.

The aim of the first chapters of this book is to contribute to the discussion about the relation between these overwhelming foreign cultural influences and local architectural traditions, by means of a factual survey of what the builders of the settlements of the Stone, Bronze, and Early Iron Ages had achieved in central Italy, and especially in Latium and Etruria (the Lazio and Tuscany of future ages). What we know about these attainments proves that those early periods of central Italy belonged to the ageless prehistoric barbarian life of Western Europe. They were barren and poor in their architecture. Antiquated evolutionistic and nationalistic

doctrine has tried to establish that the architecture and town planning of the historical periods were heralded in the primitive gropings of the Stone, Bronze, and Early Iron Ages; but as soon as we succeed in sweeping away the cobwebs, we see plainly that the Italians, not only in the eighth century but right through the great ages of Roman history, received rather than created the external forms of higher architecture. There is, however, another kind of originality which one feels in almost all their architecture: a mood, an indigenous social tradition; in short, the inner *vires* of which Pliny speaks.

A study of the prehistoric villages reveals the conditions in which the new imported culture developed. Diodorus's description of the Ligurians of the Augustan Age, who spent their nights 'in the fields, rarely in a kind of rude shanty, more often in the hollows of rocks and in natural caves which may offer them sufficient protection', could apply equally to Neolithic and Eneolithic life, so far as the remains permit us to judge. More important for an explanation of traditions persisting in the daily life of later ages is the evidence for clusters of huts. The most common huts of these primitive villages had conical roofs. They were circular or elliptical, with fireplaces in the centre, and made of wicker- or branch-work, covered with clay or perhaps sometimes with skins. Just like many buildings of the Bronze and Iron Ages, they were sometimes half sunk in the ground, sometimes more or less on ground level. Already in this early age, cave burials could be replaced by rock-cut tombs imitating huts. Here is the beginning of an architectural tradition of great importance for south Italy, Sicily, and Sardinia.

In south Italy rectangular huts of the Neolithic Age have also been found. Thus excavations on Pantelleria have revealed such huts with foundations of several layers of flat stones. At Molfetta (Apulia) a network of crooked, paved paths ties together the huts of a Stone Age village. Both in Sicily (Cannatello) and in south Italy (Coppa Nevigata) a tendency to create an open central area can be traced.[2]

Stone Age stratification has in our times been recognized in different parts of central Italy too, even near Rome; Luni affords an especially clear example, with Chalcolithic (Rinaldone) and Apennine layers appearing above the Stone Age stratum. Recently, aerial photographs of the coast of southern Etruria, south of Montalto di Castro, have shown round villages with protecting earthen ramparts akin to the great concentrations of Neolithic settlements found in Apulia on the Foggia plain (Tavoliere) and near Matera. On the Tavoliere over two hundred roughly circular sites with one to eight enclosure ditches have been traced [1]. The largest

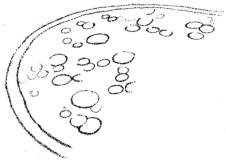

1. Tavoliere, near Foggia, settlement, Neolithic. Plan

(Passo di Corvo) measures about 550 by 875 yards. Inside these enclosure ditches lie smaller circular enclosures, individually surrounded by ditches of sizes varying from some 50 to 150 feet across. In the largest villages more than a hundred 'compounds' of this kind have been identified; smaller 'homesteads' contain only a few. No doubt dwellings were built within these enclosures for family groups and their cattle. The enclosure openings usually have the same general orientation, probably pointing towards the main entrance to the village. Otherwise no regular planning appears inside the great enclosures, and it must be noted that the villages of Latium and inland Etruria even of the Bronze and Iron Ages have not up to now afforded us any instances of regular external shapes such as

those of the Apulian sites and the coast of Etruria, nor of planning of any kind.[3]

For the purpose of this survey of the earliest architectural endeavours in central Italy, it would be an unnecessary digression to enter upon the much disputed questions concerning the population of Italy during the Stone and Bronze Ages. The country originally was inhabited probably by very sparse non-Indo-European tribes. At the beginning of historical times, peoples speaking Indo-European languages, with Latin, Faliscan, Umbro-Sabellic dialects, Oscan, and so on, predominated in central Italy, except in Etruria, where Etruscan was spoken by the entire population. To this may be added that many scholars believe, with Dionysius of Halicarnassus, the Greek historian of the Augustan Age (I, 30), that the Etruscans were descendants of the Italian pre-Indo-European tribes.

From the point of view of architecture there is no break between the Neolithic, Eneolithic, and Bronze Age periods. A really new *facies*, a clear progress beyond this primitive life in caves and wattle-and-daub huts, appears after about 1500 B.C. with the so-called Apennine culture. The Apennine culture used to be called 'extra terramaricolan'. On the Aeolian islands it is called Ausonian, and in Morgantina in Sicily Morgetian; roughly contemporary were the so-called Terramare villages in the Po valley. Of course, even this new culture was still barbaric compared with the grandiose palaces of Malta, the Minoan and Mycenaean palaces of the second millennium, and even the earliest nuraghi of Sardinia, which remained a distant horizon [6].

It has been suggested that the Apennine culture was a product of early Indo-European infiltration and represents a new racial situation created by the crossing of the immigrants with the old population. Furthermore, it has been assumed that the tribes which spread the Apennine culture over central and southern Italy were more or less nomadic shepherds, using tombs as rallying places – as were the royal tombs of the Scythians, according to Herodotus

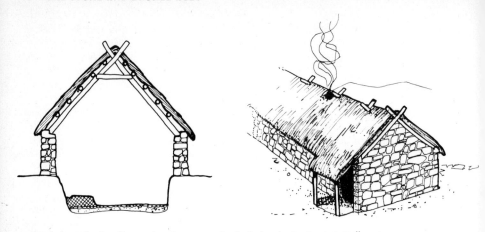

2. Luni, Apennine hut, Bronze Age. Reconstruction by Jerker Asplund and C. E. Östenberg

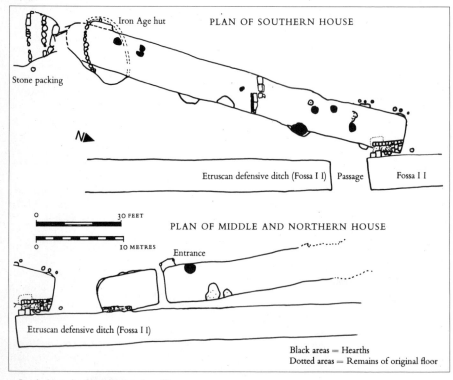

3. Luni, Apennine huts, Bronze Age. Plan

(IV, 71 f.). In Apulia, from Gargano in the north to Lecce and its neighbourhood in the south, megalithic tombs and dolmens exist akin to those of Spain, southern France, Corsica, Sardinia, and Africa, and they could have been centres of this kind. Rock-cut tombs in the neighbourhood of Bari, accessible by a vertical shaft leading down to the door of a subterranean cave, have rightly been compared with the huts of the Bedouins and referred to as reproductions of nomads' cots.

Although some of the Apennine people may have been pastoral, remains of permanent residences with agriculture and pasture-farming are typical features of the Apennine culture of central Italy. On a hill near Bolsena, called Capriola, close to Early Iron Age settlements, remains of several Apennine huts have been found. Rock-cut foundations attest to oval wattle-and-daub huts. Of great importance is the Apennine village on the acropolis of Luni, which can be dated to the centuries between 1400 and 1100 by fragments of Late Mycenaean (Late Helladic) pottery in the Apennine stratification [2, 3]. Here we meet with rectangular houses of considerable size; the largest is 138 feet long and 16 feet wide (42 by 5 m.). As in so many prehistoric buildings, their lower parts are cut down into the rock. The floors of rammed clay above a bottom layer of limestone chips lie from about 3 to 7 feet below the surface. The walls seem to have been built of rough stones and roofs were of straw or reeds. Indoors, fireplaces, portable cooking-stands and other earthenware, hand mills, bread-wheat, barley, beans, and peas have been found. The finds of bones indicate that the villagers of Luni had more cattle and pigs than goats and sheep. In short, Luni shows us in the clearest possible way how people settled and built their houses in central Italy in the centuries around 1300. Probably a rock-cut chamber tomb on the southern slope of the acropolis belonged to this village. It seems to prove connexions with the large number of rock-cut chamber tombs of southern Italy and Sicily. Below the medieval castle on the neighbouring acropolis of San Giovenale, south-west of Viterbo, where later a great Villanovan village and an Etruscan town were built, a deep stratification starting with Apennine layers and continuing through sub-Apennine times has been studied. All the layers show floors of rammed clay and postholes of huts. In one hut, which was oval, a bed of pebbles from the near-by river is laid along the inside of the wall, as also in Bronze Age villages at Manfria near Gela, and still in shepherds' huts in Sicily (below, p. 79 and Note 52).

Excavations south of the Capitoline Hill on the Forum Boarium (by the church of S. Omobono) prove that Rome also belonged to the Apennine settlements of central Italy and that her history started at least as early as about 1500 or 1400 B.C. Finds of pottery near Civitavecchia attest the existence of Apennine villages along the coast. Added to this are Apennine finds from the districts round Veii and Clusium (Chiusi), and scattered finds from the Faliscan district (round Civita Castellana). Thus we can conclude that Apennine hamlets of the type of Luni and Capriola were scattered over the area of the later Latin and Etruscan Iron Age culture during the second half of the second millennium B.C.

Towards the end of the Apennine culture we meet with strongholds fortified with wide walls of irregular blocks. It seems that the Apennine tribes, assaulted by invaders about 1000, needed *points d'appui*. One of these was Coppa Nevigata in Apulia on the Bay of Manfredonia, with walls nearly 20 feet wide, which long served as a place of resort for the Apennine people. The same seems likely regarding the rather primitive walls of Casa Carletti, near the Apennine village of Belverde in Tuscany, where there are fortified sites with dwellings comparable to those of the hill towns on the Aeolian islands and other Bronze Age strongholds of southern Italy and Sicily.

The isolated yet prosperous life of the Aeolian islands met with a sudden change after about 1250. An Apennine culture from the mainland, here called Ausonian I and II, apparently supplanted the old culture, evidently in connexion with an invasion of mainland people. The same happened in Sicily. On the acropolis of Lipari 'Ausonian' foundations, both oval and roughly square and denoting huts generally built of wood on stone, replace the older type from about 1800. This, incidentally, confirms that the Apennine tribes did live in permanent villages.

As we have seen, finds of Late Mycenaean pottery prove that after about 1400, sailors from the highly civilized kingdoms of the palaces of Cnossos, Mycenae, Tiryns, and Pylos, from Rhodes and Cyprus, came to the coasts of Sicily, to south Italy, and as far north as the Aeolian islands and Ischia. They may have been on their way to France and Spain, in search of obsidian from Lipari, copper from Sardinia, ores from the mines of Etruria, and other raw materials; perhaps they were also looking for slaves, as in Homeric days (*Od.*, XXIV, 211, 366, 389), from Sicily and elsewhere. Directly or by intermediaries this trade reached the interior of Sicily (Morgantina) and also – as the finds from Luni have already shown us – the interior of Etruria.[4]

In Sicily the so-called 'Anaktoron' at Pantalica, near Syracuse, is one construction which reveals influence from the Mycenaean palaces [4]. What remains is foundations of a rectangular building measuring about 116 by 40 feet,

built of large polygonal blocks and divided into several rooms. However, a dispassionate judgement of the known archaeological material warns us not to conjure up 'empires' and 'palaces' even here: it seems safer to avoid a terminology suggesting more than a rather primitive coalescence of villages and local improvements, even if it is true that not only the 'Anaktoron' but also the rock-hewn chamber tombs in Sicily and south Italy enhance the impression of a rising level of civilization and of influence from the Mycenaean east. At Cassibile, Pantalica, and Thapsus in Sicily hundreds of rock-cut tombs, sometimes with several chambers and with elaborately carved and decorated door jambs, have been discovered. In an earlier period entrance doorways to tombs at Castelluccio (Noto) were closed with stone slabs and decorated with spiral motifs vaguely resembling Maltese reliefs of the Tarxien period. All this may indicate that the houses had some decoration as well. Rough beehive tombs in Sicily prove that this important kind of architecture reached Italy in the period of the Mycenaean connexions. Further, when we encounter corbel-vaults in the nuraghi in Sardinia [5], and much later in the Etruscan tholos tombs, we must ask ourselves whether they were more or less distantly connected with

4. Pantalica, near Syracuse, 'Anaktoron', Bronze Age. Plan

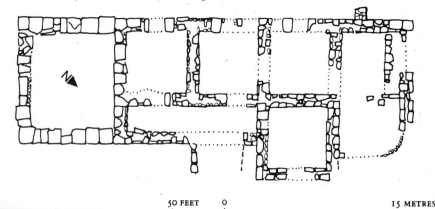

0   50 FEET   0   15 METRES

Mycenaean influence, or whether they were derived from independent origins. Traditions of early tholos architecture in Italy very likely live on today in the corbelled stone huts (truddhi, trulli) for shepherds and tools in the fields of Apulia and Sicily and in the strange beehive houses of Alberobello and its environs.[5]

No doubt Mycenaean sailors, with their ships and the tools and pottery on them, brought rudiments of the achievements of Bronze Age Greece to the Italic peoples. All the same, when discussing architecture, it is no understatement to say that nowhere in Italy did the ships from the east encounter a state of life sufficiently mature to partake in the high cultures of Mycenaean Greece.

On the northern outskirts of the Apennine culture in central Italy there appear, besides the cave-dwellers of Liguria already referred to, the much discussed lake dwellings of the Alpine and sub-Alpine districts and hut villages of the Po valley, generally described as 'Terramare', because of the black earth of their refuse dumps, or 'palafitte arginate'.

The story of the Terramare starts about 1500. It seems likely that immigrants came from Hungary at that time, bringing with them a vigorous primitive culture with a fine metal industry (probably connected with Austrian copper mines) and refined pottery with varied shapes and decoration, evidently evolved in a well-established tradition developed elsewhere, as was no doubt also the social organization. The Terramare villages were supported on piles, just like Spina and Ravenna in centuries to come (Strabo, V. 1. 7). Sometimes they were protected against the floods of the Po valley by moats, ramparts of earth, and even timber constructions, the 'gabbioni'. Typical of the Terramare sites are cemeteries, also protected by moats and with pile substructures, containing close-packed cinerary urns. It seems quite possible that the first Terramare colonists brought with them the custom of cremation.

The Terramare huts were round or rectangular. Open spaces, very likely used for cattle, always seem to have occupied the centre of the villages. But the shapes of the villages varied, and without new complete excavations nothing can be claimed as certain about them. The regular plans which have been widely reproduced and believed typical are all imaginary reconstructions, and all that has been claimed for them as prototypes for the regular towns which we shall meet with in Italy in the sixth century B.C. has no solid foundation.[6]

Among the achievements of these early ages which have never since been forgotten should be mentioned the timber constructions and corner joints in the gabbioni of Castione and the living-platform made with uprights and a floor of planks in the Grotta di Pertosa near Salerno.

The so-called lake dwellings around Lago Maggiore, Lago di Varese, Lago di Como, and Lago d'Iseo, and, farther east, the peat-bog villages of Lago di Timon and Arquà Petrarca are all older than the Terramare. It is almost certain that these lake dwellings were not built on artificial islands in the lakes but on the shores. They represent, in any case, a social organization to be compared with the circular villages in Apulia: building plots on piles with straight streets paved with planks and a common entrance. The huts were quadrangular cabins of logs and planks.

From the transitional phase between the Bronze and Early Iron Ages and through the centuries right down to the Roman conquest of 16 B.C., one has also to remember the carvings chiselled into the rocks of the Alpine mountainside in the valley of Camonica. They represent a highly characteristic log-cabin architecture.[7]

All this provides a distant background to what Vitruvius tells us about timber houses in countries 'where there are forests in plenty', and about a tower, made of larch planks, in the neighbourhood of the Alps (II, 1. 4; 9. 15).

The Terramare villages of the Po valley, the fairly rich Apennine culture of south Italy and its Mycenaean relations, and the Apennine villages in the country between the Tiber and the Arno were the centres of architectural activity on the mainland of Italy during the Bronze Age. Looking down from Populonia,

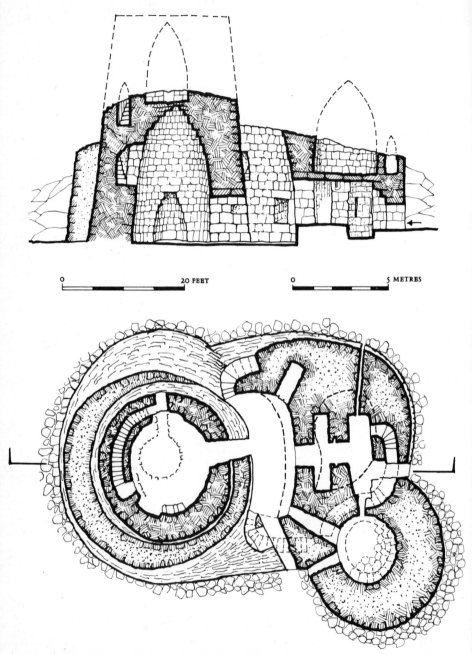

0   20 FEET   0   5 METRES

5. Palmavera, Sardinia, nuraghe, Bronze Age. Section and plan

one of the later hill towns of the Apennine district of central Italy, one can see distant Sardinia, as Strabo (v, 2. 6) remarks before entering on his charming description of that rich island. But there is an amazing contrast between the architecture and culture of Sardinia and the Apennine villages some 100 miles east of the island, a contrast much the same as that between the Apennine villages and Malta. About seven thousand nuraghi are known in Sardinia [5]. They were the most conspicuous architectural achievements of the great period of Bronze Age culture on the island from about 1500 onwards. The nuraghi were towers on hills above the plains, built all over the island within sight of each other and obviously representing a carefully planned system of defence. The oldest nuraghi were isolated circular towers of truncated conical form, containing two (or even three) corbelled round chambers set one above the other. They were constructed of blocks reminiscent of later Italian cyclopean walls. To the nuraghi belonged villages with stone-built, circular, corbel-vaulted huts [6].

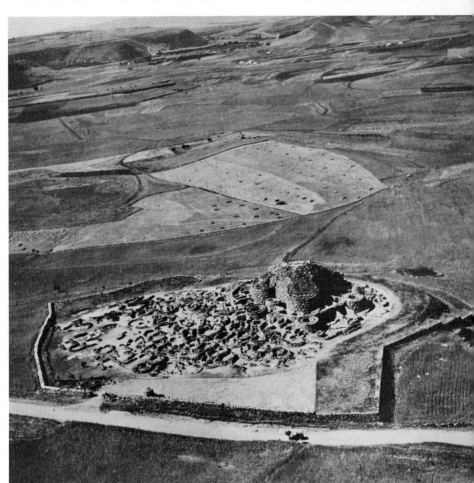

6. Su Nuraxi di Barumini, Sardinia, nuraghe, dating from *c.* 1500 B.C. and onwards

The impressive Sardinian bronze figurines, both of warriors in fantastic attire and of ordinary people, seem to show Etruscan and Greek influence and to illustrate the later periods of life in and around the nuraghi. Bastions and extensive additional fortifications which we now see around the nuraghi are remains of continued efforts to strengthen the old fortresses and use them in the stubborn resistance of the Sardinians against the Phoenicians, Carthaginians, Greeks, and finally – from the third century onwards – the Romans. Only the Roman conquest ended the free existence and Bronze Age traditions of the mountaineers of the central parts of Sardinia – one of the first instances of an interesting local culture yielding to the style of the Roman Empire. The Etruscan tholoi [95, 96] (below, p. 96 ff.) may perhaps have had some direct or indirect connexions with the corbelled vaults of the nuraghi. Otherwise we can only state the strange fact that the great Bronze Age architecture of Sardinia and Malta, so far as we can see, belonged to a quite different sphere from the Bronze Age settlements on the mainland of Italy. The Tyrrhenian Sea was the dividing line. Even the people of Iron Age Etruria seem to have made only occasional contacts with the western islands, and the Greeks never colonized Sardinia. What was, in fact, of great importance for the Sardinians, from the eighth century onwards, was the influence of the Phoenicians and Carthaginians, who built great towns with conspicuous sanctuaries on the coastal plains and penetrated inwards towards the villages of the nuraghi. The first contacts seem to have been quite peaceful, but later the resistance arose which has just been mentioned. In any case, it is significant that the Romans of Late Republican times called the cultivated Sardinians of the coast 'Punici', but used various tribal names for the despised people of the old nuraghi in the rugged interior.[8]

CHAPTER 2

THE EARLY IRON AGE

The Apennine and sub-Apennine hut builders of central Italy, whether they were partly Indo-Europeans or a local race destined to become absorbed by new invading Indo-European tribes, no doubt bequeathed some technical knowledge to the more developed architecture of the Iron Age. They may also have cut chamber tombs, as suggested on p. 13; but their architectural legacy was all the same inconsiderable. In spite of Mycenaean influence, dolmens, strongholds, and the variety of chamber tombs, not even south Italy and Sicily impress us as having reached any higher degree of cultural or architectural capability. But it seems that a new era began in the tenth or ninth century. A still primitive but all the same remarkably vigorous Iron Age culture spread over central Italy in the eighth century. At Luni (Monte Fortino) and on the western part of the acropolis of San Giovenale one sees uncommonly well how huts of a new kind were built above the Apennine villages [12, 13]. This new culture is usually called the Villanovan culture, after the first great finds at Villanova, near Bologna; but as the new types of dwelling show great variation, Early Iron Age culture is perhaps a preferable name, taking into account also the related types of the culture in the southern parts of Italy [14]. It was very rich around Tarquinia in the eighth century, but had a poorer character in Latium.

For central Italy the Early Iron Age culture meant a great reversal of conditions, the first revolution in a development which resulted in the changed appearance of the country in Etruscan and Roman times. New villages were built on hills, defensible by steep scarps, rivers, and ravines filled with brushwood. Extensive cemeteries prove a large population. Many of these large hill villages were to have a great future in Etruscan and Roman times, and in some cases have survived to our own days. It seems evident that villages on the Palatine and other hills were the first inhabited areas of this kind in Rome; in the seventh and sixth centuries Rome gradually united the settlements on the surrounding Esquiline and Quirinal Hills and also the Caelian, creating a civic and religious centre for them all on the future Forum Romanum. Already before that time, the Palatine village extended towards the forum over what had been its old cemetery along the Via Sacra. Remains of important Early Iron Age villages of the same kind have been studied on the Alban and other hills of Latin towns, such as Ardea, Lavinium (Pratica di Mare), Tibur (Tivoli), and on the future Etruscan sites of Veii, Caere (Cerveteri), Tarquinia, Vulci, Luni, San Giovenale, and others.

The tombs of these towns are to a great extent cremation tombs with ash urns in roughly circular shafts (*pozzi, pozzetti*). The urns and tomb gifts, such as terracotta vases, miniature cooking stands, fibulas, razors, and so forth, could be placed directly in the pozzetti, but frequently they were preserved in terracotta *dolia* [7],

7. Pozzo tomb from the Via Sacra, Rome, Early Iron Age. *Rome, Antiquarium Forense*

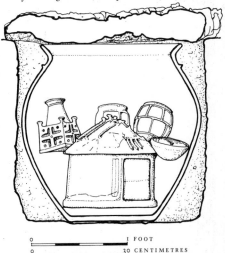

```
0                              1 FOOT
0                              30 CENTIMETRES
```

sometimes in stone receptacles or in rough rectangular coffins of stone slabs. In a tomb at Velletri in the Alban Hills the shaft is corbel-vaulted with tufa blocks, which is noteworthy [8]. One wonders whether it had any connexion

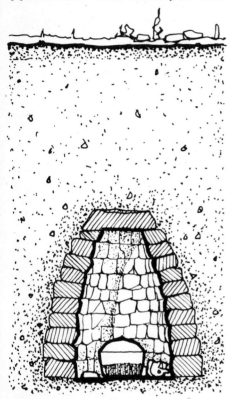

8. Velletri, Vigna d'Andrea, corbel-vaulted tomb, Early Iron Age. Section

with the larger Bronze Age structures of the same kind in Greece or was inspired by the tholos architecture of the Etruscans.

Rock-cut fossa tombs also occur, and sometimes contain coffins of oak trunks or even of terracotta imitating a tree-trunk. Iron Age Tibur (Tivoli) had a cemetery with fossa tombs of the seventh century and earlier, which are surrounded by travertine slabs forming grave circles with a diameter of 10 to 16 feet. The slabs

are about 12 inches high and 16 to 20 inches wide. Together with grave circles of the Apennine districts, they remind us of both primitive and highly developed Mycenaean grave circles, as well as of the later Etruscan *tombe a circolo*. At Vetulonia we meet with both Iron Age and Etruscan grave circles. The former are surrounded by rough unhewn blocks which herald the cyclopean and polygonal walls of later periods.[1]

These Early Iron Age villages had new, more forcible, and artistically more valuable crafts producing imposing biconical ash urns covered by helmets (or clay models of helmets) or by lids imitating roofs, ash urns reproducing huts [14–17], and above all richly developed metalwork, including helmets, shields, fibulas, and other ornaments. Life in central Italy tended to wider horizons. It is evident that the new Iron Age villages were centres for improved farming and metal-mining.

As far as archaeological evidence can tell, this development unified central Italy. It came into existence within the pale of Apennine culture and probably often in competition with the Apennine villages. The villages of the Early Iron Age converted the mainland of Italy, in a much more radical way, to a new manner of life and habitation. In this context the clearly connected but much more variegated and rich culture south of Latium must be considered, as we can see from biconical ash urns and finds of impasto ceramics from Padula, Sala Consilina [14], the Sele valley, Milazzo on the mainland of Sicily south of Lipari, and many other places.[2] The old explanation that this great change was due to a final Indo-European invasion is probably true, and may show the process by which Italy assumed its ultimate Indo-European shape. On the other hand, recent research makes it more and more probable that the Indo-European-Italic peoples of whom we know before Rome's final Latinization of Italy about 100 B.C. (the Umbrians, Sabines, Latins, Sabellic tribes, Oscans, etc.) received their characteristic ethnographic and cultural character, known from historic times, in Italy, by mingling with the probably rather sparse Bronze Age population which was perhaps to some extent already Indo-European.

When the Romans tried to visualize these old villages, they cherished stories of a round or quadrangular primitive Rome.[3] Nothing has substantiated such ancient tales about regular town planning in the Early Iron Age settlements nor the modern theories about it. It should be noted that no Villanovan village known at present displays regularity of town planning, externally or internally. Groups of huts were built on hills which offered a common natural defence – *nativa praesidia*, to use Cicero's expression (*De republica*, II, 6). Like the Apennine peoples, the Villanovans sometimes strengthened the defences of their hill-

small rough blocks of the local calcareous stone was built. A stretch of nearly a third of a mile of the wall is still to be seen, in some places some 10 feet high. A road, constructed upon a terrace wall of the same material as the enceinte, leads to the village. This strongly fortified Early Iron Age centre is indeed an early and interesting predecessor of Etruscan defensive works, especially those of Rusellae of about 600 B.C. (see p. 68). Bologna, on the other hand, offers an instance of a great Villanovan village built on a plain. The physical features of the Po valley make that, needless to say, very understandable.

In this connexion it has to be remembered that, even in Imperial times, when the Romans planned to build a colony they traced with a plough drawn by a bull and a cow yoked to-

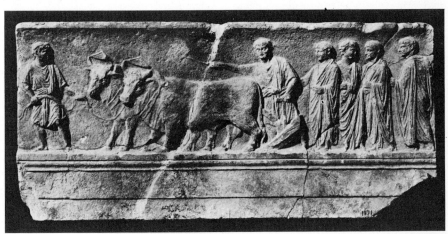

9. Relief from Aquileia showing the foundation of a colonia, fixing its border by means of a trench made by plough. Imperial Age. *Aquileia, Museo Archeologico*

sides. Most conspicuous is a place called Città Danzica south of Rapino in the country of the Samnite tribe of the Marrucini.[4] It is a big hill measuring about 3 miles from north to south and half a mile to a mile from east to west. On this plateau are dense remains of an Early Iron Age village. The western part of the settlement was defended by the steep sides of the hill, but all along the eastern side, where the slope is smooth and open to assault, a protecting wall of

gether a continuous furrow with an earthen wall on its inner side [9]. Plutarch (*Romulus*, XI) adds that a brazen ploughshare should be used, which seems to prove that the custom was very old – but this, of course, could also have been an archaistic notion. Plutarch, like Varro (*Lingua Latina*, V, 143), says that Romulus founded Rome *etrusco ritu*, 'after summoning from Tuscany men who prescribed the details in accordance with certain sacred ordinances and writ-

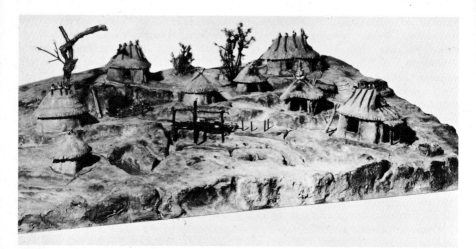

10. Reconstruction by A. Davico of part of the Early Iron Age village on the Palatine, Rome

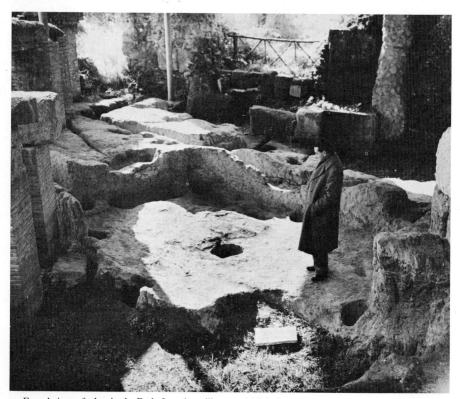

11. Foundations of a hut in the Early Iron Age village on the Palatine

ings, and taught them to him as in a religious rite' (with a sacrificial pit, *mundus*, and by ploughing).

As discussed on p. 64, the old Etruscan towns remained irregular until the sixth century, and even then only their colonies on the plains seem to have had regular patterns. It may be that both the Etruscan and the common Italic practice of the very old way of marking off the villages from surrounding agricultural lands and pasturage on the hills, or on a plain such as that of Bologna, was inherited from the Early Iron Age villages. But neither such usage nor what we know about the boundaries (*pomeria*) of Rome and other towns prove that the old settlements had fixed geometric shapes.[5]

The manner of building the huts of these settlements, with wattle and daub, which we meet on the Palatine and in all villages akin to it, is the same as in the Apennine hamlets. But otherwise the huts display a much higher standard, stabilized types, and an increased wish for adornment. On the Palatine Hill remains of two villages of the Early Iron Age have been found [10, 11], one towards the southern slope of the hill, the other below the so-called Aula Regia of the Palace of Domitian. Between them an Early Iron Age tomb has been excavated; a great cemetery along the Via Sacra north of the Palatine [7] and - it appears - another on the south slope also belonged to these villages.

The foundations of one hut on the southern slope of the Palatine are especially well preserved [11], and the village can be reconstructed in all main respects [10]. The hut measured 16 by 12 feet (4.90 by 3.60 m.). The floor is cut into the tufa of the hill to a depth of about 20 inches. The hut was rectangular with rounded corners. Six large post-holes along the long sides were evidently made for the supports of the roof. The walls were of wattle daubed with clay, as has been proved by the discovery of fire-baked fragments in different places and many huts. The huts had hipped roofs of thatch. A post-hole in the centre of the Palatine hut shows that the roof-ridge was supported by a pole. The hut had no central hearth; instead, a portable cook-ing stand of a type well known from miniature tomb gifts and fragments from many Early Iron Age villages was used for preparing food. On the southern short side is a fairly wide entrance flanked by four post-holes, two inside and two outside the door. The latter, no doubt, were made for posts carrying a canopy [cf. 17]. We see on a hut urn from Tarquinia [16], at Leontini, in the Athenaeum of Syracuse in Sicily, in Lipari, and elsewhere, as on the Palatine, that these primitive huts could be square or squarish; but other hut urns [15] and also the Early Iron Age villages of Luni, San Giovenale, and Veii prove that the most usual shape was oval.[6] The oval huts of San Giovenale are very large [12, 13]: one of them measures some 36 by 19 feet. As occurred in the Apennine hut of Capriola, the outline was drawn by a furrow in the surface of the tufa hill in which the lower edge of the wattle-and-daub walls was embedded. The hut has post-holes for the roof supports, holes which probably served to stabilize tables, beds, or other furniture (as in the shepherds' huts of today on the Roman Campagna), and a door on the western short side.

Interesting and illuminating is the burial equipment from a tomb at Sala Consilina [14]. In the tomb, together with an ash urn of the usual Early Iron Age type containing the bones of a cremated body and the usual funeral gifts, was a model of a house packed with ashes. The type is quite different from the Villanovan huts. It has a ridged roof adorned by volutes and birds, reminiscent both of ash urns and of the end acroteria of the ridge-poles of Archaic Greek and Etruscan temples. The walls are decorated with briskly painted white geometric designs. Compared with all we know about the Early Iron Age huts, the decorations of the ridge-pole and the roof construction seem to prove that the model reproduces a new type of house, probably inspired by the earliest temples and houses of the Greek immigrants, such as we know them from the Geometric Age and later.

At Luni and San Giovenale have been found square subterranean rooms of considerable size which have to be remembered among Early Iron

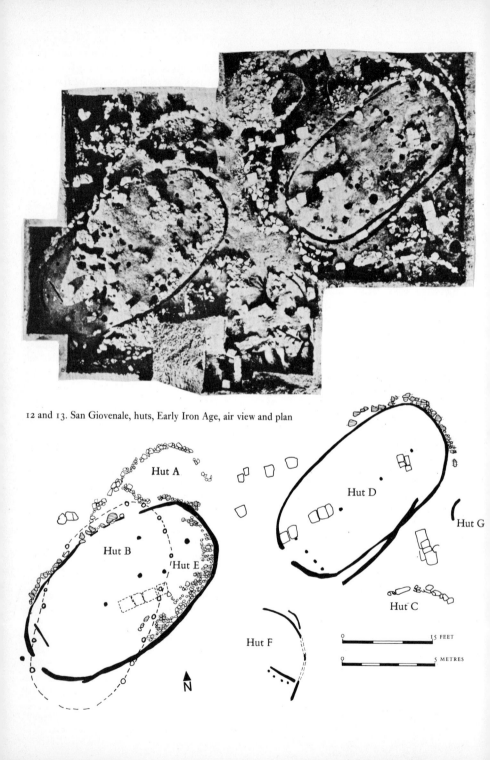

12 and 13. San Giovenale, huts, Early Iron Age, air view and plan

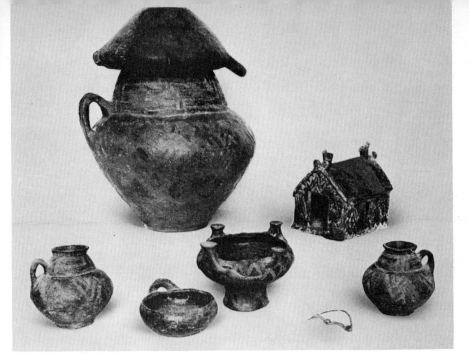

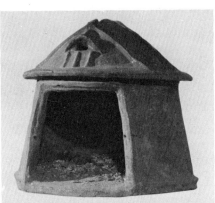

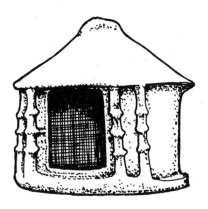

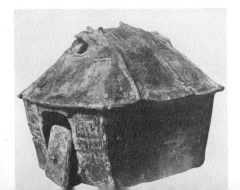

14 (*top*). Implements from tomb no. 63 at S. Antonio, Sala Consilina, with ash urn and model of a house, Early Iron Age (Oenotrio–Ausonian). *Salerno, Museo Provinciale*

15 (*above left*). Hut urn from Castel Gandolfo, Early Iron Age. *Rome, Museo della Preistoria e Protostoria del Lazio*

16 (*left*). Square hut urn from Tarquinia, Early Iron Age. *Florence, Museo Archeologico*

17 (*above*). Hut urn from Campofattore, near Marino, Early Iron Age. *Rome, Museo della Preistoria e Protostoria del Lazio*

Age instances of possible domestic or even palatial architecture. At the westernmost end of the acropolis of Luni is a shaft measuring some 60 by 30 feet and cut down in the rock about 20 feet. Between 800 and 900 cubic yards of tufa have been removed. There are charred remains of a wooden roof and walls covered with clay, though we do not know whether these once belonged to a carefully constructed basement or (as seems most probable to me) to a collapsed building constructed above the basement. There is, in any case, no entrance to the sunk room. The finds of pottery indicate that this Early Iron Age 'palace' was burnt down in the eighth century. Of later date is a similar but less pretentious structure belonging to the Early Iron Age settlement of San Giovenale. It is almost square, with sides measuring about 50 feet, and cut down to a depth of about 18 feet; stairs lead down to the lower part of the shaft. Whether basements or houses, these constructions represent a quite different, more stately architecture than the huts.[7]

The hut urns from cemeteries [14–17] complete our picture of the usual type of Italic Iron Age huts. The ash was put into the urn through its door. The diameters of most of these receptacles vary between 12 and 16 inches (30 and 40 cm.). On an average, 12 inches may be singled out as a most usual width, corresponding to a height of about 8 to 12 inches. Exceptions to those with the usual round or oval plans are huts which have curved corners and square huts. A square urn from Tarquinia (Selciatello) [16] measures $11\frac{1}{2}$ by $10\frac{1}{4}$ inches and is $11\frac{1}{2}$ inches high (29 by 26 by 29 cm.). The roof is slightly curved. It has an almost rectangular door with a window indicated to the left. Thus, except for the plan, it exhibits the common features of all hut urns. The roofs can be described as conical hipped roofs. At each end of the roof-beams on many hut urns is a vent for smoke. On the long sides of the roof they show ridge-logs to weigh down the thatched roof. The same device, usually three short ridge-logs, is often seen below the vents. The projecting tops of the logs, which cross each other at the ridge, are often elongated and shaped in a decorative way. This may seem to herald the ornamental rows of crossing rafters on archaic temples and houses from the seventh century onwards [18]. The

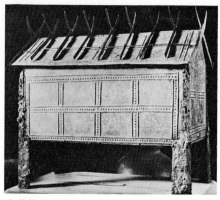

18. Faliscan ash urn, seventh century B.C. *Rome, Museo di Villa Giulia*

short ridge-logs of the vents and the cross-beam to which their upper ends are attached are also often fashioned in decorative ways. The walls of the hut urns frequently rest on a plinth and can be straight or sloping, upwards or (more rarely) downwards. A human figure outside above the door also occurs. Doors with more or less decorative door-posts or even frames are common. The doorways are closed by slabs with central knobs. They have transverse holes corresponding to holes in the door-posts, evidently intended for ropes or twigs which functioned as bars; shepherds of today can still be seen latching their doors in the same way when they leave their temporary huts. Some hut urns have fairly large windows in the wall to the left of the entrance or in both long walls. Many show incised geometric decoration filled with white or yellow colour or with strips of tin. It seems clear that the wattle-and-daub huts had incised and painted geometric wall decoration of the same kind, though the ornamentation of the hut urns may sometimes be more free and rich. The hut urns of Latium show a more primitive and simple decoration, as against the more ornate urns from the towns farther north, from Tarquinia to Vetulonia; but the latter still belong to the characteristically restricted creations of prehistoric life, even if they already display fixed types far superior to the primitive dwellings of the past.

The origin of the habit of using models of huts as ash urns has been much discussed. The technique of the decoration clearly connects the Early Iron Age pots, including hut urns, with Switzerland and Central Europe. Probably there was a link of some kind, but it has been pointed out that the hundred-odd hut urns known from Central Europe and Scandinavia seem all to be slightly later than the urns of the Early Iron Age in Italy. Other suggested parallels or prototypes seem irrelevant. The hut urns from Early Minoan to post-Minoan times on Crete, which have been adduced, were not used as ash urns and are altogether too different to be taken into serious consideration. Hut-shaped urns from Este have also been put forward, but it is uncertain whether they were hut urns, lamps, or ovens, and they do not afford us any more conclusive evidence than do the Cretan parallels.

Before we continue with architecture in the Early Iron Age, we have to consider whether these huts had any formal qualities of importance for the future. Scholars have emphasized the axial tendency of the Early Iron Age huts, with their entrances always in one of the short end walls, and have compared this with the axiality of the Tuscan temples and houses. To me it seems to display a fantastic typological bias to compare such a natural primitive disposition with the elaborate architecture which we shall meet in the next chapter. But some external features may deserve more consideration; for example, the crossing logs on archaic temples may perhaps be traditional remains of the refinements of the ridge-poles of the Early Iron Age huts [18], and the lid of an Iron Age stele [19] from Tarquinia also recalls the early Etruscan temples. On the whole, however, such characteristics, though interesting and noteworthy, seem vague and of slight importance when we consider the quite different architec-

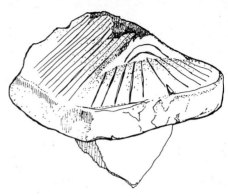

19. Lid of a stele from Tarquinia, Early Iron Age. *Florence, Museo Archeologico*

ture of the seventh and following centuries. What has been said about the Bronze Age seems in the main valid about the architecture of the Early Iron Age, in spite of its evident progress.[8]

A quite different matter is social traditions, that is, inherited habits of daily life or of defence formed in the old villages. No doubt such a legacy lived on, but architectural features of any importance which existed when the architecture of the towns of the eastern Mediterranean world conquered Italy, are very rare. One example may be the round Temple of Vesta at the eastern end of the Forum Romanum. The temple of the Imperial Age that we see today was rebuilt in marble after a fire in the year A.D. 191, and we know that it had also been reshaped previously in the styles of earlier ages. Ancient authors were convinced that the round shape was inherited from curvilinear shrines of Vesta (and from the round Early Iron Age huts). Ovid writes delightfully about the old form of the Temple of Vesta in the *Fasti* (VI, 261–82): 'The buildings which you now see roofed with bronze you might then have seen roofed with thatch, and the walls were woven of tough osiers. This little spot, which now supports the house of the Vestals, was then the great palace of unshorn Numa. But the shape of the temple, as it now exists, is said to have been its shape of old . . .' After discussing the round shape (*forma rotunda*) of the earth, he adds: 'The form of the temple is similar; there is no projecting angle in it; a dome protects it from the showers of rain.' It should be kept in mind that the Early Iron Age village on the Palatine in the seventh century extended over the old cemetery along the Via Sacra. Huts had been built even as far as the place where, much later, the equestrian statue of Domitian was erected in the Forum Romanum. Also, from all archaeological points of view it seems most probable that the traditions from the curved shrines of the Early Iron Age villages survived. Recent excavation in the neighbouring building, the 'regia', which according to Roman traditions one of the oldest kings gave to the head of the state clergy, the Pontifex Maximus, have revealed remains of a large Early Iron Age hut below the fifth-century palace of megaron type.[9]

We know that the Romans of the Imperial Age cherished memories of Latin villages with primitive huts, such as could – and can still today – be seen among shepherds throughout the countryside. Propertius wanted straw huts (*casae stramineae*) even for kings in the profligate Rome of his and Cynthia's time (II, 16. 20); Livy's Camillus talks of the famous hut of Romulus (V, 53), and Imperial coins reproduce such dwellings of the old sagas. Vitruvius also (II, I. 5) tells us about old-fashioned rustic structures kept as a reminder of olden times in Italy, referring to the hut of Romulus on the Capitoline Hill, as on the Acropolis of Athens. Dionysius (I, 79), speaking of the life of herdsmen and the struggle for existence in oldest Latium, describes the 'huts which they built, roofs and all [αὐτόροφοι], out of twigs and reeds'. He continues: 'One of these called the hut of Romulus remained even to my day on the flank of the Palatine Hill which faces towards the Circus, and it is preserved holy by those who are in charge of these matters; they add nothing to it to render it more stately, but if any part of it is injured, either by storms or by the lapse of time, they repair the damage and restore the hut as nearly as possible to its former condition.' The flavour of ancient times is still more enhanced by Cassius Dio's report from the year

12 B.C. that the hut was set ablaze by crows which dropped burning meat from some altar upon it; so there must still then have been a thatched roof (LIV, 29. 8).

Vergil was of the opinion that the rustic Romulean regia was on the Capitoline Hill (*Aen.*, VIII, 654). Dionysius makes it quite clear that the hut which he describes was situated on the south-western part of the Palatine, on the same part of the hill where the Early Iron Age village [10, 11] has been excavated. What the ancient authors affirm at least establishes that there was an old tradition dating from the Prehistoric Age alive on the spot. It seems much less likely that the huts on the Palatine and the Capitoline Hills were inventions suggested by learned hellenistic romanticism, the hut on the Acropolis of Athens, and what the Romans could see in old-fashioned dwellings in the Campagna all around them.[10]

By the time we get an equally clear picture of the somewhat later settlements in Tuscany and Latium, the cultural situation of all Italy had completely changed. From the eighth century onwards, influence from the Orient and the city-states of Homeric, Geometric, and Archaic Greece had contributed to the civilization and reorganization of the country between the Tiber and the Arno in a far more fundamental way than, for instance, the culture of the Early Iron Age had changed Bronze Age conditions. A new kind of architecture, inhumation connected with tombs of new types, a rich import of Oriental and Greek luxury, inscriptions written with Greek letters adapted for the Etruscan language, and other devices of high culture all mark the new era.

In Augustus's age Dionysius of Halicarnassus (I, 33. 4), describing the completely legendary Arcadians of the Palatine in Rome, gives us a remarkably vivid picture of how well the Romans knew that this was a revolution caused by influence from countries with a higher culture. According to him Evander, the king of the Arcadian saga, was the first to introduce into Italy the use of Greek letters, and also music performed 'on such instruments as lyres, trigons, and flutes; for their predecessors [the Early Iron Age tribes in Italy] had used no musical invention except shepherds' pipes. The Arcadians are said also to have established laws, to have transformed men's mode of life from the prevailing bestiality [ἐκ τοῦ θηριώδους, from primitive conditions, that is] to a state of civilization, and likewise to have introduced arts and professions and many other things conducive to the public good'. If we add to this list a new kind of architecture, it is indeed – attribution to the Arcadians apart – an excellent summary of the result of influences from the great Eastern cultural world which ended the Early Iron Age in Italy and overthrew its primitive and monotonous life.

What happened in Italy in the eighth and following centuries must be related to the great expansive cultural revival in the eastern Mediterranean countries after the decline about 1000 B.C. It was the age of the Assyrian and Neo-Babylonian Empires, of the Late Hittite kingdoms north of Syria with their marvellous art, of the Phrygian and Lydian kingdoms, of Urartu, of the Saitic renaissance in Egypt and of Phoenician trade and skilful imitations and new combinations of the great artistic traditions of the Near East and Egypt. As Homer, Herodotus, and later authors describe, Phoenician merchants were important intermediaries between Europe and this Eastern world in its late renaissance. Closely connected with all this was the Homeric Greek era and the unparalleled strength and originality with which the Greeks reshaped Eastern influences into their Homeric and Archaic culture. During and after this period of revived activity from the eastern Mediterranean countries, Greek Archaic culture both at home and in the Italian colonies became more important than anything else for Italy.

We must now return to the primitive villages of Italy among the wilderness and pastures and try to look at them with the eyes of the sailors from the Eastern world. They saw artefacts, such as weapons and ornaments, which proved that these barbaric western lands had consider-

able mineral resources. Along the west coast of Italy and in Sicily were vast rich plains which, whether cultivated or not, must have attracted immigrants as offering great possibilities for their more developed agriculture. The picture preserved for us of the Greek arrival in Italy is filled with acts of piracy and outrageous atrocities. The descriptions of Odysseus's landings on the barbaric west coast give us a very lively impression (see, for instance, *Od.*, X, 144 ff.), and marvellous paintings of shipwrecks on Geometric eighth-century vases from Ischia and Athens tell of the hardships of the sailors, not so different from those suffered by Odysseus. No less important is Ephorus's statement, preserved by Strabo (VI, 2. 2), that before the earliest Greek colonies (that is, before the later half of the eighth century) the Greeks 'were so afraid of the bands of Tyrrhenian pirates and the savagery of the barbarians in this region that they would not so much as sail thither for trafficking'. King Agrios in Hesiod's *Theogonia* (1013) may also belong to the era of these tales of ancient savagery at the dawn of history.

But soon the situation changed. The Greeks built their towns in southern Italy and Sicily in the style and with the organization they brought with them. All this is known history, though some of the dates are disputed. Typical and of special importance for architecture and for the entire culture of central Italy are the two northernmost Greek settlements, Cumae and Ischia. The lofty, isolated acropolis of Cumae stands above a wide beach where the ships were drawn up after their long adventurous voyages, and the settlement on Ischia lies on a hillock at the western end of the island, with a bay for the boats. Newcomers to Italy are described in the sagas in the persons of Diomedes, the Argive founder of Tibur (Tivoli), the Arcadian Evander of the Palatine, Aeolus of the Liparian islands, and others. Such tales are evidently attempting to explain the introduction of Greek culture to Italy from the eighth century onwards, even if in some cases the legends may go back to the Greeks of the Mycenaean Age. The rich country of south Italy and Sicily, with the considerable metal resources of the former, now fell into the hands of a quite new kind of people, endowed with an almost unparalleled heroic genius and energy in opposing such enormous powers as the despotic kingdoms of the Near East and the oppressive primitive life in the west. The same can be said of the Etruscans, whatever their origin was, and in spite of what they learned from the Greeks. Pictures of ships, and a few words about Aphrodite and Nestor's cup scratched on a Geometric pot from the cemetery of Ischia, bring to life for us these sailors and immigrants with their Homeric language and culture.[11]

While the Greek city-states in southern Italy remained Greek oases surrounded by native tribes, from the eighth century onwards the country between Lydius Thybris, as Vergil (*Aen.*, II, 781) styles the Tiber, and the Arno was penetrated and unified by the highly characteristic Etruscan version of Oriental and Greek culture. Where previously the Early Iron Age culture had given the same general appearance to all the villages, a new, strong nation with a language of its own arose, with rock-cut chamber tombs of a new type [cf. 70] from about 700 B.C., painted walls from the first half of the seventh century (Tomba delle Anatre at Veii), and hoards of imported Oriental and Greek tomb gifts.

The people who introduced this new luxury, the Etruscans, seem to have called themselves the Rasenna, while in the Latin and Greek languages they were known as Etrusci, Tusci, Tyrrheni, or Tyrseni. North and west of the Tiber these Etruscan-speaking tribes were spread all over the country, except for a territory with an Indo-European language round Falerii (Civita Castellana) and Capena, the Faliscan plain on the western shore of the river, which kept its Indo-European language in spite of overwhelming Etruscan influence from the seventh century onwards. All our literary sources of Late Republican and Augustan times affirm that the people on the Etruscan side, the *litus etruscum*, or *Lydia ripa*, as the riverside of Trastevere was still called in Imperial times,

knew Latin only by contact with Rome and Latium or by 'having had Romans among them as colonists' (to quote Livy, I, 27. 9). As Varro affirms in *Lingua Latina* (VII, 35), 'the roots [radices] of the words' were quite different in Etruscan and Latin.[12] How did this happen? What brought about this new cultural situation on the west coast, dissociating Etruria from Latium and its other neighbouring lands? How can it be explained that the Etruscans were prepared to make the new high culture and architecture of the Near East and Greece their own, a hundred years or even more before the Italic peoples around them – in complete contrast to what happened when Mycenaean influences had reached Italy?

The most plausible explanation is that a new people with Eastern affinities had discovered Etruria and immigrated to harbours on the west coast, especially those of Caere (Cerveteri), Tarquinia, Vulci, and other south Etrurian towns in the making. From these starting-points the newcomers would by amalgamation have reshaped the pre-existing Indo-European tribes, their language and their villages, gradually occupying the inland villages such as San Giovenale (about 630 B.C.), Luni, and – even earlier – the Faliscan district. This attempt to explain the archaeological facts by assuming an immigration from the East agrees with what all ancient historians (except Dionysius of Halicarnassus), as well as the Etruscans themselves and the Romans, believed. These old tales may be uncertain, chronologically confused, reshaped by frequently told sagas about famine-stricken emigrating peoples; but they cannot possibly be discarded *en bloc* and must be considered together with the linguistic and archaeological evidence. They all have in common the firm belief that the Etruscans were immigrants from Asia Minor.

At the head of these legends stands Herodotus's famous tale (I, 94) wherein he describes the Etruscans as a part of the Lydian people which emigrated to Italy after building ships at Smyrna, 'whereon they set all their gods that could be carried on shipboard'. Tacitus (*Annals*,

IV, 55) proves that this notion was alive among the Romans and the Lydians of the Imperial Age: he relates that envoys from Sardes in Tiberius's time quoted a decree of their kindred country Etruria, according to which a son of King Atys of Lydia, Tyrrhenus, had emigrated to Etruria with a part of the Lydian people. But there are also other tales of connexions of the Etruscans with the Near East, linking them with the Pelasgians, and of Tyrsenians (or Tyrrhenians) on Lesbos, Lemnos, Delos, and Imbros. In the Homeric hymn to Dionysus we meet them as pirates on the Aegean.[13]

But, on the other hand, there is Dionysius criticizing the prevalent idea about the Lydian origin of the Etruscans (I, 30): 'I do not believe that the Tyrrhenians were a colony of the Lydians; for they do not use the same language as the latter, nor can it be alleged that, though they no longer speak a similar tongue, they still retain some other indications of their mother country. For they neither worship the same gods as the Lydians nor make use of similar laws or institutions ... Indeed, those probably come nearest the truth who declare that the nation migrated from nowhere else, but was native to the country, since it is found to be a very ancient nation and to agree with no other either in its language or in its manner of living [οὔτε ὁμόγλωσσον οὔτε ὁμοδίαιτον].' The evident objection to this is that conditions in the Lydia of Dionysius's days must have changed entirely since the time when the Etruscans would have emigrated (though a recent find proves that the Lydian language survived into the Hellenistic period); but all the same, Dionysius's reasoning is highly interesting, especially since he makes it clear that the Etruscans were different both in language and way of life from their Italian neighbours and all other peoples – in spite of the hellenized external forms of their culture and architecture.

Modern scholars have tried to revive and corroborate Dionysius's opinion by research showing the connexions between the Etruscan culture and prehistoric life in central Italy. What is here assumed to be influence from the new tomb architecture on the old local types and other results of the merging of immigrants and the local population, they consider as proof that the Etruscan people had been living in Etruria since the dawn of prehistory. But how did it happen that this supposed aboriginal people was spared only there? Does it seem likely that the Early Iron Age culture of central Italy was created by two different races with the Tiber as a dividing line between them? Ingenious suggestions that it may have been the Etruscans who brought the Early Iron Age culture to Italy some time about 900 B.C. and that it spread from their new settlements do not, it seems, solve the difficulties.[14]

Anyhow, for the present study of the architecture of the Etruscans it is enough to state that a new architecture of common Mediterranean stamp was brought to Italy by a people that spoke Etruscan. If the Etruscans were immigrants from Asia Minor, they probably started their life in Italy with a rather low form of culture from the Near East. It seems likely that they brought with them basic architectural traditions. In any case, it is clear that refined Etruscan architecture, as we see it, was developed in the cities of the Etruscans under continuous influence from the Orient and Greece. The reshaping power of this influence was so strong that the question whether or not the immigrants brought fundamental architectural ideas with them almost becomes one of secondary importance.

CHAPTER 3

ETRUSCAN ARCHITECTURE

INTRODUCTION

The Etruscans enjoyed a free existence as independent city-states for some five hundred years, from the eighth century to the early third century B.C. Finally, in the early first century, internal warfare and Sulla's victories put an end to particularism in Italy and latinized the whole country (excepting only the Greek towns). The culture of the Roman Empire and the architecture of Augustan Rome then imposed themselves on the ancient Etruscan centres of agriculture, mining, handicraft, art, and shipping. Their ill-famed and dreaded piracy had been stopped by the Romans about 300.

Especially important for Rome was Veii, the rich and great neighbour town with painted chamber tombs already from the seventh century B.C. According to Livy, the Romans destroyed Veii in 396. Rome's next important Etruscan neighbour was Caere (Cerveteri, Etruscan Chaisre). Three famous inscriptions on golden plates, two in Etruscan and one in the Punic language, found between two temples at Pyrgi [28], one of Caere's harbour towns, show that Caere about 500 had close connexions with Carthage. From the fourth century onwards Caere became closely connected with Rome and soon lost its independence, Pyrgi receiving a strongly fortified Roman colony outside its spreading township in the third century B.C. [114]. The roster of the greatest towns, glorious coastal successors of the Villanovan villages, must include Tarquinia, Vulci, Talamone, Rusellae, Vetulonia, Populonia, and Volaterrae (Volterra); to these should be added such inland towns as Faesulae (Fiesole), Arretium (Arezzo), Clusium (Chiusi), Volsinii in the neighbourhood of medieval and modern Bolsena, Blera (Bieda), and such unidentified towns as those of the majestic, archaic tholos tomb called La Montagnola di Quinto Fiorentino [96], of Orvieto, San Giuliano, San Giovenale, and Luni (Monte Fortino). Falerii (Civita Castellana) had a special position, since it was the centre of the Indo-European Faliscans and yet politically and by its culture closely connected with the Etruscans.

Boundaries and different political associations and constitutions no doubt caused conflicts; but the Etruscan towns of the centuries which we know did not make war on each other to the same extent as the Greek city-states at home and in Italy, though they gave no aid to Veii when it was conquered by the Romans. They organized themselves into a confederation with its centre in the Temple of Voltumna in the neighbourhood of Volsinii, and even, in the seventh, sixth, and fifth centuries B.C., successfully established a dominion embracing the Po valley and Campania, with control over Latium through such Etruscan dynasties as the Tarquinii in Rome. Their architecture and culture spread over central Italy from the sixth century onwards, and it should be remembered, especially in the Campanian towns, that such features as regular town planning and atrium-houses can be explained by cultural influence and by no means necessarily imply Etruscan builders. In the Po valley Etruscan town planning and architecture asserted themselves around Felsina (Bologna), in new centres such as Spina or the Etruscan colony at the Reno River, called Marzabotto, which were both founded towards the end of the sixth century [62]. In Campania, Capua, Pompeii, and even a town on the Sorrento peninsula, Marcina (probably Fratte near Salerno), had their Etruscan periods. The Etruscans of these early days also controlled the sea around Corsica and Elba.

The period of greatest power gradually came to an end in the fifth and fourth centuries. Latium, according to the Roman tradition, was lost in 509 because of the rise of the Roman Republic. Samnite invaders from the central mountain districts expelled the Etruscans from their capital Capua and from Campania in the fifth century. By 474 their sea power had already had a serious setback in a battle against the Greeks at Cumae. North of the Alps and the Po valley the Gauls, another powerful rival of the Etruscans, developed a great military force and organization comprising cavalry with iron horseshoes (a novelty in the ancient wars). Among other material a rich tomb from the Saar shows that they had an interesting and rich culture of their own, at least the higher classes, and could import real treasures, as, for instance, the large Greek bowl from Vix. Then, towards 400, the Gauls invaded the Po valley, ending the Etruscan dominion. They proceeded to raid the towns of Etruria, and in 386 they even sacked Rome. Meanwhile, after the subjugation of Veii, a century of wars began between Rome and Tarquinia. This double warfare against the Gauls and Rome rendered necessary what proved to be one of the great architectural achievements of the Etruscans: the construction of town walls in their fully developed shape [58] (below, pp. 67–8). They confirm in a monumental way what Livy says over and over again about the military strength displayed by the Etruscans even in these late and losing wars. The end came between 280 and 241, when all Etruscans and Faliscans were brought under the sway of Rome with more or less reduced independence and territories.

For a historical study of Etruscan architecture it is most important to remember that the dependence on Rome and the decline of political power in the fourth and third centuries by no means put an end to the wealth or to the architectural activity of the Etruscans: on the contrary, after the final Roman victories, as in Pompeii, a period of increasing prosperity was inaugurated for the Etruscan towns. This was due to the peace under Rome, to Italy's contacts with the hellenistic world after the victory over Hannibal, and to great landowners and other wealthy people, protected by Rome.

The main buildings in which the Etruscans demonstrated their state, culture, religion, and family traditions were the temples and the palatial houses of kings and nobles, as we see them reproduced in monumental tombs. In contrast to these – but also to the tenement houses with upper storeys, which we shall meet with already in third-century Rome – stand out the one-storey houses of the common people which our archaeological material has revealed at Marzabotto, San Giovenale [66], Veii, Vetulonia [55], Rusellae, and in a few other places. Vitruvius remarks especially (VI, 5. 1) that the ordinary people in towns, where the rich lived in atrium-houses built in grand style, did not need such luxury.

The densely populated quarters of the common people housed a free population, though one which never seems to have attained the importance of the Roman plebs. Cicero (*De republica*, II, 16) says that even at the outset Romulus divided the Roman plebs among the aristocratic clienteles; the same system seems to have been typical of the Etruscan towns, prevailing until the decline of old Etruria. The grouping of qualified slaves, freedmen, and clients around the influential families seems to have been very important. A great proportion of the artisans were slaves, according to Livy (V, 1). They had the same kind of dwellings as the majority of the common free people which Diodorus mentions (V, 40. 3–5).

To these introductory remarks may be added a few words about Vitruvius and his description of Etruscan architecture. References to his famous Ten Books on Architecture, written about 25 B.C., have already been made and will accompany all the following chapters right down to Late Republican times in Rome. It may therefore be useful to state at once that Vitruvius was first and foremost an architect who – as he eloquently and even ardently proclaims – wished to contribute to the grandeur of Augustan Rome by reviving traditional styles of architecture. He preached to a younger generation about the honest, highly experienced architects of bygone days, expressing himself in a strong but sometimes rather ambiguous pre-classical Latin. He wanted to adapt the classical styles to the demands of his own times, but at the same time claims to have re-established their ideal proportions and forms. He thus wishes primarily to be the practising architect, not a teacher of the history of architecture, and to establish rules for all kinds of buildings in the Augustan Age. Vitruvius bases his ideal rules for Etruscan temples and their *dispositiones* upon his knowledge of the more or less modernized architecture of Etruscan stamp which he could see all over Latium and Etruria. He may even have studied Roman or Etruscan treatises on the old architecture – comparable to the compendia of Etruscan religious and political wisdom compiled in the Late Republican Age and characteristic of the learned interest of that period. While he is an unsafe guide on archaic architecture, his rules often approximate to the measurements of preserved Later Etruscan and Roman buildings. When Vitruvius tries to fix measurements for the various elements of their construction, he is evidently combating a confusion prevailing under hellenistic influence. What he intends to do is to arrive at general rules of his own based on actual buildings, but not by reproducing any one example.[1]

TECHNIQUES AND MATERIALS

When Oriental and Greek culture arrived in the eighth century B.C., the old wattle-and-daub structures soon seemed to belong to a remote past, though wattle and daub remained in everyday architecture even in Imperial times as an indestructible undergrowth. Vitruvius (II, 8. 20) expresses a wish that it had never been 'invented'. In inland places like San Giovenale we see with almost dramatic vividness how the Etruscan chamber tombs of the Oriental and Greek luxury began to appear about 630. On the acropolises of San Giovenale and Luni foundations of roughly square structures suddenly superseded the old village. We meet with rectangular houses and the common Mediterranean manners of building, which from the great Etruscan coastal towns spread to the out-of-the-way corners of inland Etruria, Latium, and all central Italy.

Timber construction appears at an early date at Veii. The ceilings, which the rock-cut chamber tombs at Caere (Cerveteri) and other Etruscan cities reproduce, show the mastery of timber-work which the Etruscans attained in the sixth century [82 ff.]. In sixth-century San Giovenale and at Veii (that is before 396), we also meet with a crude masonry of tufa blocks in various sizes in the houses. Ashlar work and polygonal walls belonged to Etruscan architecture from early times, especially in royal tombs, city walls, and the podia of temples. Sun-dried brick and half-timber on stone foundations became highly important, as seen at Veii, San Giovenale, Vetulonia, and many other places. At Marzabotto the bricks seem to be partly fired, and the foundations of the houses are of river boulders embedded in mud [63]. Sometimes walls were made of rammed clay (*pisé*), sometimes they could be built with the mud brick directly on the ground. It is evident that these modes of construction were brought to perfection and general use in central Italy in the seventh century. What reached the villages of the Early Iron Age was a technique known already from the third millennium in Malta, and from such Bronze Age villages on Crete as Vrokastro, Kavousi, Karphi, and so on.[2]

Vitruvius (II, 8. 9) describes the ancient mud-brick city wall at Arretium (Arezzo) as 'excellently built', and a description of 1536 and excavations of 1916-18 have substantiated his praise: beautifully cut bricks and scarcely visible mortar joints were revealed. At Rusellae a mud-brick terrace wall on a foundation of rough polygonal blocks was built about 600 (cf. p. 68). Vitruvius distinguishes between the square sun-dried bricks of the Greeks and the rectangular Greek Lydian bricks, 'being the kind which our people use, a foot and a half long and one foot wide'. Bricks actually found at Arretium and

Vetulonia show roughly the same proportions. The name 'Lydian' reminds us of the *Lydia ripa* of the Tiber, and may indicate real knowledge of an eastern provenance of the technique or may merely be a synonym for 'Etruscan'. In any case, though the Greeks preferred other proportions, there can be no doubt that the Etruscans learned from their mud-brick architecture, of which the enlarged city wall of Gela, of the fourth century, still affords a monumental example.[3]

Etruscan mud-brick architecture started a great new tradition in Italy. Augustus, contrasting the old Rome of brick with his marble city (that is, his city with its temples and other monumental buildings faced with marble), has in mind concrete and mud-brick. Pliny (XXXV, 173) says that in his time no mud-brick walls were built in Rome. Vitruvius (II, 3 and 8. 16) warmly defends mud-brick architecture, but he makes us understand that the Romans of the Augustan Age could not build their high houses (*insulae*), so necessary for the constantly increasing population, of mud-brick, since the space of the city was so limited that there was no room for the bulky walls needed for high mud-brick structures. In any case, a description of an inundation of the Tiber in 54 B.C. shows that mud-brick houses still survived in great numbers during the first century B.C.[4]

Mud-brick and wood evidently remained the normal building material for the walls of Etruscan temples and houses down to the last centuries of Etruscan history, in contrast to the Egyptian and Greek stone-built temples. This perishable material doomed Etruscan domestic architecture when decline came. Roman and medieval activity on the Etruscan acropolises completed the havoc. The tombs are – at least for the time being – our best archaeological evidence of what the palatial houses of the nobility were like. The case of the temples is different. Their podia and foundations were more monumental and less perishable. A rich supply of terracotta decoration and tiles often permits a reconstruction;[5] but not only in places without known Etruscan names, such as San

Giuliano, San Giovenale, or its neighbour Luni (Monte Fortino), but also in many great Etruscan centres such as Clusium (Chiusi), Volaterrae, Cortona, Arretium (Arezzo), and Perusia (Perugia), remains of temple foundations have so far been sought in vain.

TEMPLES

We learn from the tombs that the domestic architecture of the nobility and the Lucumones, as the Etruscan kings were called, assumed stately forms. But the centres of the new towns in Italy, with their foreign culture and luxury (already known from the tombs of the seventh century), were evidently the temples, with their piazzas and altars in front of them. The late compilers of Etruscan tradition report that the founders of the Etruscan towns thought that every proper town ought to have three gates, three main roads, and three temples (those of Tinia, Uni, and Minvra, i.e. Jupiter, Juno, and Minerva; Servius ad Aen., I, 422). In the Etruscan towns known to us there is no trace of such planning, but Vitruvius (I, 7) confirms that the Etruscans had rules for their temples handed down by the haruspices.

The Early Temples

A temple on the acropolis (Piazza d'Armi) at Veii seems to illustrate the first tentative beginnings of Etruscan temple building. It was a rectangular (49 feet 9 inches by 26 feet 3 inches; 15.15 by 8.07 m.) timber-framed building (with mud-brick), without pronaus or podium, and the foundation consisted of coarse tufa blocks. It had a frieze and antefixes of crude archaic workmanship. These early temples also include one at Volsinii (Bolsena) with a roughly quadrangular temenos measuring 56 feet 5 inches by 44 feet (17.20 by 13.40 m.), surrounded by a wall [20]. A cella without pronaus (26 feet 3 inches by 21 feet 8 inches; 8 by 6.60 m.) is built against the back wall of the temenos. A model of a house from an Etruscan tomb in the cemetery of Monte Abatone at Caere [21] and

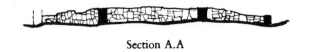

Section A.A

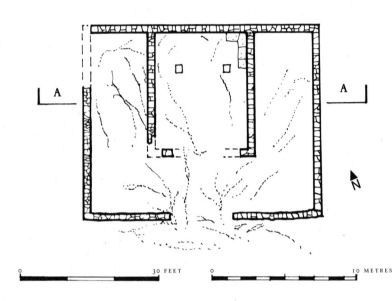

0   30 FEET   0   10 METRES

20. Volsinii (Bolsena), Poggio Casetta, temple,
early sixth century B.C. Plan

21. Hut urn from the cemetery of Monte Abatone
at Caere, seventh century B.C.
Rome, Museo di Villa Giulia

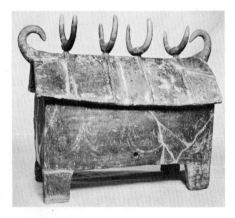

also older models of houses with decorative
crossing rafters from Falerii and from Sala
Consilina [14, 18] may be considered together
with these early sanctuaries.[6]

To a foreign architectural tradition belongs
the old Temple of Mater Matuta at Satricum,
famous for its terracotta revetments and datable
to about 500. It is surrounded by a peristyle and
has an oblong cella and deep pronaus. Like the
smaller temple at Pyrgi (p. 44), it is an interesting instance of a temple with a Greek plan. It
may, of course, have been due to Greek influence from Campania, but Dionysius (I, 21. 2)
tells us that the Temple of Juno at Falerii was
built on the model of the Temple of Hera near
Argos. Thus, temples of the Greek type, like
Greek columns (cf. p. 52), were not alien to the
Etruscans. They were probably scarce, but can
be compared with the Doric temples of Oscan
Pompeii, or to Elyman Segesta with its un-
finished columns.[7]

Funerary urns and models show small chapels with pitched roofs but without pronaus, a type which no doubt persisted *per saecula*. But of real importance for monumental Etruscan sacred

trary reconstructions. The obvious approach to our material seems to be an empirical description of common features and an unbiased classification of the various types and their long and

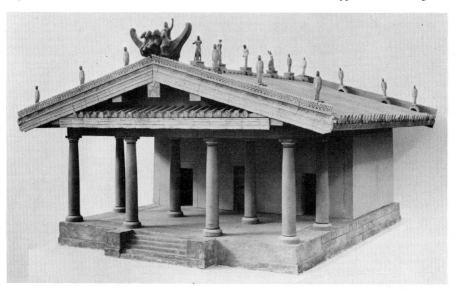

22. Reconstruction of an Etruscan temple as described by Vitruvius (IV, 7). *Rome University, Istituto di Etruscologia e di Antichità Italiche*

architecture from the fifth century down to Roman times were only what Vitruvius in his famous chapter about Etruscan temples refers to as '*tuscanicae dispositiones*', the typically Etruscan rules for temples (IV, 6 f.) [22]. There are several variations of this highly characteristic type. Vitruvius describes two of them but does not claim that they were archetypes: he just wished to re-establish an ideal arrangement and proportion, and therefore chose two types which were most in vogue in his day, because they were used for Roman Capitolia (below p. 163). However, modern scholars have assumed that all the variations of Etruscan temples were derived from Vitruvius's two types – an unfounded conclusion, which has given rise to strained categorization and arbi-

interesting career in Etruscan, Roman Republican, and Imperial architecture.[8]

As far back as we know the temples had external terracotta decoration in the Greek style [43, 44]; but their most typical features clearly were not Greek. Typical of all Etruscan temples are roomy colonnaded pronai in front of the cellas and entrances only on the front, a distinctive feature no doubt due to the nature of Etruscan religious rites. They thus had an innate axial tendency, which was also visible in the early temple areas at Volsinii (Bolsena) and Orvieto [20, 33]. In Roman times this was emphasized by altars placed in front of the centre of the entrance. Common to all the various temples with this general arrangement are wide spaces between the columns. These large intercolumniations made it impossible to employ stone or marble for the architraves, so wooden beams were laid upon the columns, and the whole entablature was of wood, which again is completely at variance with the practice in Greek temples (Vitruvius, III, 3. 5). Many temples of Etruscan type had columns along the side walls, but they never had a peristyle on all four sides as had the great Greek temples. The back walls were closed in all cases, but they could be extended right and left of the cellas if the temples had side rooms (wings, *alae*) with columns outside the walls of the central cella (or cellas), as Vitruvius says (IV, 7. 2; illustration 34, cf. illustration 126, Temple C, Largo Argentina).[9]

A very characteristic feature is the use of podia and flights of stairs or ramps on the front [35]. When a temple is built directly on rock without a podium, like, for instance, the temenos and archaic temple at Volsinii [20], it is an anomaly explained by the site, which allowed a spur of bedrock to serve as a natural podium.

These Etruscan temples have been compared with archaic Greek temples and with *megara* from Mycenaean times and later. Yet the wide pronai, the closed extensions of the back walls, and the podia give them a different and fundamentally foreign character. Neither the old simple houses of the gods nor Greek influence can give any real explanation or background to these new temples in central Italy. It is, indeed, natural that Vitruvius, trying to renew classical styles and discussing the various types, has treated the *mos tuscanicus*, the *dispositiones tuscanicae*, as something different from all other kinds of temples (IV, 7; cf. III, 3. 5). He omits variations, which will be discussed below, though they may have been as old and typical as the two kinds of Etruscan temples which he has chosen: great temples with large open pronai, on a quadrangular plan, with either three cellas against the closed rear wall or a single cella and open wings (*alae*). Vitruvius was further misled, no doubt, by later Roman and Etruscan temples with their many innovations. Both the Etruscans and the Romans started in the third century B.C. (perhaps even before) to build stone temples on the old Etruscan plan, but with high Greek columns (see below, illustration 129). In small temples, where the intercolumniations

were not too wide, they even built Greek entablatures in stone (instead· of employing the low wooden roofing of the ancient shrines). This most important combination of the principles of Greek and Etruscan buildings, occasionally mentioned by Vitruvius (IV, 8. 5), was a part of the modernized *consuetudo Italica*, as in his fifth book he called the hellenized Italic architecture of Late Republican times. Vitruvius's remarks about areostyle temples in his third book evidently show such modernisms, which were typical of Roman Late Republican architecture.[10]

All the same, partly due to Vitruvius and ancient descriptions, but more to the archaeological material now available, the genuine old Etruscan temples can be reconstructed in their main lines, with low wooden entablatures and delightfully colourful terracotta revetments in Greek style protecting the wooden parts of the buildings. In addition to these ornaments, fantastic antefixes, decorating the ends of the cover tiles above the eaves, were used, and charming rich acroteria and sometimes terracotta statues on the ridge of the roofs or on the eaves above the gables of the front [22, 51]. Before describing the superstructures of this highly original sacred architecture it is necessary to discuss what archaeological study has revealed about typical ground plans.

Types of Plan and Superstructure

There are two types of temples with the Etruscan stress on the front which Vitruvius may have had in mind when describing the Greek prostyle temples (III, 2. 2–3), but which he leaves aside in his main description (IV, 7).

One kind of temple with a deep pronaus having two columns in line with the lateral walls of the cella seems old and not unusual [23]. There is no reason to doubt that a cippus from Chiusi, dated about 500 B.C., represents a temple of this kind with two Tuscan columns [24]; in any case, a fragment of the roof of a terracotta model, also dating from about 500, proves that these two-columned temples belonged to the archaic Etruscan Age. A relief of the Imperial period suggests that the Temple of Juno Moneta on the Arx of Rome had a prodomus with only two columns, as has also the small model of a temple from Teano, which is Late Republican [25, 149].

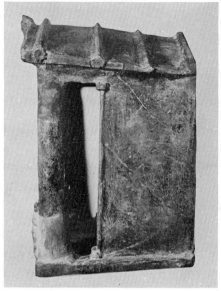

25. Model of a temple from Teano, Late Republican

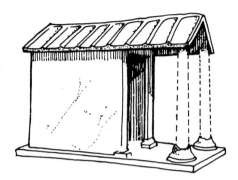

23. Model from Satricum of a temple with two columns prostyle. *Rome, Museo di Villa Giulia*

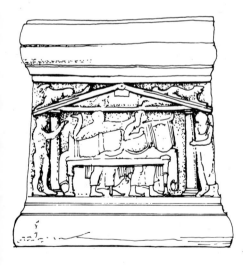

24. Cippus from Clusium (Chiusi) showing a temple with two columns in the pronaus and animals above the pediment, *c.* 500 B.C. *Berlin, Altes Museum*

A great and important group of Roman temples seems to have been related to the Etruscan ones. These Roman temples had a cella – sometimes pseudo-peripteral – without alae and with four or more columns in the pronaus. The pronaus tends to occupy the front half of the building. This type, destined to be a model for classicistic architecture in Europe and America in the eighteenth and nineteenth centuries, occurs in our present Roman material from about 200 B.C., but probably had Etruscan predecessors. The earliest instances at present known are Temples B and D and the Port Temple at Cosa, the larger temple on the acropolis of Norba, and the so-called Punic temple at Cagliari (below, p. 165). These temples may, of course, remind us of the prostyle temples in Vitruvius's list of Greek temples. Yet I repeat that the deep pronaus, the podium, and the great emphasis on the front show that the Etruscan arrangement described by Vitruvius (IV, 7) was even more important to their builders.[11]

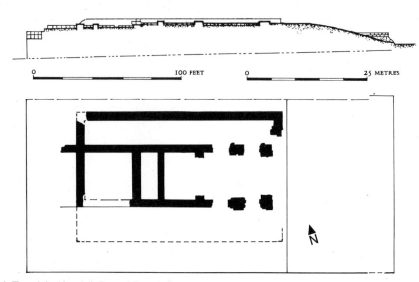

100 FEET 25 METRES

26. Tarquinia, 'Ara della Regina' Temple. Plan

We now arrive at the two types which Vitruvius (IV, 7) selected in order to represent the
ideal Etruscan temple. It is for these that he
laid down rules [22]. According to him, the
length and width of the building plot ought to
start at a ratio of 6 to 5. The length should be
divided into two equal parts, a rear part for the
cellas, or for one cella with alae, and a front part
(with stairs and entrance) for the columns. In
temples with three cellas four-tenths of the
width should be given to the central cella, and
three-tenths to the right and three-tenths to the
left cella or to the alae in temples with one cella.
The corner columns of the pronaus should be
placed in front of the antae on the line of the
outside walls (but if there are alae the corner
columns – as on the Temple of Jupiter Capitolinus [34] – terminate the row of columns along
the outside of the alae). Two other columns
should be placed between the corner columns
on a line with the side walls of the central cella.
In the space between the four front columns and
the cellas should be placed a second row of
columns, arranged on the line of the cella
walls.[12]

From the proportions of the ground plan
Vitruvius passes on to the inner arrangements,
giving first place to the three-cella temples and
merely mentioning the possibility of temples
with one cella and alae [126, Temple C]. It
seems clear that the three-cella temple can by

27. Veii, Portonaccio Temple. Plan

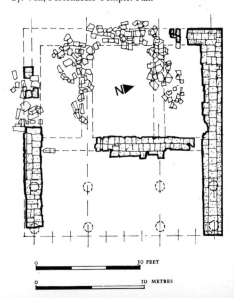

0 30 FEET

0 10 METRES

no means be claimed as necessarily dominant and especially typical of Etruscan sanctuaries. The number of the cellas depended, of course, on the number of divinities worshipped, and triads (or dyads) seem not to have played any commanding role in the organization of the Etruscan gods. Hardly any evidence from Etruria, for example, attests the triad Jupiter, Juno, and Minerva (Tinia, Uni, and Minvra) in the Etruscan towns.[13]

The 'Ara della Regina' Temple at Tarquinia [26], famous for the splendid terracotta horses in hellenistic style from its pediment, proves that great monumental temples with a tripartite inner arrangement, Etruscan disposition, and podium could be built on a quite different plan from the quadrangle prescribed by Vitruvius. It measures 253 feet 1 inch by 116 feet 8 inches (77.5 by 35.55 m.). A temple on the acropolis of

Ardea which otherwise displays Vitruvius's *dispositiones tuscanicae* measures 85 by 130 feet (26 by 40 m.). On the other hand, in the Portonaccio Temple of Veii [27, 51], which once carried the famous terracotta gods now in the Villa Giulia Museum on its ridge and which measures 61 by 61 feet (18.50 by 18.50 m.), we meet with the measurements recommended by Vitruvius. The larger temple at Pyrgi [28] measures 78 feet 9 inches by 112 feet 10 inches (24.05 by 34.40 m.). Vitruvius's description of these tripartite temples has generally suggested reconstructions of Etruscan sanctuaries with columns in open pronai in front of the cellas. This is not altogether certain (cf. p. 43 f.), but seems likely. A recently excavated temple at Vulci is Vitruvian. Thus one has to consider three possible superstructures: temples with three cellas, as Vitruvius prescribes, with three cellas and alae,

28. Pyrgi (Santa Severa), temples. Plan

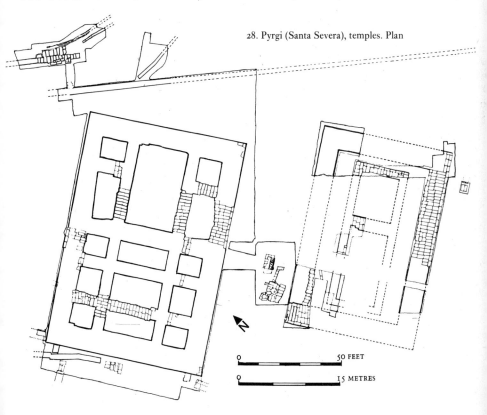

50 FEET

15 METRES

as seen in the Temple of Jupiter Capitolinus in Rome [34], and temples with one cella and open alae or closed corridors [30].[14]

Typical of the temples with alae is that the closed back wall extends right and left of the cella (or cellas like those of the Capitoline Temple of Rome). The columns in the alae along the sides of the cella were placed on the edges of the podium in line with antae, which turned off at right angles from the extended

29. Sovana, Tomba Ildebranda, second century B.C. Elevation and plan

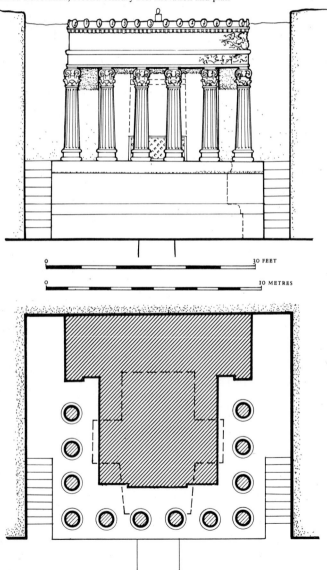

rear wall, and ended with the external columns of the pronaus. Temples with alae were very popular in Late Republican days in Rome, but the hellenized Tomba Ildebranda at Sovana, which evidently imitates a temple of the second century B.C., proves that the Etruscans also favoured this type [29]. On a high podium, below which the rock-cut chamber of the tomb is hidden, stands a colonnade in front of a broad central rock-cut block. There are six columns in front and three on the sides of this massive centrepiece. It reproduces on a reduced scale a three-cella temple with colonnades in front of the prodomus and alae left and right of the cellas as in the Capitoline Temple in Rome.[15]

The alae could also be changed to lateral corridors. Vitruvius does not mention this variation, but it has been revealed by excavations of a temple at Fiesole [30]. This temple was rebuilt in Roman times (first century B.C.), but there are older remains below the present structure. It is of great importance for a discussion of the reconstruction of the mud-brick

30. Faesulae (Fiesole), temple, Etruscan,
rebuilt in the first century B.C. Axonometric plan

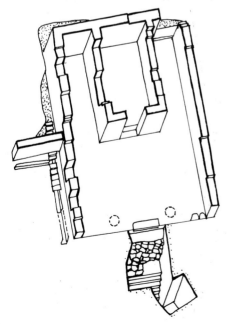

temples, for it is built of ashlar masonry, and that means that for once we can clearly see the superstructure. Against the closed rear wall is a cella measuring 27 feet 9 inches by 14 feet 5 inches (8.45 by 4.40 m.); the pronaus in front of the cella is 26 feet 8 inches (8.14 m.) deep; the proportion of cella to prodomus thus roughly corresponds to that prescribed by Vitruvius. The rear wall behind the cella continues on either side of it for 9 feet 3 inches and 8 feet 11½ inches (2.82 and 2.73 m.), and from the ends of these extensions run side walls parallel to the side walls of the cella to the front of the podium. Thus, the open colonnaded wings were, in the Fiesole temple, closed corridors along the side walls of the central cella. Between these outer walls (on the front edge of the podium) were two columns. Stairs led up to this pronaus. A special characteristic of this structure is that only the front of the pronaus – i.e. the spaces between the antae and the columns – was left open. It reminds us of what Vitruvius says (IV, 8. 5): 'Where there are projecting antae in the pronaus, some set up two columns in a line with each of the cella walls, thus making a combination of Tuscan and Greek buildings (*tuscanicorum et graecorum operum communis ratiocinatio*).'

Among the later Etrusco-Roman temples of Latium there is no structure like the Fiesole temple, but a model dating from the sixth century, found at Velletri, shows us the same construction [31]. That pushes it back to the archaic

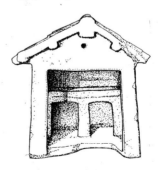

31. Model of a temple from Velletri,
sixth century B.C. *Rome, Museo di Villa Giulia*

period – in spite of the fact that in this case there are two cellas covered by a flat roof inside the building. The shrine was obviously dedicated to two divinities.[16]

The alae and the pronaus with side walls of the Fiesole temple should make us reconsider the current reconstructions of even such great and famous temples as that on the acropolis of Ardea, the 'Ara della Regina' Temple at Tarquinia, and the Portonaccio Temple at Veii [26, 27]. It is not only uncertain whether they had three cellas or alae, but we must also admit as a possibility that they had closed side walls in their pronai, like the Fiesole temple, and only four columns in front of the walls of the central cella. At Veii, inscriptions seem to indicate a triad (Artemis, Minerva, and perhaps Turan), but the remains are inconclusive. The larger temple at Pyrgi [28] seems to have been the

wealthy sanctuary of Leucothea (Eileithyia), which Dionysius, the tyrant of Syracuse, plundered in 384. Thus, it most probably had one cella and alae. The smaller temple is a peripteral temple of Greek type.

Some other temples may illustrate the different possibilities. Temple C on the temple terrace of Marzabotto, dated to the fifth century, seems to have been a temple with cella and alae, but even there different reconstructions have been proposed. The great fourth-third-century temple in the Contrada Celle at Falerii (Civita Castellana) [32] and the fifth-century temple at the Belvedere at Orvieto [33] seem also to have been three-cella temples. The former is truly grandiose. The width of the cellas is about 130 feet. They are built against the rear wall of an almost square enclosure, measuring some 260 by 260 feet. The smaller three-cella temple of

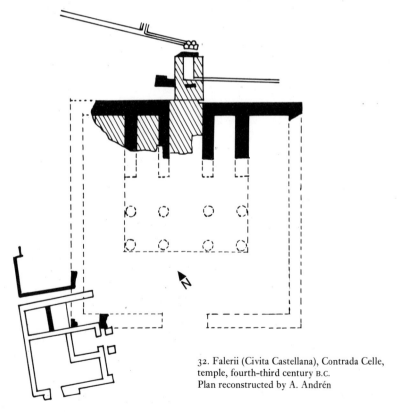

32. Falerii (Civita Castellana), Contrada Celle, temple, fourth-third century B.C.
Plan reconstructed by A. Andrén

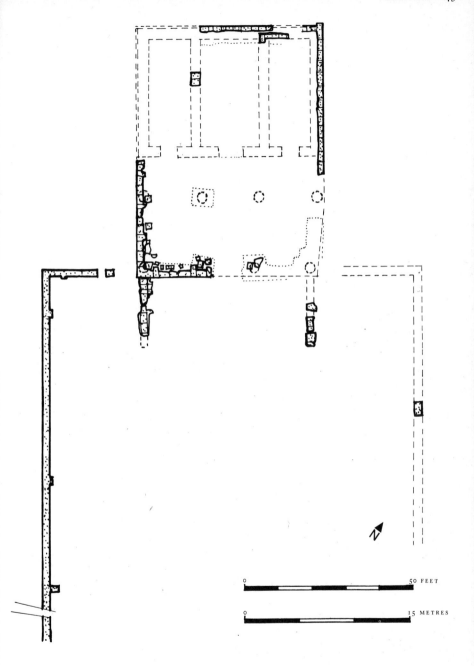

33. Orvieto, Belvedere Temple, fifth century B.C. Plan

Orvieto measures 71 feet 11 inches by 55 feet 5 inches (21.91 by 16.90 m.). To the right and left, in line with the four columns of the temple front, is a wall of tufa blocks which enclosed the sacred area. It projects some 30 feet beyond the corners of the front of the temple and then turns at right angles. Some 175 feet (53 m.) of the left side wall are preserved, and a short part of the right one. These enclosed areas in front of the temples have an archaic predecessor in the temple of Volsinii (Bolsena) [20]. Their tradition seems to live on in the Imperial fora of Rome. The arrangement implies strict axial symmetry.[17]

Plans

Indisputable evidence for the plan of an old Etruscan temple is afforded by Vulci, Pyrgi, and the already mentioned three-cella temple dedicated in 509 to the triad Jupiter Optimus Maximus, Juno, and Minerva on the Capitoline Hill in Rome [34]. Etruscan diviners, a sculptor from Veii (Vulca), and Etruscan workers were employed for the planning, decoration, and construction of the Roman temple. As the centuries went on, the temple was restuccoed and the interior lavishly modernized – as were Early Christian and medieval churches in Renaissance and Baroque times.[18] But the old-fashioned archaic temple remained as a reminder of Etruscan culture in central Italy throughout the rapid progress of Rome in the sixth century until a great fire destroyed it in 83 B.C. It was reconstructed in 69 B.C., and after that it was embellished – that is, rebuilt in the hellenistic style with high Greek marble columns – but Dionysius (IV, 61) affirms that the old plan was

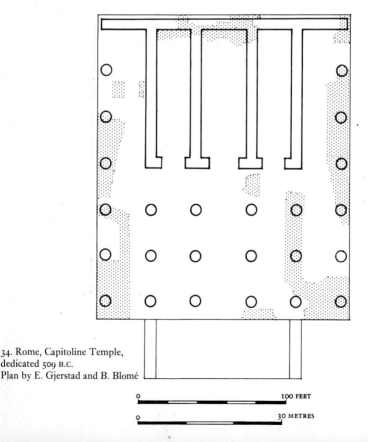

34. Rome, Capitoline Temple,
dedicated 509 B.C.
Plan by E. Gjerstad and B. Blomé

0   100 FEET

0   30 METRES

kept. Tacitus (*Historiae*, IV, 53), in addition, writes that the plan was venerated and considered sacrosanct when the temple was rebuilt in the grand Imperial marble style after fires in the Flavian Age. *Nolle deos mutari veterem formam*; the actual remains on the Capitoline Hill wholly substantiate these solemn words.

Still to be seen is a mighty substructure which, in conformity with Vitruvius's prescriptions (III, 4. I), was 'carried down into the solid ground as far as the magnitude of the work seems to require, and the whole substructure ... as solid as it possibly can be laid'. The same kind of irregular piled-up substructures below buildings can be seen in many places; for instance, below the (now vanished) podium of the temple on the acropolis of Ardea. Such irregular substructures also occur below regularly built fortification walls, as, for instance, in the outer circuit of Veii [56] and below the Etruscan fortification under the medieval castle of San Giovenale [57]. Above the Capitoline substructure an inner wall of the podium can still be seen, once destined to carry the columns in front of the eastern wall of the cellas (it now serves as a wall of the corridor between the Palazzo dei Conservatori and the Museo Nuovo). The height of the podium seems to have been about 13 feet – a height which, according to Varro, Catulus, the builder of the temple of 69 B.C., considered low (Gellius, *Noctes Atticae*, II, 10). The width of the preserved inner wall of the podium of the cellas is *c.* 13 feet 7 inches (4.15 m.). The whole podium measured 204 by 175 feet (62.25 by 53.30 m.). The relation between length and width is thus roughly 7:6; yet Vitruvius (IV, 7) prescribes 6:5 for his smaller model temple with two rows of four columns in front and no alae flanking the three cellas. Dionysius (IV, 61) says the podium was 800 feet in circumference and almost square. The excess of length over width was not a full 15 feet. This statement is incompatible with the remains of the temple, and scholars have in vain tried to explain the incongruities. In a general way, however, it confirms that the Capitoline Temple was very large and appeared squarish –

as Vitruvius prescribes (IV, 7) in his rules for an Etruscan temple without columns along the side walls. The substructure and the remains of the podium, as they stand today, further show that – in spite of Dionysius's erroneous measurements – we can safely believe his general description of the plan of the old temple. It had, he says, a closed rear wall (with extending wings right and left), and consisted of three parallel cellas under one roof, separated by partition walls; the middle shrine was dedicated to Jupiter, while on one side stood that of Juno and on the other, that of Minerva. The central part of the building, inside the peristyle, was in other words just what Vitruvius (IV, 7) demands in his prescription for a Tuscan temple. Both Dionysius (IV, 61) and the remains prove that the three cellas of the Capitoline Temple had alae with a row of columns outside the side walls and in front of the eight columns of the pronaus. Instead of Vitruvius's eight columns in front of the three cellas, the Capitoline Temple thus had eighteen columns in its monumental pro-domus.[19]

The Capitoline Temple is the largest Etruscan temple known to us. We may ask if it was the worship of the Roman triad, Jupiter, Juno, and Minerva, known already from an older temple, the Capitolium Vetus on the Quirinal (Varro, *Lingua Latina*, V, 158; below, p. 110), which first induced the Etruscan master builders, employed by the Etruscan kings of Rome, to build three cellas, thereby enlarging the type in breadth. We must, of course, also ask ourselves if there could have been still older and more distant prototypes for the arrangement with three cellas which Vitruvius regarded as the full development of the type. It may further be noted as an interesting fact that the width of the temple – that is, the distance between the corner columns on the front of the podium (163 feet 2 inches; 49.73 m.) – vies with the largest Greek temples: the corresponding measurements are for the Olympieion at Athens 134 feet 11 inches (41.11 m.), for the Temple of Artemis at Ephesus 180 feet 9 inches (55.10 m.), for the Heraion of Samos 195 feet 10 inches (59.70 m.), for Temple GT at Selinus 164 feet 3 inches (50.07 m.), and for the Olympieion at Agrigento 173 feet (52.74 m.).

To sum up: the plans of Etruscan temples, and especially the two types which Vitruvius emphasized as his *mos tuscanicus* or *dispositiones tuscanicae*, reveal a most characteristic arrangement of their own, with podia, frontal emphasis, closed back wall, and colonnades in the prodomus and in temples with alae along the side walls. These are the basic archaeological facts.

Podia

A discussion of the elevations must start with the podia. As a general rule it can be said that podia of ashlar masonry with stairs in front are typical of Etruscan temples. Vitruvius, in his third book (4. 4–5), mentions stairs in front of the podium. Already in the archaic temples we meet two kinds of podia. As already stated, the podium of the Capitoline Temple was 13 feet high. The south-east corner shows that the façade was straight and probably stuccoed. It

35. Rome, Temple C on the Largo Argentina, late fourth century B.C., podium

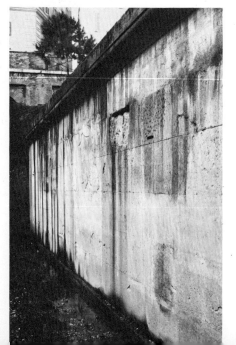

probably had a cornice on top, as has the oldest temple in the Largo Argentina (Temple C, dated to the late fourth century), where the podium is of about the same height as that of the Capitoline Temple [35].[20]

The temple in the lower town at Ardea has a rather different type of podium. It is one of the temples of Latium which, like the Capitoline Temple, attests the beginnings of Etruscan architecture south of the Tiber. It is dated by its oldest terracotta revetments to about 500. There are still some remains of swelling mouldings below the podium wall. There was, no doubt, also a cornice on top of the wall. These mouldings were connected with the rich Italic development of Greek mouldings known from the substructures of Etruscan seventh- to fifth-century tumuli [36], and also seen in the hourglass-shaped altars, with upper and lower echini, supporting sacrificial tables.[21]

The material customary for the cellas and the closed rear walls built on the podia seems to have been mud brick and timber. This accounts for the remains of the temples usually consisting only of subterranean substructures, podia, and fragments of terracotta revetments. Here one must remember Vitruvius's rule (11, 8. 17) that higher mud-brick walls should be two or three bricks thick. Instead of such clumsy walls, ashlar work may have been used for the greatest temples, as often in the sanctuaries of the latest centuries B.C.

The Orders

Vitruvius in his general rules (IV, 7) gives very clear data for the proportions of the columns and their height. The height of the columns should be one-third of the width of the temple. In some cases his rule gives fairly reasonable measurements, but in the case of the Capitoline Temple – both in 509 and 69 B.C. (below, p. 164) – as its width is 163 feet 2 inches (49.728 m.), the height of the columns should, if we follow Vitruvius's rule for a three-cella temple without alae, be 54 feet 5 inches (16.576 m.), a height which surpasses the columns of the great Doric

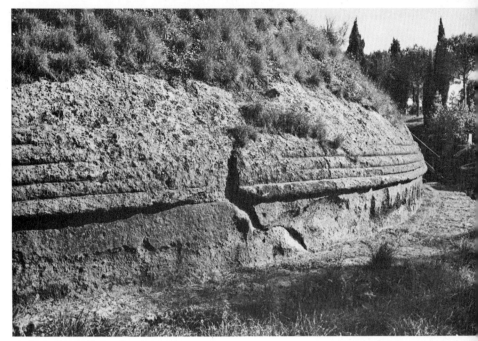

36. Caere (Cerveteri), Banditaccia cemetery,
podium of a tumulus, seventh century B.C.

temples in Sicily and almost equals the columns of the Olympieion in Athens (55 feet 5 inches; 16.89 m.). This height has been strongly advocated for the temples of 509, but I would not be prepared to allow such a scale for archaic Etruscan temples, or to accept Vitruvius's rules as a reliable basis for so sensational an assumption. Vitruvius's measurements are very likely those of the magnificent rebuilt temple of 69 B.C. In his second Verrine oration (IV, 31), Cicero exclaims that the fire of 83 seemed to him to have been almost sent by the gods 'to ensure that as the Capitol has been rebuilt with greater splendour, so it shall be adorned with greater richness than before (*quemadmodum magnificentius est restitutum, sic copiosius ornatum sit quam fuit*)'. When Dionysius (IV, 61) says that the foundations remained but that the costliness of the building was increased after the fire of 83, he evidently means the same. Finally, there is

Varro's statement that the builder of the new temple of 69 regarded the old podium as too low and out of proportion to the stately pediment he intended to build.[22]

The columns of the old temples were often of stuccoed wood. Etruria was famous for its 'very straight and very long beams' (Strabo, V, 2. 5). But in high temples, and especially in the later heightened temples, columns of stone – as, for instance, the central support of the sixth-century tholos of Quinto Fiorentino [96] – no doubt were preferred or even necessary. If the capitals and bases of wooden columns were not of stone, they were encased in terracotta.[23]

In his rules for columns, Vitruvius recommends the so-called Tuscan column, with accurate prescriptions for diminution at the top of the column, the height of base and plinth, the height of the capital, and the width of the abacus (IV, 7. 3). Characteristic of the Tuscan column

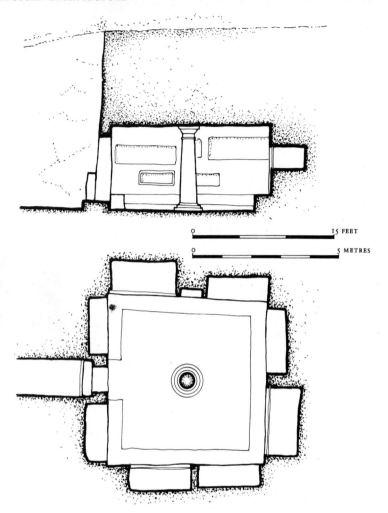

15 FEET

5 METRES

37. Vignanello, tomb with a Tuscan column,
c. 500 B.C. Section and plan

is the unfluted shaft whether straight or tapering towards one or both ends, and a capital akin to the Doric, consisting of a round cushion (*echinus*) and a square abacus. The bases were evidently inspired by Ionic columns. As in the case of the podia, a simple basic shape was enriched by influence from Greek architecture – as was the whole temple building.

We can trace columns of the Tuscan type from about 500, both in tombs and domestic architecture [37]. In the Etrusco-Roman temples of the third and second centuries, Tuscan columns and wooden Etruscan entablatures seem to have prevailed (for example, Signia, Alatri, Alba Fucens, Mons Albanus, Cosa). Tuscan columns and capitals further became popular in various kinds of Late Republican architecture, as seen in late tombs at Caere [38], porticoes in Rome and Pompeii, and, for instance, a peristyle of a sumptuous rebuilt house in Morgantina (Sicily). Imperial architecture – the Theatre of Marcellus, the Colosseum, and so on – continues this tradition.

This late renown of Tuscan columns and what Vitruvius concluded about their specific

lection for hellenistic elegance and architectural decoration which temples began to display more than a hundred years before Vitruvius.[24]

It would be wrong to assume, however, that Tuscan columns were essential from the beginning for Etruscan temples; Vitruvius is, again, too dogmatic and relied too much on the evidence of later Etrusco-Roman architecture. Casings of capitals from the archaic temples of

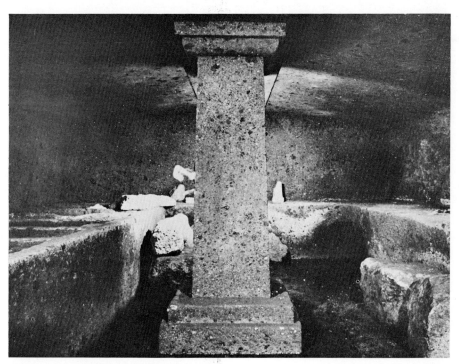

38. Caere (Cerveteri), Banditaccia cemetery, Late Etruscan tomb with Tuscan pillar

and original Italic character probably determined his choice of Tuscan columns as most appropriate for Etruscan temples: he evidently thought that they were more truly Italic. This may reveal the same romantic nationalistic tendency which can be traced in his age in Roman poetry, and sometimes also in architecture, side by side with an overwhelming predi-

Fortuna and Mater Matuta in the Forum Boarium in Rome show that as early as the sixth and fifth centuries columns with fluted Ionic shafts and capitals of a quite different shape from those prescribed by Vitruvius could be used in temples of the Etruscan type [39]. A fourth-century column from Vulci confirms that fluted Ionic shafts were adopted also in Etruria itself

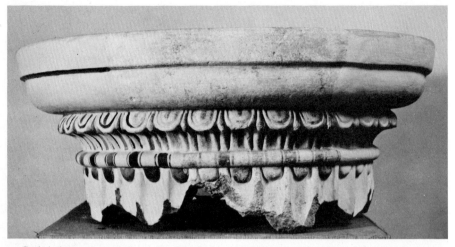

39. Capital of a temple on the Forum Boarium, Rome, sixth-fifth centuries B.C. *Rome, Palazzo dei Conservatori*

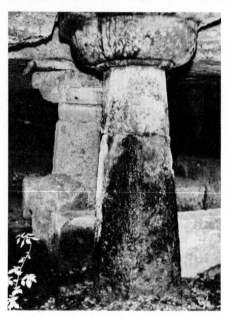

40. Caere (Cerveteri), Banditaccia cemetery, Tomb of the Doric Columns, sixth century B.C.

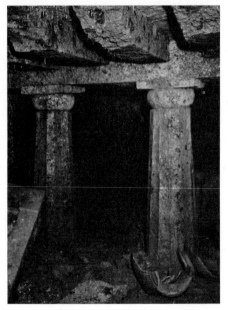

41. San Giuliano, Tomb of Princess Margrethe of Denmark, Doric capitals, sixth century B.C.

at an early date. Tombs [40, 41, 82] prove that Doric, Ionic, and especially the so-called Aeolic capitals were popular among the Etruscans from the sixth century onwards.[25]

I must restate that, at least as early as the Romans, the Etruscans could amalgamate an Etruscan plan with Greek columns and architraves of stone, as seen in the tombs imitating temple façades. Two tombs at Norchia [42] have rock-cut gables, with Doric columns and Doric entablatures displaying some characteristic Etruscan liberties. The columns were head and a Corinthian motif at the bottom. The first impression of the whole capital recalls the freely varied Aeolic capitals of many of the Etruscan tomb chambers, though capitals with

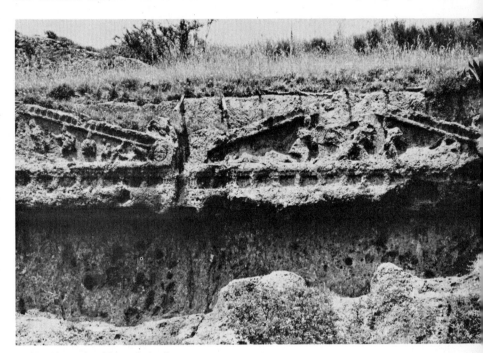

42. Norchia, tombs with temple façades,
fourth century B.C. or later

perhaps unfluted. Above a smooth architrave follows the frieze of triglyphs with guttae pointing downwards and elongated metopes with human heads on them. The unorthodox impression is increased by Ionic dentillated cornices above the frieze. In the pediments are preserved remains of highly agitated reliefs. All these details are now badly weathered. The earliest possible date seems to me to be the fourth century.

To the second century belongs a still more elaborate sepulchral temple façade on an Etruscan plan and with a most lively hellenistic elevation: the famous Tomba Ildebranda of Sovana [29]. The capitals of the colonnades have Ionic volutes to right and left of a female

figures are a hellenistic device known from the eastern parts of the Greek world. The Greek towns of south Italy or Sicily may have transferred it to the Etruscans, the Romans, and to Campania. The Ildebranda tomb stands out as a most interesting specimen of Etruscan temple architecture in the provincial, unrestrained hellenistic style with figured capitals and griffons and a rich floral pattern on architrave and frieze. The tombs of Norchia and Sovana may show what Vitruvius reacted against when he summarized his stern classicistic rules for the real Etruscan style: they are in evident contrast both to the Early Hellenistic Age in Italy and the florid and enriched decoration of the post-Augustan, Imperial Age.[26]

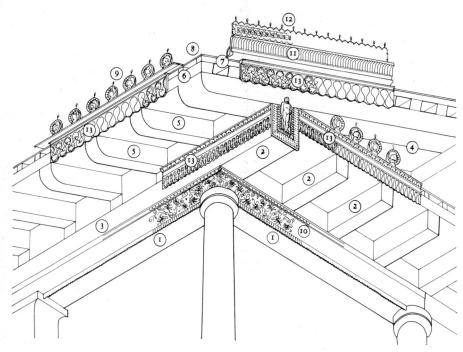

43. Cosa, Capitolium. Reconstruction

1. Architrave (trabes compactiles)
2. Mutules (traiecturae mutulorum) projecting in front of the tympanum
3. Joists (tigna)
4. Pediment (tympanum, fastigium)
5. Rafters (cantherii)
6. Purlins (templa; Vitruvius IV, 2.1)

7. Common rafters (asseres; Vitruvius IV, 2.1)
8. Sheeting of planks (opercula)
9. Antefixes
10. Frieze of the architrave
11. Sima
12. Pierced cresting
13. Revetment plaques below the sima and eaves

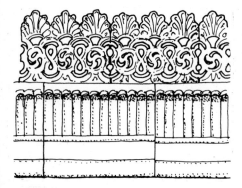

44. Cosa, strigillated sima and cresting

Pediments and Roofs

After his rules for proportions and height of columns, Vitruvius (IV, 7. 4–5) proceeds to a very clear description of the wooden entablatures of what he considered the real Etruscan temples [43, 44]:

> Upon the columns lay the main beams [*trabes compactiles*, corresponding to the architrave of a Greek temple] fastened together, commensurate with the requirements of the size of the building. These beams fastened together should be laid so as to be equivalent in thickness to the neck-

ing at the top of a column, and should be fastened together by means of dowels and dove-tailed tenons.... Above the beams and the walls [that is, above the wooden architrave] let the mutules [*traiecturae mutulorum*] project to a distance equal to one quarter of the height of a column; along the front of them nail casings; build the tympanum of the pediment either in masonry or in wood.

The *traiecturae mutulorum* were the projecting ends of the joists (*tigna*) laid lengthwise above the architrave of the side walls from the rear wall to the front of the temple. In greater temples, joists were also laid in between and parallel with the architraves of the side walls.

This description is, no doubt, reliable for temples which Vitruvius had actually seen – for instance, at Cosa – though temples without projecting mutules (pp. 58 f.) seem to have been more usual. There seems to be nothing to add to it except that the description of the pediment is chosen in Vitruvius's usual way among several different possibilities among which he codifies one as the orthodox Etruscan disposi-

tion. The paragraph ends with the much-discussed words about the *stillicidium*; that is, the eaves of the Etruscan temple. Above the pediment, Vitruvius says, 'its ridge-pole, rafters, and purlins are to be placed in such a way that the eaves of the completed roof should be equivalent to one-third [of the roof without eaves] (*ut stillicidium tecti absoluti tertiario respondeat*)'. Scholars have referred this 'one-third' to the completed roof (Morgan, Fensterbusch), to the pitch of the roof (Granger in the Loeb edition), or to the height of the columns (Frank Brown), which, since Vitruvius derived their height from the width of the temple, serve as a basic unit of the design in paragraphs 3–5. In any case, one essential fact is evident: the Etruscan temples had very wide eaves. This seems quite natural, as the walls of mud brick had to be protected. It is one of the distinctive features which must be kept in mind when trying to visualize them.

The appearance of the roofs can be illustrated by a much-discussed small terracotta model from Nemi, when the eaves which are broken are restored to the roof [45]. Confirmation comes from the actual remains. On the temple

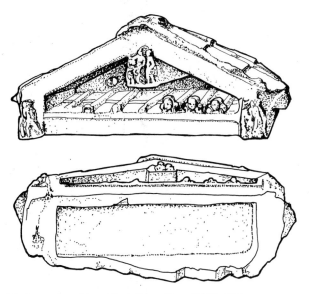

45. Terracotta model of a temple roof from Nemi. *Rome, Museo di Villa Giulia*

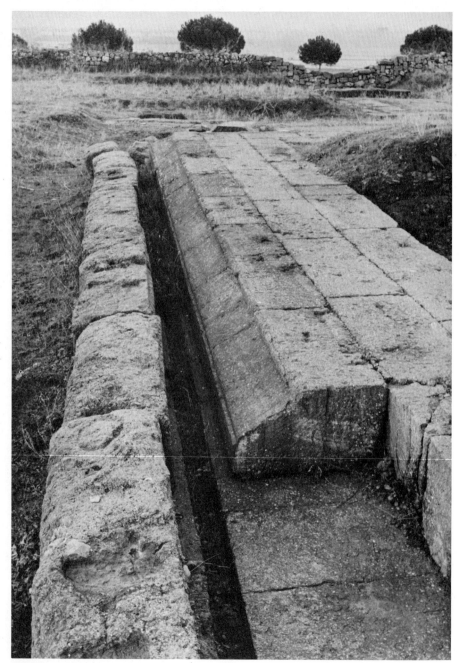

46. Gabii, temple, late third century B.C., podium with benches for statues along the sides and back

in the lower town at Ardea from the Etruscan period of Latium (*c.* 500 B.C.), the drip-line along the south-east side of the podium proves that the overhang of the eaves was at least 6 feet 9 inches (2.05 m.). Observation of the drip-line along the north flank of the Roman Capitolium of Cosa shows that its overhang was 7 feet 7 inches (2.30 m.). The recent Spanish excavations at Gabii have revealed benches for terracotta statues in front of the long sides and the back of the podium [46]. These statues were probably protected by the eaves, and as they were placed about 2 feet (60 cm.) from the wall of the podium, the eaves were probably between 3 and 6 feet wide. Archaic naiskoi in Sicily could have the same distance – some 6 feet between wall and gutter. The wide eaves belong to the many external features of Etruscan architecture of which we do not know whether they were due to Etruscan traditions or to a legacy from Archaic Greek structures, which were kept and developed in central Italy, while the Greeks often gave them up. In the case discussed here, it seems self-evident that the earlier temples of the Roman Republic inherited their wide eaves from the Etruscans. Like the Tuscan columns, they were kept until the radical hellenization of the second century.

Vitruvius (II, I. 5) speaks about thatched roofs of old temples on the Arx of Rome, and Pliny (XVI, 36) quotes Cornelius Nepos's statement that the roofs in Rome were covered with shingles (*scandulae*) until the beginning of the third century. As far back as we have material from Etruscan temples it is clear that the purlins of the roofs (*templa*), with common rafters (*asseres*) and a sheathing of planks above them, were protected by flat rectangular tiles (*tegulae*) with semi-cylindrical cover-tiles (*imbrices*) above the joints. The overhang of the lowest tiles along the eaves had a decorated underside, visible from below; and the foremost cover-tiles were protected by antefixes resting upon these eaves-tiles [47, 49].[27]

The pediments were, of course, the most conspicuous part of the roof. They could, no doubt, be differently arranged during the Etruscan

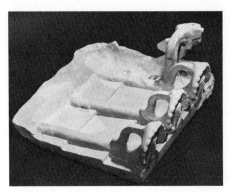

47. Roof of temple model with rectangular pantiles and semi-cylindrical cover tiles with antefixes. *Rome, Museo di Villa Giulia*

saecula. The joists (*tigna*) above the architraves (*trabes compactiles*) of the side walls, with their projecting mutules, of which Vitruvius speaks (IV, 7. 4–5; p. 54) [43], carried the ceiling of the cella (in larger temples, together with beams in between) and the rafters of the roof (*cantherii*). In each gable heavy rafters formed the pediments.

After summarizing what we know about the roof it is necessary to return to Vitruvius's rule that the mutules should project in front of the architrave, which on the front of the temple rested upon the columns of the pronaus, 'to a distance equal to one-quarter of the height of the columns'. Perhaps the model of a temple roof from Nemi [45] shows traces of this strange arrangement, illustrated by the tentative reconstruction of illustration 43. Still more illuminating is a model of a temple from Satricum [48], in spite of the columns at the ends of the mutules. We may also compare a small model of a temple from the Heraion near Argos, though there is only a flat balcony, supported by two columns, on the front of the temple. If we follow what the Roman temples of Cosa suggest, in Temple D (first phase 170–160) Vitruvius's rule would give us a projection of the mutules in front of the architrave measuring 3 feet 10 inches (1.16 m.), which seems perfectly pos-

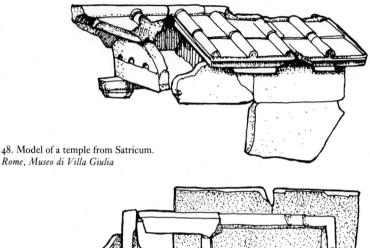

48. Model of a temple from Satricum.
Rome, Museo di Villa Giulia

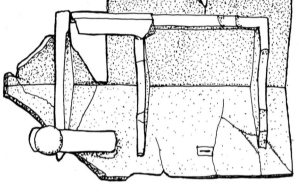

sible. On the Capitolium of Cosa (about 150) the result of Vitruvius's rule would be a projection of about 5 feet 7 inches (1.70 m.). This unsupported span is surprisingly wide, especially since the pediment had to carry terracotta figures, but it seems to be confirmed by the west end of the drip-line along the south side of the temple, which continues 5 feet 10 inches (1.78 m.) beyond the west wall.

In larger temples Vitruvius's rule for the projecting mutules is structurally hardly possible. As usual, he has probably dogmatized and codified traditional rules of proportion, which the temples did not always follow. In the case of the mutules he might have been reacting against the prevailing Greek type of temples. This fact has

been disputed, but the gist of his words cannot be ignored: he had seen temples with projecting mutules, and considered them to represent the correct Etruscan *dispositiones*.[28]

Scholars generally reconstruct Etruscan temples without projecting pediments, in clear contrast to Vitruvius's description as it stands, but with support from terracotta models [25], the tombs of Norchia [42], and later Roman hellenized temples such as the Temple of Fortuna Virilis by the Tiber in Rome and the Doric temple at Cori [cf. 151 f.]. Again, we cannot doubt that the Etruscans built temples in that way – probably under the influence of Greek temples, which never had such strange projecting pediments. But when the Etruscans first abandoned the special type of pediments described by Vitruvius cannot be established. Very likely both types were used from the earliest time of Greek influence.

From the sixth century onwards the pediment could be left plain or be decorated with sculpture. The rear pediment and pediments of small temples no doubt usually remained undecorated. A very characteristic shape could be given to the plain pediments. The model from Nemi [45] has a deeply recessed pediment with an inner flat roof probably projecting in front of the architrave. It rests on the mutules and is covered by tiles. On the cover-tiles along the edge of the inner roof are antefixes. This pediment from Nemi and other archaeological material show casings nailed on the mutules of the side walls, as Vitruvius prescribes, and on the end of the ridge-beam. To the first half of the fifth century belongs a ridge-beam revetment from the larger temple at Pyrgi [28] showing a powerful battle-scene from Greek mythology in later archaic style, but with quite a strong flavour of the wild Etruscan temperament.

A convincing reconstruction of a pediment with warriors from a small Etruscan temple or treasury in the Ny Carlsberg Glyptotek proves that as early as the sixth century the Etruscans began to use sculpture in the Greek manner. Much later, probably in the second century, the pediments from Talamone, as reconstructed in the Florence Museum, again have complicated pictorial compositions, though now in the hellenistic style.[29] Finds from Orvieto (Temples of the Belvedere and Via di S. Leonardo), Civita Castellana (Lo Scasato), Civita Alba, and the well-known team of two winged horses from the 'Ara della Regina' Temple at Tarquinia show (as do other finds) that pediment sculpture flourished in the fourth and following centuries. Sometimes it even displays capricious violations of what we consider Greek taste – for instance, the heads and shoulders of terracotta figures on the pediment of the Belvedere Temple at Orvieto project beyond the triangular space of the tympanum, intruding on the cornice of the pediment.[30]

Ornament

The pedimental sculpture was only a part of the external terracotta ornament which the Etruscans added to their temples [43, 44]. The origin of all this decoration was the Archaic Greek temples with terracotta revetments. The main Greek centre during the seventh century seems to have been the towns of central Greece. The habit of adorning temples with terracotta revetments soon spread to the Ionian towns, to Sardis (as we know from a beautiful terracotta), and all over the Greek world, assuming different stylistic characteristics in its various centres. Towards 550 it reached Etruria and central Italy. It inspired a lively, sometimes exuberant style, whether the artists were from Greek towns or were Etruscans, like Vulca of Veii (Pliny, XXXV, 157). The delightful terracottas from south Italy and Sicily also had characteristics of their own and their technically exquisite and artistically refined art persisted longer than in Greece. As a rule the Greek temples were built of stuccoed limestone, poros and other durable material, or in marble. The rock-cut tympana of the tombs of Norchia [42] as well as several sarcophagi show that the Etruscans could use alabaster, tufa, and even marble or travertine for their reliefs. But the old terracotta revetments obviously served their exuberant, lively artistic taste better, and they remained popular down to the time of Late Republican Rome.

Pliny (XXXV, 152, 157 f.) praises the artistic and technical quality of the venerable terracotta sculpture. As a matter of fact, it forms a most important part of the history of Etruscan art and is discussed in another volume of The Pelican History of Art. Here I can only briefly mention how the coroplasts retold Greek sagas, used contaminated and revived Greek ornaments, or represented their own processions, horse races, or at times historical events. With some delay, due to the use of old models for casting, conservatism, and, of course, provincial isolation, they followed the successive Greek styles from Archaic to Classical and Hellenistic, but were never quite happy with Greek discipline and showed a certain capriciousness with their fabulous beasts and half-human beings. There is in many of these reliefs a wild spirit, an unrestrained vivacity, and an agility which mark them as Etruscan.[31]

Whatever the stylistic causes of this predilection for terracottas, it is evident, in any case, that the terracottas were structurally necessary for the protection of the wooden parts of Etruscan mud-brick temples. But even after mud brick had been given up, we still occasionally see terracotta ornament persisting on temples of stuccoed tufa or limestone of the last centuries B.C. in central Italy.

Now for the antefixes along the eaves. These were more or less horseshoe-shaped reliefs. They can be merely decorative, but often represent gods, the head of Medusa, daemons, or heroic or comic groups of figures. The figures can – like the pediment sculpture from Orvieto, or like the figures in front of the terracotta gutters above the pediments – boldly swagger in front of the horseshoe-shaped antefixes or even rise in an outrageous manner above them, in which case they had decorated back supports on them, as shown by fragments of an antefix probably from the temple on the acropolis of Ardea (*c.* 500 B.C.) [49]. On these terracotta end-pieces of the cover-tiles the imagination, love of colour, and agitation of the Etruscan and Italic artistic mind found a place to work triumphs. If human figures appear they repeat Greek motifs, but it seems superfluous to seek precise Greek models for the exuberant Italic development of borrowed prototypes.[32]

The same is true of the quadrangular casings nailed on the ends of the mutules or the round discs which protected the ends of the ridge-poles and crowned the pediments. These discs were sometimes larger than the end of the ridge-pole, and were suspended from it as from a peg [50]. When Vitruvius, speaking about areostyle temples (III, 3. 5), says that the gables (*fastigia*) were ornamented in the Tuscan fashion with statues of terracotta or bronze, he is probably referring to richly developed acroteria above

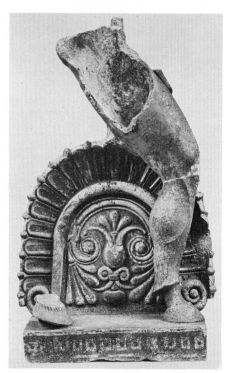

49. Antefix from Ardea, *c.* 500 B.C.
Rome, Museo di Villa Giulia

the pediments. Pliny and other authors tell of a terracotta group (Jupiter on a quadriga) on the apex of the Capitoline Temple, and Livy informs us that in 296 it was replaced by another, probably of gilded bronze. These crowning decorations could assume fantastic shapes such as high palmettes and groups of warriors. Pliny (XXXV, 154) seems to indicate that the old Temple of Ceres, Libera, and Liber on the Aventine Hill also had sculpture above both pediments. The same obsessive and tireless desire to brighten the exterior of temples with lavish ornament also inspired, from oldest times, rich acroteria on the pediments. To the temples on the Forum Boarium (dated about 500; see p. 51) belonged acroteria with volutes rising 4 feet 1 inch (1.24 m.) from an oval base measur-

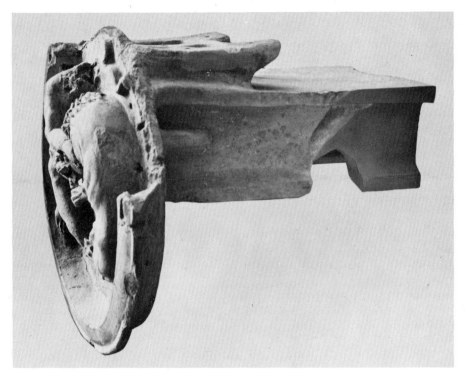

50. Ridge-pole revetment from a temple at Fratte, fourth century B.C. *Salerno, Museo Provinciale*

ing 2 feet (0.6 m.) high. Such ornaments were placed in a sloping row along the simas, facing the acroteria of the eaves, as shown on a coin dated *c.* 78 B.C. Pairs of volutes of this kind could also have crowned the apex or the whole ridge-pole of a temple, renewing a motif known already from the Early Iron Age, although there it was purely ornamental and without structural function.[33]

In the great Portonaccio Temple of Veii some of the cover-tiles of the ridge-pole were in the form of saddles, acting as bases for the famous terracotta statues of Apollo, Mercury, Hercules, and Latona (now in the Villa Giulia Museum in Rome) [51]. The gods thus seemed to move along the ridge of the roof. With these can be compared animals adorning the ridge-poles of archaic models of houses and great central acroteria of Greek temples from south Italy and Sicily, as, for instance, a horseman sitting on a ridge-tile which is shaped like a horse, from Camarina, or the youth on a galloping horse from Locri.[34]

The Roman temple at Gabii affords us another instance of assiduous endeavours to enliven the temples. As already referred to on p. 57, benches with indentations for feet and with lead dowels in them for terracotta statues were constructed in front of the long sides of the podium, reaching to the stairs, and along the back [46]. Thus, the podium was surrounded by figures on three sides; a decoration which may, however, have been a Roman addition. There is still no parallel from Etruria.

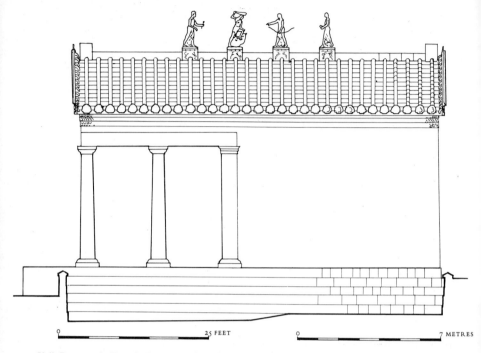

51. Veii, Portonaccio Temple. Reconstruction. Elevation

The external terracotta embellishments must, at their richest, have given the temples a fantastic appearance. Another very impressive feature was the revetments of the core of the building [43, 44]. There were ornamental reliefs nailed to the door jambs, and (as has already been said) on the ends of the ridge-poles and on the projecting mutules below the pediment. Rich, purely ornamental or figurative reliefs covered the architraves. The raking, usually strigilated simas above the pediments were crowned with pierced crests. Revetment plaques hung below the simas and in front of the purlins (*templa*) and below the common rafters (*asseres*) and planks (*opercula*) of the eaves. To what has been said about figures rising above antefixes and pediments may be added as a last example the simas from Arezzo, datable about 400, with warriors fighting.

These protective ornaments remained, on the whole, in the same position during the whole history of the temples of Etruscan type in central Italy down to the second century. At the end a classicistic taste inspired by Greek architecture reacted against the late terracotta decoration in the overflowing hellenistic style.[35]

Abundant archaeological material shows that Etruscan furniture, chariots, etc., could be covered with plates of bronze from the very beginnings of Etruscan culture in Italy in the seventh century. When we hear about 'buildings of bronze' in the Orient, Greece, and Rome, this, of course – except for some fairy tales – refers to metal-coated structures of wood or mud brick. That this common Mediterranean method of protection and adornment of buildings was regarded as ancient in Italy, as in Greece, is shown by what was told in Rome about a tiny *aedicula aenea* which was originally erected by Numa Pompilius to the Muses. Our evidence from central Italy begins with references to bronze gates of the so-called Servian Wall, an *aenea aedicula* erected on the Forum Romanum in 304, and remains of architectural ornament in bronze dating from the fourth century. The latter consists of fragments of plain bronze tiles and revetments of the same sort as those of terracotta, found at the sanctuary of Diana at Nemi and at Palestrina.[36]

Liturgical Disposition

The strict frontality of the temples may have suggested an axial planning of the areas and altars in front of them. It became the prevailing rule for the temples of the Roman Republic and for temples of the Roman type throughout the Empire. It should, of course, always be remembered that axial symmetry was fashionable, at least in later hellenistic temples.[37] However, axial symmetry cannot be claimed for the old Etruscan altars: it seems, on the contrary, that they were placed according to the demands of the cult, facing east, or as old traditions (from before the building of the temples) determined. On the other hand, from archaic times onwards we find regular square areas in front of the

temples with entrance on the central axis of the cella; for example, at the old temple of Volsinii [20] and probably the temples on the Contrada Celle of Falerii [32] and at the Belvedere of Orvieto [33]. The Capitolium of Cosa had a square area of the same type as these Etruscan temples, though with altar and entrances oriented in agreement with the city plan and the oldest traditions of the place. The Etruscans, no doubt, had rules for the placing of the temples much the same as those we know for altars and places 'set aside and limited by certain formulaic words for the purpose of augury or the taking of the auspices' (Varro, *Lingua Latina*, VII, 8). Vitruvius and some other architects recommended that temples face the western quarter of the sky, enabling the worshippers at the altars to face simultaneously the sunrise and the statues in the temple. This rule and the exceptions to it admitted by Vitruvius (IV, 5. 2) do not agree with our archaeological findings. Here we note a prevailing tendency to make the temples face south, though with considerable deviations, no doubt due to lost traditions of the different cults. In any case, it seems clear that the general direction, which we can trace in our material, comes from a basic, non-Greek, tradition present in Etruscan temples even in their hellenized form.[38]

52. Acquarossa, part of the monumental building in Zone F, with courtyard on the right, second half of the sixth century B.C. (see Note 38)

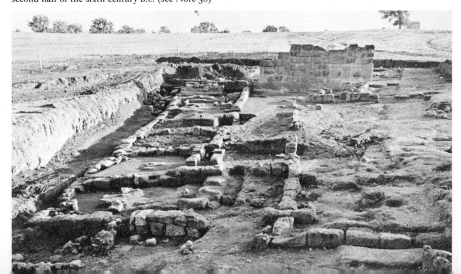

Before leaving these temples and their characteristic plan, their wide eaves, their display of colourful terracottas, and, often, most fanciful silhouettes which were formed by the acroteria on the roof, I wish briefly to sum up my opinion on the origin of their basic *dispositio* with closed rear wall, great prodomus, and frontal emphasis. It seems clear to me that these features were introduced into Italy by the Etruscan culture in the eighth and seventh centuries, either through trade, or brought to the country between the Tiber and the Arno by Etruscan emigrants from Asia Minor. The famous eighth-century Assyrian relief of the temple at Muṣaṣir in Urartu seems to me to show a part of this background of different types of temples in Asia [53].[39] In any case, I regard

resembled that of the atrium-houses, which also seem to me to display a fundamentally foreign architectural type, though in Italy such houses became hellenized by the addition of columns and decorations in the Greek style and later were largely remodelled after the Greek fashion.

TOWN PLANNING

When we turn from the temples to the towns around them, we again have to keep in mind possible aboriginal Etruscan elements, common Mediterranean culture, Greek influence, and the specific development of all of these during the six Etruscan centuries in Italy. As in the case of the placing of temples, the Etruscans developed rules for building their towns. These

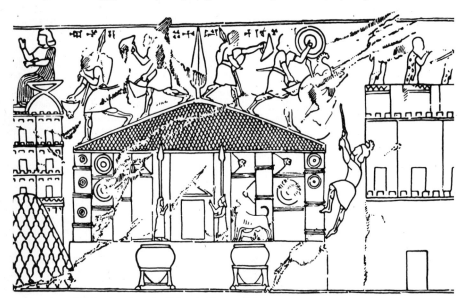

53. Assyrian relief showing the sack of Muṣaṣir, Urartu, eighth century B.C.

the basic concept of the typical Etruscan temples as of Eastern and not of Greek origin. But whatever the origin, it seems evident that a new history of this type of temple started in Italy and resulted in the monumental, externally hellenized great Etruscan and Roman sanctuaries. I assume that their history and development

rules, which we know about only from learned Late Roman elaborations, were found in the *Libri tagetici* or *sacra tagetica* of the Etruscans, ascribed to the mythical lawgiver Tages, and they include those about the foundation of towns (see p. 21) by means of a furrow ploughed around the future township [9]. Whether this

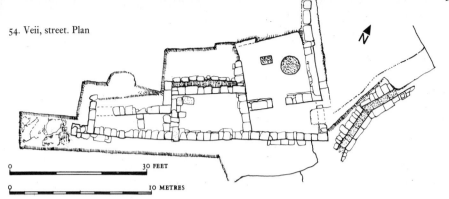

54. Veii, street. Plan

0 — 30 FEET
0 — 10 METRES

was taken over from the Early Iron Age, as I believe (see p. 23), or was part of Eastern elements in Etruscan life is not clear. To these founding ceremonies belonged also the *mundus*, a sacrificial pit in which the first fruits were deposited. The Romans employed the 'Etruscan ritual' (*etruscus ritus*) for their newly founded colonies, but also assumed that Lavinium and Rome had been founded in the same way. Roman writers have related how Romulus had summoned men from Etruria who prescribed all the details in accordance with their sacred ordinances and writings, thus giving the sanctity of old rites to their new towns.

The axial planning suggested by Etruscan temples and the rules about places for auguries and auspices may well have been a source of inspiration for the creation of regular towns. Vitruvius (I, 7. 1) quotes haruspices and rules for the location of temples from Etruscan treatises (*scripturae*), and ancient experts on the *disciplina etrusca* said that no old town was considered a proper one without three gates and three main streets (cf. p. 35). But in our archaeological evidence we cannot trace any master plan or any fixed quadrangular or circular perimeter heralding the Roman four-sided coloniae and castra among the oldest Etruscan towns or in Rome itself.[40]

Our material is scanty, but the scraps of evidence with which we must work seem to indicate that the original Etruscan settlements, *vetusta munificia*, were like the old, untidy, gradually developed Mediterranean towns such as Rome and Athens. They replaced in central Italy the Early Iron Age villages with crowds of square buildings of wood or mud brick or of stone along narrow crooked streets. This is the impression which the small excavated parts of Veii [54], Vetulonia [55], and the archaic settlement spread over the acropolis of San Giovenale give us.[41]

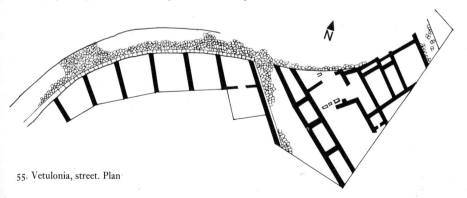

55. Vetulonia, street. Plan

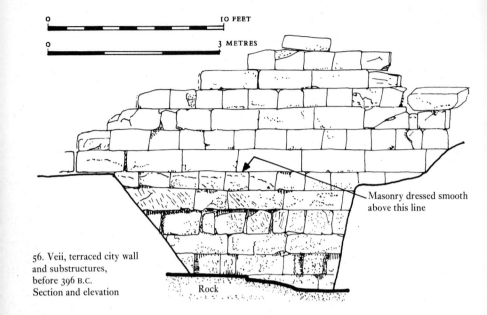

Masonry dressed smooth
above this line

56. Veii, terraced city wall
and substructures,
before 396 B.C.
Section and elevation

Rock

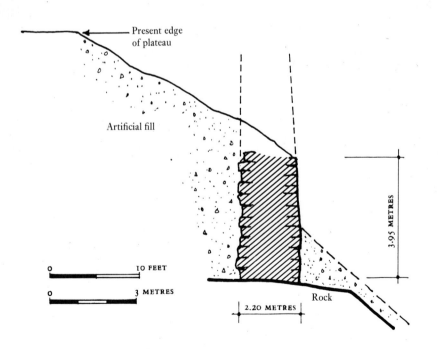

Present edge
of plateau

Artificial fill

3.95 METRES

Rock

2.20 METRES

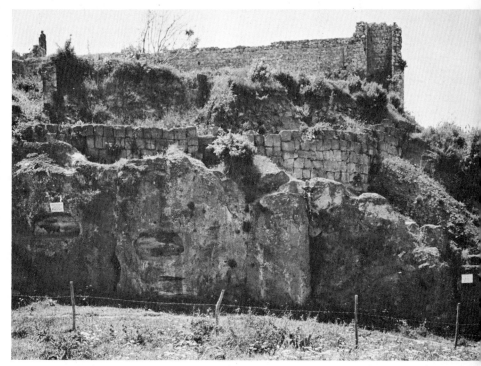

57. San Giovenale, Etruscan wall of the early fourth century B.C. below the thirteenth-century castle

Like the Early Iron Age villages, these old towns were mostly built on hills. The area of the settlement was in many cases defined by the shape of the hills and the lines of natural defence – *nativa praesidia*. Sometimes the table-lands were very large, and the settlement in such cases might have been somewhat dispersed. In the towns of San Giovenale and Luni, the larger old settlement – apparently because of the wars against Rome from about 400 – was reduced to the parts of the hills which could most easily be defended. Veii and Tarquinia are the most famous examples of such hill towns, not to speak of their offspring on the hills of Latium from the sixth century onwards: the Palatine, Esquiline, and Quirinal, Lavinium, Antium, Ardea [102], and many others.

The hillsides, if insufficient for defence, were supplemented by terrace walls [56-8]. The great period of these mighty strengthening walls came only during the wars against the Romans and Gauls in the fifth century and later. Among the most conspicuous are those protecting the lower town of Populonia, east of the acropolis, the walls of San Giovenale and Luni, and those of Tarquinia. At Veii the fortifications were strengthened by terrace walls against the Romans before the final defeat of 396. On the north-west side an *agger* was constructed and crowned by a wall supported by a solid substructure, as Vitruvius prescribes (I, 5. 1) [56]. A wall of the same kind was built against the east slope of the acropolis of San Giovenale and provided with an agger, protecting the outer side of the substructure. This wall, the steep slopes to the north and south, and a rock-cut *fossa* to the west fortified the central part of the acropolis [57]. The old, larger settlement of the

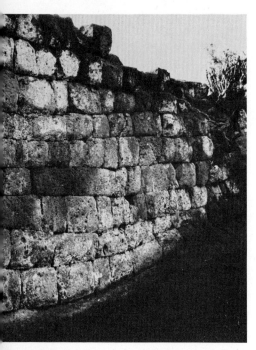

58. Luni, walls, early fourth century B.C.

easternmost point a mound was thrown up around a substructure for a crowning tower [59]. These fortress-towns obviously belonged to the time of the Roman war against Veii, or were, in any case, a part of the frontier of Tarquinia against Rome in the ensuing war in the fourth and early third centuries. Already before the Romans had conquered Veii, the Faliscans of Capena enlarged their fortifications, foreseeing that the Romans after Veii would continue the war, attacking them and the Etruscans, whom they had warned in vain.

These fortifications seem to belong to a type pioneered by the Etruscans in central Italy; no doubt they themselves were inspired by Greek town walls. At Rusellae, north of Grosseto, as early as about 600 a wall of mud bricks measuring some $2\frac{3}{4}-3\frac{1}{3}$ by 16-18 inches (7-8.5 by 40-45 cm.) was built upon a stone foundation, as in Smyrna. In the sixth century it was replaced by a stronger terrace wall of polygonal stone blocks. The walls of Rusellae may have been built against the local tribes, but they may also, of course - like the Greek city walls in south Italy - have been connected with internal feuds among the Etruscans themselves, before the system of city-states of the fifth and following centuries, as known to us, was established.[42]

Varro and other authors affirm that land surveying (*limitatio*) belonged to the *disciplina etrusca*, and the Romans (no doubt correctly) regarded the Etruscans as their teachers, though they soon developed their special *centuriatio* on

seventh and sixth centuries was reduced to this fortress. The same happened at Luni [58]. The hillsides of the east part of the acropolis were strengthened by mighty ashlar walls where necessary, two fossas protected the west side, and in a gap in the natural defences at the

59. Luni, acropolis, mound with a tower at the eastern end,
early fourth century B.C. Reconstruction

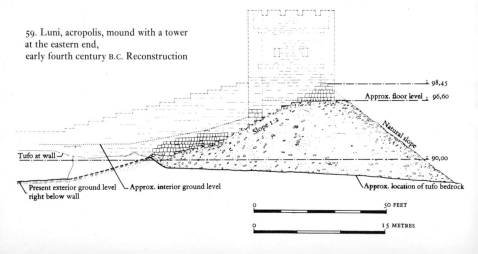

Approx. floor level · 96,60

98,45

Slope 1:2

Natural slope

Tufo at wall

90,00

Present exterior ground level right below wall

Approx. interior ground level

Approx. location of tufo bedrock

0   50 FEET

0   15 METRES

the lands around their towns, especially around their newly built colonies.

The Etruscan limitatio, no doubt from its beginnings, was connected with Greek geometry (Herodotus, 11, 109) and common Mediterranean practice, but evidently the Etruscans gradually developed this international science in their own way with typical religious precautions of their own, claiming special divine inspiration. Safe conclusions concerning the modes of their limitatio can be drawn from what the Roman land surveyors tell us: they connect it with the regular division of the fields outside the cities, as also does Varro (*Lingua Latina*, VI, 53). In old towns (*vetusta municipia*), the previous crowded settlements and the town hills (*locorum difficultates*) prevented the Roman surveyors from systematizing the town plan. But in new towns they could achieve what they considered to be the ideal master plan (*pulcherrima ratio*) of straight streets carried in from four gates and meeting in a central forum.[43]

This type, whether Etruscan or Roman, brings us from the Etruscan limitatio to a great revolution in the history of ancient town planning. In the sixth century or even before, the Greeks in Sicily, the Ionians in Asia Minor, and the Etruscans had started to plan their new towns in a rational, regular way. No doubt it had a background in the town planning of the old Oriental empires, as related by Herodotus (I, 178 f.) of Babylon.[44]

Whatever memories of their old towns may have predisposed the Etruscans to this regular type, it is evident that the new systematization was connected with the omnipresent Greek influence in archaic Etruria – in this case with the ideas formulated by Hippodamus of Miletus in the fifth century. We can clearly trace these new endeavours in the Crocefisso cemetery at Orvieto [60], where – in contrast to the dispersed great mounds of Caere (Cerveteri) [61] – chamber tombs, covered with tumuli with crowning memorial markers, are arranged in rectangular blocks, accessible by a system of straight streets. Recent excavations have confirmed that this regular planning of the ceme-

tery began in the second half of the sixth century. Later on we also see regular streets in the Banditaccia cemetery at Caere, which may give an idea of the elegance of Etruscan streets.

Interesting specimens of regular town planning belong to the centuries when the Etruscans were masters of the Po valley. In the last decades before 500 they founded the colony at Marzabotto, on the road from Etruria to Felsina (Bologna). It was built on a riverside plain where nothing interfered with the regular plan. The rectangular blocks of the grid are 540 feet (165 m.) long, but their width varies (115, 130–225 feet; 35, 40–68 m.) [62, 63]. The long sides follow the main streets (*per strigas*). Marzabotto shows the closest affinity to Greek towns such as Naples, Paestum, Olynthus, the Piraeus. Recent discoveries have elucidated the close relationship between the chequerboard pattern of the town and the terrace of temples and altars on the acropolis at the north-west corner. As along the fashionable streets of Pompeii and Ostia, the entrances of the houses faced the streets.

Most interesting is the Greco-Etruscan town of Spina in the delta of the Po, founded, like Marzabotto, about 500. Similar to Venice or, as Strabo describes it, Roman Ravenna (V, 1. 7), it was built on piles and crossed by canals provided with bridges and ferries. Aerial photographs have revealed a system of rectangular blocks, as at Marzabotto, centring upon a large straight canal (100 feet wide) which leads to the harbour. It is again the planning which Aristotle refers to when speaking of the modern fashion of Hippodamus (*Politics*, VII, 1330 b, 21 f.), though here in terms of canals.[45]

About 600, when the Etruscan city-states extended their dominion to the Oscan population of Campania, Capua became their chief town. Cato maintained that it was founded in 471, but that date probably indicates an enlargement or reorganization. Livy (IV, 37) tells us that the Etruscans admitted Samnite immigrants from the mountainous central parts of Italy to 'a share in the city and its fields', as did also the Greeks in Naples, according to Strabo

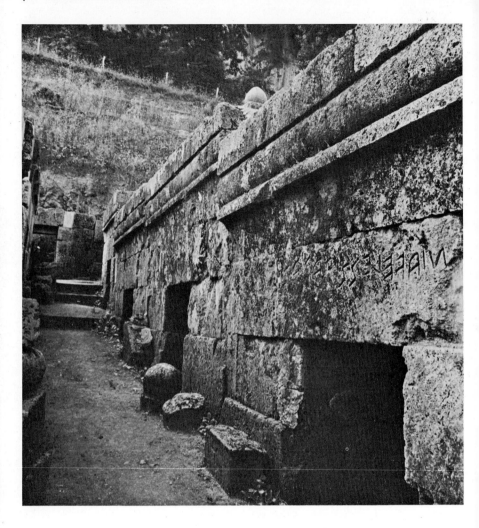

60. Orvieto, street in the Necropoli di Crocefisso del Tufo,
begun sixth century B.C.

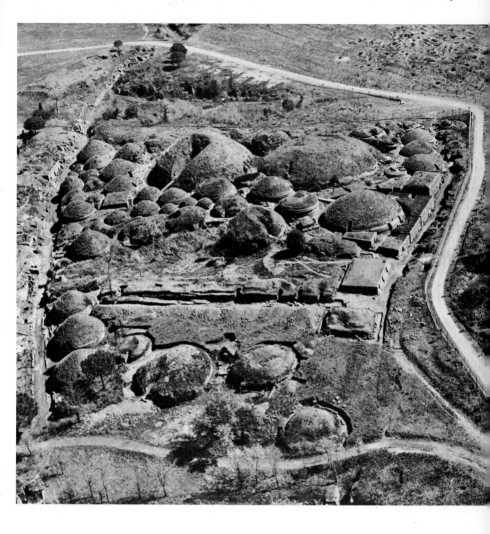

61. Caere (Cerveteri), Banditaccia cemetery, air view,
showing tombs of Early to Late Etruscan date (*c.* 650-100 B.C.)

0   100   200   300 M

ACROPOLIS

N

RIVER RENO

62. Marzabotto. Plan

63. Marzabotto, founded *c.* 500 B.C.,
the acropolis hill and part of the town, showing a street
with a drain in front of typical quarters

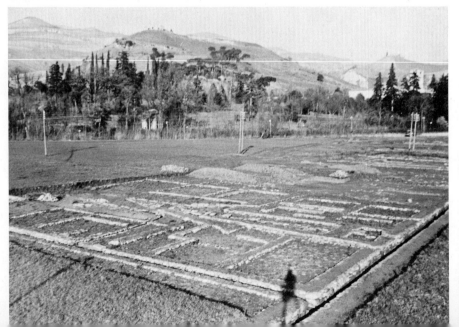

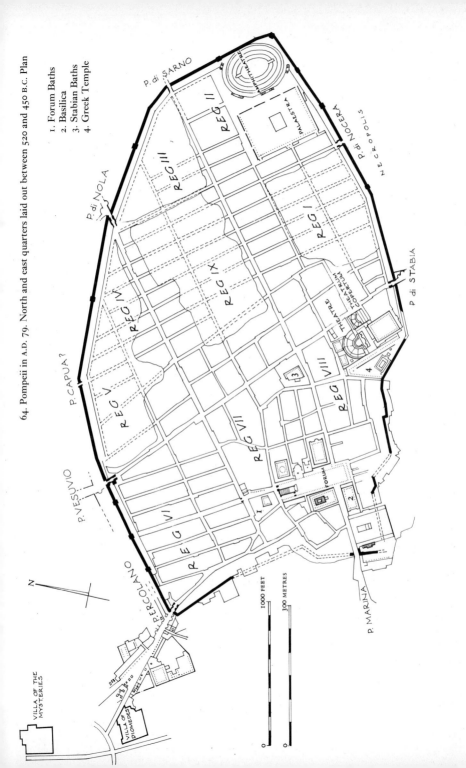

64. Pompeii in A.D. 79. North and east quarters laid out between 520 and 450 B.C. Plan

1. Forum Baths
2. Basilica
3. Stabian Baths
4. Greek Temple

(V, 4. 7). Very likely the regular rectangular blocks at Capua, shown on aerial photographs, received their final shape in the age of the great extension when Capua received the fatal Samnite immigrants who, according to Livy, were to take over the town in 423. Like Fratte (Marcina) (Strabo V, 4. 13) the old irregular parts of Pompeii (Reg. VII–VIII) were an Etruscan outpost,[46] at least for some decades around 500. It seems most likely that the extensive regular quarters north and east of the old crowded hill town were laid out some time between 520 and 450 [64]. The differing orientation and shapes of the blocks indicate that the greatly enlarged town only gradually filled up vacant parts of the level space inside the walls. It seems at least possible that some of these rectangular blocks and straight streets were outlined by the Etruscans; they may, indeed, already have started to enlarge the town to receive the Samnite immigrants (as the Etruscans did at Capua). It is, of course, also possible that the Oscans became independent and gradually reshaped their town

65. Relief from Clusium (Chiusi) showing wooden scaffolding for spectators and umpires of games, fifth century B.C. *Palermo, Museo Nazionale*

after the first great defeat of the Etruscans in Campania in the battle against the Greeks at Cumae in 474. In this case, the fortifications would have been a part of the Oscan and Greek resistance against the Etruscans. In their second, late-fifth-century period, the walls clearly belonged to the Campanians of mixed Oscan and Samnite ancestry known from Roman history.[47]

The enlarged Pompeii with its Greek wall was among the regular towns which in the fifth century became common all over Italy, when new towns were founded on plains or new quarters added to old hill towns. However, it seems clear that the Etruscans were the first to adopt the new ideas in central Italy. As town planners and land surveyors, they remained the forerunners and teachers of the Italic peoples.

Now to secular building in towns. A wall painting in the Tomba delle Bighe at Tarquinia and a relief from Chiusi (sixth and fifth centuries) [65] show that wooden scaffolding was erected around open places for spectators and umpires of the games.[48] These representations show seats raised on supports which may have been about 12 feet high, as Livy describes the 'rows' (*fori*) of the senators and knights in the

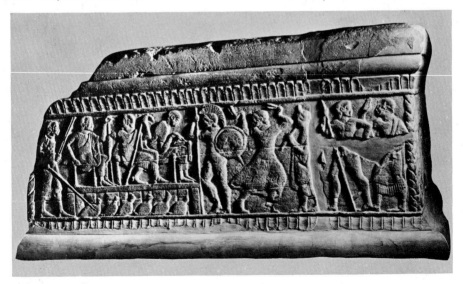

Circus Maximus of Tarquinius in Rome (I, 35. 8 f.). Vitruvius (V, I. I) attests, also from Rome, 'a custom handed down from our ancestors that gladiatorial shows should be given in the forum'. The painting in the Tomba delle Bighe shows that the Etruscans had already started to use linen awnings (*vela*) in the theatres.

DOMESTIC ARCHITECTURE

In his dramatic description of the sack of Rome in 386, Livy (V, 41. 7–8) tells us that the plebeians boarded up their dwellings, while the patricians bravely left the halls of their palatial houses, their '*domus*', open and awaited the enemy in the vestibules in front of the them, wearing their ornaments and apparel which – in the eyes of the Gauls – made them appear like gods. Literary sources and archaeological material from Etruscan towns (foundations of houses, and tombs and funerary urns reproducing houses) substantiate this distinction between the domus of the kings (*lucumones*) and aristocracy on the one hand, and, on the other, the great majority of the dwellings of the lower classes, the plebs, and, above all, of the qualified slaves, artificers (to speak with Livy, V, I. 5), clients, and affranchised, described by Posidonius (Diodorus, V, 40) and Dionysius of Halicarnassus.

The archaeological material makes up for our lack of literary information about the dwellings of the lower classes – men of ordinary means (*communis fortuna*), as Vitruvius calls them. We have remains of ordinary business quarters in the towns, the long rows of small uniform tombs in the great Banditaccia cemetery of Cerveteri, and *cippi* in the form of miniature gabled houses for the women (and pillars for the men). While skilled slaves, as Diodorus says, had houses like those of the plebs, miners and rural slaves, the *tumultuariae agrestium cohortes* referred to by Livy (IX, 36. 12), no doubt lived in barracks, the *tusca ergastula* still mentioned by Juvenal (VIII, 180). That was, in any case, typical of the great latifundia of the Etruscan countryside, which Tiberius Gracchus saw on

his way to Rome. An agricultural centre excavated near San Giovenale belongs to that time, and contains store-rooms and – it seems – a dormitory for the slaves.[49]

The archaeological material indicates that the common folk in the Etruscan towns lived in modest rectangular houses. In the confusion of low foundations inside the regular rectangular blocks of Marzabotto, small rectangular houses can be distinguished [62]. They often have party walls (*parietes communes*) and inner courtyards with wells. Rectangular houses are common, usually some 10 to 13 feet wide, with porches on the front towards the street and two rooms *en suite*. These houses resemble the Greek megara. Often they had rooms added to their right and left flanks. Usually they had a door directly on to the street. But all over the town are also *tabernae*, used as shops, workshops, or perhaps as dwellings of the proletariat, which were wide open towards the streets. Narrow rooms behind the shops or connected with the megaron-like houses were very likely staircases leading to a garret. Under the straight streets in front of the houses run common sewers [63]. The rectangular and regularly disposed blocks of Marzabotto and the distribution of rather uniform houses within them obviously represent the final achievement of Etruscan town planning of about 500.

As has already been stated, the old settlement of San Giovenale extended all over the acropolis. The eastern part of the hill is crowded with small houses which are difficult to visualize in detail. But on the slope towards the valley on the north side of the acropolis were built terraced rectangular houses on high, carefully constructed substructures of ashlar tufa [66]. They faced the valley with their northern, short sides. The stratification indicates a date about 600. The completely preserved foundations of one of the houses measure 24 feet 7 inches by 12 feet 10 inches (7.50 by 3.90 m.). Contrary to the arrangement of the chequerboard sections of Marzabotto, where the short sides of the houses face the streets, the houses of the north slope of the acropolis of San Giovenale are built

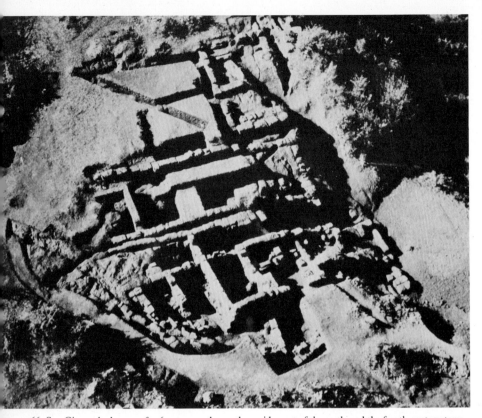

66. San Giovenale, houses of *c.* 600 B.C. on the northern side, east of the castle and the fourth-century town

in rows and obviously had their entrances on the long sides, opening on alleys between them. One street is preserved and has a width of about 8 feet, that is, as described in the Twelve Tables of the Law. There seem to have been similar terrace houses facing the valley on the south side of the acropolis.

The excavated part of Vetulonia [55] shows a winding, 10-foot-wide main street (for which the term decumanus would be quite out of place) and two oblique transverse roads. Six tabernae face the south-western half of the main street on its south side. Along the first transverse road is a row of rooms resembling those on the north side of San Giovenale, while the north-eastern half of the main road seems

to be faced by rectangular houses with open porches towards the street, resembling those of Marzabotto.[50]

On the north side of Veii we find a building of higher standard, with irregular rooms on its

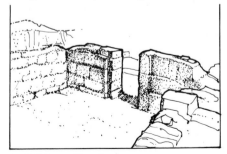

67. Veii, house. Elevation

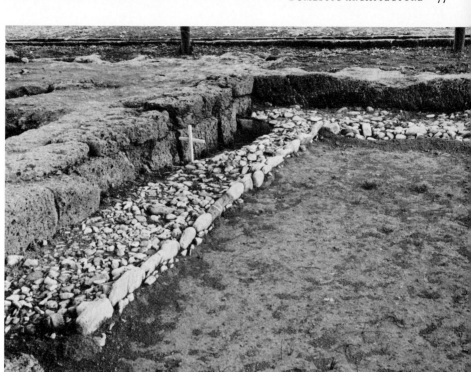

68. San Giovenale, House K in the western quarter, bedroom, *c.* 600 B.C.

west side [54, 67]. Like the houses of Marzabotto and the Greek megara, it faces the street with a porch accessible from a wide entrance. A door with tapering jambs – like those of many Etruscan tombs of all periods – leads to a room measuring 15 by $13\frac{3}{4}$ feet (4.60 by 4.20 m.). The jambs and ashlar walls are preserved to a height of 4 feet 9 inches (1.44 m.) and suggest that the entire building was constructed of tufa blocks.[51]

This megaron-like house of Veii can be compared with some of the chamber tombs and house models of the ash urns. They seem to have been better than the houses along the narrow lanes of San Giovenale and Vetulonia, and are probably the modest domus of more wealthy people. This may also be true of foundations of somewhat roomier houses with a paved courtyard and a well between them west of the fossa across the acropolis of San Giovenale [68]. The great period of these houses was that of the old, larger towns after about 600. Many seem to have resembled to a greater or lesser extent the megaron of Veii. The rear and side walls of one of the rooms in house K at San Giovenale [68] have low benches of pebbles which have been taken from rivers round the acropolis. Beds of the same kind have been noted in an Apennine hut at San Giovenale, in a Siculo-Geometric house on the lower acropolis of Morgantina in Sicily, and in the inner chamber of the tomb called the Tomb of the Thatched Roof at Caere (Cerveteri), datable to the early seventh

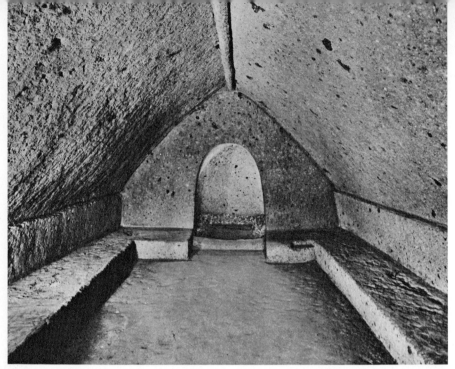

69. Caere (Cerveteri), Tomb of the Thatched Roof,
early seventh century B.C.

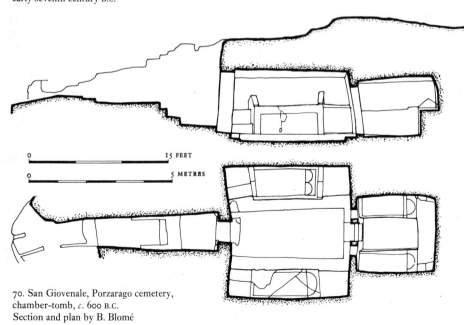

0 ————————— 15 FEET

0 ————————— 5 METRES

70. San Giovenale, Porzarago cemetery,
chamber-tomb, c. 600 B.C.
Section and plan by B. Blomé

century [69]. The excavators of Morgantina have seen such timeless resting-places, finished with grass, straw, and goatskin, among the shepherds of Sicily today. Varro (*Lingua Latina*, v, 166) tells us that the Roman soldiers in his time set up their couches in the camps (*castra*) on straw coverings (*stramenta*), grass, or wheat stalks 'in order that they may not be on the earth'.[52]

That this arrangement is to be found in the Tomb of the Thatched Roof at Caere suggests that this tomb reproduces a room in a house like that on the western side of San Giovenale. The Etruscans of the upper classes about 600 obviously had such bedrooms, in striking contrast not only to the luxury of the upper-class tombs of the following centuries but also to the royal tombs of the seventh century such as the Rego-

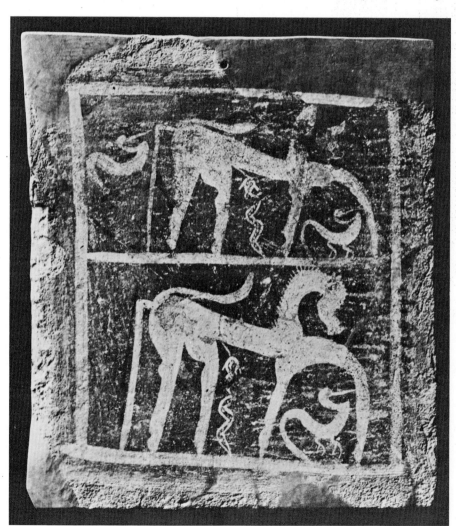

71. Painted roof tile from a house at Acquarossa of the sixth century B.C. (see Note 53)

lini Galassi Tomb at Caere, with its imposing stone-built halls and abundant treasuries [94]. After about 600 domestic architecture began to insist on more elegance. Here we can already see heralded the luxurious, over-columniated later architecture of the Etruscans. For such houses more solid roofs were, of course, required, and tile roofs superseded the wide, light, slightly curved thatched roofs, as demonstrated by the archaic tomb of Caere which has just been mentioned, by a contemporary gabled ash urn from the cemetery of Monte Abatone at Caere [21], or by ash urns like the square hut of illustration 16.

Our main sources for the domestic architecture of the upper classes after about 600 are tombs, cinerary urns reproducing houses, and Vitruvius's chapter on the architecture of the upper classes in his time (VI, 3). The great majority of the older tombs consist of one rectangular room cut in the tufa and accessible from the fields above by a sloping passage [70]. Sometimes there is an inner chamber as well. The megaron-type house at Veii [54, 67] provides a parallel from an actual town. But there are also tombs with more complex and ambitious suites of rooms. Their arrangement recalls Vitruvius's account of 'Tuscan' upper-class

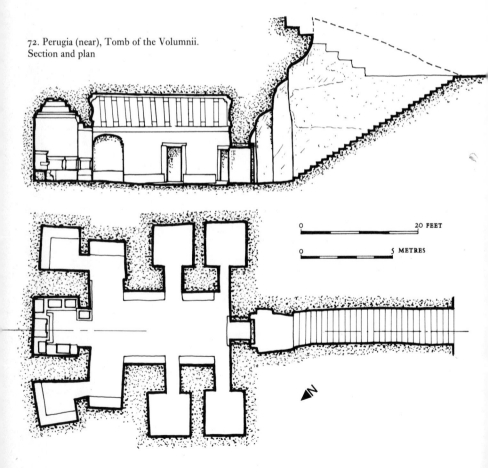

72. Perugia (near), Tomb of the Volumnii. Section and plan

0   20 FEET

0   5 METRES

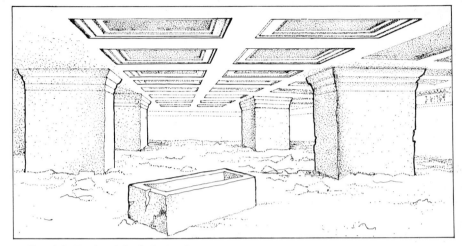

73. Tarquinia, Tomba del Cardinale. Interior

houses [82–7] (cf. below, p. 86 ff.), a type to which he gives pre-eminence.[53] Later tombs had very large halls, occasionally with several side chambers [72]. These, as has already been suggested, correspond to the palaces of the great landowners and of the monied classes of the last centuries of Etruscan history. They may, in some cases, have been the communal property of an association.

Both non-archaeological visitors and many archaeologists have often sensed that the Etruscans were inspired by the town houses of the rich when, throughout their history in Italy, they cut these chamber tombs in the tufa of the table-lands around their towns or in the slopes of the surrounding valleys, although their special purpose, and the restrictions imposed by having to cut into the living stone, naturally caused modification and simplification.

In contrast to old tombs such as the Tomb of the Thatched Roof [69], from the sixth century onwards the interiors reproduce by means of sculpture or painting beautiful roofs, door-posts, lintels, and other skilled joinery. The mighty ridge-poles, beams, and planks remind us – as do the dimensions of the terracotta revetments of the temples – of what Strabo (v, 2. 5),

Vitruvius (II, 10. 2), and others tell us about the abundance of fine building timber in the central Italian woods in ancient times. As seen in one chamber of the fifth century, the 'Tomba della Scimmia' at Clusium (Chiusi), graceful coffered ceilings were in fashion already about 500. The Tomba del Cardinale at Tarquinia (third century) [73] displays the most imposing sunk panels in the ceiling. The famous wall paintings of Greek legends, funeral feasts, races, athletic sports of different kinds, and dances, known from Tarquinia, Veii, Chiusi, Orvieto, and Cerveteri, probably belonged solely to the tombs, at least in older times, though the grand halls of the later Etruscans may perhaps have had historical paintings such as those of the François Tomb at Vulci.

The walls seem mostly to have been decorated with a high red dado with a wave pattern or parallel bands in different colours above [74]. The so-called First Pompeian Style, which we can follow in the hellenistic world from about 300 and even earlier, perhaps did not appeal to the Etruscans; but in the neighbourhood of Luni there is a chamber tomb with decoration resembling the Second Pompeian Style [75]. Tombs at Tarquinia [93] show how beautifully

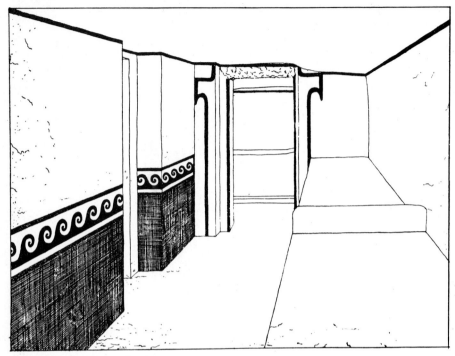

74. Ardea, tomb, *c.* 300 B.C. Interior

the ridge-poles and alternating massive planks of the ceilings were painted. The rest of the roofs were decorated with chequerboard patterns, scattered flowers, and other more or less geometric designs or gaudy motifs. In contrast to remains of monumental ceilings and house plans in Cerveteri and other towns, the famous, delightful wall paintings of Tarquinia evidently reproduce colourful tents erected for funerals, the funeral games, and even the landscape outside them. Here different ideas meet: imitation of the architecture of the houses, shelters made only for the occasion of the funerals, and temporary ornament for them. The tombs at Cerveteri, San Giovenale, San Giuliano, and other places, where the polychromy of the imitated wood constructions has largely disappeared, were at least partly furnished with painted adornments – as doubtless were the palatial houses in town and country.[54]

At San Giuliano, Bieda, Norchia, Sovana, and in other places late tombs have been provided with ornate façades, sometimes protected by projecting shed roofs above the entrance [76]. How far these decorated façades reproduce houses of the towns of the last centuries of the Etruscans it is impossible to say. On the other hand, the elegant two-storeyed tombs constructed against hillsides in the same way as the terrace houses on the south slope of Pompeii are evidently connected with real houses [77]. They belong to the flat-roofed domestic architecture of Late Etruscan times. The Crocefisso cemetery at Orvieto seems to show streets shadowed by blank walls [60]. A cinerary urn in the Museum in Florence [78], whether it had a pitched or a flat roof, gives a good idea of what simple façades in Etruscan towns were like and of how much they resembled the older façades at Pompeii; for instance, the Casa del

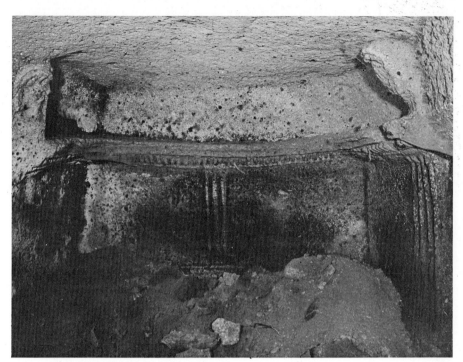

75. Luni, Tomb of the Caryatids, Late Etruscan

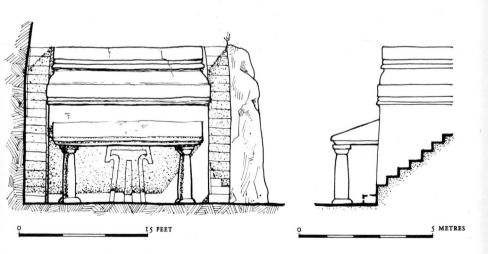

0   15 FEET   0   5 METRES

76. Norchia, tomb with porch. Elevations

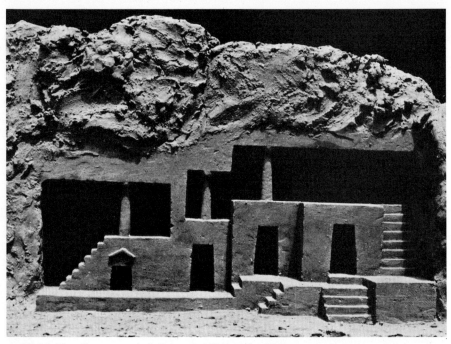

77. Model of Late Etruscan tombs built into the hillside at San Giuliano

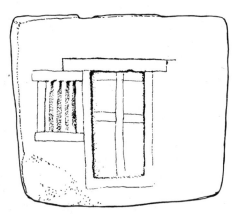

78. Cinerary urn reproducing the façade of a common type of house. *Florence, Museo Archeologico*

Chirurgo in its first period (without taberna) [85].

As for the entrances, tombs of the later cen-

turies B.C. display elegantly framed doors with lintels extending right and left of them [83] and tapering or perpendicularly framed door-posts of hellenistic type. Sometimes this motif was painted on the wall round the rock-cut door. The rock-cut outer door of the Tomb of the Thatched Roof at Caere had rough, tapering door-posts resembling the city gates of Segni [110], while the door to the inner room is a rock-cut arch [69]. A house urn, probably from Chiusi and of late date, shows that doors with arches formed of voussoirs became a part of Etruscan domestic architecture [81]. Numerous late cinerary urns represent the entrance to the underworld as an arched doorway [79] as in a real house, even to the beautiful doors. The rock-cut inner doors of the Tomb of the Thatched Roof and other archaic tombs prove that the Etruscans aimed very early at arched entrances. In the famous Tomba Campana of the seventh century at Veii, we see what is very

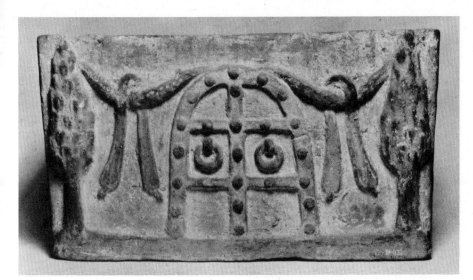

79. The entrance to the underworld on a Late Etruscan ash urn. *Florence, Museo Archeologico*

probably a clumsy attempt at imitating a rock-cut arch.[55]

Gabled houses had old traditions in Italy. The model of a house from Sala Consilina [14] shows that their history starts already in the Early Iron Age. An ash urn from Falerii (Civita Castellana) seems also to belong to the eighth or seventh century [18] (and the roof-shaped top of a stele [19] seems to reproduce a transitional form between round huts and gable-roofed houses). To the seventh century belongs the Regolini Galassi Tomb at Caere [94] with its imposing gabled halls, the Tomb of the Thatched Roof, and the gabled ash urn from a tomb in the cemetery of Monte Abatone at Caere [21] which has already been mentioned. It has highly decorative horns where the rafters meet, reminiscent of the ridge-logs of the hut urns of the Early Iron Age or the ash urn from Falerii [18], and bold snake-like decoration ending the ridge-poles. Such houses thus belonged to Etruscan architecture from its very beginnings and were considered especially appropriate for imitation in cinerary urns. Later on they also served as models for the hundreds of standard reproductions of houses which

marked female interments at the entrances of the tombs. Small gabled tomb houses dating from about 500 have been excavated in a cemetery at Populonia. To the gabled tombs of Tarquinia, Bieda, Sovana, and San Giovenale may be added the central hall of the Tomba dei Volumnii near Perugia of the second century [72, 92]. Especially interesting is a tomb at Sovana [80] with a porch recalling the houses of Marzabotto and the 'megaron' of Veii [54, 67]. The gable is of the same type as the empty pedi-

80. Sovana, gabled tomb with prodomus.
Elevation and section

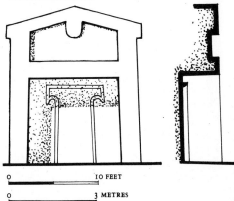

0   10 FEET

0   3 METRES

ments of the temples which are well illustrated by many models of roofs of temples.[56]

On the model of the gabled building from Chiusi [81], obviously meant to represent a

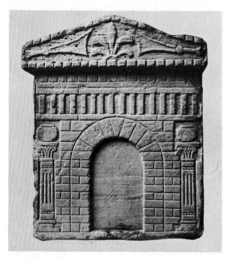

81. Ash urn with arched door from Chiusi, Late Etruscan. *Florence, Museo Archeologico*

luxurious house, the decoration of the façade is no doubt enriched in a manner not corresponding to reality, but this urn is important all the same, not only because it shows in a general way one of the rectangular houses with pitched roof but also because it indicates that such domus could have upper storeys.

These houses, reproduced by funerary urns or by tombs, show us the domestic architecture which Vitruvius briefly refers to as gabled (testudinate), and recommends, 'where the span is not great and where large rooms are provided in upper storeys' (VI, 3. 1–2).[57]

Not less typical for the Etruscan towns seem palatial houses with lavishly decorated flat roofs. A most luxurious hall of the third century is the famous Tomba dei Rilievi at Caere. At Caere (Cerveteri), at Tarquinia, and at San Giuliano tombs from the sixth century and onwards reproduce such halls with roofs supported by Doric, Aeolic, or Tuscan columns [37, 40, 41, 82–4].[58]

Flat ceilings, such as for instance that of the Tomba della Cornice at Caere [83], are typical for an especially distinguished minority of

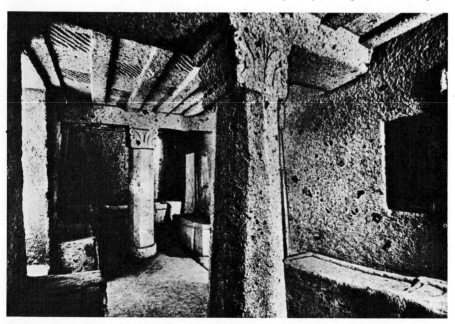

82. Caere (Cerveteri), Banditaccia cemetery, Tomba dei Capitelli, sixth century B.C.

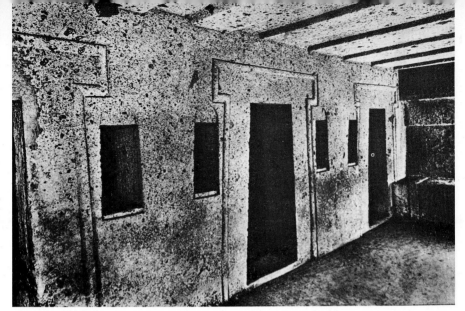

83. Caere (Cerveteri), Banditaccia cemetery, Tomba della Cornice, fifth century

noble and palatial tombs of the sixth, fifth, and following centuries [82–4, 87]. In elegance they vie with the rectangular halls already described, but they surpass them by an impressive, architecturally more differentiated arrangement of the rooms, which seems to be based on old Etruscan traditions. Even among the tombs these houses stand out as the typical domus of

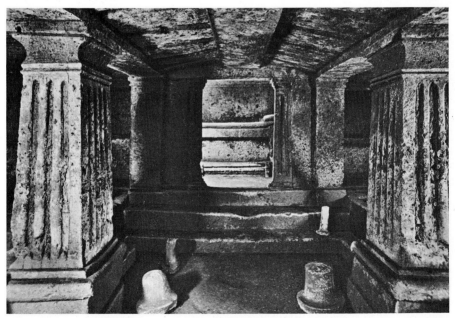

84. Caere (Cerveteri), Banditaccia cemetery, Tomba dell'Alcova, third century B.C.

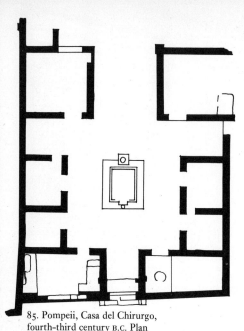

85. Pompeii, Casa del Chirurgo, fourth-third century B.C. Plan

the lucumones and patricians. They are evidently akin to the *cava aedium tuscanica*, which Vitruvius mentions first in his chapter on domestic architecture in the sixth book and which we see in late, altogether hellenized, shape throughout Pompeii and Herculaneum and in the Republican layers of Ostia [85, 91]. The most characteristic parts (tablinum and alae, see below) may appear also in some houses of Marzabotto, datable to the decades after 450.

The rock-cut tombs of this type, whether gabled, like the Tomb of the Volumnii [92], or – as was more common – provided with flat roofs, represent everything in a very reduced form, of course, and display only the basic features of the atrium-houses, as Vitruvius describes them. The main entrance to the Roman houses – the *vestibulum* in front of the house and the doorway, *ianua, ostium, fauces*, which lead to the central hall of the house, the *atrium* – is replaced in the tombs by a sloping dromos. As in the Pom-

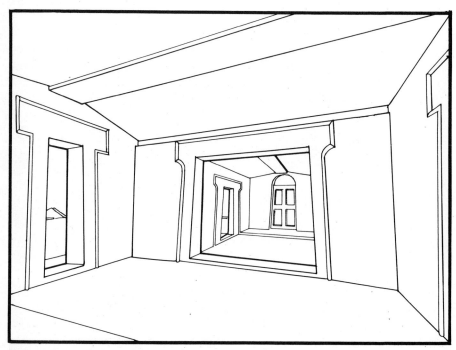

86. Caere (Cerveteri), Tomba del Tablino, fifth century B.C. Interior

peian houses, the rectangular atrium has on its far side a *tablinum* usually with flanking doors on each side built against the rear wall of the house. The tablinum was originally the main room of the *pater familias* and the mistress of the house, but the beds or benches for interments – later sarcophagi and ash urns – in the atria and side rooms of the tombs are evidently adapted to bedrooms for sepulchral use. A typical tablinum, datable to the fifth century, is in the Tablinum tomb at Caere [86]. The most famous tombs of this palatial type are the Tomba degli Scudi e Sedie, the Tomba dei Capitelli [82], and the Tomba dei Vasi Greci at Caere [87], and the Tomba Rosi at San Giuliano. In a most imposing tomb of the sixth century at San Giuliano, named after Princess Margrethe of Denmark, the tripartite division is achieved by two great Doric columns, and the same arrangement is to be seen in some tombs with plain pillars [41].[59]

Vitruvius's description of the Roman atrium-houses of his age contains important additions to what we can guess of the houses by going to the tombs. Like the paintings and all the hellenistic decoration which we see at Pompeii and Herculaneum, they evidently belong to the later development of this kind of house. Vitruvius starts his description of the *cava aedium tuscanica* with the *impluvium*, a square basin in the middle of the atrium with reservoirs receiving rainwater from an open space in the roof, which slopes inward [85, 91]. Thanks to the later excavations at Pompeii we know now that this device for collecting rainwater was a typical feature of the atrium-house during the last centuries B.C. That the older Etruscan tombs do not show this arrangement is therefore by no means surprising. In addition, it would, of course, have been most inconvenient in the reduced *cava aedium tuscanica* of the old tombs (though it is reproduced in a displuviate atrium

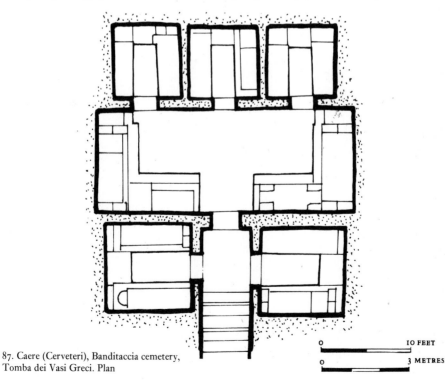

87. Caere (Cerveteri), Banditaccia cemetery, Tomba dei Vasi Greci. Plan

tomb [89, cf. 88]). Equally, neither the alae of the Pompeian houses, which ran like a transept or transverse corridor in front of the tablinum and its side doors, nor the chambers (*cubicula*, kitchens, dining-rooms) along the sides of the atrium, which we see at Pompeii and Herculaneum and which Vitruvius describes, occur in the earlier Etruscan tombs.

If we keep to the main features of the plan of the *cava aedium tuscanica*, which we can deduce both from the atrium-houses of Pompeii and from Vitruvius's description, and compare that with the tombs of the sixth- and fifth-century nobility, it seems evident to me, in spite of the differences, that Vitruvius was right in styling them 'tuscanica'. His description shows us a later development of the same palatial house type which we see in the exceptionally large and elaborate tombs just discussed and in the atria displuviata. I am convinced that the basic arrangement of these houses and of the tombs which reproduced them belong to ancient Etruscan architecture, their origin being Oriental, not Greek.[60]

Together with the *cava aedium tuscanica* and the testudinate houses Vitruvius describes displuviate houses with beams sloping outwards and throwing the rainwater off. A small model from Clusium (Chiusi) [88] and monumental

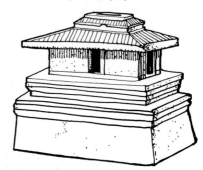

88. Model of an atrium displuviatum from Clusium (Chiusi), fourth or third century B.C. *Berlin, Altes Museum*

tombs at Tarquinia [89] give us a perfect reproduction of this kind of palatial house. They also show that they had roof openings (*compluvia*)

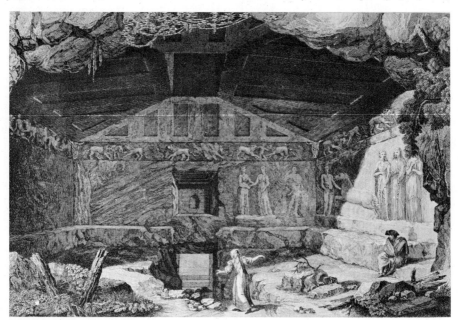

89. Tarquinia, Tomba di Mercareccia, Late Etruscan atrium displuviatum

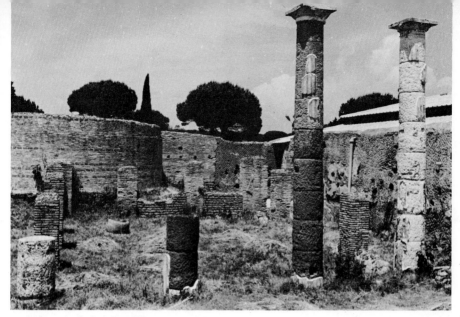

90. Ostia, peristyle, Late Republican

on the top of their hip roofs, but the woodwork and the walls were easily spoiled, because – as Vitruvius maintains – the pipes, which are intended to hold the water that comes dripping down the walls all round, cannot take it quickly enough, but get too full and run over.

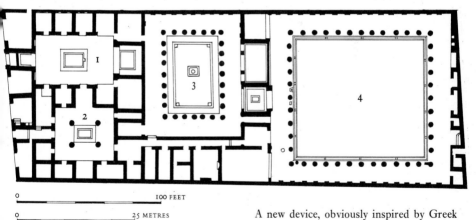

0 _____ 100 FEET

0 _____ 25 METRES

91. Pompeii, Casa del Fauno in its last period. Original building, second century B.C. Plan

1. Atrium
2. Atrium tetrastylum
3. Peristyle
4. Peristyle

A new device, obviously inspired by Greek domestic architecture, was that the atria were provided with square colonnades or peristyles [90, 91]. On the Via della Fortuna Annonaria in Ostia are remains of a peristyle dating from the beginning of the first century B.C., which stood throughout Imperial times. Peristyles became a common luxury at Pompeii in the third and

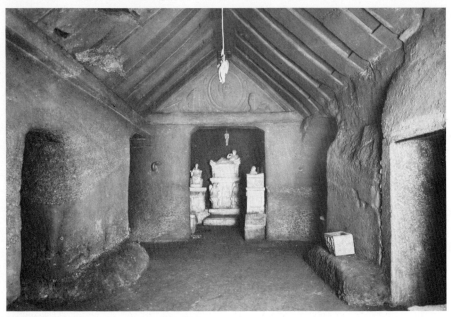

92. Tomb of the Volumnii near Perugia, second century B.C.

following centuries, and it is, of course, most probable that the Etruscans, as Diodorus affirms (V, 40), had already given peristyles – περίστωα, as he calls them – to their houses. He describes them as a 'useful device for avoiding the confusion when crowds are present'. There is no archaeological evidence for this, but if Diodorus's information is trustworthy, as it probably is, he may have thought of buildings with a plan like that of the Villa dei Misteri outside Pompeii (below, p. 192), where the peristyle is built in front of the atrium and the latter thus became a tranquil retreat. But he may also have thought of houses in which the atrium remained the traditional main reception hall for the *pater familias*, while the peristyle behind it provided privacy.

The enriched colonnaded architecture of Rome and Campania was usually connected with elegant and slender Corinthian, Ionic, and sometimes Doric columns. But – as I have said in discussing the columns of the oldest known temples

– Vitruvius, who in his rules for the temples (IV, 7) prefers the plain, Italic Tuscan columns, yet speaks of the Doric and Ionic orders for atrium-houses. Tombs from the last Etruscan centuries [38] suggest that Tuscan columns could also be used. On the other hand, many ash urns, some reproducing houses with hipped roofs surrounded by hellenistic columns, and such tombs as the monumental Tomba Ildebranda [29], show how popular Aeolic, Corinthian, and Ionic columns were in the third and following centuries in Etruria. All this shows the same process of increasing hellenistic sumptuousness and comfort as the atrium-houses of Pompeii and Herculaneum. The Tomba dei Rilievi and the Tomba dell'Alcova at Caere [84], the very magnificent Tomb of the Volumnii near Perugia [72, 92], and other large, late tombs prove how hellenistic decoration dominated among the Etruscans right down to the end of their free life in Italy. The Tomb of the Volumnii confirms in a most striking way that these tombs

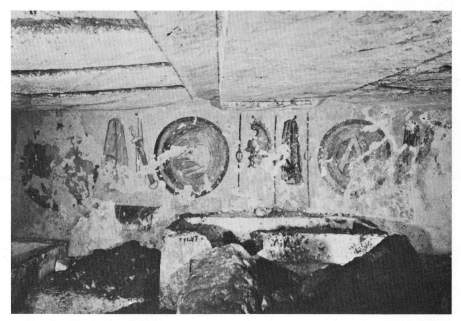

93. Tarquinia, Tomba Giglioli, second century B.C.

reproduce the later Etruscan palaces. With its gabled central hall (*atrium*), its tablinum behind, its side rooms and various types of coffered and otherwise decorated ceilings, it represents the final stage of the Etruscan palace. Here, as among the fat, complacent Etruscans on the lids of late sarcophagi and ash urns, we can realize what the Romans meant by their arrogant sneers at the luxury of their Etruscan enemies – in spite of the military decoration on the architrave of the Tomba dei Rilievi, in the atrium of the Volumnii, and in other tombs from the last centuries B.C. [93], and the determined Etruscan resistance in the wars of the fourth and third centuries.[61]

The description of domestic architecture has shown that arches built up of voussoirs became an important part of the hellenized domestic architecture of Etruria [81]. A tomb at Clusium (Chiusi), the Tomba della Paccianese (or del Granduca), has a tunnel-vault built of ashlar in the third or second century. City gates, bridges, and other public structures show that voussoir arches were common in hellenistic architecture from the fourth century onwards. The recently discovered arched city-gate at Velia proves that the Greeks were already constructing monumental arches in the fifth century B.C. At least from the first decades of the second century they also employed rows of arches for plain yet monumental façades such as those which we see at Lindos, and such as we shall see in the first century in the terrace below the Temple of Jupiter at Terracina [165] and in the amphitheatre of Pompeii [181]. Voussoir arches obviously reached Italy as a more or less complete architectural achievement. It is possible, and even likely, that the Etruscans were the first to adopt them in central Italy, but there may soon have been a parallel movement in Rome. The combination of semi-columns with arch and architrave – so famous from the Tabularium at the Forum Romanum (78 B.C.) [143], the grandiose terrace below the Temple of Hercules

Victor at Tivoli [157], and from all later architecture – had predecessors in Etruscan architecture, as shown, for instance, by an ash urn of
about 150 B.C. from Clusium now in the
Worcester (Mass.) Art Museum. Plain pilasters
with hellenistic capitals of Ionic character carry
the top border and the lid of the urn, but below
them, between the pilasters, are arches and an
architrave. The beautiful Etruscan arched city-
gates, with, for instance, heads of protecting
divinities or other heads in dramatic hellenistic
styles on the key and springer stones, as at Volaterrae (Volterra), or the great gate with shields
on the architrave at Perusia (Perugia), are all of
about 300 or later. However, the really great and
creative developments of the voussoir arches
as well as of the vault belong to Roman architecture.[62]

On the other hand, it is important to remember that the Etruscans at a very early date
brought the principle of lofty vaulting to Italy
(as shown by the corbel-vaulted tombs; below,
p. 96 ff.), and also, it seems, of light wooden
roofs. But, as far as technique goes, the vaults
which the Romans built from the second century have nothing to do with such forerunners.
They depended entirely upon the new, revolutionary Roman manner of building with concrete.[63]

I have here summarized the sacred and secular architecture of the Etruscans, which we can
follow from the seventh century as a unity,
though, especially with regard to houses and
tombs, it must always be borne in mind that the
independent city-states which formed the rather
loose Etruscan confederation had many characteristic local differences in their architecture,
art, forms of burial, etc.[64] All the same, there
was a cultural unity, the Etruscan *koiné*, which
spread all over central Italy in the sixth century
B.C., and in its main lines followed the development of Greek art from the Archaic to the
Hellenistic Age. The material just discussed
gives a reliable general idea of the old irregular
and the later regular towns, of their temples, of
the preponderance of rather small rectangular
houses, of the stately *domus* of the aristocracy
with elegant interiors and beautiful furniture.

ROADS AND BRIDGES

The admirable system of roads and streets
paved with blocks of basalt lava belonged to the
Roman systematization of Italy. But a coarse
and irregular street of stones of different kinds
and with narrow pavements has been excavated
at Rusellae; it can be dated to the last centuries
B.C. At Marzabotto, as in oldest Pompeii, step-
ping stones occur, leading over unpaved streets.
There may also have been tufa-paved streets in
the towns, as in fourth-century Ostia. Otherwise, the roads between the towns seem usually
to have been of dirt or cut in tufa, with wheel-
ruts where they passed over the tufa hills. In
comparison with their solid and durable paved
roads of the last centuries B.C. and of Imperial
times, the Romans must have regarded all the
Etruscan roads as displaying what Vitruvius
calls rural softness (*viarum campestris mollitudo*;
X, 2. 11). In any case, the Etruscan roads had
elaborate tunnels and cuttings. These could also
be used for rivers, as, for instance, the much
visited Ponte Sodo at Veii shows.

Where the roads crossed streams, wooden
bridges on ashlar piles were built, as can be seen
between the acropolis and a neighbouring hill
(the Vignale) at San Giovenale. Arched bridges
(like arches in general) belong to the later hellenistic architecture of Etruria as well as Rome.
Livy (XL, 51. 4) explicitly describes how a
wooden bridge on piles of stone built over the
Tiber in Rome in 179 B.C. was replaced in 142
by arches.[65]

TOMBS AND CEMETERIES

Among the great monuments from the centuries before 400, when the Etruscan city-states
dominated not only central Italy but also the
Po valley and Campania, belong the mounds of
the tombs [36, 61]. They changed the whole
aspect of the landscape around the cities, as seen
at Cerveteri, San Giovenale, and in other places.
Here again we meet with the Etruscan heritage
from the Near East and Greece. The great
mounds and chamber tombs of Asia Minor
show the closest affinity, as do also, for instance,

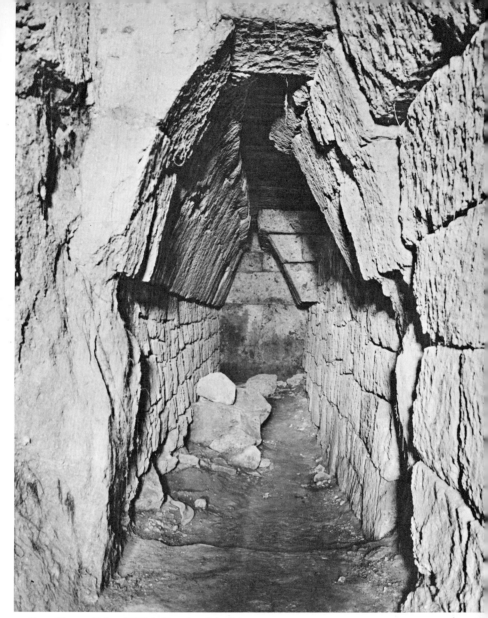

94. Caere (Cerveteri), Regolini Galassi tomb, *c.* 650 B.C.

the mounds round Cyrene, on Cyprus, the small tumuli of the Greek immigrants on Ischia thrown up from the eighth century, and what literary sources and remains attest from other Greek towns.[66]

The rock-cut chamber tombs for inhumation came suddenly to Italy about 700. The old tomb types, pozzi and fosse, lived on for a while side by side with the new types of tomb, as can be seen, for instance, at Caere in the Banditaccia cemetery. Some scholars assume an internal development in Italy from the fosse to the chamber tombs; as I see it, there are many instances of obvious influence from the chamber tombs in the latest fosse, but these transitional features by no means prove an inherent continuation, and there is neither time nor material to prove such a gradual unfolding. Here it is not possible to record more than the principal new imported types. Of them I have already discussed the rock-cut chamber tombs below the tumuli in connexion with domestic architecture. In sixth-century tombs at Tarquinia the interiors were decorated with sculptured stone slabs, placed as a door at the entrance.[67]

Monumental, round or rectangular tomb halls of ashlar masonry with corbelled roofs belonged to the first centuries of higher culture in Etruria. Of the rectangular type, the most magnificent is the Regolini Galassi Tomb with its two rectangular crypts in the Sorbo necropolis west of Cerveteri [94]. The treasures from this tomb and contemporary tombs at Palestrina are among the greatest splendours of the Museo Gregoriano-Etrusco at the Vatican and the Villa Giulia Museum in Rome. Their hoards of imported or imitated Oriental luxury date them to about or shortly after 650 – before the great importation of Greek orientalizing and later pottery and other works of art. The main corbelled, rectangular chamber of the tomb, which contained the most precious finds, measures 24 feet by 4 feet 3 inches (7.30 by 1.30 m.). A *dromos* with side chambers originally led to this main chamber, but its inner part was later provided with a corbelled roof. It thus became transformed into a large antechamber, 31 feet long and 4 feet 2 inches wide (9.50 by 1.28 m.), in front of the door to the inner original cella. The slit where the curving, corbelled-forward side walls nearly touch, is covered by slabs. This type of construction was gradually developed to a row of rude keystones forming a ridge-beam for the false vault. Among the later rectangular tombs of this kind a stately tomb, La Cocumella di Caiolo, on the outskirts of the San Giuliano cemeteries shows a steeply pitched corbelled ceiling with the top of each course chamfered so as to project beyond the course above. The same feature characterizes the corbelled tomb chambers of Orvieto from about 550 to 525.

Two or more successive corbelled rectangular chambers with side rooms are found at the so-called Meloni del Sodo tombs near Cortona, dated to the sixth century. There are also rock-cut chamber tombs with a slit at the top kept open lengthwise and covered by a lintel of stone. They obviously continued the tradition of the tombs of the seventh to sixth centuries.[68]

Archaic rectangular corbelled grave chambers seem to have been used mainly in the southern city-states of Etruria. Towards the north, we find instead corbelled domes. These beehive tombs (*tholoi*) [95] have no doubt in-

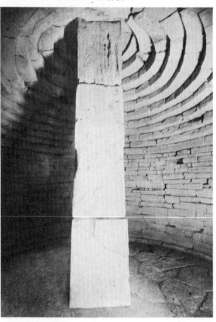

95. Tholos tomb from Casal Marittimo, *c.* 600 B.C., reconstructed. *Florence, Museo Archeologico*

herited structural traditions from the Mycenaean Age or from yet earlier primitive constructions both of the Mediterranean countries and of Asia Minor. In any case, the corbelled dome

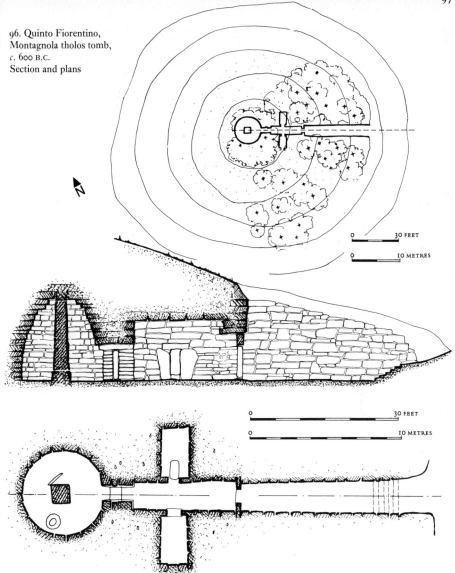

96. Quinto Fiorentino,
Montagnola tholos tomb,
c. 600 B.C.
Section and plans

N

0 ____ 30 FEET

0 ____ 10 METRES

0 ____ 30 FEET

0 ____ 10 METRES

is another monumental type which appears fully developed in Italy. Among these beehive tombs the so-called Montagnola and La Mula at Quinto Fiorentino are the most prominent examples [96]. In the Montagnola, after a dromos, which is about 45 feet long, comes a corbelled rectangular antechamber, 22 feet 6 inches (6.85 m.) long, with lateral corbelled rectangular side rooms. Behind this lies the tholos. Its diameter is 17½ feet (5.30 m.), and it is roughly the same in height. In the centre is a massive quadrangular support, carrying the corbelled vault of the dome, a feature known also from several other Etruscan tombs and taken up again by the Romans when they imitated Etruscan tombs in Late Republican times. Rich finds

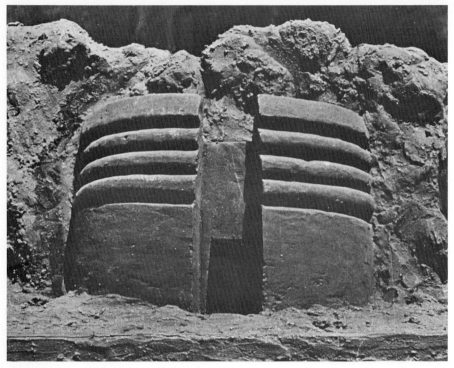

97. Model of a Late Etruscan tomb with a round façade in the valley at San Giuliano

date the tomb to about 600 at the latest. There are other magnificent tombs of this kind in the cemeteries of Populonia and Vetulonia and at Casal Marittimo near Volaterrae (Volterra) [95].[69]

At Populonia and Vetulonia occur square chambers with primitive pendentives in the angles in order to convert the rectangle into a circular shape suitable to carry the dome, as seen, for instance, in the Tomba della Pietrera at Vetulonia. Very important is that early corbelled tombs such as the Tomba della Pietrera display careful ashlar work with alternating headers and stretchers. The tombs thus prove that the Etruscans already in the seventh century (no doubt because of Eastern influence) used this building technique in Italy and had wholly mastered it. Here, no doubt, the Etrus-

cans were the teachers of the Romans. Beehive construction lived on in Roman practice, as shown, for instance, by a cistern near the House of Livia on the Palatine and by the so-called Tullianum (the lower part of the Carcer Mamertinus on the Forum Romanum).

The rows of tombs in Orvieto [60] show that mounds could be reduced to small regular tumuli. The great mounds are usually provided with a circular base of stonework. In tufa districts like Cerveteri they were piled up on beautifully profiled podia, hewn from the living rock [36, 61]. One late tomb at San Giuliano shows a high, round podium, projecting from the hill behind, which evidently reveals a living tradition from the old tumuli and their podia [97]. The so-called Tomb of Aeneas in southern Latium, which Dionysius (I, 64. 4) describes, and the mound which Vergil calls the mighty tomb of the Laurentine King Dercennus (*Aeneid*, XI, 849), show that tumuli were also constructed in old Latium, and that the revived Roman tumuli of the Late Republican and Imperial Age had antecedents in both Latium and Etruria.[70]

Tombs with a rectangular podium without mounds are seen in the rows of reconstructed tombs in the Banditaccia cemetery at Caere (Cerveteri) [61]. Quadrangular also was the podium of Porsenna's tomb, a fantastic tomb, described by Varro as having a circuit of 300 by 300 feet and being 50 feet high. In it was a 'labyrinth', evidently a legendary description of several tomb chambers. Above it stood five cones, one in the centre and four in the corners. They carried a round disc to which bells were attached by chains. The bells could be heard far and wide. If Varro's account is reliable, there were two more storeys with pyramidal pillars above the disc, carried by the five cones.

The bells on Porsenna's tomb – a device known also from Dodona – have been connected with the Columna Minucia in Rome, which also had them [98] (below, p. 206). The

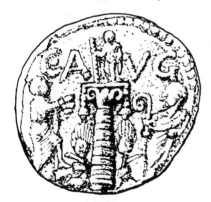

98. The Columna Minucia as reproduced on a coin of the late second century B.C.

cones of a Roman tomb on the Via Appia between Ariccia and Genzano, usually called the Tomba di Arrunte or degli Orazi, have rightly

been compared with Porsenna's tomb. It seems to show that this kind of tomb of the *reges atavi* of Etruria was among the antique tombs which the grandees of Republican and early Imperial Rome imitated, in addition to mounds – as seen at the Via Appia – and, perhaps, tholoi. An archaic Etruscan tomb with a cone consisting of superimposed tapering blocks with reliefs found at Vulci seems to be related to this kind of monument.[71]

The gabled tomb huts at Populonia, mentioned on p. 85, should also be remembered. Evidently the variety of types was due to a certain extent to the particularism of the different small city-states or groups of them.

After 400, sepulchral architecture changed. Cremation prevailed, and cinerary urns replaced the sarcophagi of the older centuries. The mounds, furthermore, were gradually given up and replaced by chambers with entrances from the hillsides of the valleys and the deep, narrow gorges which surrounded the old acropolis hills and branched out into the neighbourhood. Very impressive tomb valleys are to be found in the wilderness around San Giuliano [99], Blera, Sovana, and Norchia. The elegant, often palatial, façades and monumental doorways of the tombs which lined the valleys and transformed them into processional roads belonged to the last centuries of the life of the Etruscan cities and to the prosperity which the nobility or the *nouveaux riches* enjoyed under the sway of the Roman state during nearly two centuries of peace in Italy, after the Roman victories in the third century. In tombs like the Tomba dei Rilievi or the Tomba dell'Alcova [84], the more private of the apartments or bedchambers of the tombs of the old families had already been replaced by large halls with places for many interments. Typical of the last period of free Etruscan life are crowds of ash urns instead of beds and sarcophagi – as in the Tomba Inghirami of Volaterrae (Volterra). There may perhaps have been family crypts; freedmen and clients belonging to the closely limited clans (*familiae*) were probably buried around the family tombs. Late Republican Roman sub-

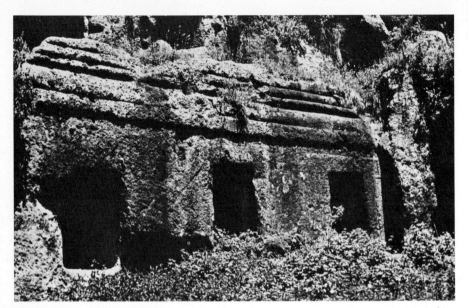

99. San Giuliano, tomb façades, after 400 B.C.

terranean corridors or rooms with *loculi*, heralding the catacombs, were obviously connected with these Late Etruscan tombs. In many of the late tombs the interiors are left rough and undecorated.[72]

To what has been stated above about temples and elegant exteriors of houses, and also about the tomb façades of Norchia and Sovana and the entrances of the houses, should now be added, as typical sepulchral architecture, the so-called cube tombs [100] and the tombs with monumental false doors [101]. The former are more or less isolated square blocks, projecting out of the rock from which they are cut. Beautiful mouldings and elaborate doors of the type already discussed characterize these tombs. False doors to the façades on these and other tomb façades became the fashion in Late Etruscan times. Below them are subterranean entrances to the tomb chambers, which were evidently filled in between each funeral.[73]

Critical descriptions of – above all – Diodorus (v, 40), Dionysius (IX, 16. 8), and also Livy (x, 16) contrast the Etruscans of these late

tombs with their forefathers of the old mounds. The Roman picture of the declining Etruscans is no doubt unfair, and must not prevent us from recognizing a genuine hellenistic renaissance among the Etruscans. Even if it is true that the noble Etruscans, on their sarcophagi, seem *obesi* indeed, and even if Greek observers saw signs of excessive good living among them, we must remember, as I have pointed out, that they resisted the Romans down to the end.

The Tomba François at Vulci with its monumental wall paintings of old Etruscan bravery, and the predilection for arms displayed by the Tomba Giglioli at Tarquinia [93], the Tomb of the Volumnii near Perugia, and other tombs, are as telling as the more frequently mentioned testimonies of luxury and terrifying representations of murder and daemons of death. The latter make many of these late tombs sinister compared with the festive splendour of the tombs of the sixth and fifth centuries. This morbid streak was connected with the pessimism about life and death common to the entire hellenistic world. When Lucretius tries to combat the superstitions of the Hellenistic Age in Late Republican Rome and to understand the true nature of the fiery thunderbolts, he refers directly to the charms of the Etruscans and the vain search of their scrolls, which are written from right to left.[74]

CONCLUSION

The Etruscan towns of the seventh and sixth centuries evidently inspired the inhabitants of the Iron Age villages on the hills of Rome and Latium to rebuild and reorganize their settlements. That is the starting-point for the architecture of historical Rome, even if the Etruscan influence – that is, the Etruscan rendering of Oriental and Greek culture – met with direct

influence from the Greeks in central Italy from about 600. For a long time the Greeks regarded Rome as an Etruscan or Greek town.[75] Roman historians and poets of the Late Republican and Augustan Ages, in spite of the common habit of caricaturing the contemporary Etruscans, loved to emphasize the importance of their Etruscan teachers. Also among modern scholars many typically hellenistic and international *communia bona* of the Late Etruscan and Roman Republican centuries have been wrongly dated and believed to be Etruscan models for Roman architecture. We have seen, for example, that we have to deprive the Etruscans of their claim to have invented the voussoir arch. On the other hand, the great tombs with high corbelled vaults, and also probably light wooden vaults,

100. San Giuliano, 'Tomba della Regina', Late Etruscan

101. Luni, Tomb of the Caryatids, false door and entrance below the door, Late Etruscan

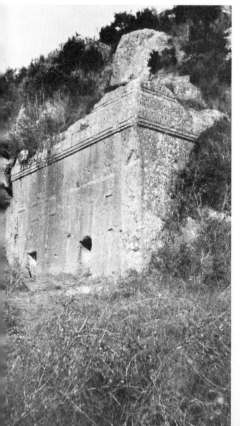

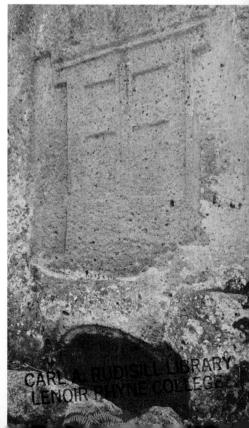

prove that the Etruscans brought the principle of lofty vaulting to Italy at an early date, though their manner of building such vaults has nothing to do with the vaulted architecture which the Romans were to develop centuries later. Already in the seventh century the Etruscans had acquired a complete knowledge of ashlar masonry, as their domed tombs show, and they also, long before the Romans, followed the Greeks in introducing regular town planning.

No doubt the Etruscans remained important as teachers, even though Romans and Etruscans went along parallel roads to Greece, and direct cultural influence from Greece on Rome replaced the one-sided influence from the city-states of Etruria. And, in any case, from the fifth and fourth centuries onwards the Romans developed a strong individuality of their own.

In the same way as the Etruscans used and transformed Oriental and Greek elements to guide their art and architecture through their five centuries of free cultural life in Italy, so the Romans digested what they received from the Etruscans and Greeks in accordance with their own traditions – as Dionysius (II, 19. 3) observed – even when hellenistic influence ran very high. He rightly distinguished (x, 55. 5) between Roman 'customs of the ancestors' and written laws, in which one could easily trace direct Greek influence and the effects of transitory political situations. Domestic 'customs of the ancestors', originating from the Iron Age and slowly changing and developing in historical times against much conservative resistance, must be remembered when Roman architecture from the fifth century onwards is examined. But because of the special architectural heritage (temples, atrium-houses, etc.), Etruscan and Greek influence was so overwhelming that Roman architecture seems to become for a while just an Etruscan dialect. The Roman 'customs of the ancestors' were, no doubt, a spiritual factor in the strength of the Romans and their capacity to learn. But the history of Roman architecture can never be understood without realizing the completely new starting-point which Etruscan building and the exchange with the Etruscans provided for all Roman building activity in Republican times and its legacy to the Imperial Age.

CHAPTER 4

ETRUSCAN ROME

When turning from Etruria to central Italy south of the Tiber, from about 600 B.C. we shall see the same development as that which started in Etruria in the late eighth century. To a great extent we have until the fourth century B.C. to rely on the one hand on conclusions from Etruscan models and later structures which seem to reveal ancient tradition, and on the other on what we can learn from scattered passages by ancient authors and from legends.

In Latium the villages were not far away from the Etruscan towns which were the source of inspiration for them. Etruscan territory extended to the Tiber, to the *alveus tuscus, ripa etrusca, ripa lydia*. The great Etruscan town of Veii was only some 8 miles from Rome. Like all the old Etruscan towns, Veii had a period of most impressive prosperity in the sixth and fifth centuries, with famous sculptors and craftsmen.

Under the influence of the rich Etruscan towns the villages of Latium – and among them those of the seven hills of Rome – were reshaped to petty city-states after the Etruscan and Greek model. We see small towns in the Etruscan style everywhere, on the hills of the old villages, and protected by their natural situation – *situ naturali munita* (to use Livy's words, XXIV, 3. 8) [102]. Already in this early period the Romans

102. Ardea, air view, showing the site of the lower town and the acropolis with fortifications dating from the fifth century B.C. or earlier to *c.* 300 B.C.

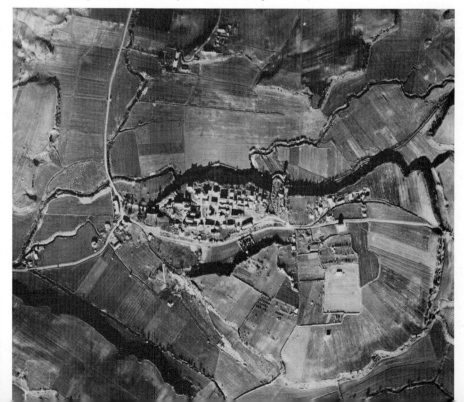

had begun to construct their famous *agger* and *fossa* (a mighty earthwork with a ditch in front) across the open table-land east of the Esquiline and the Viminal Hills [105]. At Ardea we can still see a splendid earthen agger with a fossa of the sixth or fifth century B.C. [103, 104], and

nature herself and require but a small garrison; others are protected by the river Tiber . . . [with] only one bridge constructed of timber, and this they removed in time of war. One section, which is the most vulnerable part of the city, extending from the Esquiline Gate . . . to

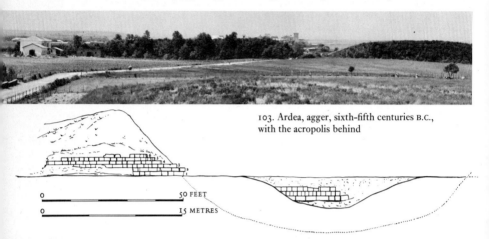

103. Ardea, agger, sixth-fifth centuries B.C., with the acropolis behind

0   50 FEET

0   15 METRES

104. Ardea, remains of the bridge leading over the fossa and of the gate (destroyed *c.* 1930), with the agger west of the fossa, sixth-fifth centuries B.C. Elevation

aggeres can be seen also at Antium – no doubt built during the Volscian wars before the Roman conquest of 338 B.C. – and at Satricum (Conca).

An ashlar wall of the local Roman tufa, *cappellacio*, on the south side of the Palatine, akin to the substructure and podium of the Capitoline Temple, shows how the Romans, like the Etruscans at Rusellae, strengthened the natural defences of the hills with terraced walls. Very likely they also built palisades or earthworks between the hills in the valleys with their groves and rivers, as the tradition mentioned by Varro (*Lingua Latina*, V, 48) about the *murus terreus Carinarum* indicates. Dionysius (IX, 68) gives a most illuminating appreciation of this archaic patchwork of natural defence and supplementary additions when he analyses the position of Rome: 'Some sections [of the town] standing on hills and sheer cliffs have been fortified by

the Colline, is strengthened artificially', that is by the ditch and the agger inside it [105].[1]

In Rome this old system of defence was of no value when the Gauls attacked the town *c.* 386 B.C. Only one of the fortified hills, the Capitoline, resisted. It is self-evident that Late Roman historians completely misinterpreted these old bulwarks when they introduced the unified wall and the agger and fossa in their fourth-century shape into the old stories and believed that all the great fortification around the seven hills, probably occasioned by the experience of 386 and built with material from tufa quarries of destroyed Veii, was the wall of King Servius (legendary date 578–535 B.C.). But no doubt all these stories incorporated memories of old terraced walls, when the hillsides did not suffice, and aggeres and fossae. Varro's description of the old aggeres and the

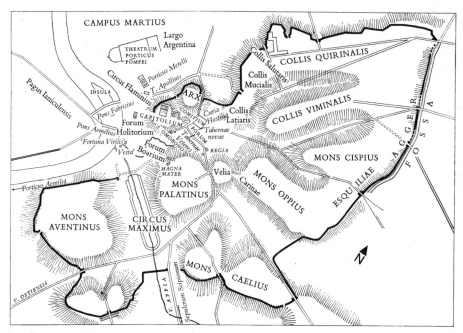

105. Rome, map of the Republican remains. The following are omitted: the Servian Wall
between the Capitoline Hill and the Aventine (see Chapters 4-6),
and the Temples of Vesta, Castor and Pollux, and Saturn on the south side of the forum

Roman *murus terreus Carinarum* show that the
word *murus* was used also for these earthworks
(Varro, *Lingua Latina*, v, 48. 143).

The Romans were always aware that higher
culture was introduced to their pastoral and
agricultural villages as a finished product, and
attributed to the Etruscans almost all the expressions of higher culture which symbolized
patrician authority and came entirely to reshape
the town life of the early Republic: the twelve
lictors and the fasces of the consuls, actually
known from a sixth-century tomb at Vetulonia;
the ivory chairs of the high officials; the array
of the triumphs; the sacred land-surveying
(*limitatio*) of the fields around the towns; the
whole code for human life and religious ceremonies (the *disciplina etrusca*), and also gar-
ments, such as the shoes of the upper classes.
Finally, there cannot be any doubt that the last

Roman kings were Etruscans, condottieri, who
stand out clearly against the earlier legendary
rulers on the Roman hills.

To this new higher culture also belonged the
alphabet, which the Augustan authors usually
styled 'archaic Greek', as was also Etruscan
writing. A famous fibula from Praeneste, the
so-called Duenos inscription on a buccheroid
impasto vase from Rome, and the much-discussed inscription on a stele from the Forum
Romanum of about 500 B.C. are the oldest Latin
inscriptions so far known. But Etruscan inscriptions – a fragment with one Etruscan word
datable to about 600 B.C. found in 1963 at the
church of S. Omobono and an Etruscan graffito
on a bucchero bowl from the Clivus Capitolinus
– have also been found in Rome. All this, together with the established traditions about the
Etruscan kings of Rome before 509, illustrates

the cultural environment which accompanied the nascent higher architecture of Rome and the Latin towns, though it is evident that direct influence from the Greek colonies in Italy also encountered the Etruscan blend of Eastern culture in central Italy. Expressions of the imported higher culture are met with on hill after hill, in town after town all over central Italy. But what we know of architecture in the town which grew rapidly on the seven hills of Rome must be used as the master key to all the towns of the small world between the Etruscans to the north and the Greeks and Etruscans in Campania. As I have remarked above (p. 101), the Greeks hesitated whether to classify Rome as a Greek or an Etruscan town; but of course we must always remember also the village traditions of the Early Iron Age and Vergil's magnificent interpretation of that legacy (IX, 603–11):[2]

Our hardy race takes to the rivers first
Its children, hardening them to frost and
    stream;
Our boys hunt through the nights and tire
    the woods,
And shoot the bow and drive their teams
    for sport:
Our men inured to work and scanty food
Harrow the earth or shatter towns in war.
The sword trains every age: we turn the
    spear
To goad our bullocks, nor do the slow years
Weaken our spirit or impair our strength.
                (Translation by Frank Richards,
                Trinity College, Cambridge)

That the Romans, as Varro says (*Lingua Latina*, V, 161), imitated the Etruscan style in architecture is evident, as I see it, in the *tuscanicae dispositiones* of the temples and of the *cava aedium tuscanica*. The same is true of the very manner of building. The podium of the Capitoline Temple, the terrace wall of the Palatine, and other remains show that the Romans had learned to use their local tufa for ashlar work. Remains of houses datable to about 300 B.C. prove that this kind of construction could be used at least for the lower parts of ordinary

houses, as in the Etruscan towns [66]. In the limestone districts hillsides were no doubt strengthened by ashlar work like that of the Etruscans. Mud brick, *pisé* (puddled earth walls), half-timbered and wooden houses on stone foundations, columns of wood (*columnae ligneae*; Livy, I, 56. 4), and terracotta revetments no doubt became as typical for the towns in Latium after about 600 B.C. as for the Etruscan cities. Archaeologically this is proved not only by the remains of temples and walls but also by the stratification along the Via Sacra of Rome and by numerous finds of archaic architectural terracottas on the Capitoline, Palatine, and Esquiline Hills of Rome, on the Forum Romanum and the Forum Boarium, and in towns all over Latium. The corbelled cisterns mentioned on p. 98 prove that the Romans also adapted that construction.[3]

Livy's description of the Gallic catastrophe (above, p. 75) distinguishes clearly between the domus of the rich and the houses of common people. From the very beginning of Greco-Etruscan culture, we probably have to assume the three types of palatial houses in the towns of Latium which Vitruvius describes (VI, 3) and which I have traced in the Etruscan tombs (p. 80 ff.): those with *cava aedium tuscanica* (though in its oldest form, without impluvium), the displuviate houses, and the testudinate houses. The atria described by Vitruvius as *cava aedium tuscanica* (p. 88) were already attributed by Varro to the Etruscans. That was evidently the current opinion in Rome – the younger Pliny refers to the atrium in his Tuscan villa as being *ex more veterum*. On the Forma Urbis [106] too one still sees the old traditional atria, and the commanding position of atria in Late Republican Ostia, Pompeii, and Herculaneum is in accord with that. But it should be remembered that our archaeological evidence is late and begins only with the oldest atria in Pompeii and Herculaneum of about 200 B.C. and with the Domus of Jupiter Fulminator (datable about 100 B.C.) in Ostia. An early atrium-house has also been excavated at Saepinum (p. 186). The Regia in the Forum Roma-

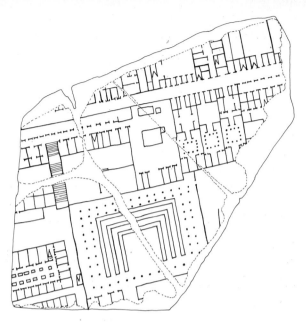

106. Fragment of the Forma Urbis Romae, A.D. 203-11, showing three atrium and peristyle houses and the usual rows of shops (tabernae) with triangles indicating staircases to the upper storeys

num, seat of the Rex Sacrorum and the Pontifex Maximus, has three rooms but does not show the megaron type with prodomus (p. 77) [54].

According to our literary sources, among the domestic architecture of the lower classes there

existed a type destined to be of the greatest importance throughout Roman history: the *tabernae* [107]. These were square or rectangular shops with a wide door, left open in the daytime, facing the street or an open space. No

107. Pompeii, Strada dei Teatri, row of tabernae

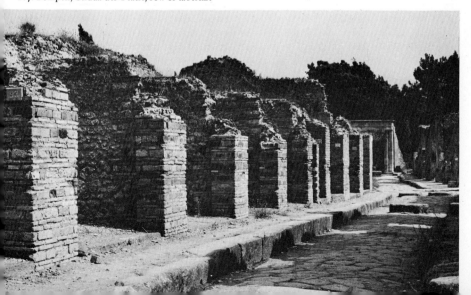

doubt they could be one-roomed units, as is still seen on Ischia and in various places in Campania. In our oldest archaeological material and the oldest descriptions they always appear in rows. The tabernae were used to house the plebs and for commerce and workshops. Livy's description of Tusculum, of what it was like in normal peaceful times, is delightful: shops with their shutters down, all wares exposed, busy craftsmen, schools buzzing with the voices of the children (VI, 25. 9). Dionysius adds shops full of arms and butchers' shops with knives on the counters on the Forum in old Rome (XI, 37. 5; 39. 7; XII, 2.8; Livy, III, 48. 5). There is no reason to doubt that already in the early days of Rome such tabernae were aligned in front of private houses along the long north and south sides of the Forum, as Varro, Plautus, Livy (I, 35), and other Augustan authors describe (although they, of course, were influenced when describing them by the same kind of architecture in their own time). The tabernae which in 179 B.C. were built (or retained) along the south wall of the Basilica Aemilia towards the Forum seem to have been constructed of timber-framing and mud brick. The row of shops along the forum of Pompeii, before its systematization in the hellenistic style in the second century B.C., may serve as a comparison (p. 145). The central parts of Pompeii show tabernae along the streets dating from the second century B.C. or even earlier. At Ostia a typical row of tabernae of the third century B.C. runs along the eastern side of the castrum [123]. It may be noted that these tabernae measure about 28 by 21 feet (8.50 by 6.40 m.) and that the portico in front is 10 feet wide.

There is abundant literary but no archaeological evidence for farmyards and villages. Often mentioned along with them are their fortified refuges (castella) and the houses of the rich. The latter may sometimes have imitated Etruscan palaces. But more typical of these times were no doubt the humble villas of the grand old days which the late Romans moralized upon. An example is Cicero's grandfather's house near Arpinum; it was small and resembled the houses of the old Romans, of the famous Curius in the Sabine country (De legibus, II, 3), and others.[4]

Together with the domus of the patricians we may at the same time remember that the Etruscan mounds were imitated in Latium (see p. 98 f.). Dionysius describes the tomb of Aeneas (or Anchises; I, 64) as 'a mound, around which have been set out in regular rows trees that are well worth seeing'. For Vergil also (Aeneid, XI, 849) the tumulus was a typical feature of old Latium, and mounds of the Late Republican and Imperial Age, referred to in Note 96 to Chapter 6, thus appear as an archaistic revival of the venerable old type.

Livy (V, 55. 2–5) speaks of the careless haste with which Rome was rebuilt after the Gallic catastrophe, in a random fashion and without straight streets. It had the appearance of 'a city where the ground has been appropriated rather than divided'. As I said on p. 69, the tombs of the Crocefisso cemetery at Orvieto (550–525 B.C.), parts of the cemetery of Caere, and both Marzabotto and Pompeii were regularly planned by the fifth century. Older Etruscan traditions, if there were any, encountered Greek ideas from the sixth century onwards here as in other fields of cultural life. But there is no evidence whatever of regular town planning in Rome itself. What Livy describes and dates to after 386 B.C. was no doubt only a continuation of the indigenous, ineradicable legacy of winding narrow streets, up and down hill, which Cicero (De lege agraria, II, 96) contrasts with the towns of the Campanian plains, where regular town planning of the fifth century could be carried out. The narrow, curved street below the wide, straight avenues of Nero between the Forum Romanum and the Palatine still shows us a fragment of the old irregular town after 386 B.C. [108].

Livy says that before the fire, sewers had been conducted through the public ways, per publicum (as at Marzabotto [63]), but that in the Rome which he knew they frequently ran under private buildings. He may be right in explaining this as a result of the chaos after the fire of

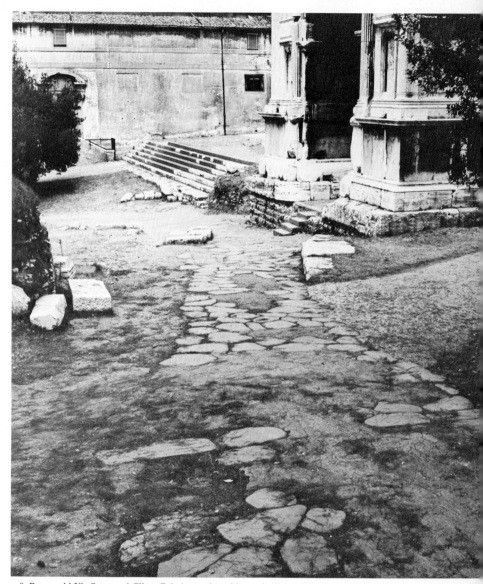

108. Rome, old Via Sacra and Clivus Palatinus, after 386 B.C., in front of the Arch of Titus

386 or as due to other random building activity. His statement about the sewers in any case supports the stories that the Cloaca Maxima was systematized by the kings, that is, in the Archaic Age, as Varro had already maintained. It may have been partly subterranean, though Plautus (*Curculio*, 476) refers to it as an open channel on the Forum. The monumental vaulted cloaca

which we see today is much later (p. 208, below).[5]

Connected with what we can see and read about the old irregular towns is the information concerning the oldest camps of the Romans and others which is given in a book on strategy by an unidentified author combined with Frontinus's *Strategemata* (IV, I. 14). He compares them with the huts (*mapalia*) and scattered cottages of the Africans, and ascribes the concentrated and fortified castra to Greek influence. In any case, the characteristic Roman castra seem to have developed later, connected on the one hand with the organization of the Roman infantry – the Roman legions – after the age of the patrician cavalry, and on the other with regular town planning.[6]

Narrow, crooked streets (like those of San Giovanle and Vetulonia) [55], sewers below streets and houses, tabernae, Etruscan atria or megaron-like houses with a porch, and aggeres supplementing the defence of the hillsides were the main characteristics of the architecture which under Etruscan influence replaced the old hut-villages. Above all, the great Temple of Jupiter, Juno, and Minerva on the Capitoline Hill in Rome and other temples in Etruscan style with terracotta decoration became the great marvels of the old crowded towns. Dionysius (III, 69) and Livy (I, 55) recorded legends which seem to contain precious recollections of the victories of the new temples in Rome over the cults of the Early Iron Age. Dionysius (III, 69) describes how 'many altars of the gods and of lesser divinities [had] to be moved to some other place' when the summit of the Capitoline Hill in Rome was cleared for the great three-cella Temple of Jupiter, Juno, and Minerva dedicated in 509 B.C. 'The augurs thought proper to consult the auspices concerning each of the altars erected there, and if the gods were willing to withdraw, to move them elsewhere.' Wherever Dionysius and Livy got this information, it may well describe what actually happened when the period when no images of the gods were made and simple hut-like shrines and altars of turf were built, was succeeded by that of temples in the Etruscan style with personified gods, occupying the cult-places of the old demons from the Iron Age villages.

The general admiration for the Capitoline Temple of 509 should not make us forget that the Romans began to build temples like those of the Etruscans as soon as the new higher culture began to prevail among them – that is to say throughout the sixth century – whether this was connected with the political supremacy of the Etruscan kings and nobles or only with influence from neighbouring Etruscan towns. It has already been said (p. 27) that the round Temple of Vesta on the Forum Romanum probably represented the survival of a tradition from the Early Iron Age villages, though it was of course rebuilt in the Etrusco-Greek style, as Late Republican coins show. Already before the Capitoline Temple there was, according to Varro (*Lingua Latina*, V, 158), a Capitolium with a temple of Jupiter, Juno, and Minerva on the Quirinal Hill. The Argeorum Sacraria, twenty-seven sacraria situated in the ancient central parts of Rome, were evidently also inherited from oldest Rome, and there were legends, too, about sanctuaries built by Romulus, Titus Tatius, and Numa Pompilius – in some cases our authors of the first century B.C. affirm that traces of them remained. As I have stated above, Vitruvius (II, I. 5) mentions the thatched roofs of temples on the Arx of the Capitoline Hill. Dionysius (II, 34. 4) even gives the measurements of the Temple of Jupiter Feretrius on the Capitoline, which he ascribes to Romulus, saying that the longest sides extended less than 15 feet. He also affirms (I, 34. 4) that he had seen the altar of Saturn built by Hercules at the foot of the Capitoline, where the ascent of the Via Sacra begins and where the Temple of Saturn was built. All this taken together only shows, of course, that the Romans themselves attributed some of their old temples to the earliest period of the kings, 753–616 B.C.; they lurked in the shadowy background of the history of their architecture. A fragment of a beautiful terracotta frieze with the Minotaur and processional friezes from the Forum Roma-

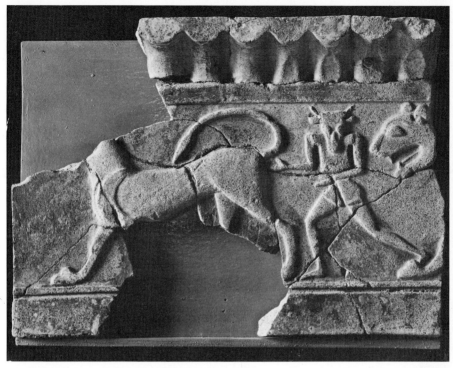

109. Terracotta revetment from the Forum Romanum, sixth century B.C.
Rome, Soprintendenza Foro Romano e Palatino

num [109] as well as finds of terracotta revetments at Ardea and various places in Rome and Latium prove by their quality that the Latin temples of the sixth century were already an important part of the Etruscan province of Greek Archaic art.

Architectural attributions to the less legendary later kings of Rome – Tarquinius Priscus (616–579), Servius Tullius (578–535), and Tarquinius Superbus – seem thus to be in substance reliable. To their period belongs the famous Temple of Diana on the Aventine Hill. Even if the tradition that Servius Tullius 'with his own sceptred hands consecrated' the Temple of Mater Matuta on the Forum Boarium (Livy, V, 19. 6 f., and Ovid, *Fasti*, VI, 479 f.) implies too early a date, the temple was clearly built in the decades about 500. Here we meet with

archaeological features belonging to the history of Etruscan architecture: terracotta acroteria in the shape of volutes rising from the base, a casing of a capital, and a small part of a fluted Ionic shaft [39].

In spite of these earlier examples, the great Capitoline Temple of 509 marked a revolution in Roman life. After 509 the town of Rome, and, of course, also the thoughts of the Romans, were dominated by this marvellous, colourful building and all that was connected with it: personified gods, terracotta images by the Etruscan sculptor Vulca (no doubt similar to the terracotta gods found at Veii), terracotta revetments as already described for Etruscan temples, a new calendar, and other innovations.[7]

According to Roman tradition, the great enterprise was started by Tarquinius Priscus.

The Romans were convinced (so Livy relates, I, 38. 7) that it was he who laid the foundations for the terrace, that is the site of the planned temple, 'with prophetic anticipation of the splendour which the place was one day to possess (*iam praesagiente animo futuram olim amplitudinem loci*)'. Already the site on the levelled Capitoline was greatly admired by the Romans. Dionysius gives a description of how Tarquinius Priscus and Tarquinius Superbus built the temple (III, 69; IV, 59-61); Pliny mentions the court of the temple among the great creations of the kings, but Livy informs us (VI, 4. 12) that the sixth-century terrace was rebuilt in the great period of the Roman city walls in the fourth and following centuries. It became adequate both for *comitia* (assemblies) and *contiones* (public meetings). Right from the first it was decorated with many monuments, and was no doubt already as spacious as the sites of the Etruscan temples discussed above [20, 32, 33]. Below were underground chambers and cisterns (*favisae*) in which – according to Varro – it was the custom to store ancient statues that had fallen from the temple and other consecrated objects and votive offerings.

Our literary sources mention several temples of fifth-century Rome; for instance, those of Mercury and of Ceres, Liber, and Libera on the Aventine and the Temples of Saturn (501-493) and of Castor and Pollux (484) on the Forum Romanum. Of the latter two, remains of Etruscan type from the first periods can be traced in the Imperial marble buildings which have replaced them and their successors of the Republican Age.[8] They were situated on the south side of the Forum, and, together with the Regia and the round Temple of Vesta to the east, they gave a new, monumental aspect to the old and rustic civic centre, which in these early days fulfilled both a commercial and political function [105].

A summary of what we know about this centre of Rome may serve as a general illustration of how fora in central Italy began. What we now regard as the Forum Romanum was then an unpaved market-place surrounded by patrician domus behind tabernae on the north and south sides. The domus disappeared only when basilicas were built on the Forum after a great fire in 210. As Varro says (*Lingua Latina*, V, 145), the Forum was the place to which people brought their disputes and articles which they wished to sell.

The political function of the civic centre was originally restricted to the north-western part of the Forum. The ancient gathering-places for public meetings were the slopes of the Capitoline Hill and the Arx towards the Forum. Later – and until the last centuries of the Republic – an open space at the north-western corner of the Forum Romanum, as we see that large piazza after its final reorganization under Sulla and Caesar, became a centre for assemblies and public meetings. It was called the Comitium and occupied the place where Caesar built his curia for the senate; indeed, that is where it still stands, as rebuilt by Diocletian. Literary sources make it quite clear that this open space was located in front of the old curia of the senate, the Curia Hostilia, which was ascribed to King Tullus Hostilius and faced the Comitium and Forum from a higher level to the north. As Livy says (XLV, 24. 12), the Comitium was the 'vestibulum curiae', the forecourt of the Curia towards the Forum. The Curia had stairs in front leading down to the Comitium. Roman public meetings could also be held on the Forum and in different places within and outside the Servian Wall, but the Regia and the Comitium seem to pertain to the Republic about 500 B.C. It has to be remembered that the Romans – in contrast to the Greeks – in accordance with their old traditions stood at assemblies and other meetings.

In the third century we meet with closed amphitheatre-shaped comitia for voters or assemblies (p. 133), but in Rome the south side of the court of the Comitium seems to have been open towards the Forum. At its boundary towards the present Forum were placed inscriptions and monuments recording political events and famous Romans. Livy calls some of the statues fifth-century, a date which the Etruscan material of course makes very likely (IV, 17. 6). Among these monuments was also a tomb said to be that of Romulus or his father Faustulus or of an ancestor of King Tullus Hostilius. Some of these old monuments, to which the Forum inscription of about 500 also relates, are still preserved below the level of the present Forum: a black memorial slab, the *lapis niger*, in the Late Republican and Imperial pavement marks the spot. The exact location and shape of the orators' platform – the *rostra*, as it was called, since after the victory in 338 it had been adorned with ships' prows from Antium – has still to be ascertained, but literary sources indicate its close connexion with the Comitium and the Curia and a position between them and the Forum. Pliny (VII, 212) makes it clear that the Rostra, a reserved place for foreign messengers (the *graecostasis*), and a later column erected in honour of the victor in the battle of 338, the Columna Maenia, stood along the south side of the Comitium. The apparitor of the consuls, the *accensus*, announced noon from the Curia when he saw the sun between the Rostra and the Graecostasis. This information makes it likely, of course, that the stairs of the Curia were visible and open to the public on the Forum. Varro (*Lingua Latina*, VI, 91) quotes an old commentary on an indictment accusing a certain Trogus of a capital offence and prescribing that an assembly should be proclaimed from the Rostra and that the bankers shut up their shops. This refers evidently to the tabernae of the bankers along the north side of the Forum, and confirms the close relation between the Rostra, the Comitium, and the Forum.[9]

A famous feature of old Rome was the wooden bridge which crossed the Tiber from the Forum Boarium. It was called the Pons Sublicius and, according to tradition, was constructed under King Ancus Marcius, without any sort of metal. Like the old Etruscan bridges, it probably had stone abutments. According to the legends the beginnings of the Circus Maximus in the Vallis Murcia between the Aventine and the Palatine Hills also belonged to this old Etruscan Rome of the kings. There is no reason to doubt that wooden platforms with vela on supports, like those known from Etruscan towns (above, pp. 74–5) [65], were erected along the sides of the long, narrow valley, as Livy (I, 35. 8) and Dionysius (III, 68. 1) describe.

As already pointed out, the Romans marvelled at the grandeur of the Capitoline Temple and explained it in various ways. Apart from the historical problem of the rise of Rome, the cultural context is quite clear, thanks to our archaeological knowledge of Etruscan temples, towns, and tombs. What we see in the Rome of the sixth and fifth centuries and in similar remains from other Latin and central Italian towns is altogether a part of the greatest age of Etruscan culture and political power in Rome, connected with the Etruscan rulers.

Pliny reports (XXXV, 154), in the course of discussing two Greek artists who were employed for the fifth-century Temple of Ceres, Liber, and Libera, that, according to Varro, before it was built everything in the temples was Tuscan work. We should not restrict that observation to Rome. Varro probably conflated the Greek Archaic and the Tuscan style without realizing that the Etruscans from their beginnings followed the development of Greek art, and that their Archaic style was only a version of Archaic Greek art. What Greek painters and terracotta artists (*plastae*) of the fifth century brought not only to Rome but to all Etruscan central Italy was certainly classical Greek tendencies. After the classical heyday of Athens and Argos they influenced all monumental architecture, monuments, and private works of art in the Etruscan and Latin towns of the fourth and following centuries.

The end of this first period of old Rome was the Gallic catastrophe of 386. The revolution against the Etruscan kings seems already to have retarded the Romans, and then, after 386 and until the victorious age after the war against Hannibal, internal struggles and continuous wars kept them busy. Though traditions from the Etruscan temples lived on and influence from the richer life of the Etruscans and Greeks can be traced, progress was delayed in the two centuries which followed after the Gauls put the great old Archaic town in flames.

CHAPTER 5

ROME DURING THE STRUGGLE FOR SUPREMACY IN ITALY

(386 – ABOUT 200 B.C.)

The old town of Rome described in the previous chapter was damaged or more or less destroyed, with the exception of the Capitoline Temple, when the Gauls, after depriving the Etruscans of their dominion in the Po valley, raided their towns and sacked Rome in 386 B.C.

The Rome which was rebuilt after the Gallic catastrophe in many ways stands out in dramatic contrast to the towns of the peoples that were brought under the sway of the rapidly increasing, overflowing town on the Tiber in the fourth and third centuries. The Romans boasted of their simple, warrior-like life and character, compared with the more luxurious hellenistic culture of the Etruscans and the Campanians; but their control of subject cities in Italy did not mean that they stood in the way of Greek influence. The classic exposition of the cultural differences between the subject states and Rome is Livy's scathing description of degenerate Capua during the war against Hannibal (XXIII, 2 ff.). We can illustrate the culture, of which Livy only gives a caricature, by reference to the refined, appealing life of second-century Pompeii (the so-called tufa period). Before the war against Hannibal, Rome remained stubbornly backward in comparison with her subjects, who had regular town planning and shared Greek cultural life.

As I have said before, Cicero contends in *De Lege Agraria* (II, 35. 96) that the Campanians with their town of Capua, which was spread out on a vast and open plain, would laugh at and despise Rome, which sprawled across mountains and deep valleys, with houses of several storeys strung along badly kept streets and very narrow lanes. Fires, floods, continual collapses of houses, and uncontrolled building were typical features of Roman life. According to

Strabo (V, 3. 7), the Emperor Augustus especially concerned himself about the defects of domestic architecture in Rome, reducing the height of new buildings and organizing a fire brigade. Yet in spite of Augustus's efforts and his speeches about improved domestic architecture, which he supported, according to Suetonius (*Augustus*, 89), old Rome – Vetus Roma before the Neronian fire of A.D. 64 in Tacitus's description – still appears as a town of narrow, twisting lanes and enormous, shapeless, and far from fireproof buildings (*Annales*, XV, 38).

In 338 Rome crushed the resistance of the Volscians around Antium, and thus became mistress of all Latium, extending her power from her strongholds there to her more cultured neighbours to the north and south. Already in the middle of the fourth century the Romans had brought the great and rich Etruscan Caere (Cerveteri) into close alliance, and they soon reduced it to a dependent state. As will be remembered, the wars against the other Etruscan towns ended with Roman victories about 280. In the fourth century the Romans had waged their great wars against the very efficient confederation of the sturdy Samnite mountaineers, culminating in the victory of 290, and it was in connexion with these wars that Naples and the Campanians came under the control of Rome. The last culturally superior parts of Italy to come under her sway were south Italy (after the war against Pyrrhus, 280–275) and Sicily, which became a Roman province after the first Punic war (227). The Sardinians of the old nuraghi (above, p. 17), with Rome's usual slander against her enemies, were defamed as useless slaves and put up for sale, but they revolted frequently, and continued brigandage even in the first century B.C.

The Romans maintained this early dominion by a network of alliances and by granting various degrees of independence or civic rights, until they reduced Italy to uniformity about 80 B.C. This multiform consolidation was controlled by strongly fortified colonies and garrisons of Roman citizens all over Italy; these fortifications are the greatest architectural expression of the system of government, corresponding to the organization and iron discipline of the legions. The consolidation was tested severely during the war with Hannibal, but emerged stronger than ever, thanks, as Livy says (XXVII, 10. 7, speaking among others of Signia and Norba), to her colonies. Later on the fortifications functioned quite differently: during the internal wars in Italy in the second and first centuries they were modernized and provided with arched platforms for catapults, etc. [170]. It is typical that even before crossing the Rubicon Caesar had begun to seize such advantageous positions, starting with Ariminum (Appian, *The Civil Wars*, 11, 5. 34 f.).

Following the legends about great city walls and gates, and the old bulwarks and the defence systems discussed in the previous chapters, there now emerges a period of truly great fortifications. The heavy terrace walls which strengthened the hillsides of the Etruscan towns during the struggles against Rome from the end of the fifth century and the Greek city walls offered the prototypes, but the Romans developed walls in their own way, as the exigencies of their own system of government and the vicissitudes of the struggle for control over Italy required. The Latins probably built walls for their last defence against Rome, though we have no certain knowledge of them. Most interesting are the rough limestone walls of a quite special, local kind which the Samnites built around their few urban centres. The circuit of Saepinum, the greatest among them, is about 2 miles wide. It still gives us an almost complete counterpart to the infinitely more refined Roman fortifications, and demonstrates the Samnite preparations for the wars with the Romans.

110. Signia (Segni), gate in the wall, fourth century B.C. (?)

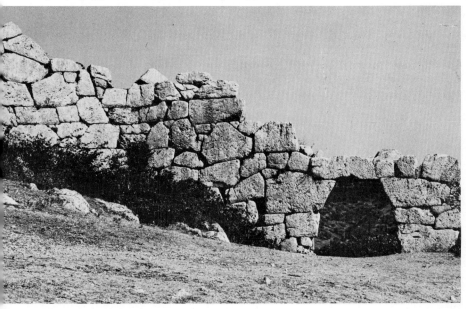

111. Norba (Norma), walls and gate, fourth century B.C. (second half)

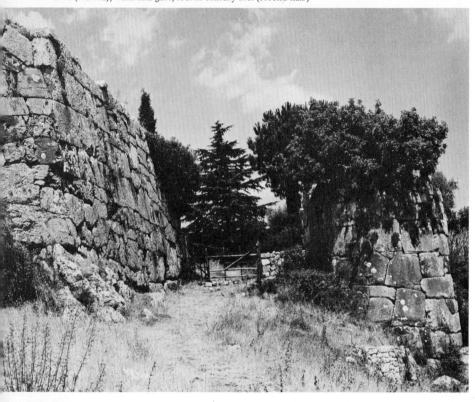

112. Cosa, city gate, with door chamber inside the wall, 273 B.C.

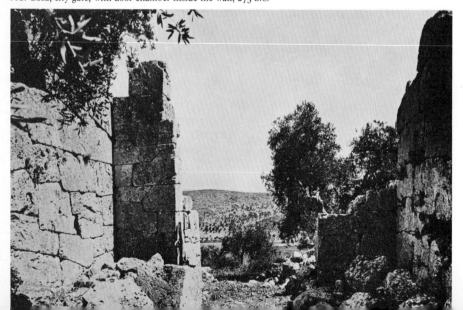

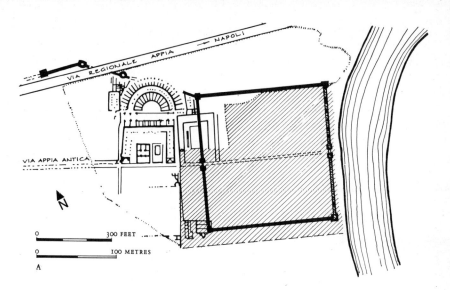

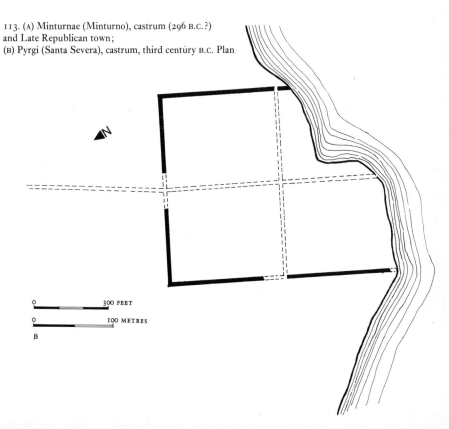

113. (A) Minturnae (Minturno), castrum (296 B.C.?)
and Late Republican town;
(B) Pyrgi (Santa Severa), castrum, third century B.C. Plan

In the Apennine limestone districts the Romans built mighty polygonal ('cyclopean', 'Pelasgic') walls similar to those the Etruscans had constructed since the sixth century; Terracina (probably about 400), Ferentinum (first period) [167], Circeii (393), Signia (Segni, probably fourth century) [110], Cora (Cori; fourth century), Arpinum (305) [116], Praeneste (fourth century), and Norba (second half of the fourth century) [111] are imposing specimens, in some cases built in connexion with the war against the Volscians. North of Rome are the well-preserved walls with which in 273 the Romans fortified their colony of Cosa [112]. They are nearly a mile long and include eighteen rectangular towers and three gateways of the interior court type, which project inward from the outside of the wall, as known already from the fourth century at Ostia [123] (below, p. 125). Rectangular walls were built on the plains to defend colonies. They were of the castrum type (see p. 125): examples are Pyrgi [113B, 114], Minturnae (probably 296) [113A], and Fondi (about 250). The majestic walls of Alatri [115]

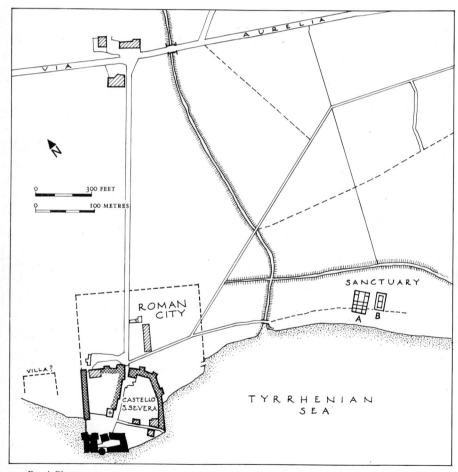

114. Pyrgi. Plan

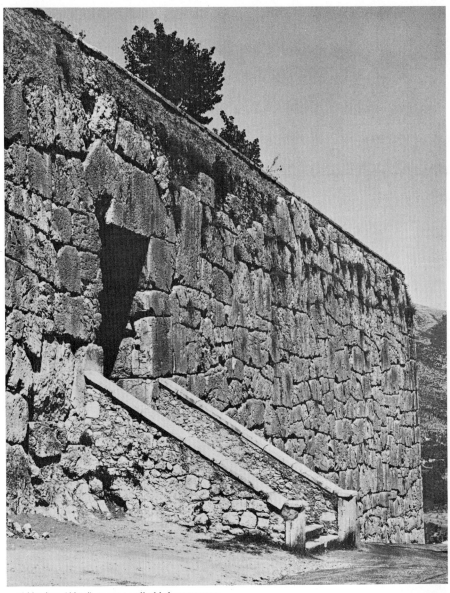

115. Alatrium (Alatri), terrace wall, third century B.C.

show the perfection this kind of construction had achieved before it was handed down to the second century.

Different kinds of structure were adapted for different functions. Large, shapeless blocks with the interstices stopped by smaller stones may once have belonged to primitive constructions, but in our material they represent only the simplest and roughest manner used for the less conspicuous parts of the walls (the so-called 'prima maniera'). A more regular wall (the 'seconda maniera') was achieved by smoothing the surface. The true polygonal masonry (the 'terza maniera') has stones accurately fitted together. They were perfectly smooth, or sometimes rusticated, and similar to a rough ashlar wall. The even more sophisticated perfection of the 'quarta maniera' was arrived at decidedly later. In Roman and Latin usage, as we know it, the first three types appear together; their various methods of construction afford no certain clue for dating. The often fantastically mighty

blocks of the fortifications seem mostly to have been brought into position by means of earthen ramps on the inside, which usually remained as an inner agger and formed a terrace for the defenders. Free-standing walls for defence, for instance the wall of Arpinum [116], seem to have been rare in this early age of Roman fortifications. Clamps and dowels were not used; mortar was a later device. The Romans continued to build polygonal walls in the last centuries B.C., as seen in villa terraces and in the Temple of Fortuna Primigenia at Praeneste (below, p. 169 ff.).

Before arched construction became the rule, gates could be constructed in the polygonal walls with corbelled, sloping walls and heavy

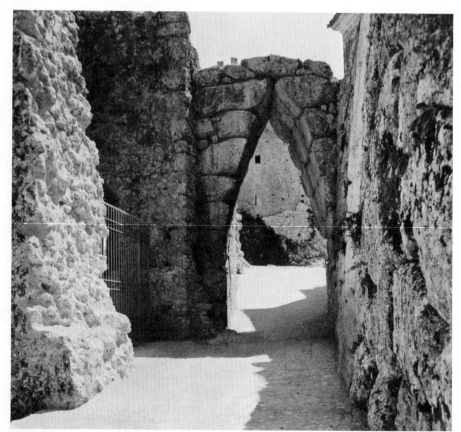

116. Arpinum, corbelled gate, 305 B.C.

lintel blocks, as at Signia (Segni), or with corbelled, pointed arches, as at Arpinum [116] and Palestrina. The corbelled arch of Arpinum has six courses rising to a height of more than 13 feet, and the lintel block of the acropolis gate at Alatrium measures about 16 feet. Minor gates were spanned by slabs. Polygonal walls were used also for podia and terraces of temples, as at Norba, Signia [117], and Cosa, and for other substructures such as those along the Via Appia, where they often seem to belong to the first period of this road, i.e. to *c*. 312.[1]

Ashlar walls were contemporary with these polygonal walls in districts where the volcanic tufa offered a suitable material. With this method of construction, in 378 and the following years the Romans built one of the greatest defensive works of their age, the so-called Servian Wall, by which they unified the seven hills into a strong, closely interrelated fortification [105, 170]. Instead of employing the rather poor and narrow local cappellaccio blocks of the previous period, they shipped a far superior building material from quarries in the recently conquered territory of Veii, the yellowish so-called Grotta Oscura tufa. The ashlar blocks measure some 2 feet (60 cm.) in height; the length varies between 2 feet 5 inches and 6 feet 11 inches (74 cm. and 2.10 m.) and the width between $17\frac{1}{3}$ and 26 inches (44 and 66 cm.). The wall is laid in alternate courses of headers and stretchers. Some of the blocks are marked with

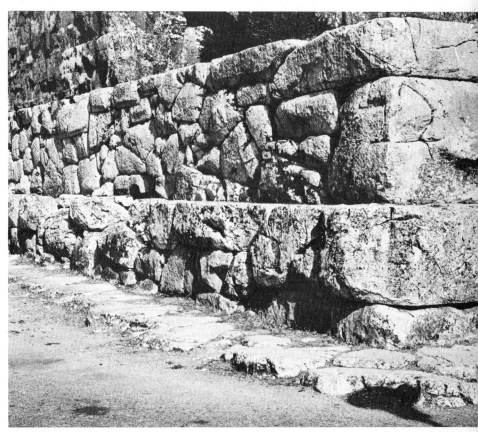

117. Signia (Segni), temple, terrace, probably fifth century B.C.

alphabetic signs, which were made either at the quarries or during the building operations. Together with other tufas from the Etruscan quarries north of Rome, the Grotta Oscura tufa remained the most important building material in the fourth and third centuries, though tufas of finer quality and firmer consistency from the Alban Hills (*peperino*), Gabii, and the surroundings of Rome were used for sarcophagi, altars, etc., and gradually replaced the Etruscan tufa even in architecture.

The colossal new town wall consisted mainly of terrace walls built against the hills and inside ramparts. The agger (cf. above, pp. 103-4), which probably earlier connected and defended the plain behind the Esquiline and the Viminal, was amplified into what may be called an artificial ridge with a height of approximately 33 feet. This agger was supported by a wall on its outer side, which continued the fortification of the hillsides and completed the circle of the town wall. Its base is 11 feet 10 inches (3.60 m.) wide. In front of this wall was a stretch of ground measuring some 23 feet, and a ditch, the *fossa*, which was 97 feet (29.60 m.) wide and approximately 30 feet deep. The artificially sloping hillside of the agger towards the town on the inner side of the wall was supported by a retaining wall of cappellaccio blocks, which, together with the huge outer wall, belong to the conspicuous remains of this most startling part of the Servian Wall. Livy tells how it deterred Hannibal from laying siege to Rome. We see the same kind of terrace walls used at Ardea, probably during the Samnite wars about 300 [118].

The lower town, which was abandoned about 300, and its old agger no longer fulfilling their function, the north-eastern side of the settlement on the acropolis needed new fortification. For this purpose a terrace wall was built against the hill with earth infilling towards the hill on the inside and a fossa dug in front of the wall.[2]

Somewhat older than the terrace wall of Ardea is the rectangular castrum of Ostia (see p. 125), a fortification which the Romans threw up in the last decades of the fourth century to protect the Tiber [123]. Fragments of terracotta revetments which seem to be of the sixth and fifth centuries suggest that this modern fort was built on a site contiguous to some older settlement, as was the castrum-fort of Pyrgi. The walls of Ostia were built in a similar manner to the Servian Wall, but with ashlar of the brownish so-called Fidenae tufa with spots of charcoal, which was quarried some 6 miles north of Rome. The thickness of the wall is 5 feet 5 inches (1.65 m.), and the highest preserved stretch measures 21 feet 8 inches (6.60 m.) from bottom to top. The wall probably had a rampart on the inner side. The four gates are of the inner-court type similar to those of Cosa [112] and run like corridors through the rampart. This type of gate may be considered a typical feature of Roman fortification. Neither at Ostia nor in Rome can we ascertain how the gates were covered, whether by lintels or corbelled.

Approximately a hundred years after the castrum of Ostia, in 241, the Romans destroyed the old Faliscan town of Falerii. They settled the

118. Ardea, acropolis, terrace wall, *c.* 300 B.C.(?), the bastion probably dating from the Gothic wars in the sixth century A.D. Elevation and plan

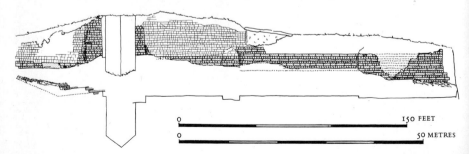

0   150 FEET

0   50 METRES

rebellious Faliscans in parts of their old territory and, as was their practice in unreliable districts, founded a strongly fortified new centre, Falerii Novi (Santa Maria di Falleri). It was connected with Rome by a straight military road, the Via Amerina, with beautiful, modern arched bridges [121]. The circuit of the city wall is about 1½ miles. In the typical Roman way it is reinforced by square towers projecting from the wall, as at Cosa. The ashlar blocks of reddish-brown tufa are only about 18 inches (45 cm.) high (they range between 44 and 47 cm.), but otherwise the wall is constructed like the Servian Wall, with the inner side generally attached to the slopes of the lower part of the town.[3]

Among the startling innovations of fourth- to third-century Latium are the elegant arched city gates of Falerii Novi and the arched bridge on the Via Amerina. A vaulted drain in front of the Temple of Saturn on the Forum Romanum has been dated to the fourth century, and the oldest Etruscan arches appear to belong to the same period also. The city gates of Falerii [119] display an unusual subtlety. Grey peperino-

tufa from the Alban Hills is used for the voussoirs and mouldings. The long, narrow voussoirs describe a circle concentric with the interior curve of the arch. The springers rest upon an impost moulding, and a moulding of the same type surrounds the outer curve of the arch. This type of arch, which is detached from the wall and limits it to right and left and carries it above, was the type usual until the age of Augustus. A fine, perhaps later, specimen is the Ponte del Diavolo at Manziana [120], which was probably constructed as part of a Roman military road to Tarquinia. The great bridge of the Via Amerina across the Fosso Tre Ponti [121] shows a different kind of arch construction. The voussoirs have five sides and are fitted into the coursing of the adjoining masonry, a type of arch which is otherwise known only from the time of Augustus onwards. But the bridge is an indispensable part of the road. There are no remains of any earlier structure; a date in the third century seems therefore certain.[4]

As stated above, Rome was rebuilt after 386 without any regular plan. In their haste after the sack the Romans disregarded the available

119. S. Maria di Falleri, gate, 241–200 B.C.

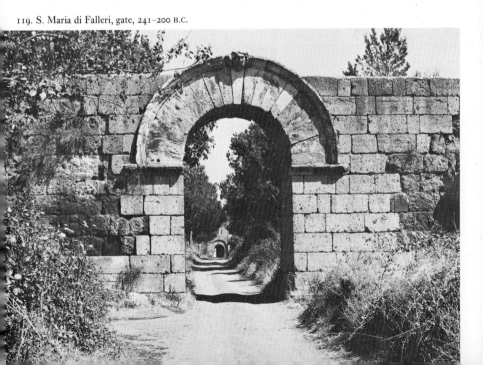

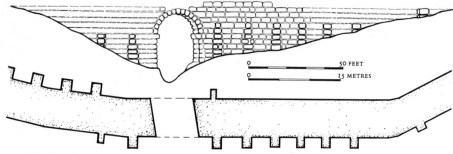

120. Manziana, Ponte del Diavolo, *c.* 100 B.C. Elevation and plan

models of Greek towns in Italy, which were regularly planned perhaps as early as the seventh century, of Etruscan towns of the sixth century, and of town planning of the fifth century in allied Campania. Elsewhere than Rome, however, the Romans began to adopt regular planning for their new towns in the fourth and third centuries, especially for colonies, where old buildings and rough and uneven surfaces did not stand in the way of modern designs. It is evident that regular planning and a street inside the walls were adapted to speedy manning of the walls, sallies, and to other military purposes. The first instance known of regular

Roman town planning is at Norba: in connexion with the great walls [111], during the war against the Volscians and Privernum in the second half of the fourth century the more level parts of the town between the hills with temples on the south-west and north-east received a regular layout. But Cosa is the first really complete regular Roman town. Although the surface was uneven, rectangular blocks of houses measuring between 107 and 121 feet (32.50 and 37 m.) in width and about 270 feet (82 m.) in length were built over the whole town inside the mighty wall. The oblong blocks and quarters arranged in a chessboard pattern show an obvi-

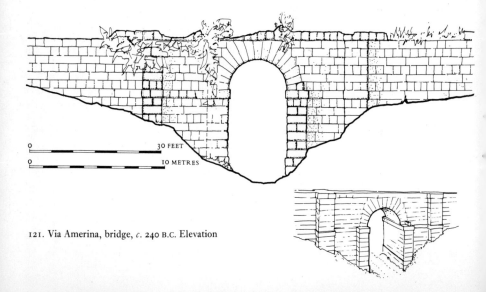

121. Via Amerina, bridge, *c.* 240 B.C. Elevation

ous affinity to Greek towns like Olynthus and Naples and the regular quarters of Pompeii (which was planned by either Etruscans or Oscans under Greek influence). The regular city plan of Cosa is clearly dated to the decades after the founding of the colony in 273.

Connected with the regular planning of the networks of streets in towns was one of the most important creations of the Roman military genius, their camps, or *castra*. Polybius elucidates this great novelty for the Mediterranean world (VI, 27-32) in a comprehensive and admiring account. He describes a camp as having two parallel main streets, the Via Principalis, which divided the camp into two sections with different kinds of barracks, and the Via Quintana. At each end of the Via Principalis were gates called the Portae Principales Dextra and Sinistra. At right angles to these streets ran a wide central passage which contained the commander's headquarters (*praetorium*), with three streets on each side. The central passage united the two halves of the camp and had gates at each end, the Porta Praetoria and the Porta Decumana. Remains of camps in Spain of the second century and from the Imperial Age as well as towns like Augustan Augusta Praetoria (Aosta) and Turin bear out Polybius's description.

The Romans not only applied regular town planning to the castra; they also, according to Frontinus (*Stratagems*, IV, I. 14), believed that they had taken the idea for their temporary castra from the Greeks. This is very likely true, but Polybius brings into special prominence the originality with which the Romans adapted the new scheme. He emphasizes the importance of the standard planning of the castra, where each soldier knew beforehand in exactly which street and in what part of the street his tent would be, and affirms that the Romans in their castra pursued 'a course diametrically opposite to that usual among the Greeks'. The Greeks, says Polybius (VI, 42), in encamping adapted the camp 'to the natural advantages . . . , because they shirk the labour of entrenching and because they think that artificial defences are not equal in value to the fortifications which nature pro-

vides'. Consequently, the Greeks adopted all kinds of shapes to suit the nature of the ground (exactly like the aboriginal hill towns). The Romans, because of entrenching and the fixed organization of the camps, did not need to take advantage of steep hillsides, rivers, and so on.

The Romans also created a somewhat different plan used especially for permanent rectangular (or quadrangular) castrum-forts with very strong, high town walls, built to house a regular garrison, such as at Ostia [123], Pyrgi and Minturnae [113, 114], Fundi, Allifae, and other fortresses resembling the castra. One may compare fortresses which Alexander the Great built on his march to distant territories of the Persian Empire [122]. The castrum of Ostia is the earliest known instance of these permanent camps, and may serve as an example. It measures 212 by 137 yards (193.94 by 125.70 m.) and has in the centre of each side gates of the type described at Cosa [123]. They are usually referred to by the names of the gates in Polybius's description of a camp. The main streets from these four gates met at right angles in the centre of the town. In modern literature these streets are conveniently called *decumanus* and *cardo*, designations which in their strict sense belong to the regular division of fields; decumanus is used for streets running lengthwise and cardo for the shorter, transverse streets.

According to the land surveyors it was ideal if the main roads from the surrounding fields could meet at right angles in the centre of the towns without interference from dwellings already in existence on the site. This system with straight, crossing main roads was not alien to the Greeks, as can be seen at Selinus and Paestum. In the enlarged fifth-century Pompeii [64], too, the main roads from the countryside resulted in a nearly rectangular grid of streets, which gave the town its basic regular layout; and Nicaea in Bithynia, a foundation of Antigonus Monophthalmus and Lysimachus and thus about contemporary with Ostia, was a quadrangular town with four gates which could all be seen from a stone in the middle of the Gymnasium, the typically Greek centre of the town.

To sum up, the city plan of the Roman castrum-forts, like all their other regular town planning, has to be seen in relation both to older and to contemporary designs all over the Greek world. But the final results the Romans achieved – exemplified by the castra described by Polybius, the castrum-forts with polygonal walls such as Minturnae and Pyrgi, and what they express of the particular Roman strength, notions, and manners in their great age – warn us not to overrate foreign influences or underlying traditions which may have lingered in the regular towns of Italy. The way in which Rome gradually developed and forcefully worked out modern ideas becomes of principal importance and should not be ignored. In the Roman Empire the castrum-forts were considered a distinctive mark of Romanity, as were also the Capitolia, the fora with statues of Marsyas, and Roman foundation rites. The remains of towns like Timgad, Egyptian Antinoopolis, and Beirut substantiate this, and the planning of many old towns in Britain, Italy, France, and Germany still reveals the legacy of the Roman castra.[5]

The colony of Cosa is remarkable because it is the most complete surviving Roman town of the otherwise scantily known centuries before 200 B.C. In addition, the method of construction of the houses demands the greatest attention. The grey limestone of the hill itself was used, cut to various shapes and sizes, but, vying with that, mud brick and wood, mortared masonry, and rubble work occurred all over the town. In cisterns barrel-vaults built of rough limestone voussoirs and rubble work or tile are connected with this kind of construction. The rubble work of Cosa ushers in *structurae caementiciae*, concrete, as described by Vitruvius (II,

122. Failaka (Ikaros), temple and fortification built by Alexander the Great on his march to the East. Plan, somewhat simplified

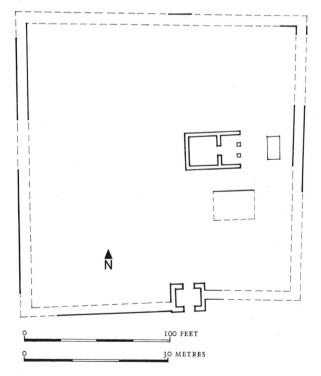

0   100 FEET

0   30 METRES

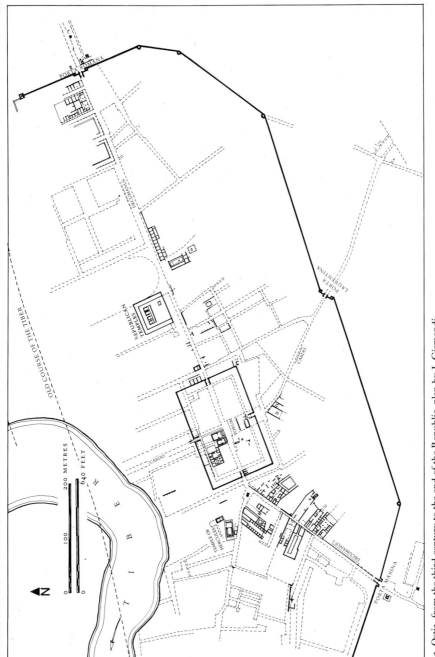

123. Ostia, from the third century to the end of the Republic, plan by I. Gismondi.
The central rectangular fortress is the castrum of the fourth century B.C.

4–8), which in the hands of Roman builders was destined gradually to revolutionize almost all Roman architecture. Roman concrete was a mixture of rubble and liquid mortar containing volcanic dust (pozzolana earth) with very great cohesive strength. Cato in *De agricultura* (14 f.), written about 160 B.C., mentions the use of mortar as a matter of course in utilitarian architecture. A barrel-vault datable to the first decades of the third century above the Upper Peirene Well on Acrocorinth is built 'of an agglomerate of sea and sand pebbles, held together by a binder . . . [with] a strong admixture of lime'. Refined concrete and concrete vaults were thus used by the Greeks in the third century, at least in utilitarian architecture. The great, but unsolved, problem is exactly when the Romans developed this kind of building to that degree of perfection and adaptability which made its overwhelming future possible.

It is necessary to pose this question already here, though there is disagreement between scholars on when this turning-point in the history of architecture of Western Europe was reached. The difference of opinion ranges between fifty and a hundred years. The lower limit seems certain: remains in Rome from about 150 B.C. onwards prove that concrete at that time was fully developed and widely used. The concrete walls were faced externally with stones of irregular shapes and thus displayed the technique which Vitruvius (II, 8. 1) praises as the old manner of giving walls a protective surface and calls *genus incertum* (the modern term is *opus incertum*) [124]. To the domestic

architecture of Pompeii belong various kinds of coarse rubble construction with a framework of limestone and tufa facing. Thanks to a fine mortar of pozzolana, towards the end of the third century walls of this type were developed to entire rubble walls without reinforcement. They resemble the Roman constructions of concrete, though they are less stable and without the more careful Roman facing. Walls of this kind were built in all quarters of Pompeii, together with façades of ashlar tufa and remaining structures of the oldest type built with the local limestone. Akin to the rubble of Cosa is the construction of the podium of the Temple of Magna Mater on the south side of the Palatine, which was consecrated in 191 B.C. It is made of irregular pieces of tufa and peperino laid in thick mortar.[6]

Many scholars believe that concrete began to prevail in Rome only about 150 B.C. But many arguments seem to prove that the new material appeared there as early as the third century, or at any rate about 200. In addition to the rubble of Cosa, the excavations of Ostia have revealed only houses of concrete with opus incertum in the quarters which grew up around the castrumfort in the third and second centuries. Of crucial importance is the dating of the imposing market hall on the Tiber south-west of the Aventine [125]. This hall and its large granaries, the Horrea Galbae, are reproduced on fragments 23 and 24 of the Forma Urbis Romae, which dates from A.D. 203-11. The remains in the Lungotevere Testaccio and Benjamin Franklin Street measure 160 feet (along the Tiber) by 285 feet (48.7 by 87 m.). This great structure is entirely built of concrete covered with opus incertum of a quality already reminiscent of that technique in Sullan times. The building has arched doors, with alternating arched windows above. Lengthwise, it follows the rising slope along the Tiber on three levels; crosswise, it is divided by barrel-vaulted transepts facing the river. It seems to me indubitable that this highly developed building is identical with the Porticus Aemilia, built in 193 and restored in 174 (Livy, XXXV, 10. 12; XLI, 27. 8). The defenders of a

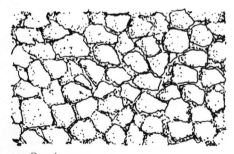

124. Opus incertum

Roman and Greek authors such as Strabo (V, 3. 8) maintained that the 'older Romans took but little account of the beauty of Rome' because they were occupied with aqueducts, paved roads, and the construction of sewers. Diony-

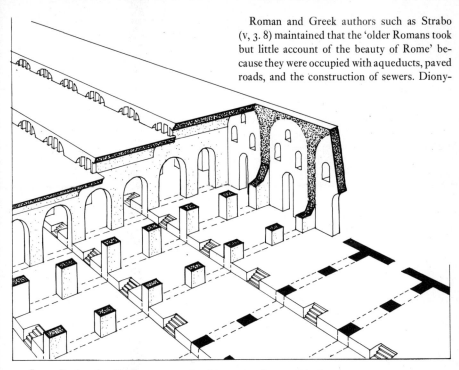

125. Rome, Porticus Aemilia(?), 193 B.C., restored in 174 B.C. Axonometric plan

later date for concrete either reject the identification or assume that the hall represents the Porticus Aemilia in a later, rebuilt form, belonging to the decades towards 100 B.C. Yet there appears to be no other building of the importance which Livy's repeated information indicates in the quarter south of the Aventine (outside the Porta Trigemina). Also, no older remains have been found below the hall. It is therefore difficult to deny that already at the beginning of the second century concrete, opus incertum, and vaulting had reached the considerable perfection which the Porticus Aemilia shows, and that the experimental age consequently was the third century. However, there are arguments against this conclusion, and the fundamental question of when such a building could have been erected in Rome must still be presented as problematical.[7]

sius says (III, 67) – in spite of the great Late Republican architecture – that the greatness of the Roman Empire can best be seen in these magnificent utilitarian works, and Strabo explains that the Greeks had taken little interest in them, and that this marks a characteristic difference between Rome and Greece. It is, of course, easy to prove that the Greeks were forerunners in the construction of aqueducts, sewers, and other utilitarian architecture. On the other hand, the Romans – later partly because of their concrete – started a new era in the field, without any of the beauty of 'the useless, though famous, works of the Greeks' (as Frontinus says in his book about the aqueducts of Rome, I, 16). Cicero (*De Oratore*, III, 179–81) even speculated on the charm which is sometimes produced by merely fulfilling practical requirements. But, as Strabo himself says, his remarks refer to the older Romans, whereas the Romans of the last two centuries B.C., and particularly those of his time, filled the city with beautiful buildings of hellenistic types.

Pre-eminent among the utilitarian structures of the fourth and third centuries were the works of 312 erected by the great censor Appius Claudius. He was the founder of Rome's first, still almost entirely subterranean aqueduct, the Aqua Appia, and the great military road to Capua, the Via Appia, with its viaducts, polygonal terraces, and, as far as possible, straight course. In the third century this famous trunk road was prolonged to Venusia, Brundisium, and Tarentum, connecting the southern parts of Italy with their new, harsh ruler on the Tiber, and at the same time creating the starting point for Rome's wars with the hellenistic kingdoms in the late third and second centuries. Both Strabo and Dionysius give the Roman roads special prominence, and they are, indeed, one of the historically most important achievements of the third century. In that century the Romans started to use selce (silex, basaltic lava) instead of gravel and tufa for paving, which, allied to

massive foundations, provided the legions with new, superior means of conveyance to hold their dominions in check. At the same time they also prepared the way for the future peaceful intercourse of the Empire. The streets of Rome and other towns were gradually reconstructed in the same way.[8]

At the same time, however, numerous temples were being built in Rome and the forum was receiving its first embellishment. Temple C in the Largo Argentina in Rome [35, 126] and the smaller temple embedded in the podium of the Late Republican Temple A were built about, and probably before, 300. The podia consist of ashlar work of the same kind as in the Servian Wall. The older temple, A, seems to have belonged to the type with two columns prostyle, discussed *à propos* the Etruscan temples (p. 38 f.) [149]. Temple C reveals the Etruscan type of one-cella temple with colonnaded alae and closed rear wall projecting right and left of the cella, mentioned by Vitruvius (IV, 7. 2) and discussed on pp. 37–8. The high podium [35] is, as always in these temples, accessible only by a flight of stairs in front of the roomy prodomus.

126. Rome, Largo Argentina, temples. Temples A and C *c.* 300 B.C. Plan

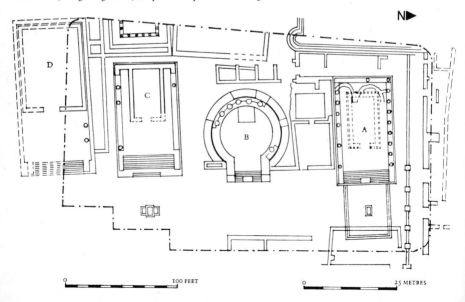

0   100 FEET

0   25 METRES

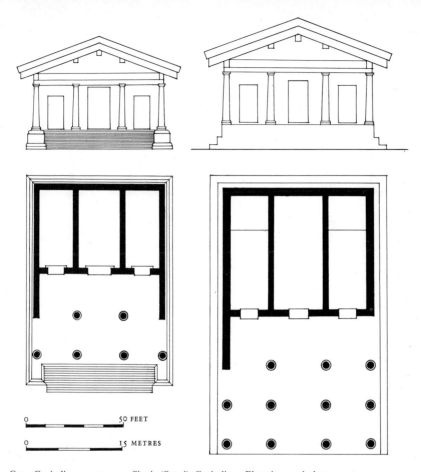

127. Cosa, Capitolium, *c.* 150 B.C.; Signia (Segni), Capitolium. Elevations and plans

These podia and temples are of stone. This, as well as the somewhat elongated proportions of Temple C, may indicate hellenistic influence. The forward orientation of the temples is emphasized, not only, as in some of the Etruscan temples [20, 33], by the open spaces in front but also by altars on the axis of the cellas.

Though the temples of Cosa, of which sufficient elements for a reconstruction remain, were built in the second century, they afford confirmation of the state of the sanctuaries in Rome before their final hellenization. The Capitolium of Cosa, dating from about 150 [127], corresponds largely to Vitruvius's description (IV, 7; and also to the Capitoline Temple of Jupiter in Rome). Smaller temples [128] are of the Etruscan type described on p. 39, with a cella without alae and columns in the prodomus. As mentioned above, the terracottas of the pediments, the revetments, and the drip-lines sometimes suggest a construction with, as Vitruvius says (IV, 7. 5), mutules projecting in front of the façade of the temple and carrying the tympanum of the pediment [43].

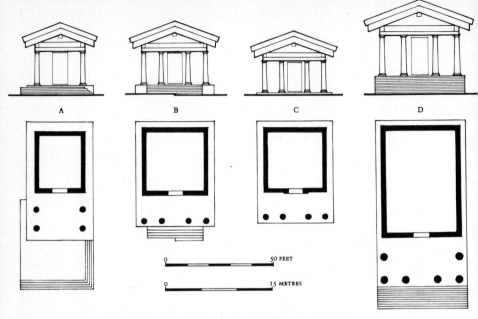

128. (A) Cosa, Temple B; (B) Cosa, Temple D; (C) Cosa, Port Temple; (D) Norba, temple.
Last centuries B.C. Elevations and plans

Tuscan columns reinforce the impression that Vitruvius learned much from exactly this type of Roman temple with its preserved Etruscan *dispositiones* and chose various items from among such temples when he attempted to reestablish what genuine Etruscan architecture had been like.

A different kind of temple was the so-called 'Tempio della Pace' in the forum of the colony which the Romans founded in 273 in the Lucanian town of Paestum, with its Greek antecedents. It has the Etrusco-Roman plan with a high podium, stairs only in front, deep pronaus, and a cella with alae [129]. In the second period

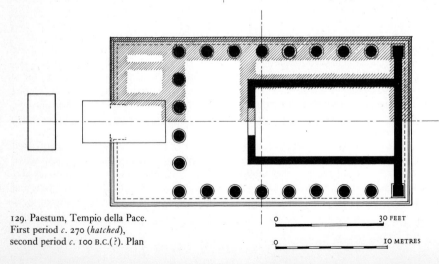

129. Paestum, Tempio della Pace.
First period *c*. 270 (*hatched*),
second period *c*. 100 B.C.(?). Plan

of the temple (about 100 B.C.?), the columns on this traditional Italic substructure were Corinthian. Its capitals belonged to the peopled type to which I have already referred as current in Etruria and which were typical of Pompeii and south Italy. From Corinthian leafage below spring two volutes of Ionic type with a head between them. The entablature was of stone with a Doric frieze above the architrave. The first temple seems to have been built during the first decades of the Roman colony, and thus – no doubt – already belonged to the Early Etruscan and Roman sanctuaries, discussed on p. 38, which introduced the combination of Italic plan and Greek superstructure and were destined to predominate in the following centuries.[9]

In spite of the temples on the south side and the paved streets around the central area, the Forum Romanum remained a rather shapeless market-place, slightly narrowing towards the main entrance road on the east side, the Via Sacra. Plautus, in *Curculio* (476), gives a wonderfully vivid description of the muddle. He also makes clear that the part of the Cloaca Maxima which passed the forum was an open channel. This old square had no axial disposition, and no dominating temple on its upper short side. Many old Italic fora probably had the same naïve, disorderly character, which contrasts strongly not only with what was to be the result of later, regular town planning but also with the axial orientation native to the Etruscan temples, and what they and their forecourts [20, 32, 33] contributed when central Italian towns were planned in agreement with modern Etruscan and Greek urbanization.

Livy (XXVI, 27; XLIV, 16) mentions the private houses which, until after a fire in 210 and later building operations, lay behind the butchers' stalls and shops of the forum – the Tabernae Veteres on the south side and the Argentariae on the north side, or Novae as they were then called. In spite of still crowded surroundings they stood out clearly as boundaries for the area of the future regulated forum. In the fourth century the dealers in victuals had been banished from the tabernae to special markets in the neighbourhood, and only money-changers and bankers were allowed to have their businesses there. This 'forensis dignitas', to use Varro's words (quoted by Nonius, 532) had a background in the Greek feeling for the dignity of central fora, expressed already by Aristotle (*Politica*, 1331a), and heralded the elegance and systematization of the Forum Romanum of centuries to come.

The conqueror of the Volsci at Antium, C. Maenius, consul in 338, constructed balconies on the upper floors of the tabernae of the forum. These 'Maeniana' projected above the columns in front of the shops, and when the gladiatorial shows were introduced to Rome, probably from Campania in 264, and it became, according to Vitruvius (V, I. 1), a custom that they should be given in the forum, the Maeniana were especially convenient and brought in public revenue. About 338 the orators' platform (*tribunal*) at the assembly-place (*comitium*) was embellished by the Rostra and the column erected in honour of Maenius, as has already been described.[10] In this forum the funerals of the great families also took place, with a peroration from the Rostra and a parade of inherited ceremonial dress, marks of honour, and ancestral masks, as splendidly described by Polybius (VI, 53). After the ceremony the mask of the man who had just died followed those of his ancestors to the family atrium, where the image was placed 'in the most conspicuous position, enclosed in a wooden shrine'.

L. Richardson has drawn attention to oval amphitheatre-shaped comitia, or voting stations. They are so far known to us only from the third and second centuries, at Cosa [138], at Paestum, and at Agrigentum. As in the case of the Comitium in Rome (the *vestibulum curiae*), a curia dominated the site, placed as it was at the top of the stairs on the central axis of the court. The same arrangement also exists in the cavea of the Theatre of Pompey, with the Temple of Venus Victrix facing the stage from the top of the spectators' gallery. The theatre temples of Latium (below, pp. 165 ff.) may also be compared. Whether the Romans followed old traditions and stood on the stairs or were seated after the Greek fashion, this architectural type of assembly building or building for voters seems to have been suggested by Greek municipal architecture.[11]

Our present material adds very little to what has been said about the atria and the domus of patricians and nobles (above, p. 106). The best archaeological evidence from the Rome region during this period is a newly excavated house at Cosa which shows an asymmetrical treatment of the atrium-tablinum plan and remains of wall-decoration closely related to examples on Delos. Among literary sources Livy (XLIV, 16. 10) relates that the domus of the Scipio family was in the quarter behind the Tabernae Veteres on the south side of the forum. Together with this domus of one of the best families in Rome he mentions butchers' stalls and shops, as we see tabernae connected with the atrium-houses in second-century Pompeii. As discussed on p. 91 f., the Etruscans may have added peristyles to their houses – in any case, peristyles behind the atria were a feature of atrium-houses in third-century Campania – but there is nothing either in our sources or in the archaeological material to prove that that luxury reached Rome at this early period, or that the gardens then existed which became such an important addition to the peristyles in Italy [91].

Far more important than what we learn about the domus is Livy's brief mention (XXI, 62; XXXVI, 37) of tenement houses with upper storeys. He informs us that in 218 an ox fell from the third storey of a house on the Forum Boarium, and that in 191 in another part of Rome, the Carinae, two cows went up the stairs of a house to the very top floor. Together with what Dionysius (X, 32. 5) relates about houses with upper storeys put up already in the fifth century by the plebeians on the Aventine, these events introduce a characteristically Roman type of building of the greatest importance for centuries to come: the high tenement house or *insula*. There is no reason to doubt that such houses were piled up on the tabernae along the streets [107, 133] and were accessible by steep staircases directly from the street – the arrangement we see in its accomplished Imperial form throughout Ostia and on the Forma Urbis, and which can still be seen in old towns or old quarters all over Italy. There are, of course, no remains preserved of these early insulae, but rambling plans, cracking walls, ladders or wooden stairs to the upper storeys, wooden ceilings and floors, and mud-brick walls were doubtless typical of them. Such defects were still complained of by historians and poets of the first century A.D., in spite of great endeavours in the last centuries B.C. to check this uncontrolled individual building activity and to erect many modern insulae.[12]

In our sources high tenement houses are considered unusual in the Mediterranean world. They are mentioned as something exceptional at Parabos in Phoenicia, at Arados in Syria, in Tyre, and in Carthage.[13] Vitruvius is no less definite when he explains the high tenement houses of Rome as a local phenomenon due to the enormous size of Rome's population, which, he says, made it necessary to increase indefinitely the number of dwellings and so to construct high houses and invent for them a less unsuitable material than mud brick. Rows of tabernae, as we see them at Pompeii and in the Republican strata of Ostia, and badly planned and badly built insulae presumably occupied great parts of the town already in the fourth and third centuries.

In 221 another circus, the Circus Flaminius of the censor C. Flaminius Nepos, was added to the racecourse in the valley of the Circus Maximus. It stood on the Tiber, with one end between the Porticus Metelli and the Pons Fabricius. The Greek hippodromes no doubt offered a model, but both the temporary theatres and the permanent circus buildings in Rome seem, until the first century B.C., to have been either surrounded by sloping earthen ramparts or provided with wooden structures for the spectators. The wooden buildings certainly left architectural traditions of importance to the monumental ashlar and concrete architecture of the centuries to come. It is typical that still in

155 a permanent theatre under construction was torn down by order of the senate, on the grounds that it was inexpedient and would damage the public character of the city. So the plebs in older times still had to stand to see theatrical performances, and the wooden theatres were always demolished after the entertainments.[14]

Livy (XL, 5) reports how the Macedonians at the court of King Philip, like the Campanians of Cicero's day, poked fun at the appearance of Rome about 200: 'It was not yet made beautiful in either its public or its private quarters.' That epilogue has its companion piece in the tomb of the Scipio family on the Via Appia. Originally it was a rough, rock-cut chamber tomb. It has many parallels among the later Etruscan undecorated tombs – for instance, the tomb of the Emperor Otho's Etruscan ancestors, the Salvii, at Ferento – but it is strikingly inferior to the rich, monumental sepulchral halls of some of the great families of Caere and Perugia [72, 73] (pp. 80–2). Perhaps in its first period, before the present façade in the hellenistic style was built about 100 B.C., the tomb had an adorned rock façade, as did so many Late Etruscan tombs with entrances from the hillsides [99]. The famous sarcophagus (now in the Vatican Museum) of the consul of 298, Lucius Cornelius Scipio Barbatus – even if it was added to the tomb during the golden age of the Scipiones in the second century – and a beautiful sarcophagus found south of Rome, outside the Aurelian Wall [130], reveal eloquently the progress of Greek influence and taste among the leading Roman families in the third century.[15]

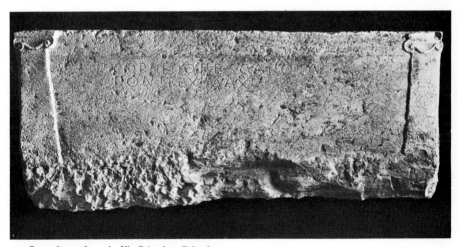

130. Sarcophagus from the Via Cristoforo Colombo, third century B.C. *Rome, Palazzo dei Conservatori*

CHAPTER 6

HELLENIZED ROME 'CONSUETUDO ITALICA'

'The beginnings of foreign luxury were introduced into the city by the army from Asia' about the year 187 B.C., says Livy (XXXIX, 6. 7). He also affirms (XXV, 40. 2) that already during the war against Hannibal an enthusiasm for Greek art had been awakened in Rome by the statues and paintings from Syracuse seen at Marcellus's triumph (212 B.C.).

Statements of this kind should not make us forget that direct influence from Greece or, still more, such influence in its reshaped Etruscan form, had guided Roman architecture and art from their very first beginnings. What Livy and Pliny mean is that the harsh centuries of 'the early Romans' (to speak with Strabo, V, 3. 8) and of the wars in Italy and against Hannibal were over. The theatres of war were now in the hellenistic world. Rome was transformed by a landslide of influence not only from southern Italy but also directly from the great Eastern capitals of the hellenistic kings. It is of great importance to remember that the culture of the Greek city-states with their restricted aims and scope after Alexander appeared in a far more irresistible and international shape throughout the Mediterranean world. It meant a new epoch for the hitherto obstinately old-fashioned town on the Tiber. In the second century B.C., Cato and the consul and senate, who forbade permanent theatres, were still trying to uphold ancestral customs, old usages, and the unwritten laws of Rome.

Livy speaks about the new charms of town life and new ways of living; Pliny, and even Tertullian, still resound with the contemporary reaction against these hellenistic 'licentious profligacies'. Archaeological material and literary sources prove that hellenistic taste pervaded not only the Roman way of life but also architecture. According to Vitruvius (VII, Preface, 15. 17), the Seleucid king, Antiochus IV (175-

163), commissioned a citizen of Rome, Decimus Cossutius, to rebuild the Olympieion in Athens. Vitruvius adds that this was done 'with great skill and supreme knowledge'. This startling information shows, apart from anything else, that there were already contacts between the architecture of the hellenistic states and Rome during the sixties of the second century. In Rome, its colonies, and central Italy, we see the beginning of an inspiring struggle between Etrusco-Italic traditions and the overwhelming riches from the hellenistic towns. This created a new sort of hellenistic architecture. Only very rarely is piety towards old buildings as such attested. The Romulus huts are a special case (above, p. 28); another is the fact that in the midst of the rich resources of Imperial Rome, Pliny (XXXV, 158) speaks of the fine terracotta sculpture in Rome and other towns of Italy as 'more deserving of respect than gold, and certainly less baneful'. On the other hand, Cicero in the second Verrine Oration (11, 4. 68, 69) says that the Capitoline Temple rebuilt after the fire of 83 B.C. was adorned 'as the majesty of the temple and the renown of our empire demand' – that is, with modern hellenistic monumentality. 'Let us feel,' he continues, 'that conflagration to have been the will of heaven, and its purpose not to destroy the temple of Almighty Jupiter, but to demand of us one more splendid and magnificent.' Nothing can better express the victory of hellenistic taste and luxury. But before the curia of the senate rebuilt in Sulla's age, Cicero makes a halt (*De finibus*, V, 2) saying that the old Curia Hostilia evoked thoughts of Scipio, Cato, and other famous men of the olden days, while the new, Sullan curia 'seems to be smaller since its enlargement'.

Vitruvius, in the fifth and sixth books, describes the new variety of hellenistic architecture, which Italic builders could not resist, as 'consuetudo italica'. He points out, over and over again, recurrent Italic features, but he also specifies typical architectural designs of the Greeks which remained alien to the Roman branch of hellenistic architecture – such as fora in the form of a square (V, I. I) and Greek theatres (V, 7). In the sixth book he brings out specially prominently that the Greeks did not use atria (as the Etruscans and the Romans did) and therefore 'do not build their mansions as we do' (VI, 7). The atrium-houses of Pompeii [85, 91, 131] and Republican Ostia preserve the exclusively Italic plan. Vitruvius thus discloses

Egyptian and Cyzicene oeci (saloons), which none the less were imported to this new Rome (V, 11; VI, 3. 7-10). What Vitruvius calls 'consuetudo italica' was neither pure old-Italic nor a copy of hellenistic towns: it was a new interpretation of the Roman commonwealth aided by modern adornments, which the increasing renown of the Empire demanded. The influence of Roman traditions upon foreign elements and the amalgamation of Roman architectural patterns with hellenistic taste created something new. However, foreign influence is readily perceived everywhere.

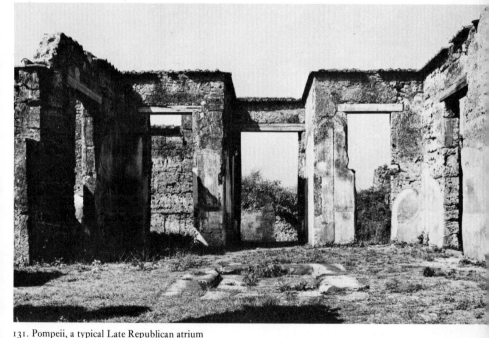

131. Pompeii, a typical Late Republican atrium

to us on the one hand the legacy of old Rome, its Etrusco-Roman temples, its atria, and its indigenous or long-established buildings, and on the other hand the hellenistic influence which pervaded Roman architecture of the previous centuries. Further, he describes Greek buildings with no Italic tradition, such as the palaestras, the peristyles, and, in private houses, the

TECHNIQUES AND MATERIALS IN PUBLIC BUILDINGS

In discussing theatres (pp. 134-5), it has already been said that the Romans before Augustus's time rarely used costly material in public buildings. The marble quarries of Luna (Pliny, XXXVI, 14; Strabo, V, 2-5) were discovered only

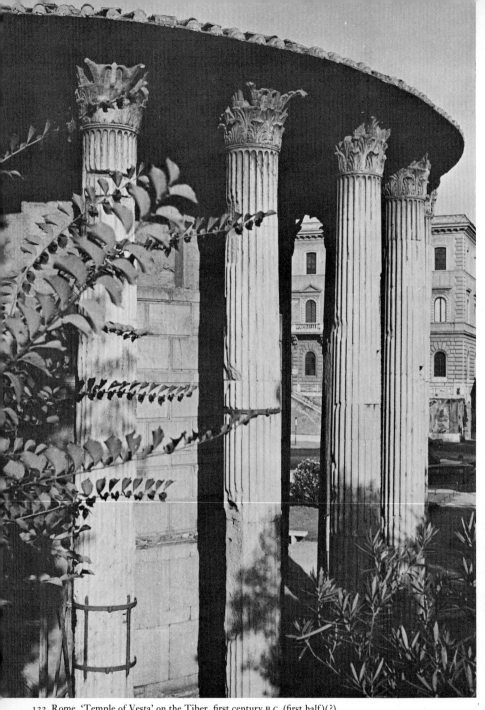
132. Rome, 'Temple of Vesta' on the Tiber, first century B.C. (first half)(?)

in the Augustan Age. In 149 B.C., however, the first floor of the Capitoline Temple was constructed with a diamond pattern (according to Pliny, XXXVI, 185), and in 146 the ceiling was gilded (Pliny, XXXIII, 57). Catulus, who rebuilt the Capitoline Temple after the fire of 83 B.C., was still both criticized and praised for having gilded the brass tiling of the roof. The victor over the Macedonians, Q. Caecilius Metellus, was the first to build a marble temple in Rome. That was in 146 B.C. His Temple of Jupiter Stator in a portico by the Tiber (later known as the Porticus Octaviae) was pointed out as the first instance of 'the magnificence or luxury of marble' among Roman public buildings. The charming, round marble temple by the Tiber (usually called, without foundation, the 'Temple of Vesta') [132] seems to belong to the first half of the first century B.C. Preserved from the predecessor of the present temple are foundations of tufa. The marble walls remain to about two-thirds of their height, and three different types of capital and column (twelve later replaced by columns of the Imperial Age). The entablature is lost, but the Corinthian columns with Attic bases, the capitals, fragments of coffering, the cornice, and the elegant plinth and masonry of the walls indicate that the temple – as has been aptly said – was a hellenistic 'intruder upon the Roman scene'. In contrast to the probably somewhat later Italic round temples on podia (p. 162 f.), it was also, in the Greek fashion, surrounded by steps. Some of the Roman generals may have brought a Greek architect and the marble from Greece to Rome, as Sulla sent Corinthian marble columns from the Olympieion in Athens to the Capitoline Temple after the fire of 83.[1]

However, as a rule Late Republican public buildings in Rome, though more and more influenced by hellenistic styles and proportions, were constructed until the age of Augustus with tufa from Rome and its surroundings and additional travertine from Tivoli. In the first century B.C., travertine was even used for entire buildings, thus embarking on the career on which it was to continue in Imperial times.

Rubble and concrete could also be employed. Walls, entablatures, capitals, and columns of tufa or travertine were always covered with stucco and painted, whether the buildings were of tufa, travertine, rubble, or concrete. Colourful terracotta revetments on the entablatures remained in favour throughout the Late Republican Age. In Vitruvius's eyes the traditional parsimony with costly materials detracted from Republican buildings; had they been refined by 'the dignity conferred by magnificence and great outlay' (VII, Preface, 17), they could, according to him, have been included among the first and greatest works of architecture.[2]

As Pliny preaches, morals had already lost the battle against hellenistic luxury about 100 B.C. in the domus and the villas of the rich. A house which was regarded as luxurious in 78 B.C., after thirty-five years no longer ranked among the first hundred in Rome. Sumptuous marbles flooded Rome and were even dragged past the earthenware pediments of the temples to private houses and to temporary theatres.[3] Pliny sometimes (XXXVI, 8 and 113) even thinks that Late Republican luxury, in architecture and otherwise, surpassed that of the Imperial Age, or – at least – introduced it (XXXVI, 110).

Ashlar work and mud brick persisted. As the temples and other public buildings of Cosa have shown, rubble came into use already in the third century; in temples from about 100 we meet with walls of concrete. For the podia of the temples and for the walls of utilitarian buildings, *opus caementicium* (concrete) more and more replaced the older techniques. The concrete podia were faced with ashlar of tufa or travertine. In the old temple terraces of Norba, the podium of the Capitolium of Signia [117], and even in some terraces of Roman villas we still see the old-fashioned polygonal work (though, of course, stuccoed) on podia. The small irregular cover-blocks of tufa, limestone, or selce (*opus incertum*) [124] used for second-century concrete walls became tidier after about 100. The modern name for these more regular, but still uneven, facing-blocks is 'quasi- (or pseudo-) reticulate'. It heralds the famous regular reticulate work (*opus reticulatum*) of the Imperial Age, which, on the evidence we have at present, first appears in the Theatre of Pompey (55 B.C.) and also in a few structures erected just before that sensational building. According to Vitruvius (II, 8. 1), in his day everybody used such a regular network, though, with his usual conservatism, he maintains that the old incertum was less likely to crack. Excavations at Alba Fucens, a sanctuary in the neighbourhood of Sulmona (the so-called 'Villa d'Ovidio'), and several buildings in other places show that incertum could persist together with other later techniques. Small blocks (*tufelli*) protected door-posts, corners, and other exposed parts of walls, and in these centuries were also used for arches.[4]

TECHNIQUES AND MATERIALS IN DOMESTIC ARCHITECTURE

The most spectacular, original, and important employment of opus caementicium was connected with the improvements of the tenement houses (insulae; see p. 134) and with the Roman vaults. Vitruvius states (II, 8. 17) that high houses of mud brick needed walls two or three bricks thick, while Roman laws forbade walls in public property to be more than $1\frac{1}{2}$ feet thick. All the same, Rome's crowded population made it necessary to increase the number of dwelling-places and to build high. For this dilemma, Vitruvius recommends insulae with concrete walls, strengthened by piers of stone and protected by a layer of baked tiles on top of the concrete walls below the roof.[5] He otherwise distrusts concrete – as he does most novel inventions – and he reports that concrete walls were not expected to last more than some eighty years (II, 8. 8). But high tenement houses with fairly slender walls could be built with concrete. Vitruvius therefore accepts the material for this purpose and even praises the excellence of the increased accommodation provided by these modern high buildings. Vitruvius's keen interest in insulae makes us understand just how

frantic builders' activity of that kind was in Rome during this period, though rows of tabernae without superstructure no doubt also remained along many streets.

Added to that are both Augustus's endeavours to improve the town in a rational way (cf. p. 114), continued uncontrolled building, and the more than five hundred slaves of Crassus 'who were architects and builders'. He bought the plots for his most successful speculative investments – building new tenement houses after fires and collapses when previous owners had let them 'go at a trifling price owing to their fear and uncertainty'. From all this irrational or careless building activity there finally arose the perfection of well-planned, brick-faced insulae which we see all over Ostia from about A.D. 100 and on the Forma Urbis [106]. Thus, domestic architecture developed which was unprecedented in the towns of the ancient world, even if in certain respects it may seem defective to us.

Certainly in Vitruvius's Rome, nobody had conceived the idea of a homogeneous, sturdy, brick-faced town such as second-century Ostia presents. The far less perfect tenements of concrete, which Vitruvius hails as solving the problems of housing in Rome, were by no means as frequent as his words imply. Dio Cassius (XXXIX, 61), describing the great flood of 54 B.C., mentions as something typical walls constructed of mud brick, which 'became soaked through and collapsed while all the animals perished in the flood'. Seneca Rhetor (*Controversiae*, II, 1. 11), like other authors of the earlier Imperial Age and like Strabo (V, 3. 7), reports that fires and collapses were still frequent in Rome, adding that the houses were so high and the streets so narrow that there was no escape from such disasters.

From the decades after 100 we have archaeological evidence showing the kind of domestic architecture which Vitruvius recommended some fifty years later. At Terracina five tabernae of a large insula remain from the beginning of the first century B.C. [133]. The house is built of concrete with a cover of opus incertum. Its piers and arches are of small blocks of local lime-

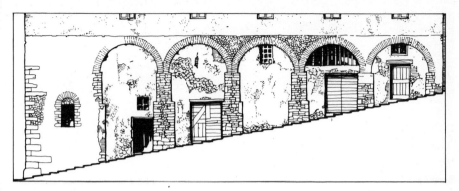

133. Terracina, Via dei Sanniti, tabernae of an insula, early first century B.C. Elevation

stone. In the street along the south side of the Palatine the remains of a great Late Republican building, erected some decades later, has piers and arches of tufa blocks and concrete walls covered by quasi-reticulate [134]. The same kind of technique is used in various remains of walls along the Via Sacra and in a part of the crowded old Rome with a brothel and a bath, below the Neronian portico and south of the Via Sacra, towards the Clivus Palatinus. In the Republican layers below the rebuilt Ostia of Imperial times, concrete covered by incertum and quasi-reticulate occurs everywhere after a first period of concrete and larger tufa blocks.

The most perfect specimen of a Late Republican tenement house of concrete, from the point of view both of planning and of building technique, is the Roman baths on the north side

134. Rome, building on the south side of the Palatine, the left-hand arch. Late Republican

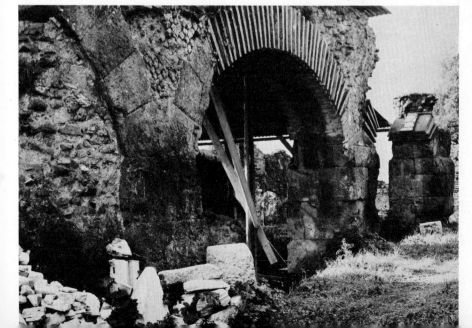

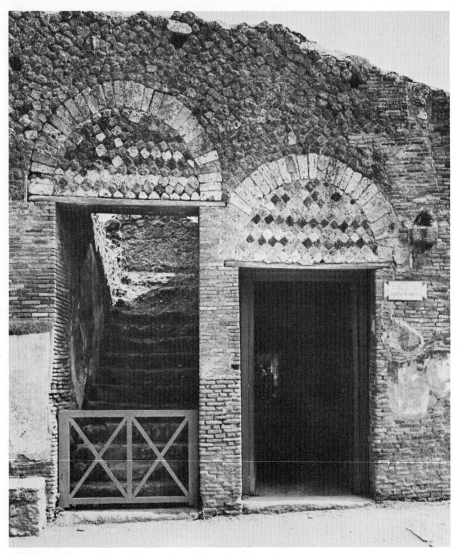

135. Pompeii, Forum Baths, staircase and corridor to the baths, *c.* 80 B.C.

of the forum of Pompeii (Terme del Foro) [178]. Together with other buildings, they were put up for the colony of Roman veterans, *Colonia Cornelia Veneria*, established in 80 B.C. to punish the Pompeians for their resistance to the Sullan army in the Social War. This building stands out from the usual architecture of Pompeii as a typical Roman insula. It is built of concrete and faced with a quasi-reticulate of lava. On the east and north side of the bathing establishment, which occupies the whole inner part of the site, against Via del Foro and Via delle Terme, rows of tabernae are built with at least one upper storey, accessible by a direct staircase from the street; a corridor leads to the baths themselves [135]. In other words, here we see the standard for the rapidly increasing number of tenement houses with upper storeys in Rome after their first shapeless beginnings: a tenement house built above rows of shops.

their own down to the pavements. As Varro says (*Lingua Latina*, v, 162): 'After they began to take dinner upstairs, all the rooms of the upper storey were called cenacula.' An interesting attempt to build a tenement house with upper storeys and small apartments around an inner court appears in the so-called 'Casa a Graticcio' at Herculaneum, but it should not be confused with the great, well-planned blocks, with central courts surrounded by tenements

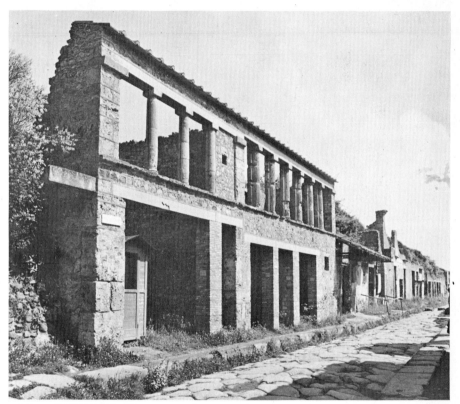

136. Pompeii, Via dell'Abbondanza, houses with porticoes on the second floor, built and rebuilt during the last centuries of Pompeii

Both at Pompeii and at Herculaneum one or even two storeys were often built above atrium and peristyle houses, with elegant colonnaded dining-rooms (*cenacula*) open towards the street [136], or apartments with staircases of

and with windows and shops towards the street, which we see in Imperial Ostia and which their discoverer Guido Calza called Palazzi di Tutti.

Tabernae round the Terme del Foro at Pompeii exhibit the form common to all shops of the

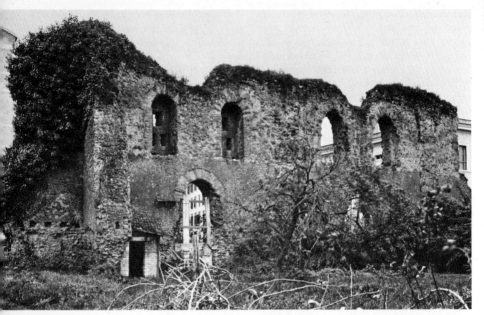

137. Rome, Porticus Aemilia, begun 193 and restored 174 B.C.(?), before the modern buildings on the site, showing the alternating arches on the first and second floors

Imperial Age. Above them are the remains of a balcony like those on the tenement houses of Rome and Ostia. The shops had a wide, open entrance from the street and inside a barrel-vault with a garret provided with a small window above the lintel of the door. As in Imperial times, the garret was certainly reached by wooden stairs or ladders within the shop.[6]

Together with the progressively higher tenements of concrete, I have already singled out as one of the most important Roman innovations the vaults, constructed of a mass of concrete cast over a wooden form in contrast to the stone-built vaults of the East. Here starts a tradition of craftsmanship of enormous importance for the Imperial Age, comprising not only the gradually improving ability to handle a new material but also an efficient organization of carpenters to make the centering of the vaults. Vaults on the principle of the arch, wooden vaults, and the old corbelled vaults were now replaced more and more by the durable concrete vaults

of less weight and more convenient construction. The Porticus Aemilia [125, 137] has already shown us the most common type, the barrel-vault, as it was probably introduced to Rome in the first decades of the second century B.C. The barrel-vaults of the shops of Terracina and Pompeii show how common this manner of vaulting had become by the beginning of the first century.

As seen in the cooling rooms (*frigidaria*) in the baths of Pompeii, domes with a large circular opening in the centre and resembling the old corbelled domes were moulded of concrete. The portico along the façade of the Tabularium on

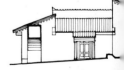

the Forum Romanum and the shops of the terrace below the Temple of Hercules at Tivoli show that rectangular domical vaults also existed in Late Republican Rome.[7] Insulae and concrete vaults were developed in Rome with an energy and to an extent which created new, exclusively Roman types, reducing the possible basic influences from abroad or from the Etruscans to a matter of secondary interest.

FORA

Monumental architecture, porticoes round the fora, baths, private palaces, etc., are a different matter; here one must distinguish between the imported architectural achievements of the hellenistic towns – 'non italicae consuetudinis', in Vitruvius's words – and the Italic traditions from Etruscan architecture of the seventh century and through the Roman centuries.

Of great consequence for the future was the development of the Italic market-place towards the axial monumentality and splendour of the Forum of Caesar and the other Imperial fora. Different elements seem to have contributed. First, the old traditions of the Etrusco-Italic temples, with their frontal orientation and their open space in front of the stairs of the pronaus [20, 33]. Second, the old market-places with their rows of shops, which, as the history of the Forum Romanum shows, were no less deeply rooted in Italic life. However, to take the rectangular forum of Pompeii as an example, before systematization this space had a different orientation, with a row of common tabernae without portico along its eastern side, and no dominating temple at its north short side.[8]

A third formative component was rectangular hellenistic piazzas surrounded by porticoes and having a temple on the longitudinal axis, such as the Kaisareia of Alexandria, Antioch, and Cyrene.[9] In contrast to the monumentalized Italic fora of the last centuries B.C., with a dominating temple built against the rear wall at the upper side, the temples of the Greek piazzas were detached. This can also be seen in the precinct of the Temple of Apollo outside the western portico of the Pompeian forum [64]. A temple area dedicated to Ptolemy III and Berenice at Hermopolis Magna (Ashmunein) in Egypt of before 221 B.C. already exhibits the fully developed type of this piazza, with porticoes and axial symmetry.

It has to be remembered – together with these direct counterparts to the axial Italic fora – that in the fourth-century revival of Greek towns before and after Alexander, there appears a

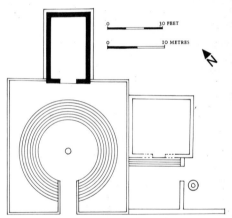

138. Cosa, forum and comitium:
(*above*) plan showing early buildings only;
(*below*) reconstructed section across the front of the basilica, comitium, etc. at a later phase

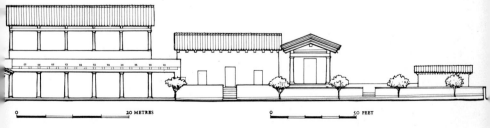

general, increasing predilection for axiality and symmetry. It stands in strong contrast to the charming free disposition and independence of the majestic architectural units of Olympia, for example, or of the Samian Heraeum and the Acropolis of Athens. The agoras of Assus, Miletus, the planning of the acropolis of Pergamum, or of the centre of Morgantina in Sicily, remind us that also in hellenistic times quite different principles for monumental planning remained with other kinds of beauty than what the new fashion of axiality offered. Yet, the latter inspired such great, strictly ordered complexes as the Temple of Asklepios in Cos or the acropolis of Lindos with the Temple of Athena.[10] It is evident that this axial hellenistic architecture made an overwhelming impression upon Roman builders, but it would be rash and without historical common sense to overlook that because of their traditions from the Etrusco-Italic temples and sacred precincts, they were predisposed, anyway, towards hellenistic symmetry, though they adapted it to the axial tendencies of Etrusco-Italic architecture. The great Roman shrines – such as those of Praeneste and Tibur (Tivoli; below, pp. 166 ff.) – display in fact a more stringent and rigorous axiality than the hellenistic ones. At Lindos, for instance, no straight axis leads to the temple and porticoes interrupt the open view to it.

At present, the fora of Cosa [138] and Pompeii [64] are the first known regular Italic piazzas. Aligned along the northern long side of the forum of Cosa are monumental buildings: a basilica, two temples, and the comitium (see p. 133). A central axis ran from Temple C transversely over the forum – as did the central axis from the Temple of Augustus in Vitruvius's basilica at Fanum (Fano) (V, 1. 7). In the forum at Pompeii, with its longitudinal central axis, we can see still more clearly how the traditions of Etruscan temples and old Italic market-places united with hellenistic magnificence. Even before the Roman colony, c. 150–120, the old forum received a temple of Etruscan type at its upper north end, with stairs and prodomus towards the forum. It thereby obtained a central

axis running lengthwise from north to south. The tabernae were demolished, and in the second century, along the east, south, and west sides of the rectangular space, suggested by the orientation of the Etrusco-Italic temple, two-storeyed porticoes with columns and architraves of tufa were built in the hellenistic style. Behind them, on the east and south sides, there seem to have been private buildings or public offices. The porticoes of the west side formed a screen in front of the Temple of Apollo with a differently orientated peristyle and a basilica, which seems to have been built about 120. An important change in this pre-Roman monumental piazza, caused by the Roman colony, was that the temple was transformed into a Capitolium for the Capitoline triad. From this combination of an Italic market-place and a Greek colonnaded piazza is derived Vitruvius's rule (V, 1. 2) that Italic fora should be oblong. He prescribes that the breadth should be two-thirds of the length.

The forum and the Portico of Hercules at Alba Fucens [139] afford us most instructive specimens of axial systematization, both deriving from the regular planning of the entire colony at the beginning of the first century B.C. The oblong forum – and this seems to have been an innovation – had a longitudinal axis running from a tribunal on the south-eastern rear wall of a basilica (discussed on p. 183), across the basilica and a portico in front of it, and on to a temple at the north end. Like the forum of Cosa, it recalls Vitruvius's description of the forum of Fanum, with a central axis running across the basilica and the middle of the forum to the Temple of Jupiter on the opposite side. We see the same arrangement in the oblong Imperial forum of Augusta Raurica near Basel, though the fora of Alba Fucens and Augusta are longitudinal, not transverse like the fora of Cosa and Fanum. The very narrow Temple of Hercules behind the basilica faced south. In it has been found a splendid statue of Hercules in a grand hellenistic style, and a ciborium built against the rear wall. Before the present temple was built the whole precinct seems to have been

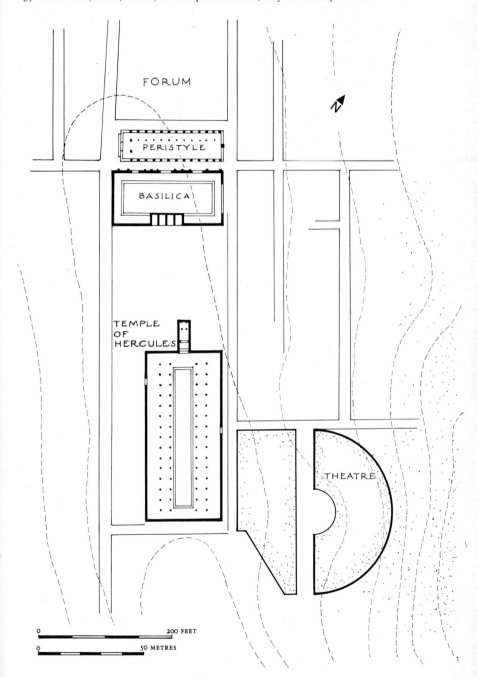

FORUM

PERISTYLE

BASILICA

TEMPLE
OF
HERCULES

THEATRE

0   200 FEET

0   50 METRES

a shapeless open space, though perhaps still a forum. Now a great portico measuring some 115 by 245 feet (35 by 75 m.) and surrounded by walls was built in front of the temple, with a central axis running from the northern rear wall of the temple to the presumed exit on the south side of the portico. The central court was open to the sky and only some 30 feet wide. The large porticoes right and left of it had two rows of columns. The whole scheme reminds one both of the basilicas and of the future Imperial fora, and is of importance for the understanding of both.

It is interesting to compare the forum of Brixia (Brescia) as it was regularized when the town was transferred from an old hill site to the plain. The forum of the new, regularly planned town had about the same size and shape as that of Pompeii. However, at its upper end, four small hellenized temples were built and decorated in the so-called Second Pompeian Style. They are datable to the decades after 89 B.C., when Gallia Cisalpina became closely attached to Rome. This seems to be an instance of Roman regard for local deities and cults after the victory in the internal wars of the eighties (as seen also in the Temple of Fortuna Primigenia at Praeneste and the Hercules Temple of 'Villa d'Ovidio' near Sulmona [158, 159]).

The forum of Paestum is another colonnaded, rectangular hellenized market-place, though it had no temple at its upper end to emphasize its longitudinal axis. The monumental buildings around, such as the comitium (p. 133), the somewhat later 'Tempio della Pace' on the northern long side [129], and what probably was the Shrine of the Lares on the western short side, are arranged without any regard to symmetry.[11]

When the new fashion of systematizing the market-place reached the Forum Romanum, the points of departure were the old tabernae along the northern and southern long sides (p. 133) [105]. The Comitium at the north-west corner, on the other hand, was an obstacle to any axial planning. The beginning of modern systematization came evidently after a great fire

in 210, which, according to Livy (XXVI, 27. 2), destroyed the shops on the north side. The private houses behind the tabernae were replaced later by basilicas: the Aemilia, built by the censors in the year 179, M. Fulvius Nobilior and M. Aemilius Lepidus, behind the tabernae on the north side, now named Argentariae Novae; and the Sempronia, built in 169 on the site of the old domus of the Scipio family behind the Tabernae Veteres by Tiberius Sempronius Gracchus. The latter basilica and the Tabernae Veteres were demolished when Caesar's and Augustus's basilica, the Basilica Julia, was built. It seems likely that the Tabernae Argentariae Novae, with maeniana (second storey to the portico), were rebuilt in ashlar in connexion with a restoration of the Basilica Aemilia in 80–78 B.C., if not before. At any rate, the Basilica Aemilia and the tabernae, though separated by independent walls, remained a unity throughout the Imperial Age. In the manner well known from Greek agoras, there were shops in the two-storeyed porticoes, superseding the old tabernae. That is how Vitruvius describes them; and the fora of Paestum and Lucus Feroniae (north of Rome) also show us this kind of two-storeyed structure in the shape he prescribed: at Lucus Feroniae, at the end of the Republican Age (no earlier than 50), a portico with Tuscan columns and a series of tabernae were built along the west side of the unpaved rectangular market-place with staircases to the upper storey.

For the porticoes in the cities of Italy, Vitruvius prescribes fairly wide intercolumniations because of the shows given in the fora. In contrast to the Greek stoas and the porticoes of the forum of Pompeii, forum porticoes (such as those of the Aemilia at the Forum Romanum) therefore probably still had wooden architraves in Late Republican times.

In 78, the irregular group of structures on the sloping west short side of the Forum Romanum was given a monumental background in the shape of the Tabularium [143], a repository for the state archives built on the south-east slope of the Capitoline Hill. Another modern feature had been added to the old ensemble when in 117 the Archaic Temple of Castor and Pollux was rebuilt in a hellenized style. From hellenized Roman architecture also came *fornices*, honorific arches bearing statues. L. Stertinius had erected such arches, from spoils brought from Spain, in the Circus Maximus and on the Forum Boarium in front of the Temples of Fortuna and Mater Matuta in 196; Scipio erected another in 190 at the entrance to the precinct of Jupiter Capitolinus at the top of the Clivus Capitolinus. This architectural device of unknown origin, the forerunner of the glorious line of marble Imperial triumphal arches, was also introduced to the ensemble of the hellenized Forum Romanum by the Fornix Fabianus of 121. It spanned the entrance of the Via Sacra at the east end of the forum, commemorating a victory over the Allobroges. No remains of these fornices are preserved, but we know that the Fornix Fabianus was rebuilt in 57 B.C. – no doubt with tufa and travertine – and probably represented then the final shape of these monuments before the Augustan marble arches. The central area of the forum had been paved with tufa slabs before it was covered with the travertine pavement of the two uppermost levels. This reminds one of the elder Cato's complaint about the modernization of the forum; according to him, it ought to have been paved with small sharp stones in order to prevent people from lounging about.

Cato's words recall the political and social temper of his time and the altercations connected with the development of the forum which are revealed by formal analysis. Very important for the development of the axial piazza of the Imperial Age is a characteristic change in the the use of the Rostra, which took place in the second half of the second century B.C. All earlier popular orators, so Cicero and Plutarch affirm, had, while speaking, turned their heads towards the Curia of the senate and the traditional place of public assembly, the Comitium. But – it seems, in 145 – a politician 'set a new example by turning towards the forum as he harangued the people . . . , thus by a slight deviation and change of attitude . . . to a certain extent chang-

ing the constitution from an aristocratic to a democratic form; for his implication was that speakers ought to address themselves to the people' behind the Rostra, not to the Senate.

Such new fashions in the life of the forum – the hellenized Temple of Castor and Pollux, the porticoes, and the basilicas – were the immediate forerunners of the monumental systematization which the Late Republican Age left to Caesar and Augustus. In contrast to such compromises between modernization and the old disorder of the slightly V-shaped area, outlined by the tabernae, stood the inspiring models of hellenistic piazzas and such accomplished Italic fora as that of Pompeii. It must have seemed quite natural that Caesar should try to make an axial piazza of the Forum by radical measures, abolishing the Comitium, transferring the Curia to its present place on the Forum, and building new Rostra in the centre of the western short side.[12]

BASILICAS

With the basilicas of the Forum Romanum a new kind of building with a great future enters the history of architecture. Its origins and its Greek name have been widely discussed. Here it may suffice to state that the oldest basilicas known are Roman, in spite of the adopted Greek name. Their antecedents were evidently Greek peristyles and colonnaded piazzas. As a basic conception valid for all the various types of basilicas, this may be proposed: a peristyle with a central space (the nave) covered by a roof supported by timber trusses and surrounded by ambulatories (the aisles) on all four sides.[13] The best archaeological evidence for Late Republican basilicas is provided by the basilica of Pompeii, probably built about 120 [64, 142]; and by those of Cosa [138], Ardea [140], and Alba Fucens,' which has already been mentioned [139], all dating from about 100.

Livy (XXXIX. 44. 7) informs us that Cato, in the face of considerable opposition, bought a building plot west of the Curia and the Comitium in 184 and built the first basilica in Rome.

Plautus speaks in *Curculio* about a basilica near the Sacellum of Cloacina, and parts of walls in the lowest strata below the Basilica Aemilia may well be remains of this probably insignificant structure.[14]

Vitruvius (v, 1. 5 ff.) describes two types of two-storeyed basilicas. One had columns in two storeys, those of the upper tier being smaller than those of the lower; an upper flooring, he says, should be constructed in the aisles, carried by the lower columns. The other, of somewhat different character, is represented by the basilica at Fanum, the building of which Vitruvius himself supervised. There the columns round the nave went all the way up, but engaged columns against the walls of the building carried an upper flooring between them and the columns of the nave. According to Vitruvius, it was desirable that the parapets of the balconies in the aisles should be so high that people walking in the upper storey would not be seen by those transacting business in the nave.

To understand the function of Roman basilicas, one has to realize that in Late Republican times they were attached to the fora as shelters for businessmen and the public at large, or added to precincts of temples for the benefit of the pilgrims. The basilica of Ardea [140] is clearly connected with a great temple below the acropolis. It was probably a shelter for pilgrims attending the famous sacred rites of the Laurentine and Rutulian coast, believed to have been handed down from the time of Aeneas. It had an open front, and two doors, one in the rear wall and one to what Vitruvius calls a 'Chalcidian porch' (*chalcidicum*), a portico outside the wall of the south-eastern short side towards the temple. A water cistern behind the rear wall corroborates the explanation of the building as a resort of visitors to the temples. Neither the cistern nor the doors display any axiality.[15]

Vitruvius prescribes (v, 1. 4) that the basilicas should be constructed on a site adjacent to the forum and 'in the warmest possible quarter, so that in winter businessmen may gather in them without being troubled by the weather'. Like the Greek stoas, they of course also served as shelters against sun and rain. The first indications of the magistrates beginning to move from the fora into the basilicas are the 'tribunals' of the basilicas of Pompeii and Alba Fucens, and Vitruvius's statement that he built the tribunal

140. Ardea, basilica, *c.* 100 B.C. Plan

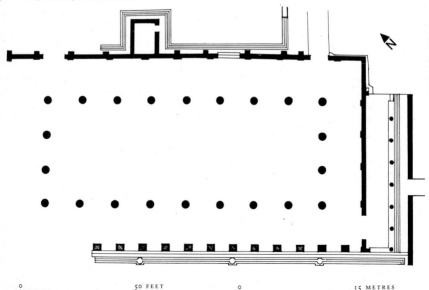

in his basilica at Fanum in front of the pronaus of the Temple of Augustus as a semicircle with a curvature inwards 'so that those who are standing before the magistrates may not be in the way of the businessmen in the basilica'.

Vitruvius shows us how he wished to transmit the principles of basilica building to the great Augustan Age, giving his usual detailed prescriptions of measurements and proportions of the ideal basilica and of Egyptian *oeci* (saloons) in private houses, which resembled basilicas (VI, 3. 8 f.). Our main sources are the basilica of Pompeii and preserved remains of walls at Cosa, Ardea, and Alba Fucens, which exhibit two different kinds of basilica plans: the two great basilicas of the Forum Romanum and the small basilicas of Cosa, Ardea, and Alba Fucens turned their long sides towards the public squares in front of them [138, 139, 140]; the basilica of Pompeii, on the other hand, faced the forum with an open entrance on the eastern short side. The Aemilia and Sempronia were screened off from the Forum Romanum by the rows of two-storeyed shops and the porticoes in front of them, but they were, of course, provided with entrances to the Forum, as we know from the Aemilia of the Imperial Age and the forum basilica of Alba Fucens, which was separated from the colonnade and the forum in front of the north-western long side by a wall with three doors [139]. The basilicas of Ardea and Cosa were open towards the squares in front of them. Their façades are controversial. The Tabularium of the Forum Romanum [143] and the Basilica Julia had arcaded façades, but it is of course also possible that the aisles of the basilicas at Ardea and Cosa were open colonnades along the front like those in front of the rows of the shops of the Aemilia and Sempronia. In each case this kind of building must have been especially useful as a sheltered, directly accessible appendage enlarging the public open space.[16]

The Aemilia was completely rebuilt on a higher level between 55 and 34 B.C., but some 16½ inches (42 cm.) below the floor of the Imperial basilica are remains of parts of a sub-structure of Grotta Oscura tufa and three bases for columns of tufa with a diameter of about 3 feet 5 inches (1.05 m.). It seems clear that this old tufa structure had spacious ambulatories (aisles) round the nave and a front wall along the rear wall of the porticoes and the tabernae towards the Forum. The Basilica Aemilia had two-storeyed aisles with lower columns on the upper floors (as Vitruvius demands, V, 1. 5), as had the porticoes with tabernae outside the south front wall of the basilica. A coin of 59 B.C. confirms this, reproducing the basilica as it was

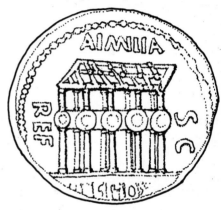

141. Coin of 59 B.C. showing the Basilica Aemilia as it was after a restoration in 78 B.C.

after a restoration in 78, with two-storeyed aisles [141].[17]

All the basilicas had of course some kind of top lighting for the nave. There is nothing to indicate that naves with two-storeyed aisles had clerestories above them in the centuries under discussion. Vitruvius's basilica at Fanum was lit by windows between the pilasters of the upper storey of the aisles, and we must probably assume the same arrangement in the great forensic basilicas in Rome as well as in the basilica of Pompeii (see below). In the so-called Egyptian *oeci* of private palaces, which Vitruvius describes (VI, 3. 9), an architrave above the columns of the lower storey carried joists between them and the surrounding walls 'with a floor in the upper storey to allow walking under the open sky'. Columns, three-quarters the height of those of the lower storey, carried the roof of the nave, and windows set in between them faced the promenades or verandas above the aisles. The tablinum behind the atrium in the so-called 'Casa dell'Atrio a Mosaico' of the Early Imperial Age at Herculaneum was built in this way.[18] The basilicas of Ardea, Cosa, and Alba Fucens were probably built in the same way too, though with lean-to roofs above their one-storeyed aisles.

The basilica of Pompeii [142] is the best preserved of the known early basilicas. Behind the walls of the basilica, supporting a series of semi-columns above them. The interior of the basilica resembled Vitruvius's basilica at Fanum. The nave was surrounded by twenty-eight great Ionic columns and roomy ambulatories on all four sides. The columns were constructed of kiln-dried bricks, an exceptional procedure in Late Republican architecture. They were obviously of one giant order and carried the timber truss of a pitched roof above the building. It is uncertain if the lower semi-columns along the south and north walls carried upper flooring in the aisles, as at Fanum, though the presence of

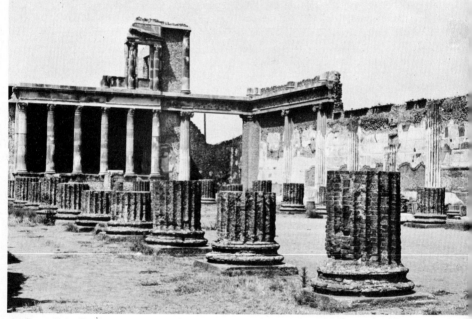

142. Pompeii, basilica, c. 120 B.C.(?)

two-storeyed porticoes of the forum there was a chalcidian hall, probably also two-storeyed, with five intercolumniations towards the portico on one side and the basilica on the other. The columns in the open entrance from the chalcidicum to the basilica were of the same height and type as the engaged Ionic columns which were aligned along the lower parts of the side a second tier of semi-columns suggests such a motif. It seems most probable that the building was lit by windows between the upper semi-columns. The basilica of Pompeii was, of course, not so big as the sensational Aemilia in Rome, but was still much larger than the basilicas of Ardea and Cosa, measuring 79 by 196 feet (24 by 59.85 m.).[18a]

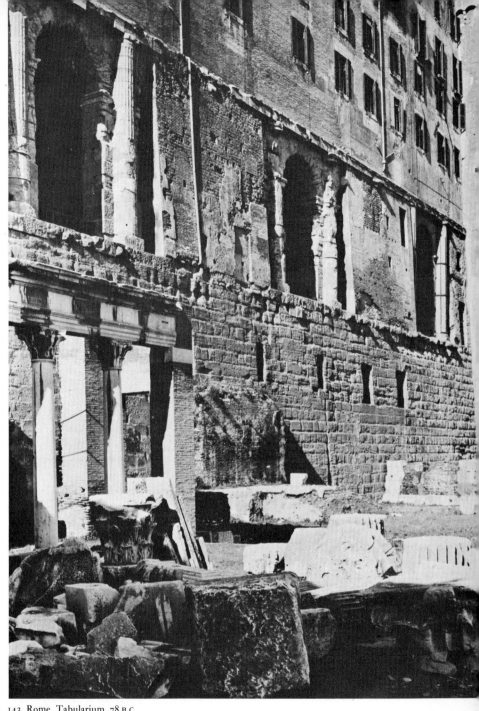

143. Rome, Tabularium, 78 B.C.

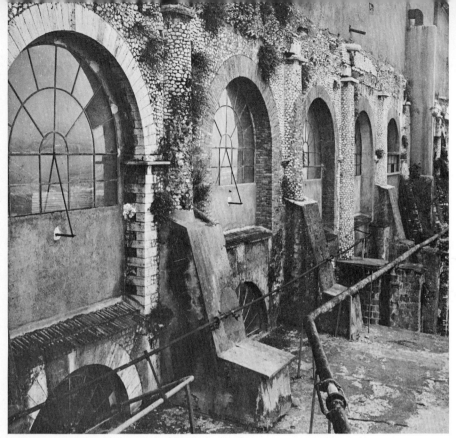

144. Tibur (Tivoli), Temple of Hercules Victor,
Late Republican, western façade of terrace

The basilica of Pompeii differed from that of
Ardea and the Aemilia in being planned axially.
It had a two-storeyed tribunal at its western
short end, flanked, like the tablina of the atria
in private houses, by entrances right and left.
This structure would have dominated the interior, if the view had not been obstructed by
the columns on all four sides of the nave. Here
we meet with a conflict between the architectural idea of a Greek peristyle and the un-
Greek, Italic arrangement with concentration
upon a principal room built against or behind
the centre of the rear wall. We shall see the same
conflict between tablina and peristyles in the
peristyles of the domus. As the basilicas of Cosa
and Alba Fucens [139] have shown, the tribu-

nals in basilicas with their long side towards the
public space were placed in the middle of the
rear wall with a central axis running transversely through it.

Vitruvius's basilica at Fanum was arranged
in this way, but Vitruvius – feeling the conflict
between peristyle and axiality – omitted the two
middle columns of the long side in front of his
tribunal and the prodomus and Temple of
Augustus behind it. He did this in order not to
interrupt the axis running transversely from
that structure in the middle of the rear wall of
the basilica to the Temple of Jupiter on the
other side of the forum. The Hercules Portico
of Alba Fucens had already achieved an open
view along the central axis to the temple on its

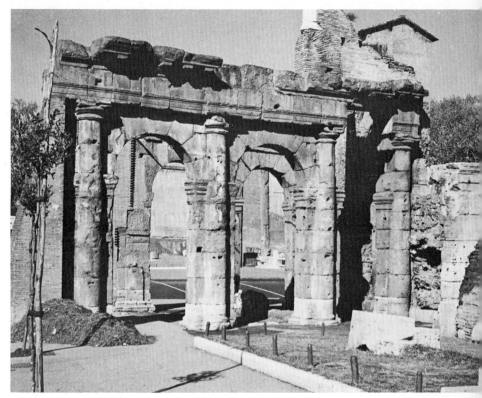

145. Rome, Forum Holitorium,
Late Republican portico on the eastern side

upper side [139]. Vitruvius's views inaugurate the attempts to focus direction on a dominating structure in the centre of the rear wall, thus enabling basilicas to function as monumental assembly rooms, as an expression of the Roman state, represented by its officials, and later of Imperial power, and finally for the Christian cult. In this last case the axial tendency was yet further accentuated and the final goal became the altar in the apse. No doubt a variety of influences contributed to this type of building, which was to achieve such world-wide and millennial significance, but the conflict, given expression by Vitruvius, between Greek peristyles and the straight line from the main entrance to a tribunal in the centre of the rear wall

is one of the stimuli that requires to be remembered.

The Tabularium on the Forum Romanum [143], referred to on p. 151 as a part of the systematization of the west side of the forum and because of its arcades and domical vaults, is the only building of the Late Republican Age which kept its place in the ensemble of the Imperial forum.[19] The building was erected in 78 by the consul Quintus Lutatius Catulus for the state archives. It has a high substructure of concrete covered by tufa ashlar from Gabii. This substructure faced the forum and served as a retaining wall against the Capitoline Hill. A corridor, lit by a row of small windows, connected the north and south ends of the building. It was accessible from the forum by a door with a flat masonry arch and a relieving arch above. A direct, barrel-vaulted staircase of sixty-six steps led from the forum side of the slope of the Capitoline Hill to this corridor and to the famous open gallery above it, with its domically vaulted compartments and rooms inside the building. Nothing can be safely confirmed about upper storeys above the gallery. However, the preserved façade of the first storey, with its arcades framed between engaged Doric columns, and an entablature built on the flat arch principle, with *guttae*, belongs to a group of buildings with the same decoration: the Late Republican terrace of the Temple of Hercules Victor at Tibur (Tivoli) [144], part of the portico round the piazza in front of the round Temple of Fortuna Primigenia at Praeneste, and a Late Republican portico in the Forum Holitorium in Rome [145]. As I have pointed out on p. 93, both Greeks and Etruscans knew this architectural motif, but the Thèatre of Marcellus and the Colosseum in Rome demonstrate the new monumentality and importance which it acquired at the hands of Roman builders.

TEMPLES

We now come to the temples of the last centuries B.C. and their evidence concerning Roman respect for the Etrusco-Italic religious tradition, even where hellenistic influence changed the external appearance of temples and sacred precincts. Here the most deep-rooted creative forces were at stake. In the chapter on Etruscan architecture, I have tried to trace the various kinds of temples which the Etruscans built and their early appearance in Etruscan towns (pp. 35–64). Of the third, second, and first centuries B.C., which are represented by a large number of temple remains in central Italy, it should first of all be stated that these late, hellenized temples still display the main features of Etruscan architecture: the podium, the frontal emphasis, the deep pronaus, and the closed back wall [126]. The podium of Temple C on the Largo Argentina in Rome – like the temple in the church of St Peter at Alba Fucens – was 13 feet high. It had a simple, vigorous cornice at the top and a straight base. The base and cornice of the podium of the Capitolium of Cosa (*c.* 150) have Tuscan tori of elliptical curvature. The later temples have elegant mouldings at top and bottom of the podia, reminding us of the development of Italic altars. The height of the podia of the second century is mostly between about 6 and 10 feet. When the Capitoline Temple was reconstructed after the fire of 83, its builder, Q. Catulus (cf. p. 47), wished to heighten the old archaic podium to make it match the scale of his pediment, though it was already some 11 feet (3.352 m.) high. Temples of the Imperial Age – such as the Temple of the Magna Mater on the Palatine as reconstructed by Augustus in 3 B.C., the Temples of Apollo Sosianus and Divus Julius, and, later on, the Capitolium of

146. Roman temples: (1) Largo Argentina; (2) Jupiter Stator, 146 B.C.; (3) Forum Holitorium. Plans

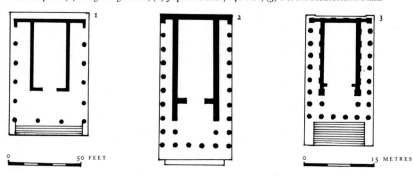

147. Rome,
Forum Holitorium,
temples. Plan

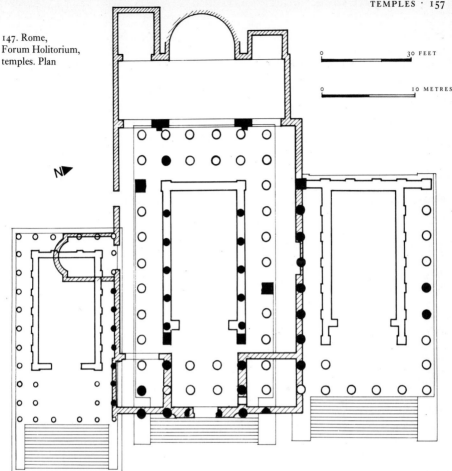

Ostia – show that this predilection for high podia lived on.

Various Etruscan types of temples reappeared in Late Republican architecture [127, 128, 146]. But it must be clearly stated that between the old Etruscan and the Late Republican structures lies much independent development during the rather dark centuries after the Gallic catastrophe of 386. As in the atria of the private domus (below, p. 186), it is often only basic elements which connect Late Republican buildings with their distant Etruscan prototypes. Often the traditional pattern is so changed that the similarities may seem less important than the differences. This is also true of Campanian temples, as shown by models and – above all – by the pre-Roman Temple of Apollo at Pompeii with its combination of peristyle and Italic orientation [64]. The same combination of Italic plan and Greek peristyle occurs also in Temple A on the Largo Argentina in Rome in its third period, i.e. about 100 B.C. [126, 153], and in the two southern temples of the Forum Holitorium in Rome, Doric and Ionic hexastyle peripteral buildings [147] connected with a third temple to the north which has a closed back wall. These are perhaps to be dated as late as Augustan times.[20]

Ornament

Two main types of embellishment are characteristic of these late temples. On the one hand, the terracotta revetments were richly developed, as can be seen all over central Italy and can be especially well studied in the second-century temples of Cosa [43, 44]. Art historians can follow a most fascinating gradual unfolding of early hellenistic style, 'perhaps the finest classic style ever achieved in temple terracottas', and Augustan classicism.

As I have already pointed out, remains of pedimental terracotta sculpture from the sixth and fifth centuries show that such decoration in a Greek style appeared early in the Etruscan temples. Pedimental sculpture seems to have been abandoned in Greek temples after the fourth century, though the Hieron at Samothrace and the Temple of Dionysus at Teos indicate a revival in the mid second century. In Etruscan and Roman architecture, pedimental decoration of terracotta flowered in the centuries after 300, as shown by the splendid pair of horses from the so-called Ara della Regina Temple at Tarquinia, by remains from Falerii Veteres and Orvieto, by the vivid scenes on the pediments from Talamone (reconstructed in the Museo Archeologico at Florence), and by fragments of pedimental groups from Cosa.[21]

In contrast to the swan-song of traditional terracotta decoration stands a more radical, new-style hellenization with stuccoed Doric, Ionic, or Corinthian columns of tufa or travertine or tufa columns with travertine capitals, as, for instance, in the great unidentified temple at the Via delle Botteghe Oscure in Rome. As I have said, marble was still rare in temples and public buildings. In smaller temples the entablatures were of stone in the various Greek styles [151, 152] with architrave, Ionic frieze or Doric frieze of triglyphs and metopes, and cornice. The terracotta revetments had always followed the successive phases of Greek styles, but these new hellenized superstructures above Italic-plan temples revolutionized temple architecture [151] and created models for the Imperial Age. Vitruvius, conservative as always, recommends Tuscan columns for his Etruscan temple. At Cosa all the temples originally had Tuscan columns. The same is true of the temples of the Capitolium of Signia (Segni), and of Alatri, Alba Fucens, and other places. Tuscan columns gained increasing popularity in the architecture of the last centuries B.C. and in Imperial times; but in the latest Republican temples, Greek columns predominated, as, for example, at Cosa, where Temple D in its second phase (100–75) had Doric capitals, as had the southernmost peripteral travertine temple in the Forum Holitorium and the Temple of Hercules at Cori [152] of the end of the second century. Neither Tuscan nor Doric prevailed in Roman Late Republican temples after about 150: the remains display, above all, a predilection for Corinthian capitals [148], capitals with inserted human heads, typical of Pompeii, and bunchy Corinthian capitals adorned with a

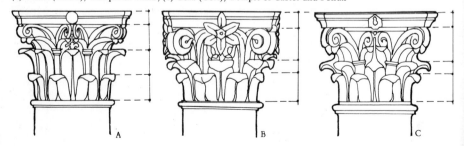

148. Late Republican capitals. (A) Morgan's interpretation of Vitruvius;
(B) Tibur (Tivoli), Temple of Vesta; (C) Cora (Cori), Temple of Castor and Pollux

great flower.[22] As in the case of the terracotta revetments, this hellenistic exuberance, which in Italy became still more excessive, was restrained by late hellenistic classicism – as can be observed, for instance, in the Ionic capitals of the so-called Temple of Fortuna Virilis by the Tiber [151]. The combination of Corinthian columns and Doric triglyphs and metopes or Ionic frieze was now accepted – even by Vitruvius (IV, 1. 2–3). The Tempio della Pace on the forum of Paestum shows this combination in its second period (first century B.C.) [129].

Types of Plan and Superstructure

As regards Italic (Etruscan) plans, which were retained for sacred architecture, something has been said already about the first period of this temple, about Temples A and C on the Largo Argentina [126, 146], and also about Dionysius's golden words concerning the rebuilt Capitolium: it 'was erected upon the same foundations [as the temple of 509], and differed from the ancient structure in nothing but the costliness of the materials' (marble columns; cf. p. 46, and Dionysius, IV, 61).

A relief showing the Temple of Juno Moneta on the Arx in Rome, according to Roman tradition dedicated in 374 B.C., proves that temples with two columns prostyle were still visible in Imperial times [149], but especially important for the future among these hellenized temples with Italic plan was the type with one or two sets of four columns in front of a cella without alae; the type, that is, already discussed in Etruscan temples (above, p. 39) and the temples of Cosa [127, 128] and most important for Imperial times. We meet with Ionic semi-columns decorating the walls of the cella – as a pseudoperipteros – and Ionic columns in the tetrastyle temple at Tibur (Tivoli) [150] next to the Tempio di Vesta, and in the so-called Temple of Fortuna Virilis by the Tiber in Rome [151]. The temple at Tivoli is built of travertine ashlar on a podium of concrete, faced with travertine slabs. The cella walls project as antae half the length of the prodomus, with its columns and stairs in

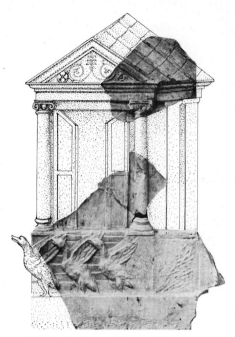

149. Relief of the Imperial Age, probably representing the Temple of Juno Moneta on the Arx in Rome, dedicated 374 B.C. *Ostia, Museum*

front. The elegant small pseudo-peripteros by the Tiber has six Ionic columns with capitals in pure Greek style, four in front of the prodomus and one on each side of it. Travertine is used for the facing of the concrete podium, and for the six free-standing columns of the pronaus and the four engaged corner columns of the cella. The walls of the cella are built of tufa. The building was, of course, covered by stucco, as remains show, and it is one of the most elegant combinations of Italic plan and Greek taste. Both these temples were probably built in the second half of the second century B.C. The same plan reappears in Temple D on the Largo Argentina in Rome, with its ten columns round the prodomus. The magnificent pseudo-peripteros of the Temple of Jupiter Anxur at Terracina [164] had six columns on the front above the stairs and two columns on each side of the prodomus. It is one of the great structures

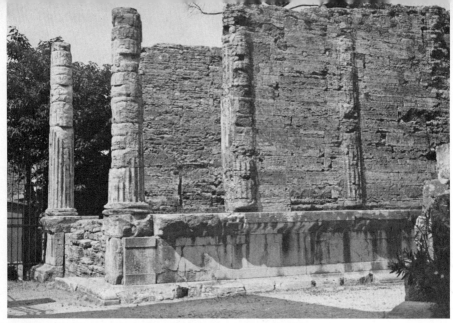

150. Tibur (Tivoli), tetrastyle temple, second century B.C. (second half)(?)

151. Rome, 'Temple of Fortuna Virilis' on the Tiber, second century B.C. (second half)(?)

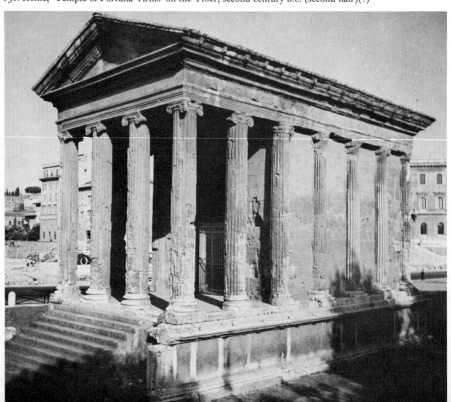

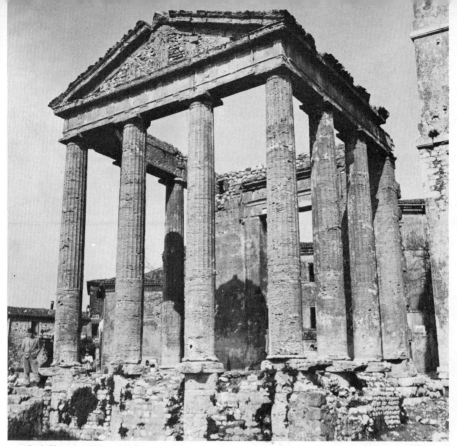

152. Cori, Temple of Hercules, late second century B.C.

typical of the age of the Sullan régime (82–79). The small Doric temple of Cori [152] illustrates the preceding decades. It has four slender columns in front of the deep Italic prodomus and two on each side of it. The columns have low bases and an unfluted lower part, which – as is often seen at Pompeii – was probably stuccoed red. To this group of temples belongs also the Tempio Tetrastilo next to the Temple of Hercules at Ostia [123] and the four small temples on a common podium on the north side of the piazza next to the theatre of Ostia (on the Late Republican level of Regions 1 and 2, i.e. of *c.* 100–80).

In the second century the type with one or more cellas, alae, and closed rear wall became very popular. Rear-wall wings extended right and left of the cella and often returned at right angles towards the front with short stretches of walls ending in antae. We have already seen this arrangement in the Archaic Capitoline Temple, in the first Tempio della Pace at Paestum, and in Temple C on the Largo Argentina.

A famous group of temples of this kind which I would date to the second century B.C. (though more ancient dates have been proposed) consists of the so-called Temple of Juno at Gabii [155, 156]; the Temple of Jupiter Stator in the Porticus Metelli (later Octaviae) in Rome [146], built in 146 and drawn on a fragment of the Forma Urbis; the Temple of Diana Tifatina (S. Angelo in Formis), as rebuilt in Roman times; the northernmost temple of the Forum Holitorium in Rome, built in the Ionic style [147],[23] and finally Jupiter Anxur at Terracina. Then follow the temples of the Imperial Age, a great number of them marble-faced and exhibiting variations of the type, such as the Temple of Divus Julius on the Roman forum, the temple at Vienne, the Temple of Minerva in Nerva's forum in Rome and others.

The temple of Fiesole [30] has, as I have discussed on p. 43, instead of rows of columns along the alae of the long sides, side walls extended from the rear wall to the front of the prodomus. The temple was rebuilt in the same way in Roman times (first century B.C.).

The round Temple of Vesta very likely – as the Romans believed (above, p. 27) – inherited its shape from old Italic huts, but later restorations in the Greek style reshaped it entirely. The marble temple by the Tiber [132] (p. 139, above) has already given us one instance of direct contact with pure Greek architecture of this kind: the Romans combined this Greek influence and their own traditions in the round temples, too, providing them with podia and steps only opposite the entrance to the round cella.

Temple B on the Largo Argentina [126, 153] had a cella surrounded by sixteen high slender Corinthian columns with bases and capitals of travertine. The image of the god, in harmony with the axiality of the rectangular temple, stood against the rear wall opposite the stairs. The columns and the base and cornice of the podium allow us to date the temple to about the middle

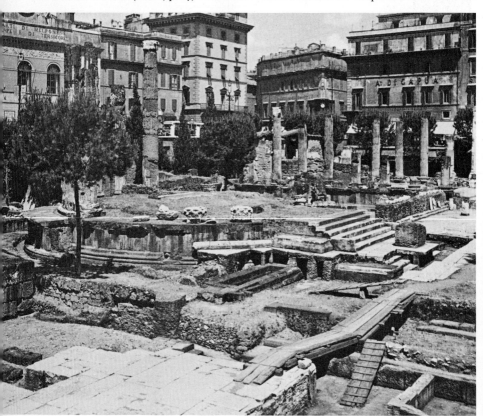

153. Rome, Temples A and B on the Largo Argentina, c. 100 B.C.

of the second century, but nothing remains of the entablature.[24] Of the first decades of the first century is the so-called Tempio di Vesta at Tibur (Tivoli) [154]. The round cella is of concrete with a facing of opus incertum. The podium has a sturdy base and an elegant cornice. The eighteen Corinthian columns of travertine have capitals of the bunchy hellenistic type [148B], and the frieze has heavy ox-heads (not bucrania, as became common during the Imperial Age), connected by rich festoons. The elegant door-jambs and windows slope slightly towards the top. Between the cella walls and the cornice above the frieze is a panelled ceiling of travertine with two concentric rings of sunk panels with rosettes. Nothing indicates how the roof was constructed.

Most important for the centuries after Rome's victories in Italy and in the hellenistic world, and for the Imperial Age, were the temples with three cellas for the Capitoline triad, Jupiter, Juno, and Minerva, to which Vitruvius (IV, 7) gives much prominence.[25] As discussed earlier on p. 46 f., the great Capitoline Temple of 509 was the glorious model [34], both in its archaic grandeur and in its rebuilt forms of 69 B.C. (after the fire of 83) and of the Flavian Age. The Capitolia became symbols of the Roman Empire all over the Mediterranean world. The great prototype in Rome was rebuilt after the fire of 83, as Cicero emphasizes in the second Verrine Oration (see above, p. 136), as the Roman Empire demanded, but – as the actual remains confirm – it preserved the orig-

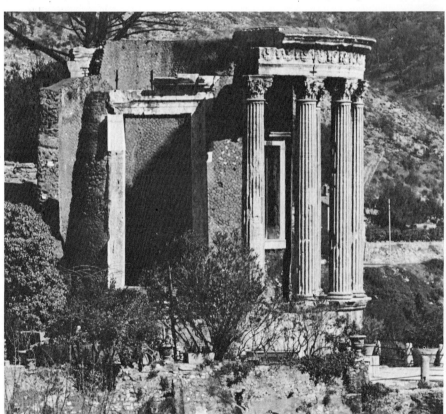

154. Tibur (Tivoli), 'Temple of Vesta', early first century B.C.

inal Etruscan plan with three cellas, colonnaded alae, and eighteen columns in the pronaus both in 69 and in the Flavian Age. Ovid further reports in the *Fasti* (II, 669 ff.) that even an old altar of Terminus, with a hole in the roof above, was retained from the old temple, and Pliny relates the same about an aedicula of Juventus in the cella of Minerva (XXXV, 108). The podium of the Capitoline Temple was heightened by a top layer of ashlar about 16 inches (40 cm.) high, above the twelve earlier courses of blocks measuring about a Greco-Roman foot (also about an English foot; 30-2 cm.).

As I have remarked in discussing the temple of 509, Vitruvius demands that the height of the columns of an Etruscan temple should be 'one-third of the width of the temple', that is in the Capitoline Temple 54 feet 5 inches (16.576 m.), which seems unlikely for the building of the sixth century. But Pliny informs us (XXXVI, 45) that Sulla – who followed the reconstruction of the Capitoline Temple with special interest – brought columns from the Olympieion in Athens 'to be used for temples on the Capitoline Hill'. The height of these Athenian columns is 55 feet 5 inches (16.89 m.), which would be close to Vitruvius's rule for columns. It therefore seems probable that Vitruvius has accepted a height connected with the hellenized Italic temples, and especially with the high columns of the Capitoline Temple. Pliny's statement proves – even apart from the precise information about the columns from the Olympieion – that the rebuilt temple vied in height with the highest Greek temples, and that the Capitoline, by virtue of its columns, belonged to the early marble temples of Rome.

For the entablature of the great temples which preserved the Etrusco-Italic ground plan and wide intercolumniations, Vitruvius (III, 3. 5) prescribes architraves consisting of a series of wooden beams laid upon the columns. Vitruvius mentions this old-fashioned roof construction both for the Capitoline Temple and for Pompey's Temple of Hercules. His conclusion that these temples are 'clumsily roofed, low, broad' is indeed most startling in being ex-

pressed some forty years after the highly admired Capitoline Temple had been built, with its great new pediment and high Greek marble columns. We know (above, p. 47) that the builder of the temple of 69 thought that the podium was too low, but contemporary coins seem to prove that the pediments of the new temple were a sensation. Vitruvius's words may contain recollections of archaic Tuscan temples, but it is also possible that he and his contemporaries really thought that the temple, in spite of its high columns, was wanting in height, as did the Romans of the Flavian Age, according to Tacitus (*Historiae*, IV, 53). Vitruvius's statement, in any case, should not be ignored. Tacitus confirms that the high Sullan marble columns of 69 B.C. carried a wooden superstructure. In his description of the riots in Rome in A.D. 69, he tells that the pediments, *aquilae*, which supported the roof of the Capitoline Temple, being of wood, caught and fed the flames of the fire thrown on the roofs by the insurgents (*Historiae*, III, 71).[26]

The plans of these temples transmitted Etruscan traditions to the Imperial Age; some of them proved to have magnificent futures, as I have pointed out in discussing their Etruscan predecessors.

A Roman innovation, it seems, was the Temple of Veiovis, behind the Tabularium, between the Arx and the Capitolium. It was built in 196 B.C. and rebuilt in the middle of the second century, but it was enlarged and received its final shape in connexion with the building of the Tabularium in 78. Probably in the earlier period, and in any case by about 150, the temple assumed its peculiar plan: a transverse, closed cella, facing south, with a tetrastyle pronaus and stairs in the centre of the southern long side and of the transverse central axis. The type was kept with slightly different orientation in 78 and during a restoration in Domitian's time, and it returns in the Augustan Temple of Concord on the Forum Romanum and in the Capitolium which, in Flavian times, replaced the Sullan temples at the upper end of the forum of Brixia (p. 148).[27]

Late Republican temples could not only be connected with fora and temple precincts with altars but could also be used in the context of other architectural schemes. The rows of co-ordinated temples, such as those of the Largo Argentina [126], of the Forum Holitorium [147], and of the Republican forum of Brixia must have made a great impression. The temples of the Largo Argentina originally had rectangular forecourts with altars on the central axis of the temple, recalling in a strictly system-atized way the old Etruscan precincts. Later the area in front of them was unified, paved, and finally surrounded by porticoes.

A special, highly monumental group of temples were related by virtue of having semi-circular staircases leading up to the façade and imposing terraces and porticoes [155 ff.]. The comitia of Cosa [138] and Paestum, with their curiae above the amphitheatrical stairs, were like this, as well as Morgantina, with its monu-mental stairs between the upper and lower agora; no doubt the comitium of Rome was similar, too.[28] Of these theatre-temples the earliest are one at Cagliari on Sardinia,[29] which is certainly Roman and was probably built in the second century, and the temple of Gabii [155, 156] (see also Note 23) already discussed. The hexastyle Corinthian temple with alae and flanking rows of terracotta figures (cf. p. 57) [46] lies in the centre of a great rectangular precinct, surrounded by walls and facing south. The walls of the northern half of the precinct are adorned by colonnades; those of the western and eastern

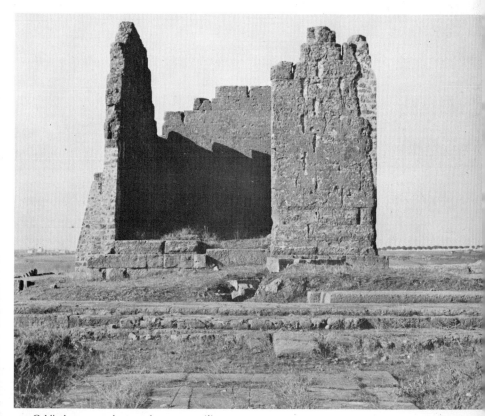

155. Gabii, theatre-temple, second century B.C.(?)

long sides had shops in the porticoes, like the Tabernae Novae on the Forum Romanum and other Italic and Greek porticoes (p. 148, above). It has the same width as the orchestra and projects outside the centre of the south wall of the precinct. It seems evident that this theatre was

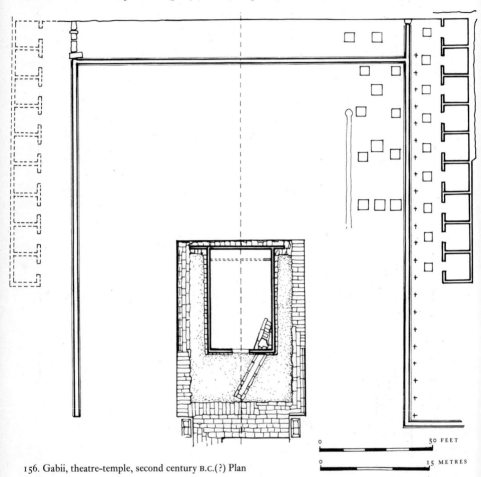

156. Gabii, theatre-temple, second century B.C.(?) Plan

It is typical of these great sanctuaries that they are surrounded by a large number of shops. The festivals seem to have been fairs, with a bustle of dealers and workers. In front of the temple, on its central axis, is the monumental staircase with an orchestra below. It is some 200 feet wide and has about twelve flights of stairs which reach the level of the temple. Behind the orchestra are remains of what certainly was a stage building.

constructed for shows or ceremonies in front of the temple, and that – in contrast to temporary theatres in Rome at the same time (below, pp. 198 ff.) – it imitated the permanent hellenistic theatres.

Some hundred years after the probable date of the theatre-temple of Gabii, about 50 B.C., a still more grandiose sanctuary of the same kind was built at Tibur (Tivoli) and dedicated to

Hercules Victor [157]. The temple, perhaps reconstructed in Imperial times, lies in the centre of the back of a great transverse, rec-

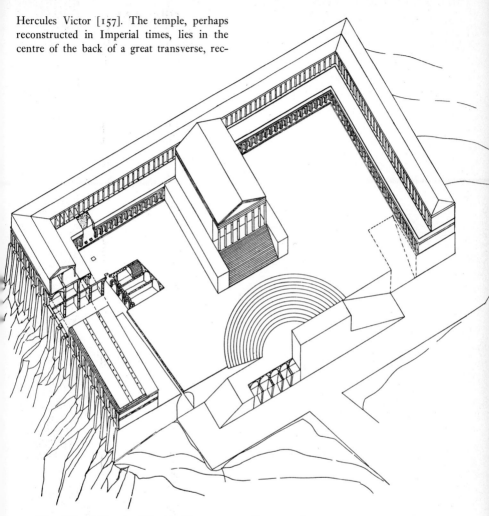

157. Tibur (Tivoli), Temple of Hercules Victor, *c.* 50 B.C. Reconstruction

tangular terrace. Along the eastern long side behind the temple and along the north and south short sides runs a triple portico with Tuscan columns. Above the two outside passages of the portico was a double colonnade. In the centre of the western, open, long side of the terrace is a semicircular staircase leading up from the orchestra to the stairs of the temple. Behind the orchestra projects a stage building,

as at Gabii. It seems clear again that this sanctuary was a theatre-temple built for performances in front of the temple.

The temple, its porticoes, and the stage building are set on a majestic terrace, constructed, like the porticoes, of concrete covered with opus incertum. The mighty wall on the north side of the terrace is most spectacular. It has an elaborate system of inner buttresses and a

158. Praeneste (Palestrina),
Temple of Fortuna Primigenia,
c. 80 B.C. Axonometric plan

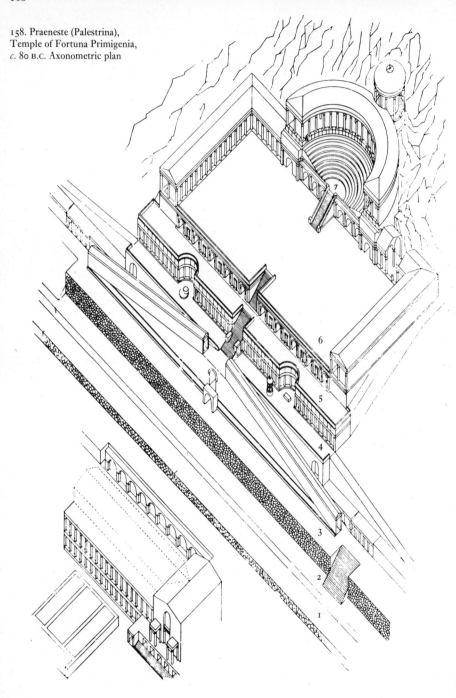

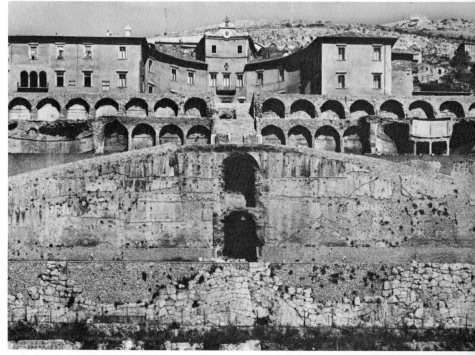

159. Praeneste (Palestrina), general view

façade decorated by arches in two storeys. The lower arches are flanked by strong buttresses of travertine ashlar, while the upper row of arches has engaged semi-columns and an architrave like the Tabularium [143]. A vaulted tunnel, 28 feet (8.50 m.) wide, runs through the northern part of the terrace, to carry the Via Tiburtina. It has quadrangular roof lights; rows of shops with barrel- or domical-vaults make it obvious that the tunnel served as a shopping centre.[30]

A semicircular staircase is also a part of yet another large sanctuary, which belongs to the best early pieces of Roman concrete construction and vaulting, vying with the great hellenistic ensembles (above, p. 146): the Temple of Fortuna Primigenia at Praeneste (Palestrina) [158, 159]. Praeneste was famous for a sanctuary connected with sortilege and for an image of

Fortuna Primigenia seated, with the infants Jupiter and Juno in her lap – evidently one of the statues of maternal goddesses so common in Italy in the centuries before Christ. Carneades, visiting Rome in 156-155 as a member of the famous Athenian delegation of philosophers, remarked that the Fortuna at Praeneste was more fortunate than most oracles of lots. Cicero (*De Divinatione*, II, 85-7) mentions this, and tells us that the origin of the lots was that dreams admonished a distinguished man of noble birth at Palestrina to dig into the rocky hillside of the mountain on which the old independent Praeneste with its rich Etruscan past of the seventh century was built (the present village of San Pietro). Now this hill town was defended by polygonal walls with extensions to a later, lower town with a forum of its own, lying far below on the southern slopes. It is to this lower town that the Temple of Fortuna Primigenia belonged, though it extended up the hillside. When the noble Praenestine, 'disregarding the jeers of his fellow-townsmen, split open the rock at the designated place, close to the statue of Fortuna with Jupiter and Juno in her lap, lots carved on oak with ancient characters appeared in the pit'. And at the same time, Cicero says, honey flowed from an olive tree in 'the spot where the Temple of Fortuna now stands'. There were thus three sacred spots which belonged to the lower, pre-Roman Praeneste: the pit where the lots were found, the statue of Fortuna, and the temple.

The end of the ancient town and its freedom came when Sulla gave the place to plunder and executed some 12,000 Praenestini after his victory over the younger Marius, who had taken refuge there in 82 B.C. Sulla then founded a third Praeneste, a colony of his veterans, on the plain below the lower pre-Roman Praeneste. For historical and archaeological reasons those scholars seem to be right who assign both the buildings around the forum of the middle town and the grandiose upper sanctuary with its theatre, which was built above it, to Sulla's re-establishment of the old cults of towns he defeated and to his intense building activity in connexion with the colonies of veterans.

Concrete, covered by opus incertum and of course stuccoed, and columns of tufa with bases and capitals of travertine of the local calcareous stone characterize the last great structure. The whole slope on which the lower pre-Roman town was built was systematized by parallel terraces running east-west, starting at a terrace wall and a propylon towards the road below the hill (Via degli Arconi). A row of barrel-vaulted shops, built against the terrace wall, is the lowest part of the sanctuary shops, which continue on the upper terraces above the forum and the buildings around it. On the highest terrace of the town below the upper sanctuary is the forum of the middle pre-Roman Praeneste, now the piazza of Palestrina; along its north side were a temple built of tufa ashlar (partly preserved in the cathedral), the curia [163], and the treasury (aerarium) of the town. The temple and two

picturesque caves in the rocky hillside behind the forum are clearly earlier than Sulla, but all scholars agree that the other monumental buildings round the forum were built after Sulla's victory of 82.[31] On a terrace behind and above the temple and the forum a large basilican building was erected with a bipartite central nave running east-west [158, 162]. On the south side was a Doric colonnade on the lower level towards the forum, and above that, on the level of the floor of the basilica, an upper colonnade with Corinthian columns [160]. Along the north side of the bipartite central nave ran an aisle with a rear wall decorated with engaged Corinthian columns [161]. Between them were elegant high windows with a slight inclination inwards and ornamental tablets right and left. Between this wall and the steep hillside behind it, which reaches the level of the lowest terrace of the upper sanctuary, is a narrow barrel-vaulted space to guard against humidity.

It is still an open question whether and how this high building was roofed. As there are no gutters, it seems clear to me that the two central naves were covered with a ridge roof, as the section [162] suggests. They were no doubt two-storeyed. A row of arcades above the rear wall of the north aisle and its engaged Corinthian columns suggests that (to speak with Vitruvius, VI, 3. 9) it 'had a floor in the upper storey to allow of walking under the open sky'. The same was probably true of the portico along the south side of the basilica. The whole structure would thus resemble the Egyptian oeci of Vitruvius, with verandas on both sides of a central nave and windows between pilasters or columns in the second storey to light it.[32]

This somewhat strangely mixed monumental basilican structure connected buildings in front of the two grottoes in the hillside above the temple. Especially important is a rectangular hall which was built along the eastern short side of the basilica, the curia [163]. It faces the forum, but is on the same higher level as the basilica. Right and left of the entrance above the stairs from the forum were Corinthian semi-columns, and above the lintel is a large arched

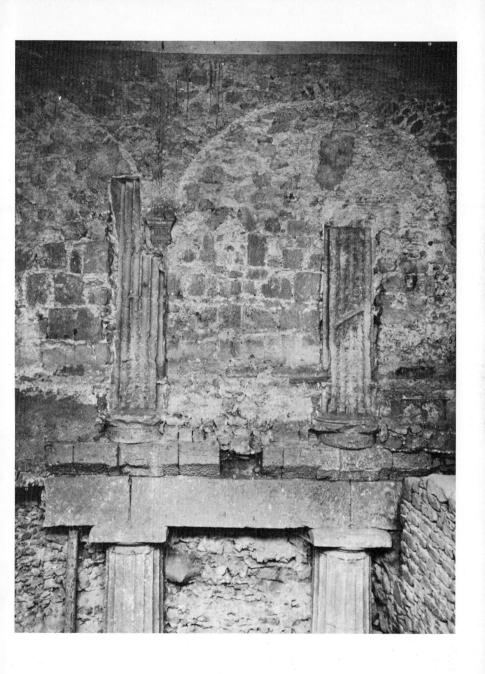

160. Praeneste (Palestrina), Corinthian above Doric portico in front of the basilica behind the temple, *c.* 80 B.C.

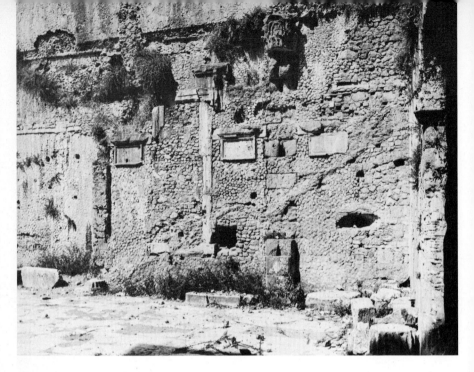

161. Praeneste (Palestrina), basilica, *c.* 80 B.C., north wall

window. The interior is decorated by Ionic semi-columns, niches between them, and a podium with a triglyph frieze along the wall – no doubt for statues. The central axis ran from the entrance from the forum to the old east grotto, which now became the apse of the high hall.

In both grottoes mosaics have been found. In the eastern hall was a great landscape of the Nile valley (now in the museum of Palestrina), and in the western grotto delightful marine motifs still remain. It seems likely that these mosaics were added in the Imperial Age. Pliny (XXXVI, 189) mentions 'lithostrota' before discussing tessellated floors in Sullan Praeneste, but it seems evident that in both Varro's and his usage 'lithostrota' means 'opus sectile', in contrast to the typical earlier Late Republican

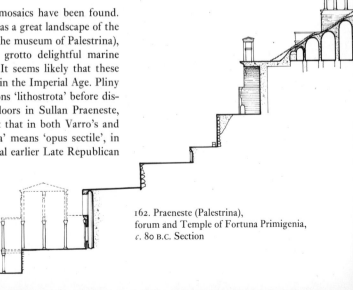

162. Praeneste (Palestrina), forum and Temple of Fortuna Primigenia, *c.* 80 B.C. Section

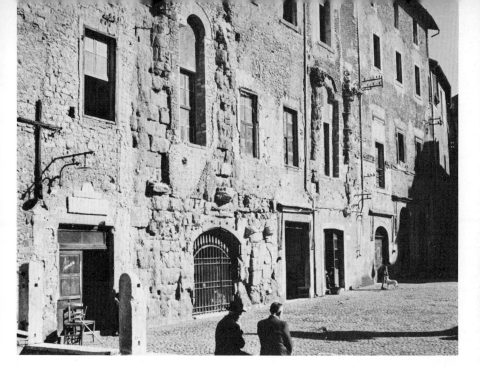

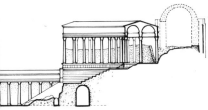

163. Praeneste (Palestrina), curia, with aerarium on the left, *c.* 80 B.C. (The present ground level is some six feet higher than the Sullan level)

cement floors with small inserted travertine chips, the so-called *opus signinum*.[33]

Whoever visits Praeneste or analyses the plan of the upper and lower sanctuaries [158] sees that the buildings round the forum and the upper part of the sanctuary are unconnected and that there is no central staircase between them. The upper sanctuary is independent of the forum and a real masterpiece of hellenistic Italic axiality, a triangle with its base on the terrace high above the basilica between the grottoes. Seven terraces lead up to a round temple, which is the apex of the triangle. The third terrace rests upon a wall of polygonal work. To its right and left rise staircases from the second terrace, ending in front of colonnaded well houses. From them great ramps led up to the fourth terrace, where the staircase of the central axis starts. Along the outer side of the ramps ran covered porticoes with a closed outside wall (towards the south). In the centre of the ramp building on the third terrace are niches for statues, which mark the beginning of the central axis. Along the entire rear wall of the fourth terrace a portico was built with a row of shops interrupted by the central staircase and by two hemicycles with Ionic columns and coffered barrel-vaults, some 50 feet east and west of the central staircase. In front of the portico at the west end of the eastern hemicycle was a small round Corinthian shrine with triglyph friezes above the architrave and on the high base (now in the museum). Between the columns above the base were a decorative railing and gratings. Below it was a pit. It seems most probable that this was the 'religiously guarded place' where the lots were found.[34]

Following the staircase of the central axis to the fifth terrace we meet with another row of barrel-vaulted shops with purely decorative blocked doors and engaged columns on the walls between them. Above them extends the sixth terrace, a large piazza with double Corinthian porticoes on the east and west sides and along the western and eastern ends of the northern rear wall as well. In the centre of the north wall, right and left of the central staircase, which continues to the seventh terrace, are arches, and between them piers adorned with engaged columns; behind the compartments of this façade, which recalls the Tabularium [143] and the terrace of Hercules Victor, runs a barrel-vaulted corridor from south to north, a so-called cryptoportico. A cryptoportico of this kind evidently offered a sheltered walk for the public on hot summer days, and cold winter days as well, as did the cryptoporticoes on the terraces of rich landowners' villas. Above this piazza, with its commanding view towards the Campagna and the sea, towers the seventh terrace. Here we encounter, as at Gabii and Tivoli (above, pp. 165 ff.), an orchestra and semicircular stairs. They are crowned by a semicircular double portico. Behind its centre, in line with the staircase of the central axis, stands the round temple. It is the culmination of the whole layout above the forum buildings, and no doubt had a superstructure visible from the terraces which lead up to it. The theatre indicates that the round temple had a central importance for the religious performances of the sanctuary, very likely choirs and ritual dances on the piazza in front of the theatre stairs (the sixth terrace).

How can the piazza (forum) and the upper sanctuary be explained? It is of course possible that the old temple on the forum of the middle town was the Temple of Fortuna and that the basilica, the hall on the east side of it (the curia in my view), and the two grottoes belonged to it, and this has usually been assumed. One of the grottoes could then have been the place where the lots were found, though Cicero's description makes a site higher up on the slope more likely. There is, at any rate, nothing to disprove that the forum was an ordinary civic centre with basilica, aerarium, curia, and an old, unidentified temple. To me it seems most probable that this was so: that the round temple and the theatre stand on the place of the cult of Fortuna, and that the upper sanctuary connected the holy places of the Fortuna cult. All the great upper sanctuary, viewed as a whole, is focused on the round temple, and the theatre would have been used for ceremonies in front of it, as at Gabii, and later in the sanctuary of Hercules Victor at Tivoli. Up there – according to the suggestion accepted by me – the honey would have flowed from an olive tree when the lots were found a little lower down the slope.[35]

Another great sanctuary of the Sullan Age was built in the old cult centre of Jupiter Anxur on the mountain east of Terracina [164]. Instructed by the experience of Pyrrhus's and Hannibal's wars, or perhaps because of the danger of internal warfare, in the second century the Romans strengthened the defences of the great roads leading to Rome. In a gorge by the Via Appia between Formia and Terracina a strong fortress was built. The original Via Appia, which reaches the old fortified hill town of Terracina over the hills on its east side, was blocked by a strong wall. This wall connected the town with a quadrangular castrum fort with barracks perched on the top of the mountain of Jupiter Anxur. This great fortification had round towers, a strongly fortified gate where the Via Appia passes the wall, and barracks on the west, east, and north sides of the castrum. Unlike all earlier known Italic defence-works, it was built entirely of concrete covered by coarse opus incertum. Below the open south side of the castrum was added a monumental terrace for the cult of Jupiter Anxur. Like the fortifications, it was built of concrete but covered with a more

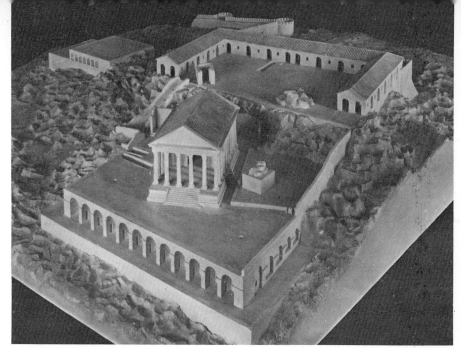

164. Terracina, Temple of Jupiter Anxur, *c*. 80 B.C. Reconstruction showing the terrace, temple, and castrum (with the beginning of the wall which connected it with the wall of the town). *Excavations Museum*

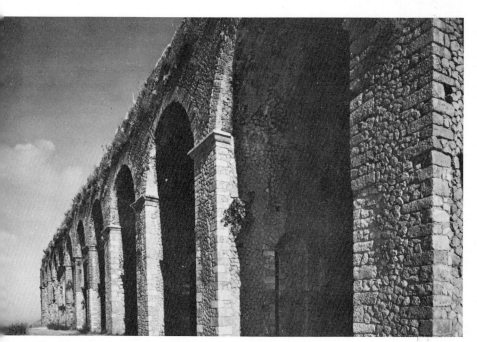

165. Terracina, Temple of Jupiter Anxur, *c*. 80 B.C., terrace

refined opus incertum of – so it seems to me – unmistakably Sullan type. The terrace had a most imposing arcaded façade without any applied semi-columns or other Greek adornments. It was like, for instance, the amphitheatre and the podium of the Villa dei Misteri at Pompeii [165; cf. 175], and of the Late Republican pavilion on the beach of Sperlonga. The terrace of Lindos has already reminded us of the fact that this kind of straightforward façade was not at all alien to hellenistic architecture. As on the north side of the sixth terrace of Praeneste, a barrel-vaulted cryptoportico was built behind the equally barrel-vaulted compartments of the façade. The great Temple of Jupiter Anxur, previously described, with ten columns in the prodomus (p. 159, above), was built on this terrace with a surprising oblique orientation, no doubt due to the old ceremonies of the place. Behind the temple, in front of the hillside of the castrum, a portico offered further shelter for the pilgrims who came.[36]

Another of the great Sullan sanctuaries is the Temple of Hercules Curinus, south of Sulmona, usually called the 'Villa d'Ovidio'. Against the steep hillside which overlooks the plain 'rich in ice-cold streams' (as Ovid says), corn, grapes, and olives, three terraces were built. On the highest terrace is the Temple of Hercules, partly constructed of rammed clay (*pisé*). Its location recalls that of the Temple of Dionysus on the theatre terrace of Pergamon. The second terrace has a portico and a monumental stairway, which connects it with the third terrace and reminds us of the imposing

steps between the upper and the lower agora (forum) at Morgantina, Sicily. Below it protrudes the lowest terrace, built of concrete covered by opus incertum and reticulatum. On it are shops, as in the other great sanctuaries of the countryside, evidently constructed for fairs connected with the sacrifices.[37]

The Romans were more original in other fields of architecture, but a survey of the Late Republican temples gives us the best notion of traditionalistic hellenism in the centuries from Naevius and Ennius to Cicero and the young Vergil. The theatre-temples show us how the fundamental Etruscan and Italic traditions could become almost effaced by the variegated combinations and decorations of hellenistic architecture. They also show that stone-built theatre buildings were constructed around Rome earlier than in the capital itself. Cicero, Vergil, and Horace saw the beginning also of the next age, when this architecture met with the marble and classicism of Augustan Rome. Vitruvius was a champion of the latter; the use of marble in Italy depended, however, upon whether it could be found and made ready without great expense (I, 2. 8), but he mentions it, for instance, in connexion with the tombs of the rich (II, 8. 3).

Closely related to the great systematizations of the sanctuaries of Praeneste, Tivoli, and Terracina is an imposing bastion which in the second half of the second century was added to the acropolis of Ferentinum [166, 168]. There also one recognizes inspiration from the hellenistic world and the riches which the Eastern wars

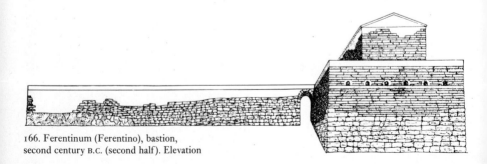

166. Ferentinum (Ferentino), bastion, second century B.C. (second half). Elevation

brought to Italy. In the second century the polygonal walls of Ferentinum above the Via Latina (above, p. 118) were heightened by a superstructure of ashlar masonry and provided with arched gates [167]. In addition to this strengthened outer defence, the acropolis was reshaped, probably between 150 and 100, by the erection of the bastion overlooking the

which thrusts forward towards the valley, has a low foundation of very rough and large polygonal blocks, most likely remains of an older fortification. Upon this base rests a wall of more refined polygonal work, and above this stands the main part of the bastion, built of ashlar. The uppermost part of it contains a great rectangular subterranean concrete basement con-

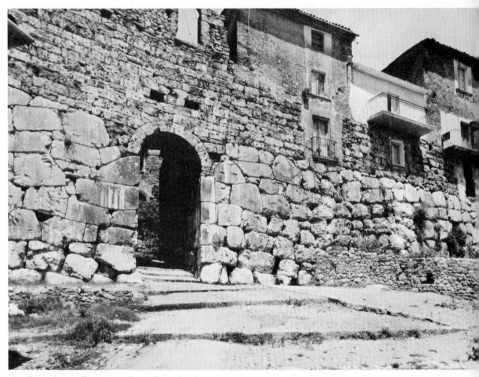

167. Ferentinum (Ferentino), Porta Sanguinaria, second century B.C.

valley with the road on the western side of the town [168].[38] This is another of the reconstructions of old towns around Rome which display evident influence from the hellenistic world. In the small towns they were more freely converted into Italic modes than in Rome itself, where dense quarters and strong traditions hampered even the schemes of a Caesar, an Augustus, and later emperors. The bastion,

sisting of a rectangular central structure with somewhat lower, barrel-vaulted cryptoporticoes on all four sides. Small, oblique arched windows pierce the ashlar façade. They were no doubt built here also as sheltered walks for hot or cold days. At Aosta and in several French towns shelters of exactly the same kind as on the acropolis of Ferentinum were added to fora of the Imperial Age.[39] The central structure sur-

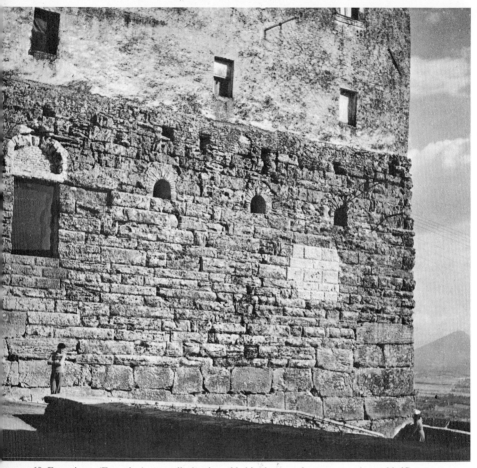

168. Ferentinum (Ferentino), acropolis, bastion added in the second century B.C. (second half)

rounded by the cryptoporticoes was divided into two parallel longitudinal naves covered by barrel-vaults. Above them, on the top of the bastion, stood a large hall with columns on benches along the side walls. It can be compared with the Capitolium of Pompeii (above, p. 146), but was perhaps rather a curia or some other public building. Together with the eastern hall on the forum of Praeneste, it may give an indication of what the old Curia Hostilia of the Roman Senate became like when it was enlarged and rebuilt by Sulla in 80 and by his son Faustus in 52 B.C.

TOWN PLANNING

After the fora, the temples, and the monumental layouts which herald the great architectural schemes of the Imperial Age, we must now seek out, in the numerous tabernae in the towns of central Italy and in the tenement houses in Rome, other prominent and characteristic features of the hellenized Italic town: town houses of the wealthy and the bourgeoisie, market halls, baths, and theatres. As an introduction to these partly typically Roman innovations, something about the continued development of town

bend of the old polygonal wall on the south-east side of the town.[40]

Openings in the walls for later catapults were also arched. A fine specimen is in that part of the Servian Wall which defends the Aventine [170]. It evidently belongs to repairs of the year 87, when the consuls fortified Rome with trenches,

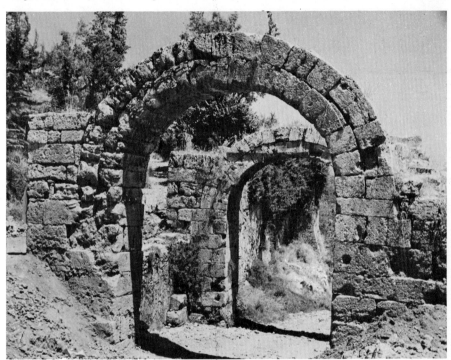

169. Ferentinum (Ferentino), Porta Maggiore or 'di Casamari', c. 80–70 B.C.

walls and city planning may be added to what has already been said.

As to the shape of the gates, the type known from the so-called 'Servian Wall' of Rome, from the castrum of Ostia [123], and from Cosa, with a gatehouse projecting on the inside of the wall, persisted in the first century. The Porta di Casamari of Ferentinum [169] is a very fine example from the seventies. It is built of ashlar, provided with two arches, and attached to a

restored the walls, and planted catapults on them.[41]

Among the specially characteristic late walls are the following. The colony of Alba Fucens, which the Romans founded about 300, was an important rural centre but also a strong fortification with the function of keeping watch over the Samnites and the Etruscans. Alba Fucens was refortified at the beginning of the first century, in connexion with the internal wars in

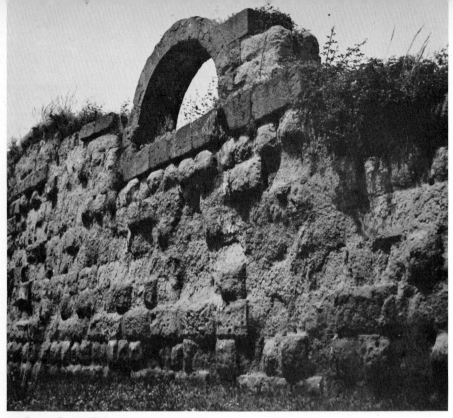

170. Rome, 'Servian Wall' at the Aventine, begun
378 B.C., rebuilt with an arch for catapults in 87 B.C.

Italy, by imposing polygonal walls, replacing
older fortifications of the same kind [172]. They
have an oblong polygonal terrace on the west
side of the town, with strong towers and a superstructure consisting of a concrete wall with
semi-columns – or perhaps a portico with shops
on the inside – and an apse at the south-western
extremity. The walls are built of concrete covered with opus incertum on the outside and
opus reticulatum inside. The apse, no doubt,
had a wooden roof and may have housed a
statue. On the central axis towards the north
end of the terrace stands a high tomb. Whether
this elegant piazza was built on the top of an
older outer defence work or whether, with its
three types of constructional technique, it stood
alone, it seems most probable that the great rec-

tangular court with its apse was arranged for
fairs and religious gatherings, like the terraces
of the Temple of Hercules south of Sulmona.[42]

Concrete became more and more usual both
for entirely new buildings, such as the great
wall between Terracina and the hill of Jupiter
Anxur, and for more or less extensive repairs
and additions to polygonal or ashlar structures.
Outside the west gate of Terracina the city wall
was extended some 200 yards along the north
side of the Via Appia. The most conspicuous
remains are a round tower on the north side of
the same kind as those of the great wall and an
imposing square tower standing at the west end
of this outer work. The lower part of this tower
consists of a structure of very refined polygonal
work of calcareous blocks, with a decorated

frieze above the seven bottom layers. The upper part is built of concrete covered with opus incertum and has two arched windows. It seems most likely that this additional fortification was contemporary with the great south-eastern wall, and thus should be dated to the second century B.C.[43]

Very extensive are the repairs of concrete with opus incertum on the third-century polygonal walls of Fundi. Like the repairs and round concrete towers of Cora (Cori)[44] they are an eloquent witness of the internal wars in Marius's and Sulla's times. No less eloquent, moreover, on the side of the rebellious Italic people, are the repairs to the fifth-century wall of Pompeii, where, before the final defeat in 89, square concrete towers and other reinforcements of concrete were added to the old walls of tufa ashlar, as it stood with its Italic agger on the inside, more or less in disuse, in the second century.[45]

The great outer wall of Ostia encircles the outer town, which after about 300 B.C. grew up round the old castrum-fort [123].[46] This en-

larged Ostia became the seaside suburb of Rome, busily trading with the Mediterranean and the coastal towns of Italy from the mouth of the Tiber. Most probably the wall was built after the city had been plundered by Marius. It is a concrete wall faced with opus incertum, which sometimes tends to be reticulate and often assumes the aspect of quasi-reticulate. The wall evidently left the river side unfortified. It starts with a strong square tower of ashlar work at the north-east corner of the town and has round concrete towers at each bend. The gates are of the internal gatehouse type (see pp. 118 and 122, above), with the interior faced with ashlar. Their strong military character is emphasized by square flanking towers right and left of the entrances.

The enlarged Ostia, which was surrounded by this wall, represents one of the two main types of Late Republican town. It can be studied in the layers below the brick-faced Ostia of the centuries after A.D. 100. A few temples remained in the Imperial town [171], but almost all the

171. Ostia, Late Republican temple on the lower level (next to the Temple of Hercules), with stuccoed tufa columns and opus incertum

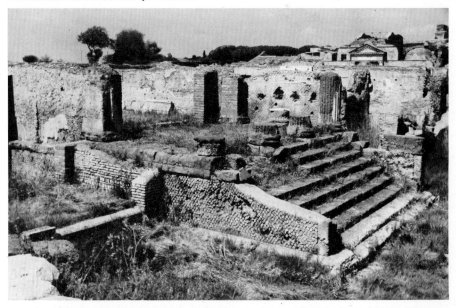

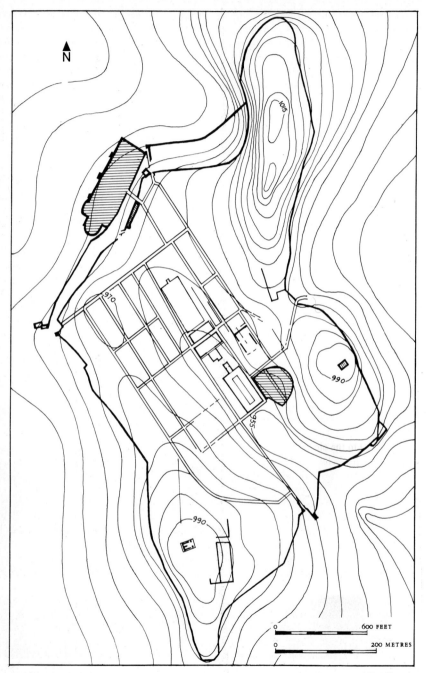

172. Alba Fucens, founded *c.* 300 B.C., the walls and the final, regular town-plan early first century. Plan

atria and shops were destroyed and buried below the level of the new town, which had the entirely changed stamp and technique of the greatest days of the Empire. Roads ran from the gates of the old castrum to Rome (Via Ostiensis), to the sea and the river mouth, and on the south side of the town to the villages and villas and to the towns with their obsolete river harbours along the west coast of Latium: Laurentum, Lavinium, Ardea, and so to Antium. They now became the main streets of Late Republican Ostia and remained such, though widened, in the Imperial town above it. Inside the old castrum fort were two straight, main streets: one is the Via Ostiensis, running east to west and in modern usage called *decumanus*; the other, usually called *cardo*, traversed the castrum fort from north to south, crossing the decumanus at right angles in its centre. The decumanus passed the eastern part of the added quarters in a straight line; the riverside between it and the Tiber was reserved, it seems, for warehouses, etc. But all the rest of the new outer town is old-fashioned oblique streets and irregular quarters. It reminds us of Tacitus's description of the old Rome before Nero's fire, with narrow lanes and sprawling blocks. The plan of Ostia shows how, during centuries of peace, trading towns developed haphazardly if military demands or special planning did not impose regularity. The outer wall of Ostia illustrates how, when war came, the defence had to accept such a town as it stood. Lucus Feroniae of the Augustan Age is an example of another town that grew up in the same way, according to the needs of daily life.

Many towns in Italy no doubt grew up like the enlarged Ostia, but regular town planning seems to have prevailed. Its development in the first century is well illustrated at Alba Fucens [172]. The old grid of the town (no doubt regular from its beginnings) was renewed. The main streets, which passed through the town from the south-east (where the gate of the great highway from Rome, the Via Aurelia, was located), were probably inherited from the earlier periods, as were the streets which crossed them at right angles running north-east-south-west. All this reappeared now in a modernized, ele-

gant shape. Between the two great streets running south-east-north-west were the forum, the basilica with a portico in front, both facing north, and behind them, facing south, the Temple and Porticus of Hercules, as described above, pp. 146–8. Porticoes, a theatre, and rows of well-built tabernae along the main streets and facing south, below the tribunal of the basilica, were typical of this replanned, elegant town. It is worth noting that in most other towns the short ends of the rectangular house blocks (*strigae*) face the main street perpendicularly (as, for instance, at Cosa) while at Alba Fucens and some other towns long sides of the blocks run parallel with the streets. *Scamna* seems to have been the usual term for blocks orientated in this way.[47]

It is interesting to compare Cosa with Alba Fucens, as it was rebuilt some two hundred years later. The polygonal walls and the plan of a temple on a hill east of Alba Fucens, now incorporated with the church of S. Pietro, have preserved the old Italic style, but the concrete faced by opus incertum shows a striking difference from the rubble of Cosa. Altogether, Cosa shows us a Roman colony in the stern age of the earlier wars and conquests, while Alba Fucens displays the enriched and refined colonies of Sullan times.

DOMESTIC ARCHITECTURE

In his description of the Rome of the Neronian fire in A.D. 64, Suetonius (*Nero*, 38) speaks about 'the immense number of tenement houses' – in country towns one would say *tabernae* – and, in contrast to them, an aristocratic minority of 'domus of the leaders of old, still adorned with trophies of victory'.

Pompeii, Herculaneum, and the Late Republican layers at Ostia show that the one-family houses of the rich and the well-to-do bourgeoisie filled a much larger place in Late Republican towns than in the Imperial Age, with its apartment houses. There are also different kinds of domus. The closed (testudinate) type of atrium in the Casa dello Scheletro at Herculaneum,[48] a stately atrium displuviatum such as the Tomba di Mercareccia (above, p. 90) [89], shows that several old Italic one-family house types known from Etruscan tombs and by Vitruvius lived on.

Vitruvius's main recommendation for domus, that is, for houses of a higher standard (VI, 3), concerns the houses with reception halls called atria and hailed also by Varro (*Lingua Latina*, V, 161) as originally Etruscan. In my opinion, Vitruvius and Varro are perfectly right in deriving these atrium-houses from the Etruscans. Their main features seem to be derived from Etruscan palaces such as they are represented in tombs like the Tomba a Tablino, the Tomba degli Scudi e delle Sedie, the Tomba dei Capi-

telli, the Tomba dei Vasi Greci at Caere, and the Tomba Rosi at San Giuliano in the modified form of the rock-cut chamber tombs [82–4].

Together with the plans of temples, this seems to me to be one of the most spectacular instances of how traditions from archaic Etruscan architecture influenced the building activity of the subsequent centuries, although we have only Vitruvius's description and the tombs to substantiate the Etruscan ancestry. It seems quite clear that Vitruvius's and Varro's atrium-houses became the preferred upper-class mansion of the Etruscan *koine*. Consequently, as in the third chapter (see pp. 75 ff.), I continue to

173. Pompeii, Casa del Chirurgo,
fourth or third century B.C.

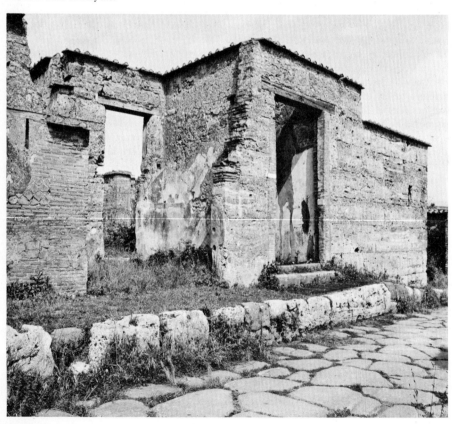

compare the main features of these Late Republican houses with archaic Etruscan tombs. All the same, however, the most interesting task is to describe this virtually new kind of house, created in the last centuries B.C. by innovations such as the impluvium (p. 186, below) and by the victorious Greek taste, and then handed over to Imperial times.

Like the Etruscan tombs, the Roman atrium-houses of the third century onwards [85, 91] were strictly axial and symmetrical. They were accessible by a forecourt and lobby, the *vestibulum*, inside which was the main entrance to the house, the *fauces*. In old atrium-houses the chambers right and left of the fauces were closed towards the street – as still can be seen on the right side of the Casa del Chirurgo [85, 173].

On the opposite side of the atrium, facing the entrance from the street, was the *tablinum*, which in Vitruvius's description (VI, 3. 5, 6) and in other sources, and in the houses as we see them at Pompeii, appears as the original main room and centre of the household. Pliny (XXXV, 7) tells us that the tablinum also served as an archive room and was filled with family documents. Originally the tablina seem to have been the bedchambers of the master of the house and his wife. As we see them today, they have one side completely open towards the atria, but the wooden screen in the Casa del Tramezzo di Legno at Herculaneum and arrangements for hangings show that they could be – and they probably usually were – separated from the atria.[49] Of old there was a dining-table, the *cartibulum*, at the entry to the tablinum, as Varro (*Lingua Latina*, V, 125) describes it from his boyhood days. The known Pompeian cartibula are elegant marble tables which were no longer used for meals in the atria. To the right and left of the broad entrances to the tablina are usually doors to side rooms or passages. We meet this kind of house, described as Etruscan by Vitruvius and Varro, all over Pompeii, Herculaneum, and in the Republican strata of Ostia.[50] It is evident that Vitruvius, as he often does, has chosen the best-liked traditional type of house from the last centuries B.C. for his special model.

The Late Republican houses which are known today have bedrooms (*cubicula*) along the side walls. In front of the tablina and their flanking doors are open wings (*alae*) extending right and left to the outer walls of the houses, as described by Vitruvius (VI, 3. 4). Very likely this arrangement was inherited from the Etruscan palaces, though it could not be reproduced in the tombs, where the beds of the dead are placed along the walls of the main hall, in the side rooms of the tablinum, and in the tablinum itself.

In the old days the atrium-houses seem to have been mostly free from the bustle of streets with their tabernae, where wares were displayed, where the daylong pounding of the coppersmiths' hammers, the early-rising bakers, the humming voices from the school, the clinking from the moneychangers' are all described for us by Livy (VI, 25. 9), Martial (XII, 57), and others. Later, in connexion with the intensified commercial life of the last centuries B.C., the owners of atrium-houses yielded, and opened tabernae to the right and left of the entrances to the atria. This occurred throughout the town and resembled the butchers' stalls and shops which Livy (XLIV, 16) describes at the atrium-house of the Scipiones, their *aedes*, by the Forum Romanum. These tripartite entrances in the façade are a typical feature of Pompeii as we see it.

In the material which we have at present, we come across at the very beginning both aristocratic houses, such as the noble Casa di Sallustio in Pompeii, and middle-class houses with plain façades, such as the Casa del Chirurgo, interrupting the rows of shops along the business streets. Refined Pompeian houses of the late second and first centuries had pilasters with flowery Corinthian or Ionic capitals flanking the main entrances, anticipating the hellenistic decoration of the interior.

The development during the centuries of hellenistic luxury and increasing civic activity and splendour evidently exerted a great influence upon the atrium-houses (whatever their origin), before they attained the rich and varied appearance which we see in Pompeii and Herculaneum. A difference between the old Etruscan tombs and the Late Republican houses is that the back walls of the tablina have wide windows or are left completely open towards gardens (*horti*) behind them. When old-fashioned gardens were replaced by elegant Greek peristyles [91], the tablina, which had had such an important function in the tombs and older atrium-houses, became chiefly elegant passages and could be remodelled in various ways or even omitted.

As was pointed out on pp. 80-1, the Etruscan tombs reproduce reception halls, in front of the tablina and side rooms, with flat, richly decorated roofs and supporting Doric or Aeolic-Ionic columns. But in the third century we meet with the *cava aedium tuscanica*, atria with valleys tilting inward to a roof opening, the *compluvium*, with a rectangular tank, the *impluvium*, below.[51] This contrivance was useful in towns for keeping rainwater away from neighbouring houses. A still more important reason for the device was probably to collect water from the tiles of the inward slopes of the roofs. Cisterns were built below the atria for this rainwater (*collecti imbres*), which Horace in one of his epistles (I, 15. 15) seems to disapprove of, but which for many places and during sieges were indispensable. Late Republican atria have gracefully decorated frames round the tops of the tanks (*putealia*) in front of the tablina.

Material which would allow us to follow this development between the fifth and the third century is very scarce. We cannot even establish when, in the fifth century or later, atrium-houses became the most typical kind of dwelling for the upper and middle classes throughout central Italy and Campania. At Saepinum, a town in the Abruzzi rebuilt by the local population after 293, when the old Samnite town was destroyed by the Romans, a regular atrium has been excavated, and an impluvium of terracotta with Oscan inscriptions found below the later stone impluvium. Livy mentions a palm tree which grew in an impluvium in 169 and was considered a prodigy.[52] Pliny's famous description of the ancestral atria with wax models of the forefathers in special cupboards (XXXV, 6-7) refers to the old Roman traditions of the atria; evidently the younger Pliny is right in speaking of an atrium built in the ancestral manner (*ex more veterum*) among all the various modern halls and courts in his Villa Tusca (*Epist.*, V, 6. 15; 11, 17. 4).

In the third century we begin to get an overwhelming mass of evidence from atrium-houses at Pompeii and Herculaneum, and, about 100, at Ostia.[53] Like the Etruscan towns, the Osco-Samnite towns of Campania in the third and second centuries still had their own language, city life, and upper classes, which developed their own brand of hellenistic culture and built beautiful atrium-houses. These houses were evidently influenced by Rome, directly by the hellenistic world, and, of course, by Greek neighbours in Naples and farther south. The public buildings show that the Roman colony, the Colonia Cornelia Veneria, affected the life of the towns in many ways from about 80, but in the domus we can hardly discern any difference. The hellenistic *koine* in its Italic shape, the hellenized *consuetudo Italica* of Vitruvius's fifth book, had impressed its common pattern upon all refined domestic architecture in central Italy.

Already in the second century, both at Pompeii and at Herculaneum, we see houses with high atria surrounded by rooms in two storeys. The Casa delle Nozze d'Argento from the Samnite times of Pompeii (second century B.C.) and the Casa del Tramezzo di Legno at Herculaneum (first century A.D.) show especially well these heightened atria. The rooms of the upper storeys sometimes had windows towards the atria and towards the street in front of their entrances (the *fauces*); in many cases these upper apartments were accessible by direct staircases from the street. Neither these flats round the atria nor flats round central courts (as in the Casa a Graticcio at Herculaneum) developed into the high tenement houses of the future; they seem like a transitional patchwork when compared with the fundamentally different insulae which we know from the Terme del Foro at Pompeii and from Imperial Ostia. As seen, for instance, in the Via Stabiana or the Via dell'Abbondanza at Pompeii, galleries with elegant Greek columns could be arranged above the entrances to the houses [136]. These, as has already been said, were connected with the *cenacula*, the upstair dining-rooms, discussed by Varro (*Lingua Latina*, v, 162), which in his day became common and gave their name to all the upper rooms. In the Casa Sannitica at Herculaneum an open gallery with Ionic columns ran round the upper part of the high atrium.

For the sake of greater elegance, the old impluvia of tufa or terracotta were replaced in the later atria by marble basins. As Vitruvius says and as can be seen in many houses at Pompeii and Herculaneum,[54] the compluvium could be supported by Greek columns at the four angles or all around the impluvium [91]. The former arrangement was called 'tetrastyle' and the latter 'Corinthian'. Corinthian columns became the fashion of the day. Cicero mentions in the second Verrine Oration (147) that columns intended for an impluvium were brought (probably to some villa) a long way over bad roads. Pliny (XVII, 6) reports that six columns of marble from Mount Hymettus were erected in the atrium of the orator Lucius Crassus about 100 B.C., and makes clear that this was considered a great luxury during these Late Republican centuries, when marble columns were rare even in public places.

Another most important part of the hellenization of atrium-houses was the peristyles (*peristyla, peristylia*), the square courts surrounded by colonnades described by Vitruvius (VI, 3. 7 and 5.2) and, in their most luxurious shape, by Cicero in his account of Clodius's domus on the Palatine (*De domo*, 116) [91]. Peristyles were built behind the atria and tablina in town houses (Vitruvius, VI, 5. 3). The colonnades, which presented a delightful view behind the open back walls of the tablina, had various kinds of columns – slender modernized Doric columns as well as Corinthian, Tuscan, and Ionic. They were surrounded by living-rooms (*conclavia*)

with a new convivial luxury. As suggested by Diodorus (V, 40) and mentioned above on p. 92, it is possible that the Etruscans introduced or even 'invented' peristyles. In any case, from the second century they represent the most outstanding and charming parts of the atrium-houses that we know so well in Pompeii, and, to say it again, at Ostia a peristyle of about 100 remains in the Via della Fortuna Annonaria.[55]

The origin of these porticoes poses no problems. The old Italic mansions had gardens (*horti*) behind the tablina, surrounded – as Livy describes it from the third century at Capua (XXIII, 8. 8; 9. 13) – by a wall facing the adjacent street (*maceria horti*). In the Casa di Sallustio there are remains of a colonnade surrounding the back of the atrium block, as Vitruvius (VI, 5. 3) describes it when discussing villas, and as we actually see it in the Villa dei Misteri outside Pompeii. It must have been natural to substitute for this old arrangement porticoes in the Greek style, at a time when places made varied by countless columns became characteristic for hellenized Italic towns, and when even in wall paintings of the Second Pompeian Style a predilection is shown for colonnaded architecture. The Greek peristyles, known from private houses such as those of Olynthus and Delos, palaces, gymnasia and palaestrae, marketplaces, and other sophisticated town architecture, underwent characteristic alterations in their Italic context. The peristyles of the atrium-houses remained gardens. They were a most characteristic expression of the Roman love of nature.[56] The space in the middle, open to the sky, was embellished by greenery. Walking in the open air is very healthy, explains Vitruvius, speaking of colonnades and walks in general (v, 9. 5). The 'iucundissimum' murmur of elegant fountains, which the Romans loved, was often to be heard, as can be understood from Pompeii and as is described by the younger Pliny (*Epist.*, v, 6).

The Romans introduced strict axiality and symmetry into their peristyles too. Of course, this also exists in Greek peristyles (for instance, in the hellenistic gymnasium of Miletus), but more characteristic of Greek architecture is a free disposition of rooms round the peristyle. At Pompeii, on the other hand, over and over again tablina occur with side rooms in the centres of the upper sides of the peristyles, repeating the principal motif of the atria. The palaces of the Imperial Age, with their predilection for open doors or niches flanked by side doors as the centre motifs of the back wall of their courts and halls, still carry on the axiality of Late Republican atrium-houses and peristyles. In addition, actual atrium-houses survived, as is seen on the Forma Urbis, in Imperial Ostia, and also in the younger Pliny's villas (cf. p. 106).[57]

Among the conclavia and dining-rooms drawn up round the peristyles were Corinthian tetrastyle and Egyptian oeci. The side of the oecus towards the peristyle was left open. As in the Casa del Labirinto at Pompeii, the Corinthian oeci had barrel-vaults and side rooms with flat ceilings to allow walking above them under the open sky. The best-known tetrastyle oecus belongs to the left side wall of the peristyle in the Casa delle Nozze di Argento at Pompeii. It has an antechamber in front of the barrel-vaulted saloon with its four columns. Still more elaborate were the Egyptian oeci. A fine specimen from Imperial times is the *oecus Aegyptius* that serves as tablinum in the Casa dell'Atrio a Mosaico at Herculaneum,[58] but Vitruvius already gives us a full description (VI, 3. 9). The Egyptian oeci resembled basilicas, though the

aisles had only one storey, and above that, as in the Corinthian oeci, an upper floor for promenading under the open sky. Windows in the walls between the upper columns of the nave admitted light to the interior. Vitruvius further singles out so-called Cyzicene oeci as being particularly foreign to Italic manners of building. They had two sets of dining-couches, facing each other, and windows on the right and left 'so that views of the garden may be had from indoors'. The Casa di Giulia Felice at Pompeii and the main triclinium of the reception wing of the Domus Flavia on the Palatine show how this disposition lived on in the Imperial Age.[59]

In the eighth region, in the southern part of Pompeii and accessible from the Via della Regina, there is a row of atrium-houses originally dating from the third century. On the level of the town they have atria and tablina of the usual kind. But when at the end of the second century the fortifications on this side were given up, and especially in the age of the Sullan colony, the old houses were enlarged by structures which covered the hillside. Projecting lower storeys supported by terraces were provided, and corridors, staircases, loggias, and windows facing the marvellous view towards the plain, the sea, and the mountains [174]. The sources here must be Etruscan terrace houses and coastal villas of stepped outline known from wall paintings at Pompeii [177].[60]

The beautiful Casa dei Grifi, excavated below the Domus Flavia on the northern slope of

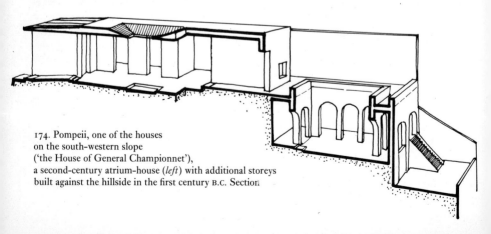

174. Pompeii, one of the houses
on the south-western slope
('the House of General Championnet'),
a second-century atrium-house (*left*) with additional storeys
built against the hillside in the first century B.C. Section

the Palatine in Rome, is a terrace house of a similar kind. Against the hillside are built elegant barrel-vaulted rooms with pavement mosaics and paintings and stuccoes in the earliest Second Pompeian Style. The date must be the early first century. The rooms were probably lit by doors or windows in the destroyed north wall. Very likely there was an atrium on the surface of the Palatine, from which the still-existing staircase led down to the rooms in front of the hill. At the southern edge of the Palatine, south of the early Augustan 'Casa di Livia', are also Late Republican remains, state rooms decorated in the typical style of *c*. 90–60. It seems at least possible that terraces built against the southern slope of the Palatine with a view towards the Circus Maximus were added to this house, just as on the southern hillside of Pompeii. Perhaps this was the house of one of Augustus's friends and freedmen, from which Augustus, and later Tiberius, used to watch the games in the Circus.[61]

Houses of this kind in Rome, the remains of large atrium-houses in Late Republican layers below Imperial Ostia, and the peristyle mentioned on p. 187 show us the Roman background of the kind of town architecture which Pompeii and Herculaneum reflect in such a charming way. Wholly to understand Campanian towns and villas, we must look to Rome and to the hellenistic towns of Italy and the eastern countries. This delightful domestic architecture, which spread to towns in the countryside such as Pompeii and no doubt received something of a new flavour there, was accompanied by wall paintings in the so-called Pompeian styles. To the period discussed in this chapter belong the so-called First and Second Pompeian Styles. Painters from Rome, Greek towns, and, no doubt, local painters who adopted the metropolitan ways of decoration gave the rooms an entirely different appearance. The old-fashioned walls, with a fairly high dado and a wave pattern above [74], were no longer acceptable (cf. p. 81). The First Style (or Masonry Style) was evidently hellenistic and international. It imitates 'different kinds of

marble slabs' (Vitruvius, VII, 5. 1) and is known in the Greek world from the fourth century onwards. We have met it in Sicily during the early third century and see it in Rome and at Pompeii from the second century or even earlier. The Second Style reproduces the overwhelming architectural motif of the day – the colonnaded exterior and interior. It widened the impression of the room by painted columns, which appeared to jut out, 'although the picture is perfectly flat' (Vitruvius, VI, 2. 2). The colonnades were, to use Vitruvius's words again, 'copied from actual realities' (VII, 5. 3). The Second Style began in the early first century.

Besides the paintings there were pavements with variegated sectile work, *lithostroton*, mosaics, and an increasing wealth of other luxurious decorations such as costly marbles – in short, all the elegance of the house of Lepidus, built in 78 and then considered the finest of its age, but thirty-five years later not considered fit even to occupy the hundredth place (Pliny, XXXVI, 109). Decorations at Pompeii of about 100 and later show elegant modillions and other refinements, which later became typical of the marble architecture of Early Imperial Rome. There is no reason to doubt that they were also to be found in the decoration of Late Republican palaces of the capital. In the Caesarian and early Augustan Age the most important type of decoration was the great garden paintings and paintings like the megalography of the Villa dei Misteri and of the Boscoreale villa, as well as the Odyssey landscapes from the Esquiline (now in the Vatican Museum). Vitruvius devotes a special paragraph to this (VII, 5. 2).[62]

Suetonius (*Augustus*, 72) implies that people were amazed that Augustus in his house on the Palatine had only small peristyles, that the columns were of stuccoed Alban stone (*peperino*), and that 'the rooms [were] without any marble decoration or handsome pavements'. Vitruvius (VI, 5. 2), summarizing the demands of the new age, recommends handsome and roomy apartments for advocates, public speakers, and their meetings. 'For men of rank', he continues, must be constructed 'lofty entrance courts in a regal style, and most spacious atria and peristyles, with plantations and walks of some extent in them, appropriate to their dignity. They need also libraries, picture galleries, and basilicas, finished in a style similar to that of great public buildings [like the Egyptian oecus; above, p. 188], since public councils as well as private lawsuits and hearings before arbitrators are very often held in the houses of such men.'

If one compares these modern Italic houses with their hellenistic counterparts – such as the houses of Delos, the peristyle houses of Morgantina, or the House of the Columns at Ptolemais near Cyrene[63] – the first general impression is so very similar that one can almost forget the basic difference not only between Greek megara and Italic atria (emphasized by Vitruvius, VI, 3 and 7) but also between the symmetry always aimed at in Roman houses and the easy-going arrangement which prevailed in Greek mansions. Of the intention in these Late Republican houses to be hellenistic and relaxed there can be no doubt, even if we did not have Strabo (V, 4. 7) to tell us of it with reference to Campania.

VILLAS

The attitude is still more evident in the Roman villas, whether, like Horace's small farm in the Sabine country with its household of five coloni (*Epist.*, I, 14), they remained agricultural (as the word villa originally implies), or whether they became villas in our sense of the word, country residences, to which the owners – as Bassus says in a witty epigram by Martial (III, 47) – went for relaxation with a carriage crammed full of all the abundance of the rich countryside bought in town. As a contrast, with Seneca (*Epist.*, LXXXVI, 5), we may hail Scipio cultivating the soil with his own hands, as the old Romans used to do. In the second century B.C. the luxury of the towns invaded these villas, though the really rural villas evidently often kept their old form and probably, in many cases, remained rustic. Cicero makes the difference very clear when speaking of his family home, the farm on the

rivers Fibrenus and Liris below Arpinum (*De Legibus*, II, 1). While his grandfather was alive it was as small as the old villas of unshorn Cato and other idolized heroes of ancient and simple times. Cicero's father rebuilt and enlarged it and thus achieved the right hellenistic atmosphere for his 'life of study'. Yards for cattle and farming purposes were typical of the old rural mansions. There are a few such villas preserved with yards surrounded by a crowd of rooms without any axial disposition. The whole was purely utilitarian, judging by Roman descriptions of these rural dwellings. Apart from these larger villas there were also, of course, villages and farms with small and simple buildings. Such unpretentious holdings were revived in veteran colonies from Sulla's time onwards.[64]

The Villa dei Misteri near Pompeii demonstrates best of all the changes due to the elegance of the houses in town. Though remaining a farming centre, about 200 the villa became what the ancients called a 'villa pseudo-urbana', or 'suburbana' or 'urbana'. It was built on a high podium with plain arches [175], a *basis villae* as Cicero styles it (*Ad Quintum fratrem*, III, 1. 5). Such podia, family tombs, and cisterns became typical of all country seats. The podia were built of concrete covered by incertum, reticulate, or polygonal work and had internal, barrel-vaulted cryptoporticoes with slanting side openings along the sides, a convenience for walks on hot or cold days, as was discussed in relation to the public buildings of Praeneste, Ferentinum, and Terracina.

We can follow these villa terraces back to the third century. On the rich plain around Cosa there are several very extensive terraces built of rubble which date from the second century [176]. They obviously reveal the presence of great Roman estates which, after the victories over the Etruscans in the third century, safeguarded by the fortified colony of Cosa, reorganized agriculture in this fertile countryside. One of these villa terraces in Valle d'Oro, the so-called Ballantino, is faced by polygonal work and has along its western side projecting round towers, constructed of coarse rubble covered

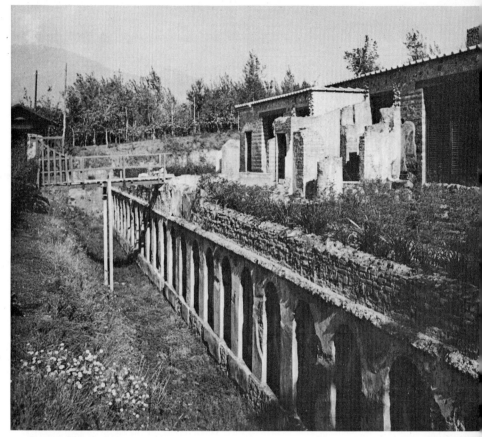

175. Pompeii, Villa dei Misteri, *c.* 200 B.C.,
basis villae (podium)

by rather slipshod ashlar work. Above the lower part of these turrets lies a protective layer of roof tiles with fringes, as Vitruvius prescribes (11, 8. 17, 18) for walls both of concrete and of wattle and daub. This solid lower part of the turrets carries an upper structure with two successive sets of arched dovecots. Above the upper row of these arches is a second protecting layer of roof tiles. The most imposing basis villae around Cosa is called Sette Finestre. It consists of three wide terraces built of coarse rubble and facing north-west. Along the façade of the low-est terrace are turrets with dovecots of the same type as in the Valle d'Oro villa. They alternate with sturdy buttresses. Below the second terrace is a system of barrel-vaulted corridors, which may have served as cryptoporticoes or storehouses or both. They are accessible from the lowest terrace by a row of arches. Between them are sloping buttresses crowned by travertine slabs with simple mouldings. On the highest and third terrace the manor house was built, dominating the plain as nowadays a medieval farmhouse does.[65]

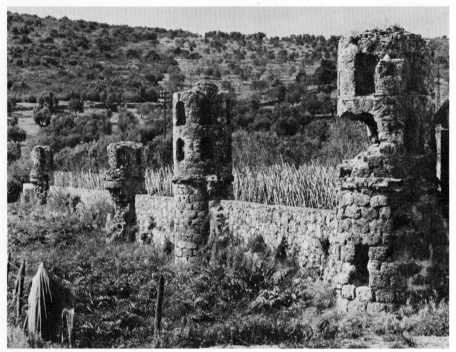

176. Cosa, villa, second century B.C.

The first structure on the large terrace of the Villa dei Misteri outside Pompeii was a rectangular building of about 200 with a courtyard – and probably also a rural side yard – surrounded by walls. From the entrance to the main court a central axis leads to an atrium without alae and to a tablinum, accessible by two doors at the corners of the atrium. A portico of the same kind as that in the Casa di Sallustio in Pompeii, with a view towards the coast and the sea, was at the back of these central rooms and chambers. During the first century the villa received paintings in the Second Pompeian Style, with architectural and figured motifs, including the famous Dionysiac paintings. In the second half of the second century a peristyle was built round the main court in front of the atrium. The final result was thus exactly in accordance with what Vitruvius records (VI, 5. 3): 'in town, atria are usually next to the front

door, while in country seats peristyles come first, and then atria surrounded by paved colonnades'.[66]

This arrangement seems to have been adopted in the Late Republican Villa Suburbana dei Papiri (Villa of the Pisones) outside Herculaneum in its first stage and in the so-called Villa di Diomede near Pompeii, also in its first stage. To these can also be added a large, luxurious villa below Tivoli with walls covered by incertum and reticulate. It was partly re-used when Hadrian built his famous villa on the same site.[67]

The atrium and peristyle villas and their podia – as also the tripartite arrangement for the upper sides of halls and courtyards – were extremely important for the development of Roman palaces. The same is true of the two other kinds of villas: the so-called portico and landscape villas. The one- or two-storey façades of seaside portico villas are a favourite subject of the Pompeian painters of the Early Imperial Age [177]. Many of these villas had a quite different origin from the peristyle villas. Like the Roman insulae, they evolved from a row of rooms with wide openings facing a courtyard, a

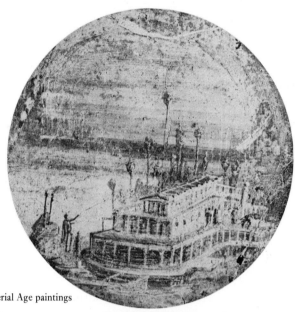

177. Early Imperial Age paintings
from Pompeii
showing terraced villas by the sea

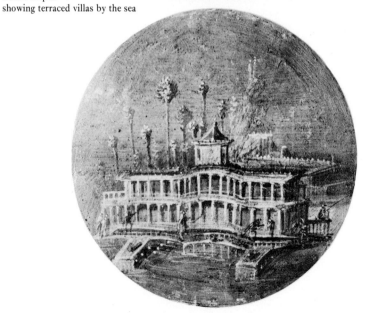

road, the coast, or a view. This type of house is known all over the Mediterranean countries from the Bronze Age onwards. At the very end of the Late Republican period architects apparently took it up and gave it all the hellenistic charm of paintings, colonnades, and terraces with fine views. The portico could also be used as a screen in front of a peristyle villa – as in the western half of Nero's Golden House in Rome – but the original form was a long, narrow house with a row of open rooms behind a colonnade, as we see it in the delightful 'Villa di Arianna' at Stabiae (above Castellammare di Stabia).[68] In all the villas one should also remember Agrippa's speech, referred to by Pliny (XXXV, 26), about pictures and statues banished to the villas (*in villarum exilia*), which he wished to make public property instead. Pliny (XXXV, 130) gives an illustration of this, reporting that the famous Late Republican orator Hortensius had Cydias's painting of the Argonauts in a special pavilion at his villa in Tusculum.

Artificial or natural grottoes also still exist, with elegant decoration, mosaic floors, walls adorned with shells and pumice stone, and so on. Roman poetry very often dwells upon romantic specus or speluncae, like the Cave of the Muses, mentioned by Juvenal (III, 10 ff.) south of the Caelian in Rome; their Late Republican refinement is obviously due to hellenistic influence, as the descriptions of Greek grottoes and the names *nymphaea* and *musaea* suggest. In Greek Locri models of caves with wells and nymphs have been found, and a small barrel-vaulted, apsidal grotto with a well outside the walls of Bovillae, near Albano, obviously continues this tradition. Vault and walls are built of rather rustic stone and should probably be dated to the second century. Soon this kind of shelter for hot days assumed monumentality; highly sophisticated nymphaea were built in front of natural grottoes, but could also be wholly artificial. A charming building of this kind is the barrel-vaulted so-called Doric Nymphaeum below Castelgandolfo, facing the Alban lake, which has three beautifully decorated entrances to a cave behind the rectangular

hall. Similar is a nymphaeum in the Villa di S. Antonio at Tibur (Tivoli). This has an apse, and along the side walls semi-columns carried four arches below an architrave. The capitals of these semi-columns, of the four arches, and of two columns which flank the apse were all Corinthian and of travertine. Mosaic panels decorate the apse ceiling. On the lowest terrace of a large villa at Formia, the so-called Villa di Cicerone, there are two Late Republican nymphaea with wells in the apses and a marvellous view towards the sea. They were redecorated and partly rebuilt in the Imperial Age, but the larger of the two evidently had a nave with columns of somewhat Tuscan type, narrow aisles, and a barrel-vaulted nave. It is 29 feet (8.70 m.) wide. These grottoes are the predecessors of the still grander nymphaea of the Imperial Age – like, for instance, the fantastic cave, with its pools and its four Homeric marble groups and other sculpture, which, like a gigantic heathen presepio, faces the sea at Sperlonga. Together with the nymphaea and the crypto-porticoes one has to remember subterranean halls, 'aestivi specus', constructed as shelters against the heat of the warm summer months.

The speluncae are often connected with the type of villa which I venture to call the 'landscape villa'. The stuccoes from the Villa Farnesina in Rome give us a delightful picture of them. We see before us grounds laid out in imitation of natural scenery, towers, bridges, pavilions, statues, trees, and fields. Besides this, Pliny (XXXV, 116) gives an enchanting summary of the paintings of all these rural amenities, including arriving or departing ships, donkeys or carts, and anglers, hunters, and labourers in the vineyards. Horace (*Od.*, II, 15) tells us of lakes larger than Lake Lucrino, and Atticus (in Cicero's *De Legibus*, II, 1) derides 'the artificial streams which some of our friends call "Niles" or "Euripi"', comparing them with the real rivers Fibrenus and Liris at Cicero's family villa and the lovely island in the Fibrenus. Varro (*De Re Rustica*, III, 5. 8–17) describes his villa at Casinum, which, according to him, surpassed the improvements of the villa of Lucullus at

Tusculum: there were a canal with bridges, groves, fishponds, and colonnades covered with a hemp net, and filled with all kinds of birds. Another aviary was round and domed, with columns and a net again preventing the birds from escaping into a surrounding wood planted with large trees. Inside the dome, the morning and evening stars circled near the lower part of the hemisphere, and a compass of the eight winds indicated the direction of the wind.

In the Roman villas a love of nature, the old agricultural traditions of Italy, and the fanciful luxury and refinement of hellenistic palatial architecture and pleasure grounds (παράδεισοι) met. All that has to be kept in mind also for what Martial (XII, 57. 21) calls 'rus in urbe', i.e. landscape gardens in Rome itself, like that of Nero's Golden House. According to Tacitus (*Ann.*, XV, 42), in the eyes of the Romans the greatest marvel of this palace was that it was a villa brought to the town, with its groves, pastures, herds, wild animals, and artificial rural solitude.[69]

BATHS, THEATRES, AND OTHER PUBLIC BUILDINGS

Pompeii shows, and Vitruvius in his fifth book describes, how hellenistic accomplishments were offered to the public at large and became *consuetudo italica* in the last centuries B.C. The display of works of art, for instance, and the *fornices* (triumphal arches), also with statues, were now part of the everyday life of the citizens. An example is the fornix at Cosa, dating from after 150. The so-called decumanus at Ostia has, in front of a granary of the early first century A.D., porticoes facing the theatre on the opposite, north side of the street. This kind of public amenity was obviously inherited by the Imperial Age from Late Republican towns.[70]

Baths and Palaestrae

The domus and villas, with their peristyles and other luxuries, also had baths (*balneae, balineae, balnea, balneolae*), and they grew larger and

larger, and more and more luxurious too. Seneca notes that the bath (*balneolum*) in Scipio Africanus's villa at Liternum in Campania was small and dark, 'according to the old style', 'for our ancestors did not think that one could have a hot bath except in darkness' (*Epist.*, LXXXVI, 4). That was no doubt also true of the old public baths, but in the second century at Pompeii they began to grow more elaborate. After a dressing-room (*apodyterium*) followed the warm *tepidarium* and the hot *caldarium*. We see this system, obviously Greek in origin, in the Stabian Baths of the second century and the Forum Baths at Pompeii built for the Roman colony about 80 B.C. [178]. The *caldaria* have an apse with a round basin for cold water (*schola labri*) and, at the other end of the room, a rectangular bath-tub with hot water. Both these baths have domed rooms with an aperture left in the middle of the dome and round basins for cold water (*frigidaria*), attached to the dressing-rooms. Vitruvius (V, 10. 5) recommends rooms of the same kind next to the tepidarium for steam baths. In such *laconica*, as Vitruvius calls them, a bronze disc hung from the aperture in the dome; 'by raising or lowering it, the temperature of the sweat bath can be regulated'. These features remained unchanged in all later baths, however grand and sumptuous they became in the Imperial Age. In the Late Republican baths, domes seem to have been the only form of masonry vaulting. Vitruvius discusses wooden vaults with a framework tiled on the underside, and describes how they should be constructed (V, 10. 3). Great vaulted halls came only with the Imperial Age. The first instance known to us is a large rotunda with a mighty dome built of concrete on the seashore at Baiae. It belongs to the Late Republican or Augustan Age.[70a]

The balnea of the towns and villas became hot-air baths, but to start with they were heated by pans containing charcoal. A brazier remains in the tepidarium of the Forum Baths of Pompeii. About 100 B.C. another system existed with hot air conducted from a furnace room below the floors, which were supported by pillars of brick. The advantage of the new sys-

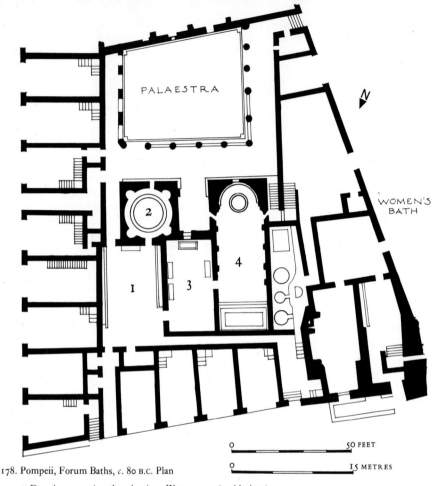

178. Pompeii, Forum Baths, *c.* 80 B.C. Plan

1. Dressing room (apodyterium)   3. Warm room (tepidarium)
2. Cold room (frigidarium)   4. Hot room (caldarium)

tem was that the rooms were free of smoke, dust, etc. This system spread to baths, and also palaces and private houses, throughout the Roman Empire. It lived on in Byzantine and Turkish baths and also in medieval Europe. The Romans ascribed the 'invention' of *pensiles balineae* to a rich and enterprising Roman, G. Sergius Orata, who lived at the beginning of the first century B.C. and was also the first to have oyster ponds. However, excavations in Greece have shown that the Greeks were again the first.

From the Augustan Age onwards we see in Rome and the provinces large-scale bathing establishments, known as *thermae*, built on large terraces, surrounded by gardens, and with central halls, palaestrae, etc., planned with strict axiality. All this – as far as we know – was unfamiliar to the Late Republican architects, but as the Stabian and Forum Baths at Pompeii show, peristyles were then already added to the balnear rooms. The swimming pool of the Stabian Baths confirms that palaestrae at the back were there for the purpose of gymnastic exercise.

This combination of bath and palaestra marks an important step towards the great symmetrical unities of the centuries to come. Vitruvius affirms that palaestrae were not part of the Roman tradition (v, 11. 1), but were Greek meeting-places, where 'rhetoricians and others who delight in learning' gathered in the peristyles, while gymnastics were practised around them. Behind the principal palaestra, Vitruvius describes stadia, running tracks, etc., such as had existed in Late Republican and Augustan times on the Campus Martius, with the yellow Tiber for swimming and diving. According to Livy (XXIX, 19. 11 ff.), the conservative Romans censured Scipio Africanus because in Magna Graecia he strolled about in the palaestrae, wearing a Greek mantle and sandals, and giving his attention to books in Greek and physical exercise. In contrast to this, the Osco-Samnites of Pompeii already in the second century added a great square peristyle surrounded by porticoes (a palaestra-inspired feature) to their theatre, as Vitruvius recommends (v, 9. 1), and as Pompey did when he erected his theatre in Rome. The peristyle was built behind the stage, but above the theatre the Osco-Samnite Pompeians also had a small, gracious palaestra, a rectangular peristyle, but without running tracks, etc. [64]. The function of this palaestra was proclaimed by a very fine copy of Polyclitus's Doryphorus in front of the south portico. In Imperial times this palaestra was shortened by a Temple of Isis on its eastern side, and the great quadriportico behind the stage was reshaped and used as a barracks for the gladiators.

We cannot say if second-century Rome approved of the combination of a typically Greek palaestra with the bath-houses as they developed in Italic practice. It may have been connected with the uninhibited way of life of the Campanian towns. In any case, the Forum Baths of the Roman colony at Pompeii prove that the novelty was accepted in Rome about 100 B.C. Among many other baths, the Central Baths of Pompeii and the Terme di Nettuno on the decumanus of Ostia show that the asym-metric plan of the balneolae which the architects of Late Republican days had provided for practical demands in hellenized Italic towns, lived on side by side with the majestic, axial architecture of Imperial Age thermae. Several small baths on the Forma Urbis with irregular courts and the usual bathrooms alongside them prove the same. The catalogue of the regions of Rome in the fourth century A.D. lists 11 thermae and 856 balneolae. The latter, no doubt, usually kept the informal Late Republican pattern.

The Forum Baths at Pompeii and the Terme di Nettuno of Imperial Ostia have one more feature worth mentioning: narrow rows of tabernae surrounded the whole establishment, with upper apartments accessible by direct staircases from the street. This of course made the baths more profitable. In Imperial times we see the same rows of shops with lodgings above them facing the streets around the peristyles of the granaries (*horrea*), and even in the portico around the façade of the Circus Maximus in Rome and of the theatre at Ostia.[71]

Circuses

Another aspect of town life, the entertainment of the people, was provided for in olden days by the Circus Maximus, for horse-races and different kinds of games. It lay in the long valley between the slopes of the Palatine and the Aventine [105]. Later, other circuses and theatres followed, and finally in the Flavian Age the Colosseum was dedicated in A.D. 80. As I have said above, there is no reason to doubt that the tradition of the circus went back to the age of the kings. Livy (VIII, 20. 1) reports that the first permanent carceres (starting gates) were built in 329 B.C., though they were probably of wood. They were at the straight, western end of the circus. Cicero (*De divinatione*, I, 108) quotes Ennius describing how the spectators waited eagerly for the chariots to come out of the painted gates. In 174 the censors restored the carceres. Some twenty years before, in 196, L. Stertinius, as an *ex voto* for his victories in Spain, had erected an arch with gilded statues, the Fornix Stertinii (of the same kind as is known somewhat later from the Forum Romanum and Cosa), at the curved east end of the racecourse. Gradually the course was surrounded by wooden seats. It was divided lengthwise by a low wall, the *spina*, around which the races were run. Conical columns, the *metae*, stood at the ends of the spina, marking the turning-points. In Augustan days (Dionysius, III, 68) the spectators' stands had three storeys, the lowest with stone seats and the two upper with wooden seats. On the outside of the circus were shops with dwellings over them, and between the shops were entrances with stairs for the spectators. Probably the lowest rows of seats were built on the slope of the northern and southern hillsides, whereas the upper seats and the building around the curved eastern side were supported by wooden structures.

In 220 the censor C. Flaminius built another circus, the Circus Flaminius, on the low, flat riverside by the Tiber, with its southern end at the crossing to the Tiber island. How was this circus constructed, since there was no natural slope? Perhaps, like a theatre at Capua of about 100 B.C., a small theatre at Gioiosa Ionica, or the stadium of Olympia, the seats were on artificial embankments around the stage; but it seems more probable that wooden structures were erected and that they were among the first of their kind.[72]

Theatres

The history of the Roman theatres exemplifies especially clearly how Greek culture was grafted on to the old and warlike Italic life. Theatres came late. No doubt in central Italy rustic dances and recitations of verse were performed in the early days by 'fauns and native bards', to quote Cicero (*Brutus*, 71), but, according to Livy (VII, 2), a change took place in Rome in the fourth century. Among attempts to mitigate the effects of a plague in 364 B.C. was the addition to the Roman circus of players who had been brought from some Etruscan town, just as, according to Herodotus (I, 167), the inhabitants of Caere, in an attempt to get rid of a national

scourge, had introduced Greek games and horse races in the sixth century, following advice from Delphi. These *histriones*, as they were called (from *ister*, the Etruscan word for players), 'danced to the strains of the flute and performed not ungraceful motions in the Tuscan fashion without any singing, and without imitating the action of singers'. This tale of Livy's illustrates the beginnings of Roman scenic entertainments. Already about 240 B.C. a Greek from Tarentum, Livius Andronicus, had devised for the Romans a play with a plot. Other Greek theatrical performances - comedies, tragedies, and satirical plays in Latin - soon became a feature of Roman festivals such as the Ludi Romani, Plebeii, Apollinares, Megalenses, Florales, and Ceriales, as well as of burials and the consecration of temples. Plautus and Terence bring all this to life for us.[73]

The theatres which were erected for these early plays in Rome itself were of wood, and evidently imitated temporary stages in the towns of south Italy, while - as the history of sanctuaries around Rome has shown - outside Rome and its closest environs permanent, stone-built theatres were admitted, at least if they were connected with temples, already about 100 B.C. It should always be remembered that both the great hellenistic permanent theatres, embodying traditions from the fifth century, and the temporary wooden structures of south Italy were known from the beginnings in Rome. In south Italy, after the fashion of the neighbouring Greek towns, permanent theatres were erected a hundred years earlier than in Rome: the highly hellenized Osco-Samnites of Pompeii, for example, built a permanent theatre in the second century [179]. In Rome, Pompey's theatre, built when he had returned from Greece with the theatre of Mitylene in mind, was the first, and dates only from 55 B.C.

At first the theatre at Pompeii simply had tufa or limestone seats resting on the southern hillside of the town, which was north-east of the archaic Greek temple. We can follow this development with the help of Vitruvius (V, 6. 2) and see how sectors of seats (*cunei*) were divided from each other in a regular way by passage-

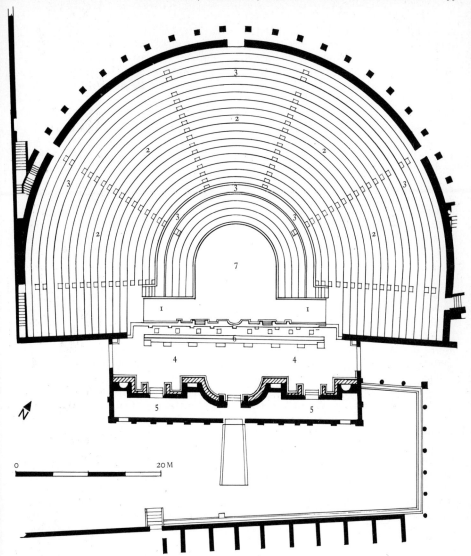

179. Pompeii, Large Theatre,
second century B.C. Plan of final state

1. Parodoi
2. Cunei
3. Praecinctiones
4. Pulpitum
5. Scaena
6. Slot for aulaeum
7. Orchestra

ways, and how curved cross aisles (*praecinctiones*) after Greek models became accepted practice. The large, square peristyle mentioned on p. 197 lay behind the stage. Elegant, stuccoed Doric columns, with an unfluted lower part that was painted red, adorned the porticoes on all sides of the peristyle. Vitruvius (v, 9) gives detailed rules (no doubt Greek) for building these porticoes behind stage-houses, explaining how useful they were for the public when showers interrupted the plays, for walks in the open air, and for 'getting ready all the stage properties'. He also strongly emphasizes how indispensable they became for storing wood in times of siege and war. The theatres of Pompey and Balbus in Rome and the theatre of Ostia with their large peristyles prove that what Vitruvius recommends, and what the Osco-Samnites had built at least a hundred years before, became accepted in Late Republican and Augustan Rome, whether the Romans took the idea from Campania and south Italy or whether Pompey brought it with him from Greece.

From the first, like the Greek theatres, the theatre at Pompeii had a narrow stage-house behind the stage. The stage podium (*pulpitum*, λογεῖον) was wide, but, perhaps also after the Greek fashion, raised fairly high above the orchestra. It had side wings (παρασκήνια) which converged inwards to the façade of the stage-house. This façade (the *scaenae frons*), the stage-front, and the stage itself could all – with some degree of confusion – be referred to as the *proscaenium*.

Wide and low stages were characteristic of the wooden theatres in Rome and of their later tradition. It is obvious that Rome took the main elements of theatrical architecture from the Greeks, though to start with not from the hellenistic theatres known from excavations in Greece and described by Vitruvius, but from the roomy stages of the popular comedies in Italy. These could be high and supported by columns, or low with stairs leading up to the pulpitum from some open space – a sacred precinct, the arena of a circus, or wherever the shows were performed – as retained in Roman theatres. The contemporary Greek stages are delightfully illustrated in south Italian vase paintings. In contrast to them and to the Roman stages, hellenistic theatres had narrow stages raised up some 10 feet. The chorus and supporting artists gave their performances in the orchestra, in front of the stage. These orchestras were roomier than the Roman ones. A characteristic of the latter – as the theatres of Gabii,

Praeneste, and Tivoli [157, 158] show – is that they were semicircular.

Vitruvius (v, 6–7) contrasts the final arrangement in Italy with that of hellenistic theatres. According to him, the stages (*pulpita*) of Roman theatres should always be deeper than those of the Greeks and 'raised not more than five feet': this was because the orchestras in Roman theatres contained seats reserved for the senators. Here we see how the demands of Roman social life, together with the kind of shows performed, contributed to the final shape of the Roman theatres.

A terracotta model of a stage building of about 300 B.C. [180] from a town in southern Italy displays a permanent scaenae frons with the same main characteristics that the Romans adopted. It seems that they almost immediately imitated Greek stage-decorations and – if a short note did not suffice to indicate the setting – that for tragedies they were decorated as palace façades with columns, for comedies as private dwellings with balconies, windows, and upper storeys (*cenacula*: Plautus, *Amphitruo*, 863), for satyr-plays with trees, caverns, mountains, and other rustic properties (Vitruvius, v, 6. 9). According to Vitruvius, and as the stage model just referred to shows, the palace sets had double doors in the centre decorated like those of a royal palace and to the right and left the 'doors of the guest chambers'. Another original feature inherited from south Italy and the Greeks was revolving pieces of machinery (περίακτοι) to the right and left of the doors, each with three decorated faces, to indicate the mood. The exits on the short sides were considered to be entrances, 'one from the forum, the other from abroad'. The Romans also adopted from the Greeks curtains (*siparia*) which were hung before parts of the scaenae frons and could be drawn up or to the side, and others (*aulaea*) that were lowered at the beginning of a show and raised at its end from a trench along the front side of the stage. The theatre at Pompeii shows such an arrangement, and we are told that pictorial hangings were brought to Rome already in the second century from the royal palace of Pergamon and

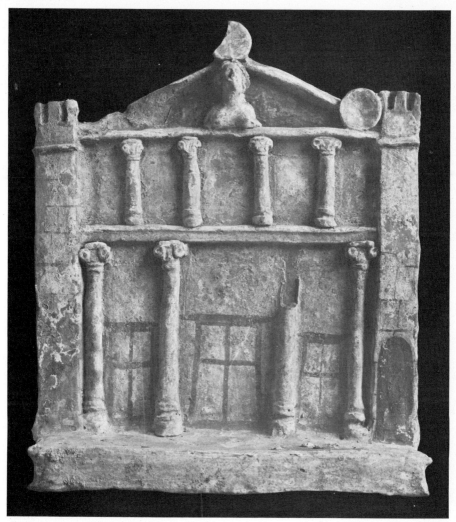

180. Terracotta model of a stage building,
c. 300 B.C. *Naples, Museo Nazionale*

used as drop-scenes. But, like all the other elements of the Roman stage, this achieved its final shape only in the Imperial Age, and for Late Republican times can only be traced in literary sources and from insufficient remains.

At the beginning there were objections not only to Greek entertainments as such but also to allotting seats to the plebs in temporary theatres. Our sources sometimes confuse this with the reaction against permanent theatres, but Tacitus (*Ann.*, XIV, 20) gives a precise summary of the main facts: 'To go further back into the past, the people stood to watch. Seats in theatres, it was feared, might tempt them to pass whole days in indolence.' In any case, in Plautus's comedies we already encounter a theatre with wooden seats: a *cavea*, as the Latin word is. Until 194 plebeians and senators were accommodated together, but in that year Scipio Africanus and the censors ordered the curule aediles to separate the senatorial seats from those of the commoners at the Ludi Romani. The seats could be constructed on earthen embankments or hillsides – like the stone seats of Greek theatres and the theatre at Pompeii – but they could also, of course, be erected on a flat site, a technique which became important for the large permanent theatres of Rome in the centuries to come.[74]

The seating regulations in Scipio Africanus's time, i.e. in 194, show us how one of these temporary structures operated. In 179 Livy (XL, 51) mentions a stage building and seats for spectators at the Temple of Apollo, no doubt the temple behind the Theatre of Marcellus that in its rebuilt Augustan shape was called Sosianus. Like the theatres of Gabii, Praeneste, and Tivoli, the theatre here was closely connected with a sanctuary; the Augustan Sosianus Temple and the Theatre of Marcellus certainly renewed this connexion. Livy's words (XLI, 27. 5) referring to 174, about 'a stage placed at the disposal of the aediles and praetors', whose duty it was to arrange plays, may indicate a more permanent building. However, as already mentioned, after the censor Lucius Cassius had begun to build a permanent theatre in 154, it was demolished on a motion of P. Scipio Nasica, as a potential hotbed of sedition and because it seemed 'far from desirable that the Romans should be accustomed to Greek pleasures'. According to Velleius Paterculus, it was 'located in the direction of the Palatine from the Lupercal', that is, on the south-western slope of the Palatine, below the Temple of Magna Mater, and had seats facing the valley of the Circus Maximus. The Ludi Megalenses were celebrated in front of this temple, 'in the very sight of the goddess', as Cicero says (*De haruspicum responsis*, 24). Cicero clearly indicates that there were two theatres on the slope of the Palatine

facing the Circus valley. He is indignant when he tells how Clodius at a celebration of the Megalensia let slaves loose in one theatre and ejected every free man from another (25, 26). This, as well as the mimes of the Ludi Florales in front of the Temple of Flora on the Aventine, directly recalls the theatres in front of the temple at Gabii and the round Temple of Fortuna Primigenia at Praeneste (as I interpret it), the theatre below the great temple of Pietrabbondante, and that of Hercules Victor at Tivoli. One should, in any case, remember that plays were performed at funerals as well and that in 167, according to Polybius (Athenaeus, XIV, 615a-e), Lucius Anicius built a very large stage in the Circus Maximus. He summoned distinguished musicians from Greece and posted them with the chorus in the orchestra 'at the front of the stage' (ἐπί τό πρυσκήνιον). Finally, four boxers climbed on to the stage, accompanied by trumpeters and horn players.[75]

The theatre that Lucius Mummius built after his victory in Greece, in 145-144 (cf. Tacitus, *Annales*, XIV, 21), was no doubt decorated by marbles which he had brought from Corinth. It appears to have been an early and sensational stage building. Among the wasteful luxuries of these temporary structures were cloths that were used as awnings. This convenience, used by the Etruscans already in archaic times (see p. 75), now became common; in Caesar's time it spread to the gladiatorial games on the Forum Romanum and to the adjoining streets (Pliny, XIX, 23). In 99 Claudius Pulcher adorned his theatre with paintings, which, according to Pliny (XXXV, 23), were so realistic that crows tried to alight on the roof tiles, and at the games of Scribonius Libo in 63 the architect Valerius of Ostia (Pliny, XXXVI, 102) roofed the theatre. Roman stage-houses (*scaenae*) soon came to be decorated with gold, silver, ivory, or marble façades and columns from Mount Hymettus, and later on from still more famous quarries, and columns from the temporary theatres were later used in the palaces of the Roman politicians. Pliny echoes the contemporary indignation at this corrupting private luxury. The climax of all this short-lived magnificence – the Romans outdid the luxury of the Campanians and Greeks in the first century – was the theatre erected by M. Aemilius Scaurus during his aedileship in 58. Pliny affirms that it 'surpassed not merely those erected for a limited period but even those intended to last forever'.

Details no doubt became exaggerated and even legendary before they reached Pliny, but his description makes the main arrangement clear and shows how Roman architects enriched the stage. It is also of considerable interest for the great theatres of the Imperial Age. To understand the link between the stages of south Italy and the later splendours, it is essential to read Pliny's chapter about Scaurus's theatre, even if it is too highly coloured. Tacitus dryly remarks (*Ann.*, XIV, 21) that it was a measure of economy to build permanent theatres instead of wooden structures which had to be reared and razed, year after year.

Scaurus's stage had three storeys: the lowest was of Lucullean marble (either veneer or solid blocks), while the middle one was faced with glass mosaic and the top one with gilded plates. According to Pliny there were 360 columns in front, the lowest to be 38 feet high. For the bronze statues in the spaces between the columns, Pliny gives the fantastic number of 3,000. He also reports that the auditorium accommodated 80,000 spectators, while Pompey's theatre some ten years later had seats for only 40,000 (though the fact is that the latter had room for only about 10,000). To this we have to add the luxurious costumes of the actors, and paintings such as those in the Theatre of Claudius Pulcher. Whether the canal (*euripus*) in which a hippopotamus and five crocodiles were exhibited at the games during Scaurus's aedileship was actually part of the theatre is not certain.

The next sensational innovation seems to have been a theatre erected in 52 by C. Scribonius Curio in honour of his father's funeral. Curio, as Pliny says (XXXVI, 116–20), could not hope to outstrip Scaurus with costly embellishments, but he built two large wooden theatres

close to each other, facing in opposite directions and balanced on revolving pivots. Here, as in front of the Temple of Magna Mater, we have two theatres in which performances of different plays were given simultaneously. These theatres could revolve, even with spectators remaining in their seats, so that Curio was able to convert his two theatres into an amphitheatre for gladiatorial combats. For practical reasons we must assume that this amphitheatre was round, like the Imperial amphitheatre of Lucus Feroniae, or the cistern represented in the Egyptian landscape of the great mosaic at Praeneste. We do not know by what means it was rotated and thus have the same problem as with the main, circular banqueting hall in Nero's Golden House, which, according to Suetonius (*Nero*, 31), revolved constantly night and day. According to Pliny, the device put Curio's spectators in as great danger as the gladiators. When the pivots wore out, he kept the amphitheatre and re-erected in it two stages, back to back. They could then be moved aside to make room for the gladiators. As in the case of some of the theatres, Curio's amphitheatre was built on flat ground with free-standing spectators' seating which had to be wholly constructed.[76]

The amphitheatre at Pompeii, built by two Roman magistrates (*duoviri*) for the veterans of the Colonia Cornelia Veneria after 80, shows us how early amphitheatres were constructed [181]. They did not yet have subterranean quarters for the gladiators, animals, equipment, etc. Like the later and more famous ones, this first-known amphitheatre was oval. It measured 500 by 350 feet (150 by 105 m.) and could hold some 20,000 spectators. To start with, the spectators evidently sat either on earthen slopes or on artificial embankments converging towards the arena, with or without wooden benches. The mass of earth – as in the theatre of Pietrabbondante – was surrounded by a broad structure of concrete, covered by opus incertum and strengthened by buttresses joined by arches. This is one of the most impressive plain arcaded façades in Italy. Stone seats were added later. The two lower rows – evidently reserved for

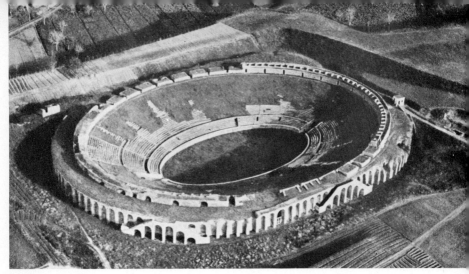

181. Pompeii, amphitheatre, after 80 B.C.

magistrates, etc. – were accessible from a corridor which was built on the level of the arena and had special entrances. The two main entrances to the arena were on the main north-west–south-east axis; the latter was blocked by the city wall, but was reached by a corridor from the west façade. Two great double staircases outside the west side of the amphitheatre and single outside staircases towards the northern and southern ends of the structure led to the top of the galleries – in striking contrast to the inner entrances to the cavea of the theatres and amphitheatres of the Imperial Age. Below the central double staircase on the west side was a narrow passage, which has been explained as a reserved entrance for the magistrate in charge of the games or as a gate of Libitina, the goddess of corpses, through which dead gladiators were carried out. The sectors of seats were divided into three tiers, the uppermost perhaps for women. The upper terrace as we see it, with arched boxes, was evidently of later construction, for its building material is different from that of the lower parts of the façade. A parapet with a metal fence protected the spectators from the arena, and another parapet separated the distinguished spectators in the lower seats from the upper tiers (just as the aristocracy came to be separated from the plebs in Roman theatres).

As in the theatres, awnings were stretched from poles above the whole interior.[77]

What we can trace of the first period in the theatre of Pompeii and see in the Roman amphitheatre of Sulla's Colonia Cornelia Veneria is obviously important for a full understanding of some of the greatest Roman architectural creations: the great theatres and amphitheatres of the Imperial Age. They reveal formative and creative traditions stemming from south Italy and from the great permanent hellenistic theatres with their pedigree going back to the sixth century, and their encounter with the social and political conditions of Rome and the demands of Roman taste, as well as from the temporary wooden theatres in Rome.

From these early attempts of a temporary character – an outburst of a *nouveau riche* passion for show – it is a far cry to the first great permanent theatre in Rome, the Theatre of Pompey, and also to the two slightly earlier theatres at Pompeii (as remodelled for the Roman colonia), the theatres of the Latin sanctuaries, and the contemporary theatre of Alba Fucens. In them the low, wide stage and the cavea became a unified block, in contrast to the Greek theatres with their open side entrances to the orchestra (*parodoi*), right and left of the stage. Instead, barrel-vaulted entrances to the semicircular orchestra were built on both sides. Rows of seats continued above the barrel-vaults, exactly as Vitruvius prescribes; this innovation can be seen in the theatre at Pompeii as rebuilt to serve the Roman colony [179]. At this time it received a low Roman stage, and also a curious circular water basin in the orchestra with a diameter of 23 feet (7·10 m.), whose use has been much discussed. Most likely the water was introduced for performances by nude pantomimists. It could hardly have been used in the orchestras of Roman theatres, where the senators had reserved seats. There was an extensive restoration of the theatre in Augustan times, but the stage took its final form only after the earthquake of A.D. 62. During the Augustan period a covered corridor (*crypta*) with six doors (*vomitoria*), leading to the six staircases between the five sectors (*cunei*) of the cavea, was built above the cavea.[78]

Together with the amphitheatre, the small Roofed Theatre at Pompeii is, together with the theatre-temples, the earliest complete archaeological evidence of the great achievements of Roman architects (such as Valerius of Ostia) during the two hundred years or so of temporary theatres. This *theatrum tectum* (to use the name given to it in the dedicatory inscription) was built at the expense of the same Roman magistrates who constructed the amphitheatre for the Roman colonia. It was a concert hall for music and recitation, added to the enlarged and modernized great theatre on the east side of its stage. Thus Roman Pompeii received what Statius in his *Silvae* (III, 5. 91) describes from Naples: a great group consisting of an open and a covered theatre. The hall had a wooden roof without supports. Such roofing was one of the great prides of Imperial Rome, and the Theatrum Tectum is the first specimen known to us of that daring construction. The theatre is of concrete, surrounded by a rectangular outer wall and faced with opus incertum which has strengthening additions of tiles and tends towards being reticulate. The high walls slice the cavea to right and left. The back corners of the rectangular building were used for entrances,

in addition to semicircular stairs right and left of the seats round the orchestra. Calculated to hold an audience of 1,500, the five sectors of seats and their passageways were not interrupted by cross aisles (*praecinctiones*). As in the remodelled larger theatre, vaulted entrances lead to the orchestra; above them were platforms (*tribunalia*) and behind them three rows of seats. The stage was low and wide.

The theatre of Alba Fucens belongs to the same epoch. It was enlarged in Early Imperial times, and only some parts of its cavea remain. Most of the seats rested upon the living rock of the Pettorino Hill east of the town, but the north-west side of the cavea was completed by a structure of concrete. The ends of the tiers of seats were supported by grandiose terrace walls (*analemmata*) of polygonal work. In front of them was a portico leading to the side entrances (*parodoi*), which otherwise were open, as in Greek theatres. There are no vaulted entrances, and the theatre of Alba Fucens was thus not, in the Roman way, united in a great block comprising stage-house, stage, and cavea. We meet the same arrangement in the plan of Pompey's theatre on the Forma Urbis. On the stage are pits for movable scaffolding, but behind its low and wide platform only vestiges of the stage-house remain. The portico and a short cross street connected the theatre with the eastern main street of Alba Fucens, the Via dei Pilastri, and with the Temple and Portico of Hercules on the other side [139].[79]

The final summing-up of this stage of Roman theatrical architecture is the Theatre of Pompey, built during Pompey's second consulship in 55 B.C. and dedicated in 52. We know this revolutionary structure from the plan on the Forma Urbis, numerous literary sources, the considerable remains of the substructure of the cavea, which was built in concrete covered by reticulate, and other parts of the great group on the Campus Martius.[80] Tacitus (*Ann.*, XIII, 54) tells us of the barbarians who visited Rome in Nero's time and were guided to 'the usual places shown to barbarians, among them the Theatre of Pompey'. To Nero, who on one occasion gilded the whole façade, it seemed small, especially compared with the gilded façade of his Domus Aurea; but Dio Cassius (XXXIX, 38) affirms that the Romans took pride in the theatre even in his time, and Ammianus Marcellinus mentions it as one of the great monuments of fourth-century Rome (XVI, 10. 14). It was variously referred to as 'the marble theatre', 'the great theatre', and sometimes simply as 'the theatre'.

The plan on the Forma Urbis, dated between A.D. 203 and 211, reveals the same arrangement as the theatre of Alba Fucens: a low, wide stage, open parodoi with porticoes, and a semicircular orchestra. To begin with the stage-house was probably wooden, but Pliny mentions that it held copies of celebrated sculptures of high quality and that around it were statues of fourteen nations (VII, 34; XXXVI, 41). As in the theatre at Pompeii, there was a great rectangular peristyle behind the stage-house with roomy recesses (*exedrae spatiosae*) provided with seats for philosophers, etc., in conformity with Vitruvius's rules (V, 9; 11. 2). The senate was probably assembled in one of these *exedrae*, which contained a statue of Pompey, or perhaps in some other hall connected with the peristyle, on the occasion when Caesar was murdered.[81] An important novelty was that the entrances were no longer external but placed inside, as in the later theatres and amphitheatres of the Imperial Age; we do not know whether this reflected the arrangements in the wooden theatres or was a new architectural scheme.

In contrast to the rectangular building of the small theatre at Pompeii, the façade of Pompey's theatre followed the curved outline of the cavea. Our sources praise especially the fact that Pompey placed a shrine of Venus above the cavea, and that the steps to it served as a most monumental ascent to that temple. It was said that Pompey did this to disarm opposition to the permanent theatre as such, and indeed in his public invitation to the dedication he announced it not as a theatre but as a Temple of Venus, 'under which we have placed steps for spectators of shows'. On top of the cavea there

were other shrines of Honor, Virtus, Felicitas, and one more goddess.[82]

Plutarch (*Pompey*, 42, 4) says that Pompey very much admired the theatre of Mitylene and 'had a model of it made, intending to erect one in Rome to the same design, but larger and more magnificent'. There has been much speculation about this statement and about what Pompey actually took over. It should certainly be kept in mind that all the main features of Pompey's theatre agree with what the Romans and Campanians had already achieved from the third century onwards in their adaptation of Greek features. For example, the concave or amphitheatrical comitia [138], with a curia on the central axis on top of the stairs, show the same disposition as the Theatre of Pompey. The theatre-temples of Gabii, Praeneste, Tivoli, and Pietrabbondante afford equally striking parallels.[83]

UTILITARIAN ARCHITECTURE

To turn now to utilitarian architecture, one must first of all recall the Porticus Aemilia (see p. 128 f.)[125] on the quay of the Tiber, south of the Aventine. Behind, warehouses – granaries – were built by Servius Sulpicius Galba, who was consul in 108 B.C. Evidently Rome adopted the system of the hellenistic world known from Rhodes, where, according to Strabo (XIV, 2. 5), the people were supplied with provisions and the needy supported by the well-to-do. As early as the fifth and fourth centuries, and long before any far-reaching Mediterranean trade had started, our sources repeatedly tell us about supplies of corn and food from Sicily, Cumae, and the Etruscan coastal towns that were brought to Rome in river-boats via the Tiber, or from Ostia. Famine threatened if the Tiber became unnavigable, if internal strife hampered agriculture, or if the magistrates lacked proper care. It is evident that some kind of granaries became necessary along the riverside long before these. The Romans ascribed the Columna Minucia (above, p. 99), which was erected somewhere outside the Porta Trigemina in the south-western part of the great city wall of 378

B.C., to Lucius Minucius, a magistrate who in 439 B.C. was in charge of the provision of Rome's grain and food, and who took possession of the stores brought to the town by the demagogue Maelius and distributed them on easy terms to the people. This tale, legendary or not, attests that the surroundings of Galba's granary were thought of as an early centre for the import of victuals. Horrea publica are known to us only from the Imperial Age; Late Republican horrea may have been walled and citadel-like, like the granaries of Syracuse, and they probably had courtyards surrounded by storage rooms of the same type as the tabernae. All the horrea of Imperial Rome exhibit such a plan, and the markets of hellenistic towns seem to have been the origin. In the Near East the tradition has lived on through the centuries in caravanserais (khans).[84]

Strabo, with Greek towns and their harbours in mind, notes (V, 3. 5) with amazement that the port-town of Rome was 'harbourless on account of the silting up'. The merchant ships anchored outside the mouth of the Tiber at Ostia. Tenders then took their cargoes, brought them to the riverside harbours of Rome, and took back cargoes in exchange; or they relieved the overseas ships of part of their cargo so that they could be towed to Rome. In other words, Ostia had only an old-fashioned river harbour like those along the Laurentine and Rutulian coast, from which the new commercial centre took over the legend of Aeneas. The need for granaries, etc., at Ostia for its own consumption and for temporary storage was probably met by wooden warehouses on the riverside east of the castrum and north of the decumanus [123], which was vacant until the first century B.C. In the second half of the century, rows of tabernae in reticulate (the so-called Magazzini Repubblicani), surrounded by porticoes with tufa piers, were built on the north side of the decumanus, towards the east gate of Ostia's city wall.[85]

As seen in the Hercules Victor terrace at Tivoli (pp. 166–9), streets lined with shops were sometimes united in a way that suggests a shopping centre and are reminiscent of the tunnels of tent-makers and saddlers in the old bazaars

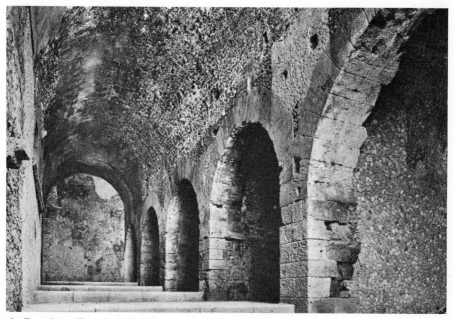

182. Ferentinum (Ferentino), Via Latina, market hall, c. 100 B.C.

of Aleppo. Buttressing the citadels of Ferentinum and Tibur (Tivoli) are warehouses of concrete, dating from about 100 B.C. and faced with opus incertum. They had high, broad barrel-vaulted corridors running transversely from the streets towards the hillsides [182], and they recall the stone-built barrel-vaulted structures, on which a great podium was raised, that Herod built at Caesarea Maritima in Palestine. The latter were probably warehouses too, but the warehouses at Ferentinum and Tivoli were more accomplished and had a row of five shops along one side. At Ferentinum these tabernae are barrel-vaulted. The floor of the 'nave' in front of them rises by low and broad steps towards its inner end. The entrance was about 26 feet high. The Tivoli warehouse is more elegant, and, moreover, the height of the entrance was about 30 feet, and that of the first shop inside the entrance arch some 35 feet. The first two shops have high barrel-vaults, and the three inner ones are covered by apsidal vaults.[86] It seems evident that the souks, warehouses, and covered streets of the Orient served as models, but concrete and vaulting made it possible for the Roman builders to develop the borrowed ideas in a new and monumental way. The architectural tradition stemming from these Late Republican innovations was evidently an inspiring factor when, in the second century A.D., the monumental warehouses were built outside the Forum of Trajan and at Ostia.

As the lofty entrances to the warehouses of Tivoli and Ferentinum show, in the last centuries B.C. arches became the rule for city gates and for façades with or without flanking columns, as well as for fornices, heralding the triumphal arches of the Empire. They are also a most important part of utilitarian architecture. In 179 the Pons Aemilius in Rome was equipped with stone-built piers of tufa ashlar work supporting a wooden bridge; Livy (XL, 51. 4) reports that the censors of 142 built arches (fornices) on these supports. Later, in 62, the magistrate in charge of roads, L. Fabricius, built the beautiful Pons Fabricius between the left bank of the Tiber and the Tiber island. It

was constructed of tufa ashlar blocks faced with travertine. In 109 the Pons Mulvius (Ponte Molle) of 220 on the Via Flaminia north-west of Rome was replaced by a bridge of tufa ashlar with arches of travertine – part of which can still be seen in the present bridge. Livy (XLI, 27. 5) relates that the censors of 174, when reordering the roads outside Rome with gravel and footpaths, also built bridges, and these were probably arched. Beautiful early examples are the bridge on the Via Amerina, constructed in the third century [121], and the old, low one below the Ponte di Nona on the Via Praenestina.[87]

The arch also revolutionized a field of utilitarian architecture where even a Greek like Strabo (V, 3. 8) admits that the Romans were outstanding: aqueducts and sewers. Marzabotto shows how the Etruscans solved the problem of sewerage by channels covered by slabs. We have seen that the largest of the Roman sewers, the Cloaca Maxima – originally a stream running obliquely through the forum – was probably an open channel still in the second century, at least on the forum. Otherwise, the sewers may have been more or less similar to those of Marzabotto. In any case, at the end of the second century the Cloaca Maxima was vaulted with close-fitting stones (Strabo, loc. cit.) and widened. Strabo writes that 'sewers in some places were roomy enough even for wagons loaded with hay to pass through them'. Perhaps that was due to reconstructions during the Augustan Age, but parts of vaults survive which must be much older than that; for example, the three concentric arches at the mouth of the Cloaca Maxima on the left bank of the Tiber opposite the island (to judge from the material) must be dated as early as about 100 B.C., though some attribute them to Agrippa.[88]

The first aqueduct built by the Romans was the Appia of 312 B.C. The channel was almost entirely subterranean, like that of its successor Anio Vetus of 272. After countless centuries with the provision of water by the Tiber and by wells, and after the great, though primitive, undertaking of Appius Claudius, the great revolution in this field was the Aqua Marcia, built in 144-140 by Quintus Marcius Rex. The channel (*specus*) was lined with a thick cement of lime and pounded terracotta, and, like the Etruscan sewers, covered by slabs. Since the flow of the current was carefully calculated, it brought a constant stream of water into the town. It was carried by arches, which starts one of the greatest architectural traditions of Imperial Rome. The arches and their piers were built of tufa ashlar, a proof of how the Romans trusted their various tufas and also of how ingeniously they economized by using especially strong blocks only where they were needed, and cheaper kinds where they were not. This is typical for the Late Republican centuries. Frontinus, in his famous work on the aqueducts of Rome, in discussing the Marcia (I, 7) tells us that when the officials in charge of the Sibylline books were consulting them for another purpose, they discovered that the water from the River Anio, which furnished the Marcia with water, ought not to be brought to the Capitol. Marcius Rex's influence overcame these scruples, but the episode indicates that the new high aqueducts were felt to have broken the continuity of time-honoured traditions.[89] This is one of the most impressive instances of the clash between old Roman habits and new structural ideas.

TOMBS AND CEMETERIES

Something of the contest between ancient traditions and Etruscan and hellenistic influences appears also in the Roman cemeteries. The tomb of the Scipiones has already shown us a chamber tomb in Rome of the Etruscan type. It was enlarged in the second century and embellished by the great sarcophagus of the consul of 298, L. Cornelius Scipio Barbatus. It displays a mixture of elements of the Doric and Ionic styles which is characteristic of the second century. Of the same time is the present main façade of the tomb, facing a cross-road between the Via Appia and the Via Latina. It consists of a high podium, crowned by a heavy, moulded

cornice. Above was a wall of ashlar with demi-columns of tufa (peperino); only a piece of the wall and the base of one Attic-Ionic column are preserved. To the right of the original rock-cut door of the podium is an arched entrance of tufa blocks (Anio tufa) which leads to an added gallery. The podium was once decorated with a historical painting, but was covered by plain paint both before and after that decoration. While the façade of the Scipiones is typical of stuccoed and painted Roman architecture, the rock-cut chamber tomb of the Sempronii on the slope of the Quirinal has an elegant travertine façade with an arched entrance through a high podium, crowned by a delightful floral frieze and dentils under the moulding of the cornice.

Tomb chambers of tufa ashlar have been excavated on the Esquiline. A much-discussed historical painting in one of them represents a transaction between a Roman general and probably an enemy and is generally dated to the late third or early second century. In the Via di S. Croce in Gerusalemme, south-east of Republican Rome, are chamber tombs with plain façades of tufa ashlar, built by well-to-do freedmen of noble Roman families. One is decorated with sculptured shields, as were the halls of archaic Etruscan tombs and as is seen in Roman architecture through the centuries. Above the doors of two others were travertine slabs with portraits in niches, characteristic of the Roman realistic portraits of people of all classes, but probably resembling the cupboards in the atria of the aristocracy in which portrait masks were kept. On the one hand these middle-class tombs recall Etruscan grave-streets as seen in sixth-century Orvieto [60]; on the other, they are the predecessors of the endless rows of small tomb-houses outside towns of the Imperial Age.[90]

In one of his *Satires* (I, 8), Horace describes a burial place for paupers outside the agger of the Servian Wall, before Maecenas laid out his gardens, 'where of late one sadly looked out on ground ghastly with bleaching bones'. This was a cemetery for inhumation tombs to which slaves carried their fellows' corpses, cast out from narrow dwellings. The graves between the tomb-houses of the middle class in the cemetery of Isola Sacra between Ostia and the Imperial harbours, which are marked only by amphorae or concrete covers, show a considerable improvement on the former inhumation graves of the proletariat. Burials of this kind probably also took place outside the densely occupied areas of Imperial Age tomb-houses. Perhaps a martyr such as St Peter was buried in such a place.

Although influences from the East may have contributed to the establishment of the vast system of Jewish and Christian catacombs in Imperial Rome, one should remember that as early as Late Republican times chamber tombs could be enlarged to galleries with tiers of coffin-like recesses for inhumation. A subterranean rock-cut tomb north-west of Antium has three galleries connected by a vestibule. Along the side

walls are table tombs (*loculi*) in two or three storeys, closed by tiles (or in one case tiles and a marble slab) as in the catacombs.

In the last centuries B.C. cremation became the prevailing form of burial. Rectangular enclosures were surrounded by 6- or 7-foot-high concrete walls. As there are no entrances, they must have been entered by ladders. The finds prove that funeral pyres for burning corpses were lit in these *busta*, and that the urns containing the ashes could be buried there. Sometimes there is also an added enclosure for the pyre, an *ustrinum*. Niches in the walls for urns were added to the busta later – no doubt the origin of the columbaria of the Augustan Age. Enclosures of this kind, from the very end of the Late Republican Age and Early Imperial times, have been excavated in a cemetery outside the Porta Laurentina of Ostia, among the crowded

183. Rome, tomb of S. Sulpicius Galba, consul of 108 B.C.

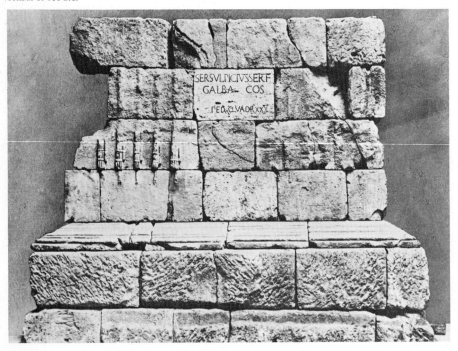

burial grounds north of St Peter's (below the present car park), and among the graves round S. Paolo fuori le Mura.[91]

Associated with the cremation tombs are the most conspicuous and typical burials of the age: the monuments in the hellenistic style which were aligned along the roads outside the city gates, as can still be seen among the Imperial tombs of the Via Appia. The surroundings of Pompeii display this new and charming feature of the towns. Such monuments were erected by wealthy and cultivated citizens and became the fashion. To this day they bring us personal messages from the Pompeians and their hellenistic culture as we approach or leave their towns. A tombstone of a Vestal Virgin on one of the green banks of the Anio at Tibur (Tivoli) and Cynthia's injunctions, preserved in a delightful poem by Propertius (IV, 7. 81 f.) composed the night after she had been cremated, prove that tombstones were also erected where rivers entered towns:

> Where fruitful Anio broods among its
>   branchy fields, . . .
> There on a pillar write a phrase worthy of
>   me,
> But short, to catch the Roman traveller's
>   eye:
> Here in the earth of Tiber golden Cynthia
>   lies,
> A glory added, Anio, to your banks.[92]
>   (Gilbert Highet's translation)

Between the Porticus Aemilia on the Tiber and the horrea of Galba was erected a tomb for S. Sulpicius Galba, the consul of 108 [183]. It is a quadrangular monument of Monte Verde tufa with an inscription tablet of travertine. The preserved lower part of the monument rests upon a substructure of two courses of tufa blocks with a moulded cornice, and was decorated by ten fasces, five on each side of the inscription. Nothing remains of the structure which crowned the tomb. The tomb of the Sempronii on the Quirinal (see above, p. 209) should also be mentioned once more in this connexion.

Two Roman tombs outside Agrigento, dating from the beginning of the first century, give us a full impression of the elegant new style of repositories for urns. In these two the structures above the high podia are preserved and prove clearly the dependence of these podium tombs on the hellenistic architecture of Asia Minor. In the 'Oratory of Phalaris' a low podium containing the tomb chamber supports a small prostyle tetrastyle Ionic temple with a Doric entablature, used for the memorial services. The 'Tomb of Theron' [184] is a quadrangular cella raised above a high podium with a heavy moulded cornice containing the tomb chamber. The Doric entablature rests on Ionic columns at each of the four corners of the small building. On all four walls are elegant blind doors. Clearly this kind of tomb had no relation to indigenous Italic burial traditions.

184. Agrigento, 'Tomb of Theron', hellenistic

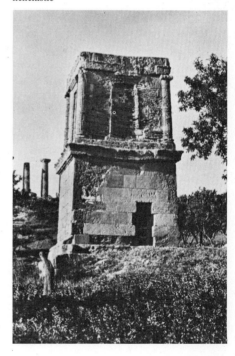

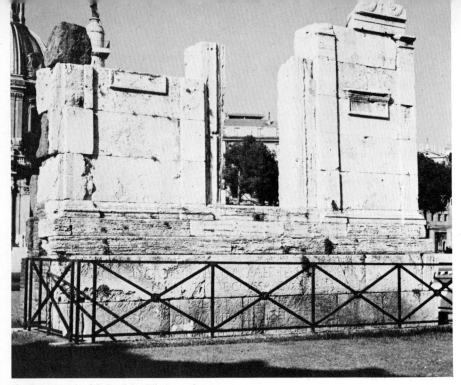

185. Rome, tomb of C. Poplicius Bibulus, *c.* 60 B.C.

Contemporary with these tombs and closely related to them is the tomb of C. Poplicius Bibulus, which stood outside a gate of the Servian Wall in front of the northern slope of the Capitoline Hill [185]. It was an oblong, rectangular tufa structure with a facing of travertine, oriented north-westwards. The inscription towards the street outside the gate testifies that it was erected by the Senate 'honoris virtutisque causa'. The building above the podium seems to have been a small temple *in antis* with a narrow prodomus resembling the 'Oratorio di Falaride'. In the centre of the south-west side is a fairly wide door, where perhaps a statue was placed. Right and left of this door and at the corners of the back wall are Tuscan pilasters. Resting on them is the architrave and a frieze with garlands hanging from bucrania and decorated also by libation bowls above the garlands. Between the pilasters were tablets with a protecting cornice above, probably intended for

painted decoration, as in the great basilica of Praeneste [161]. Though this monument has some Roman flavour, the general hellenistic character is obvious.

Altogether hellenistic is the charming Tomb of the Garlands (Tomba delle Ghirlande), one of the monuments outside the Porta Ercolano on the western side of Pompeii. It is all ashlar work. Upon a low podium the tomb is raised, rectangular in shape, probably containing a cella for the urn. The wall is decorated by elegant short flat pilasters with garlands between them.[93] The hellenistic tombs on the Via Appia also remain.

Tombs of a different kind adorn the Via Appia outside the great wall which connects the town of Terracina with the castrum on the Hill of Jupiter Anxur. They are constructed of coarse concrete covered by opus incertum, which, as always, was once stuccoed and painted. The tomb chambers have their façades towards the Via Appia. Above a podium, with a cornice, stands the monument. It has semi-columns at the corners, of baked brick, like the strengthening layers which Vitruvius describes. The bases of the semi-columns and the quoins of the podium are of stone. These façades were probably crowned by a tympanum, suggesting a temple cella with two columns prostyle.[94]

Occasionally tombs now also show romantic historical associations, a caprice which, however, became more popular only in Imperial times. Pyramids, for example, as tombs in cemeteries and references in poetry prove, became fashionable in Augustan times. A corbelled tholos tomb outside Cumae, generally dated to the third century but very likely later, seems to be an archaistic imitation of Bronze Age Greek beehive tombs. One of these, as we know from Pausanias (II, 16. 6), perhaps the so-called 'Treasury of Atreus', remained famous and was visited in Roman times. The Italian imitation has a dome with straight walls resting upon a high dado with moulded cornice.[95]

It has already been mentioned (p. 97) that Etruscan tombs with a central column supporting the apex of a vault or rock-cut ceiling inspired Late Republican builders. That seems clearly to be the case also with regard to Pliny's description (XXXVI, 91) of the tomb of King Porsenna at Chiusi. A tomb of the Imperial Age on the Via Appia outside Ariccia displays all the most characteristic features of the early model. But, while such fancies remained rare, the old Etruscan and Latin mounds had a renaissance of great importance and long duration all over the Empire. How far they surpassed their Etruscan prototypes in monumental height and grandeur is manifested by the mausolea of Augustus and Hadrian, or – to adduce an example from the provinces – the 'Tombeau de la Chrétienne' in Numidia. This predilection for the tombs of the *atavi reges* (to use Horace's phrase from his first ode) had begun already in a more modest and genuinely Etruscan way in Late Republican times. On the Via Appia some five miles south of Rome are three mounds

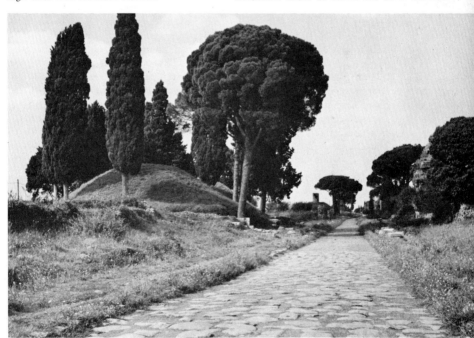

186. Rome, Via Appia, tumuli, from the south. The nearest pair are the 'Tumuli degli Orazi'; in the distance the 'Tumulo dei Curiazi'

showing the most patent Etruscan ancestry, the Tumulo dei Curiazi and the two Tumuli degli Orazi [186]. The northernmost of the Orazi tumuli is pre-Augustan and stands, as far as our knowledge goes, at the beginning of the series. Like the smaller Etruscan mounds of the sixth and fifth centuries, such Roman tumuli often have tomb-chambers in the centre, accessible by a dromos. The podium is reminiscent of the Etruscan rock-cut podia [36], but was built up with a façade of tufa ashlars, backed up by internal semicircular supporting walls. On top of the podium, round the lowest part of the mound, small upright stone slabs seem to have been arranged. Strict axiality and the height and monumentality of the podia became more and more accentuated later on, and constituted a difference between the colossal Roman tombs and the greatest old Etruscan mounds – especially those with scattered chambers; but the beginnings show the closest affinity with what could be seen in so many places between the Tiber and the Arno, and in Latium as well.[96]

CONCLUSION

Rarely does the beginning of a new epoch stand out as clearly as does the Age of Caesar and Augustus – in contemporary testimonies, in art, in the whole political system, and also in architecture, as the *nova magnificentia* (Livy, I, 56. 2; cf. 55. 9) and a severely classical style broke with the freer architectural decoration in the Greek style as it had characterized the last century of the Republic and the time of Caesar. The marble of Luna (Carrara) was discovered, or, in any case, first fully exploited; it was easy to export, since the quarries stood above the harbours of Luna, and the cargoes could be conveyed to Rome on the Tiber. Strabo tells us that marble from Luna, monolithic slabs and columns, became used for superior work of all kinds, both in Rome and in other towns.[97] The final victory of marble in all public buildings, the perfect Augustan reticulate, and many distinctive external features mark this new start in Roman architecture. Vitruvius comments bitterly upon

the innovators: yet he himself was tireless in drawing up rules for achieving a purified style in the new public buildings and for expressing in them the authority sought by Augustus. Like Caesar before him, Augustus aimed in this way at revealing the greatness of Rome's finally stabilized power by his modernized Rome. Yet the great new programme of the city of Rome was mainly a new, more splendid, classicized version of the hellenized Late Republican town, described by Vitruvius in his fifth book. As Pliny points out (XXXIII, 151, and *passim*), the new luxury was inspired by hellenistic splendour; but no one can understand the leading architectural devices of Augustan and Early Imperial Rome who does not keep in mind that they enshrined the traditions of some six centuries. These centuries began with the great Etruscan architecture of the seventh and sixth centuries and the early Roman version of it, at a time when Rome became a forceful, more independent branch of the Etruscan culture of central Italy. In the course of increasing commerce with the Greek towns, both the Etruscans and the Romans created their own architectural dialect and their own patterns for towns, to be remembered beside the great Greek solutions: the Homeric and Archaic towns, which inspired the early Etruscans, and the classical and hellenistic towns, which had such world-wide influence. Cicero once wrote to Atticus (XIII, 35) that he thought it scandalous that Caesar, wishing to enlarge Rome, should summon a Greek architect, who 'two years before' had never even seen the city: 'O rem indignam.'

Examining Late Republican Rome, one sees everywhere that the starting-points for Imperial development were principally the hellenized Roman features analysed in this chapter, and that it was not a question of making direct copies of contemporary hellenistic architecture. The monumental axiality which we see at Praeneste, at Tibur, at Terracina, had acquired its own characteristics; in its Roman shape it now became the guide for the builders of the Imperial fora, the thermae, and almost all the monumental architecture of the Empire. No less decisive for the future was the combination of Greek, Etruscan, and Italic idioms in the temples and in various types of upper-class houses. Theatres and tenement houses were left to the Augustan architect to perfect, but the principles were already in existence, as were also the use of concrete, vaulting, warehouses, paved streets, high aqueducts on arches, and vaulted sewers in their improved Roman shape.

The inner propylaea of Eleusis, built by Appius Claudius Pulcher about 50 B.C., and, among other Roman architectural achievements, the capitolia and the axiality created by the odeion in the Agora in Athens, prove that the Roman variety of hellenistic architecture had made its way in the Eastern world even before Imperial times.[98] It is most illuminating to read the comments of Strabo (XVII, I. 10) on the suburb of Nicopolis, outside Alexandria, and its Roman architecture of Caesar's time, which even in a centre such as the capital of the Ptolemies already surpassed the hellenistic buildings. He mentions especially an amphitheatre and a stadium, and here we should again remember the amphitheatrical cistern in the Egyptian landscape of the Praeneste mosaic.

Behind all this architectural progress, we must recall Vitruvius, brooding over the perfect styles of building, and affirming in the introduction to his seventh book the great knowledge of Roman architects of the Late Republican Age. This is his comment on an early-first-century temple in Rome: 'If it had been of marble, so that besides the refinement of art it possessed the dignity which comes from magnificence and great outlay, it would be reckoned among the first and greatest works of architecture.'

LIST OF PRINCIPAL ABBREVIATIONS

NOTE: Other abbreviated titles are given fully in the general bibliography or in the relevant chapter bibliography.

Acta Ath. Suec.	*Acta Instituti Atheniensis Regni Sueciae*
Acta Rom. Suec.	*Acta Instituti Romani Regni Sueciae (Skrifter utgivna av Svenska Institutet i Rom)* (cf. *Opus. Rom.*)
A.J.A.	*American Journal of Archaeology*
Andrén, *Origine*	A. Andrén, 'Origine e formazione dell'architettura templare etrusco-italica', *Rend. Pont.*, XXXII (1959-60), 21-59
Anz.	*Archaeologischer Anzeiger* (in *J.D.A.I.*)
Arch. Cl.	*Archeologia classica*
B.A.S.O.R.	*Bulletin of the American Schools of Oriental Research*
B.C.H.	*Bulletin de correspondence hellénique*
B. d'Arte	*Bollettino d'Arte*
Blake (1947)	Marion Blake, *Ancient Roman Construction in Italy from the Prehistoric Period to Augustus*. Washington, 1947
Boëthius–Ward-Perkins	A. Boëthius and J. B. Ward-Perkins, *Etruscan and Roman Architecture (Pelican History of Art)*. Harmondsworth, 1970
B.P.I.	*Bollettino di paletnologia italiana*
Bull. Comm.	*Bullettino della Commissione Archeologica Comunale di Roma*
C.I.L.	*Corpus inscriptionum latinarum*
Civiltà del ferro	*Civiltà del ferro. Studi pubblicati nella ricorrenza centenaria della scoperta di Villanova. Documenti e studi a cura della Deputazione di Storia Patria per le Province di Romagna*, VI (1960)
Cosa I, II	F. Brown and Emeline H. and L. Richardson, *M.A.A.R.*, XX (1951), 12–113; XXVII (1960)
Crema	L. Crema, *L'Architettura romana (Enciclopedia classica*, III, vol. XII, *Archeologia (Arte romana))*. Turin, 1959
Dionysius	Dionysius of Halicarnassus
Ducati	P. Ducati, *Storia dell'arte etrusca*, 2 vols. Florence, 1927
Dura	*The Excavations at Dura Europos. Preliminary Reports*. New Haven, 1929-52
Encicl. Art. Ant.	*Enciclopedia dell'arte antica classica e orientale*. Rome, 1958-73
Fontes	G. Lugli, ed., *Fontes ad topographiam veteris urbis Romae pertinentes*
Forma Urbis	G. Carettoni, A. M. Colini, L. Cozza, G. Gatti, eds., *La Pianta marmorea di Roma antica, Forma Urbis Romae*. Rome, 1960
Giglioli	G. Q. Giglioli, *L'Arte etrusca*. Milan, 1935
Gjerstad, *Early Rome*	E. Gjerstad, *Early Rome*, I-VI (*Acta Rom. Suec.*, in 4°, XVII). 1953-73
G.G.A.	*Göttingische gelehrte Anzeigen*
I.L.N.	*Illustrated London News*
Itinerari	*Itinerari dei Musei e Monumenti d'Italia*. Rome, Libreria dello Stato
J.D.A.I.	*Jahrbuch des Deutschen Archaeologischen Instituts*
J.H.S.	*Journal of Hellenic Studies*
J.R.S.	*Journal of Roman Studies*
Lugli, *Tecnica edilizia*	G. Lugli, *La Tecnica edilizia romana con particolare riguardo a Roma e Lazio*. Rome, 1957
M.A.A.R.	*Memoirs of the American Academy in Rome*
Mél. Rome.	*Mélanges d'archéologie et d'histoire de l'École Française de Rome*
Mem. Linc.	*Memorie dell'Accademia Nazionale dei Lincei*

Mem. Pont.	*Atti della Pontificia Accademia Romana di Archeologia, Memorie*
Mon. Ant.	*Monumenti antichi*
Nash	E. Nash, *Pictorial Dictionary of Ancient Rome.* 2 vols. 2nd ed. London, 1968
N.S.	*Notizie degli scavi di antichità*
Opus. Arch.	*Opuscula archaeologica*
Opus. Rom.	*Opuscula Romana.* Studies collected in special volumes of *Acta Rom. Suec.*
P.A.A.R.	*American Academy in Rome, Papers and Monographs*
P.B.S.R.	*Papers of the British School at Rome*
Platner-Ashby	S. B. Platner, *A Topographical Dictionary of Ancient Rome.* Completed and rev. by T. Ashby. London, 1929
Polacco	L. Polacco, *Tuscanicae dispositiones.* Padua, 1952
P.P.S.	*Proceedings of the Prehistoric Society*
Proc. Brit. Ac.	*Proceedings of the British Academy*
P.W.	Pauly-Wissowa, *Realencyclopädie der classischen Altertumswissenschaft*
Rend. Linc.	*Rendiconti dell'Accademia dei Lincei*
Rend. Nap.	*Rendiconti della Accademia di Archeologia, Lettere e Belle Arti di Napoli*
Rend. Pont.	*Atti della Pontificia Accademia Romana di Archeologia, Rendiconti*
Rh. M.	*Rheinisches Museum für Philologie*
R.M.	*Mitteilungen des Deutschen Archaeologischen Instituts. Römische Abteilung*
San Giovenale	*Etruscan Culture, Land and People. Archaeological Research and Studies Conducted in San Giovenale and its Environs by Members of the Swedish Institute in Rome.* Columbia University Press, New York, 1962
Scavi di Ostia	G. Calza, Maria F. Squarciapino, G. Becatti, Raissa Calza, *Scavi di Ostia,* I-V. Rome, 1953–64
Serv. ad Aen.	*Servii grammatici qui feruntur in Vergilii commentarii.* Recensuerant G. Thilo et H. Hagen. Aenaidos librorum commentari. Recensuit G. Thilo. Leipzig, 1881. (Servius on the Aeneid)
St. Etr.	*Studi etruschi*
von Gerkan, *Gesammelte Aufsätze*	A. von Gerkan, *Von antiker Architektur und Topographie. Gesammelte Aufsätze* (ed E. Böhringer). Stuttgart, 1959

NOTES

Bold numbers indicate page references.

CHAPTER I

9. 1. Augustine, *De Civitate Dei*, IV, 31 (Varro); Plutarch, *Numa*, VIII, 7–8. Tertullian, *Apologeticus*, XXV, 12.

10. 2. Diodorus, V, 39; IV, 20. For the latest discussion of Stone and Bronze Age settlements and material, see A. M. Radmilli, 'Dal paleolitico all'età di bronzo', *Popoli e civiltà dell'Italia antica*, I, 1 (1974), 69 ff. See also T. E. Peet, *The Stone and Bronze Ages in Italy*, and G. Patroni, *Architettura preistorica generale ed italica. Architettura etrusca*. Especially important, in addition, are: G. von Kaschnitz-Weinberg, 'Italien mit Sardinien, Sizilien und Malta', *Handbuch der Archäologie im Rahmen des Handbuchs der Altertumswissenschaft*, VI, 2 (Munich, 1950), 311–402; M. Pallottino, 'Le origini storiche dei popoli italici', *Relazioni del X Congresso Internazionale di Scienze Storiche*; C. F. C. Hawkes, *The Prehistoric Foundations of Europe to the Mycenaean Age*; V. G. Childe, *The Dawn of European Civilization*, 6th ed. (London, 1957), and *Prehistoric Migrations in Europe* (Oslo, 1950); A. M. Radmilli, *La preistoria d'Italia*. For Sicily: L. Bernabò Brea, *Sicily before the Greeks*. For caves: F. Biancofiore, *La civiltà dei cavernicoli delle Murge baresi* (Bologna, 1964). Round villages of Apulia: J. Bradford, *Ancient Landscapes* (London, 1957), 86–103; J. B. Ward-Perkins, 'The Early Development of Roman Town-Planning', *Acta Congressus Madvigiani*, IV (Copenhagen, 1958), 109 ff.

11. 3. C. E. Östenberg, *Luni*; A. Boëthius, 'La continuità dello habitat etrusco nella zona di S. Giovenale di Bieda', *Fondazione per il Museo Claudio Faina, Orvieto, Collana di Quaderni d'archeologia e di storia* (1964), 5 ff.

14. 4. For the Apennine culture: A. M. Radmilli, *op. cit.* (Note 2); U. Rellini, 'Le stazioni enee delle Marche', *Mon. Ant.*, XXXIV (1931), 130–280; 'Sulla civiltà dell'età enea in Italia', *B.P.I.*, LIII (1933), 65–94; D. Trump, 'The Apennine Culture of Italy', *P.P.S.*, XXIV (1958), 165–200; R. Peroni, 'Per una definizione dell'aspetto culturale "subappenninico" come fase cronologica a sè stante', *Mem. Linc.*, ser. 8, IX (1960), 3–253; S. M. Puglisi, *La civiltà appenninica*, especially 43–54, with A. C. Blanc's critique of Puglisi's excavations, *Rivista di antropologia*, XLIV (1957), 243–63. For south Italy, see Chapter 2, Note 2. Bolsena: R. Bloch, *Recherches archéologiques en territoire volsinien de la protohistoire à la civilisation*

étrusque (Paris, 1972), 17–40. Bed of pebbles in an Apennine hut at San Giovenale: *San Giovenale* (Swedish ed., Malmö, 1960), 306, figure 265. Manfria near Gela: A. W. van Buren, *A.J.A.*, LXV (1961), 387, plate 125; Boëthius, 'La tomba del tetto stramineo a Cerveteri', *Palladio*, XV (1965), 3–6. Sant'Omobono: *Bull. Comm.*, LXXVII (1959–60), with studies by E. Gjerstad, R. Peroni, E. Paribeni, and G. Colonna; Gjerstad, *Early Rome*, III, 387, 400–13, 460, 462 ff. Apennine huts around Civitavecchia: F. Barbaranelli, *B.P.I.*, N.S. IX (1954–5), 381–400; *Anz.* (1957), 260 f. Casa Carletti: *St. Etr.*, X (1936), 330, plate 32.2. Fortifications: Puglisi, *op. cit.*, 60, 79, 81, 85. Aeolian islands: Bernabò Brea and Madeleine Cavalier, *Civiltà preistoriche delle isole eolie e del territorio di Milazzo* (Rome, 1956); *B.P.I.*, N.S. X (1956), 7–98; Bernabò Brea, *Sicily before the Greeks*, 103 ff. For Sicily also: E. Sjöqvist, *A.J.A.*, LXII (1958), 157 (Morgantina). Mycenaean finds: W. Taylour, *Mycenaean Pottery in Italy and Adjacent Areas* (Cambridge, 1958); F. Biancofiore, *La civiltà micenea nell'Italia meridionale* (Rome, 1963); Luigia Achillea Stella, *La civiltà micenea nei documenti contemporanei* (Rome, 1965), 218, note 71; C. E. Östenberg, *Luni*, 128–45.

15. 5. 'Anaktoron' of Pantalica: Bernabò Brea, *Sicily before the Greeks*, 162 ff. Tombs: *ibid.*, plate 33 ff. For truddhi, trulli: Patroni, *Architettura preistorica*, 92, 125; G. Chierici, 'I trulli in pericolo', *Palladio*, N.S. I (1951), 125–7.

6. The Terramare were first distinguished from the Apennine culture by Rellini (cited Note 4), Patroni, *Athenaeum*, N.S. VIII (1930), 425–51, and E. Ciaceri, *Le origini di Roma* (Milan, 1937), 153–6. The comprehensive work is: G. Säflund, *Le Terremare delle provincie di Modena, Reggio Emilia, Parma, Piacenza* (*Acta Rom. Suec.*, VII, 1939); see Rellini's review in *B.P.I.*, N.S. III (1939), 113–26, with additional remarks *loc. cit.*, IV (1940), 169–73, and in *Il Lazio nella preistoria di Roma* (Rome, 1941), 29. For the date: J. E. Forssander, 'Europäische Bronzezeit', *Kungl. Vetenskapsamfundet i Lund. Årsberättelse 1938–1939*, III, 76–91; F. Matz, *Klio*, XXXIII (1940), 143–8; XXXV (1942), 303 ff. For the earlier urnfields of the Iron Age and their supposed connexion with the Terramare see Trump, 190, 194, and Puglisi, 78, both cited in Note 4.

7. Pertosa: Peet, *The Stone and Bronze Ages in Italy*, 405 ff., and Patroni, *Architettura preistorica*, 76, figure 97. Delia Brusadin, 'Figurazioni architettoniche nelle

incisioni rupestri di Valcamonica. Ricostruzione della più antica dimora camuna', *B.P.I.*, N.S. XIII (1960-1), 33-112; E. Anati, *Camonica Valley* (New York, 1961).
18. 8. G. Lilliu, *La civiltà dei sardi dal neolitico all'età dei nuraghi*; Margaret Guido, *Sardinia*; G. Lilliu, *I nuraghi, torri preistoriche di Sardegna* (Verona, 1962). [The date of the earliest nuraghi is still disputed: E. Contu, 'La Sardegna dell'età nuragica', *Popoli e civiltà dell'Italia antica*, III, 2 (1974), 146 ff., 198 f.] For Malta: J. D. Evans, *Malta*. Relations between Iron Age Etruria and Sardinia: G. Bartoloni and F. Delpino, *St. Etr.*, XLIII (1975), 40 ff. Important is a find of one of the Sardinian figurines in a tomb of the Early Iron Age: M. T. Falconi Amorelli, *Arch. Cl.*, XVIII (1966), 1-15, plate 2. Carthaginians and Phoenicians in Sardinia: G. Pesce, *Sardegna punica* (Cagliari, 1961); S. Moscati, 'The First Inland Carthaginian City to be found in Sardinia', *I.L.N.* (3 April 1965), 19; F. Barreca, *La Sardegna fenicia e punica* (Sassari, 1974). Famous is the Roman gibe preserved by Festus, 'Sardi venales, alius alio nequior'.

CHAPTER 2

20. 1. Iron Age huts at San Giovenale: *San Giovenale*, 292 ff. For recent discussions of Early Iron Age cemeteries in Etruria, see H. Hencken, *Tarquinia, Villanovans and Early Etruscans*; (for Veii) Close-Brooks, 'Considerazioni sulla cronologia delle facies arcaiche dell'Etruria', *St. Etr.*, XXXV (1967), 323 ff.; I. Pohl, *The Iron Age Necropolis of Sorbo at Cerveteri* (Stockholm, 1972). [For Iron Age Rome and Latium the researches of Gjerstad (*Early Rome*, I-VI) and Gierow (*The Iron Age Culture of Latium*) are fundamental, but their chronological conclusions have not found general acceptance: see the review by D. Ridgway, *J.R.S.*, LVIII (1968), 235-40; M. Pallottino, 'Le origini di Roma', in H. Temporini (ed.), *Aufstieg und Niedergang der römischen Welt*, I, 1 (Berlin and New York, 1972), 22-47 (with useful bibliography); G. Colonna, 'Preistoria di Roma e del Lazio', *Popoli e civiltà dell'Italia antica*, II, 4 (1974), 275-346.] Velletri tomb: *N.S.* (1893), 198 ff., figure 1. Tivoli grave circles: *B.P.I.*, XV (1964), 187 ff. Vetulonia: Blake (1947), 71.
2. For south Italy: B. d'Agostino, 'La civiltà del ferro nell'Italia meridionale e nella Sicilia', *Popoli e civiltà dell'Italia antica*, II, 1 (1974), 10-91; see also L. Bernabò Brea and Madeleine Cavalier, *Mylai* (Novara, 1959), and L. Pareti in *Greci e Italici in Magna Graecia* (Naples, 1962), 155-7, with the review of Emeline Hill Richardson, *A.J.A.*, LXVIII (1964), 408 f. Sala Consilina: J. de la Genière, *Recherches sur l'âge du fer en Italie meridionale: Sala Consilina* (Naples, 1968).
21. 3. By 'Oscans' I mean the old, Indo-European

tribes of Campania and Samnium before the Etruscans and before the Samnites of central Italy and the eastern coast invaded Campania in the fifth century B.C. The Oscans of the coastal plain were no doubt akin to the Samnites of the mountains of central Italy and the eastern coast (see E. T. Salmon, *Samnium and the Samnites* (Cambridge, 1967), 28 ff.). Primitive Rome: Plutarch, *Romulus*, IX, XI; Dionysius, I, 88; F. Castagnoli, *Ippodamo*, 67-72; 'Roma quadrata', *Arch. Cl.*, XVI (1964), 178-80, with references and bibliography, to which Y. Hedlund, 'Mundus', *Eranos*, XXXI (1933), 53-70, must be added. For the Terramare and their supposed regular planning, see Chapter 1, Note 6, and Castagnoli, *Ippodamo*, 9-10.
4. Rapino: *Anz.* (1959), 224 f.; *Studi Calderini-Paribeni*, III (1956), 311 f.
23. 5. Dionysius, I, 88; Macrobius, V, 19.13; C. O. Thulin, *Die Ritualbücher . . . Göteborgs Högskolas Årsskrift*, I (Gothenburg, 1909), 3-10. For the rite in the Roman colonies see the well-known relief from Aquileia [9] in addition to coins like those of Beirut: R. Mouterde and J. Lauffray, 'Beyrouth, ville romaine', *Publications de la Direction des Antiquités de Liban. Villes libanaises*, I (Beirut, 1952). Pomerium and Argeorum Sacraria: Platner-Ashby, *s.v.* Tacitus, *Ann.*, XII, 24; Livy, I, 44; Serv. ad Aen., V, 755. See also Momigliano, *J.R.S.*, XXXIII (1943), 121; Agnes Kirsopp Michels, 'The Topography and Interpretation of the Lupercalia', *T.A.P.A.*, LXXXIV (1953), 35 ff.; von Gerkan, *Rh. M.*, XCVI (1953), 27 ff., and Gjerstad, *Early Rome*, III, 44. Bologna: *N.S.* (1960), 291.
6. Huts at Rome: Gjerstad, *Early Rome*, II, 282-6; III, 48-78, reviewed by Romanelli, *Gnomon*, XXXVI (1964), 816-23; Romanelli, 'Certezze e ipotesi sulle origini di Roma', *Studi Romani*, XIII (1965), 165 ff. Palatine cemeteries: G. Carettoni, *B.P.I.*, N.S. IX (1954-5), 261 ff. Leontini, Syracuse, and Lipari: Bernabò Brea, *Sicily before the Greeks*, 142 f. and 172 f. Huts at Luni and San Giovenale: *San Giovenale*, 293 ff., 321 ff.; Riemann, 'Die schwedischen Forschungen in Südetrurien 1956-1962', *Gymnasium*, LXII (1965), 331-3.
26. 7. The model from Sala Consilina: *Mostra della preistoria e della protostoria nel Salernitano, Catalogo 1962*, 64, 71, no. 168 (Tomb 63), figure 19; *Apollo*, II (1962), 85, figure 11. Cf. lavish acroteria on the roofs of Etruscan temples, Chapter 3, p. 61. Semi-subterranean huts at Luni and San Giovenale: P. Hellström, *Luni sul Mignone*, II, 2 (in *Acta Rom. Suec.* in 4°, XXVII: II, 2 (1975)); *San Giovenale*, 298. Flood danger makes it perhaps less likely that the sunk rooms were themselves habitations rather than basements below protecting buildings above. For contemporary Greek houses cf. H. Drerup, 'Zum geometrischen Haus', *Marburger Winckelmann-Programm* (1962),

1-9; 'Griechische Architektur zur Zeit des Homers', *Anz.* (1964), 180–219; A. Cambitoglou, *Zagora*, I (Sydney, 1971).

27. 8. J. Sundvall, *Die italischen Hüttenurnen* (*Acta Academiae Aboensis Humaniora*, IV: 5) (1925); W. R. Bryan, 'Italic Hut Urns and Hut Urn Cemeteries', *P.A.A.R.*, IV (1925); Gjerstad, *Early Rome*, II; Gierow, *The Iron Age Culture of Latium*; 'A Latial Iron Age Tomb-Group', *The Museum of Mediterranean and Near Eastern Antiquities, Bulletin No. 2* (Stockholm, 1962), 32–8; Andrén, 'An Italic Iron Age Hut Urn', *ibid.*, *Bulletin No. 4* (1964), 30–7; Müller-Karpe, *Vom Anfang Roms* (with unfounded theories about affinities with Crete and Este), 45–51. Interpretation of the ridge-logs: Andrén, *Architectural Terracottas*, XXV f. Strips of tin: Berta Stjernquist, 'La decorazione metallica delle ceramiche villanoviane in una nuova illustrazione', *Civiltà del ferro*, 431 ff. The lid of the stele from Tarquinia [19] is discussed by Andrén, *Origine*, 53 f.

28. 9. Solinus, *Collectanea rerum memorabilium*, I, 21; Ovid, *Tristia*, III, I, 29–30; Cassius Dio, fragment 6.2; Serv. ad Aen., VII, 153. Gjerstad, *Early Rome*, III, 310–20 with references to A. Bartoli's excavations, *Rend. Pont.*, XXI (1945–6), 5 ff., *Mon. Ant.*, XLV (1961), 19–68, and others. Regia: Plutarch, *Numa*, XIV, I. Excavations by F. E. Brown have revealed remains of the Early Iron Age village along the Via Sacra below the Regia of – probably – about 500 B.C.: F. E. Brown, 'New Soundings in the Regia; the Evidence for the Early Republic', *Entretiens sur l'antiquité classique*, XIII (Fondation Hardt, 1967), 45–60 (rectangular huts with curved corners); 'La protostoria della Regia', *Rend. Pont.*, XLVII (1974–5), 15–36.

10. Romulus's hut appears still in the *Libellus de regionibus Urbis Romae, Regio X* in the fourth century A.D.; Romanelli, *Studi Romani*, XIII (1965), 156 ff. For other sources: *Fontes*, VIII, I. liber XIX; Regio X (Palatine), 51 ff. There was also a *tugurium Faustuli*: Solinus, *Collectanea rerum memorabilium*, I, 18. Both were on the south-western slope of the Palatine: Castagnoli, *Arch. Cl.*, XVI (1964), 174 f.

30. 11. A useful analysis of the influence from the Eastern world: J. Boardman, *The Greeks Overseas* (London, 1964). For summaries about the Greeks and Italy: E. Wikén, *Die Kunde der Hellenen von dem Lande und den Völkern der Apenninenhalbinsel bis 300 v. Chr.* (Lund, 1937); T. J. Dunbabin, *The Western Greeks* (Oxford, 1948), and more recently D. Ridgway, 'The First Western Greeks', in C. and S. Hawkes (eds.), *Greeks Celts and Romans* (London, 1973). [New light on the transmission of Greek ideas to the Etruscans is shed by the excavation of a Greek sanctuary of Hera at Graviscae, the ancient port of Tarquinia, which proves the presence of a Greek community here in the sixth century: M. Torelli, 'Il santuario di Hera a Gra-

visca', *La Parola del Passato*, XXVI (1971), 44–67.] For Ischia: G. Buchner, 'Pithekoussai, oldest Greek Colony in the West', *Expedition*, VIII, 4 (1966), 4–12; and D. Ridgway, *loc. cit.*, gives a full bibliography. Margherita Guarducci's explanation of the inscription about Nestor's cup, *Rend. Linc.*, ser. 8, XVI (1961), 3–7, seems to me evident. Suggestions that Nestor was only one of the seamen are far-fetched and contrary to the Homeric style of the text, which, in any case, proves Homeric influence.

12. I have collected material proving that Etruscan was the language of the whole population of Etruria and wholly different from Latin (*San Giovenale*, 36). The names of the Tiber prove the same: *Lydia ripa*, Statius, *Silvae*, IV, 4. 4; *ripa veientana*; *paterni fluminis ripae*, Horace (to Maecenas), *Odes*, I, 20, 5 f.; and others. Important is Dionysius's statement (I, 30) that the Etruscan language was unlike all known languages, cf. V, 28; Livy, IX, 36; X, 4. Latin occurs only in the latest of the thousands of Etruscan tomb inscriptions, when the Roman influence gradually became more dominant than before.

31. 13. For the different tales about the Etruscans see *P.W.*, *s.v.* Tyrrhener; and H. Hencken, *Tarquinia, Villanovans and Early Etruscans*, 603 ff. Important is what the Emperor Claudius says about Etruscan history in his decree about Lyon; *C.I.L.*, XIII, I, 1668. Pallottino is the leading authority among the defenders of the Italic origin of the Etruscans: see his *The Etruscans*, 2nd ed. (London, 1975), and 'Le origini storiche dei popoli italici', *Relazioni del X Congresso Internazionale di Scienze Storiche*. See also *The Ciba Foundation Symposium on Medical Biology and Etruscan Origins* (1958); J. B. Ward-Perkins, 'The Problem of Etruscan Origins', *Harvard Studies in Classical Philology*, LXIV (1959), 1–26; H. Hencken, 'A View of Etruscan Origins', *Antiquity*, XL (1966), 205–11.

For different opinions: A. Furumark, *Det äldsta Italien*, 161 ff., discusses the tradition about the Tyrsenians from Lemnos as the most probable ancestors of the Etruscans in Italy. G. Säflund, *Historia*, VI (1957), 10–22, identifies the population of the Early Iron Age and their new settlements ('the Villanovans') with Etruscan immigrants. Recent excavations at the Banditaccia cemetery of Cerveteri reveal Early Iron Age tombs among and below the Etruscan tombs. They have been interpreted as remains of a continuous development and intermediate links. To my mind, here the complex only proves that the Etruscans usurped the Iron Age cemetery and that their new types of tomb in some cases influenced the old, local population. Very important in any case is R. E. Linington's article 'Prospezioni geofisiche a Cerveteri', *Palatino*, X (1966), 147–57. See also P. Bosch-Gimpera, 'Réflexions sur le problème des Étrusques', *Mélanges offerts à A. Piganiol* (Paris, 1966), 639–53.

14. It has to be borne in mind that nothing in our present material from Lydia reveals an emigration corresponding to Herodotus's tale and the different dates suggested by ancient sources, which can be combined with what archaeological finds from Italy attest. For Lydia: G. A. Wainwright, *Anatolian Studies*, IX (1959), 197 ff.; G. M. A. Hanfmann, 'Sardis und Lydien', *Akademie der Wissenschaften und Literatur in Mainz. Abhandlungen. Geistes- und Sozialwissenschaftlichen Klasse, 1960*, especially 510 f. and 523 f., and the annual reports of the excavations at Sardes in *B.A.S.O.R.* from 1958 on; also J. G. Pedley, *Sardis in the Age of Croesus* (University of Oklahoma Press, 1968). Hellenistic Lydian inscription: *B.A.S.O.R.*, CLXXVII (1965), 10.

CHAPTER 3

34. 1. For the archaeology of the Etruscan cities: G. Dennis, *The Cities and Cemeteries of Etruria*; Luisa Banti, *Il mondo degli Etruschi*; F. Coarelli (ed.), *Le città etrusche*; M. Pallottino, *The Etruscans*. The period of political decline brought about by the struggles with Rome is discussed by H. H. Scullard, *The Etruscan Cities and Rome*; see also W. V. Harris, *Rome in Etruria and Umbria* (Oxford, 1971). [For further discussion of what Vitruvius means by *tuscanicae dispositiones*: F. E. Brown, *Art Bulletin*, LIV (1972), 342 f.]

2. Wattle-and-daub: Blake (1947), 309. Ashlar masonry in Etruria: Blake (1947), 71-8. Timber construction at Veii: Ward-Perkins, 'Excavations beside the North-West Gate at Veii 1957-1958', *P.B.S.R.*, XIV (1959), 58-65. Stone construction at Veii: E. Stefani, *N.S.* (1922), 379 ff. Mud-bricks at Vetulonia: I. Falchi, *N.S.* (1895), 272 ff. Marzabotto: Mansuelli, *I.L.N.* (13 October 1962), 557; R. A. Staccioli, 'Sulla struttura dei muri nelle case della città etrusca di Misano a Marzabotto', *St. Etr.*, XXXV (1967), 113-26.

35. 3. [At Rusellae not only a stretch of the town wall but also some entire buildings were constructed in mud-brick: Clelia Laviosa, *St. Etr.*, XXXIII (1965), 49 ff.; 'L'urbanistica delle città arcaiche e le strutture in mattoni crudi di Roselle', *Atti del Convegno sulla città etrusca e italica preromana* (Bologna, 1970), 209 ff.; F. Coarelli (ed.), *Le città etrusche*, figure on page 114.] Wall of Arretium published by L. Pernier, *N.S.* (1920), 171-90. Average measurement: 44 by 29 by 14 cm. (17⅓ by 11½ by 5½ in.), roughly corresponding to Vitruvius's Lydian bricks (II, 3. 3) and bricks from Vetulonia measuring 45 by 30 by 11 cm. (17¾ by 11⅘ by 4⅓ in.). A brick from Veii 30 by 23 by 15 cm. (11⅘ by 9 by 6 in.): Blake (1947), 276 ff. See further: Ducati, 365 ff.; R. Naumann, *R.M.*, *Ergänzungsheft*, III (1958), 17 f. Mud-brick wall of Gela: *Encicl. Art. Ant.*, III, 801, figure 994.

4. For the flood of 54 B.C.: Dio Cassius, XXXIX, 61. 2. The famous words ascribed to Augustus (Suetonius, *Augustus*, XXVIII) generalize in a misleading way. He adorned the town with marble columns and marble-faced temples, but the domestic architecture of his age was mostly built of concrete and covered with opus reticulatum.

5. Mud-brick: Blake (1947), 277 ff.; Lugli, *Tecnica edilizia*, 529 ff. Terracottas: Andrén, *Architectural Terracottas*; L. and Emeline Richardson, *Cosa*, II; Å. Åkerström, 'Untersuchungen über die figürlichen Terrakottafriese aus Etrurien und Latium', *Opus. Rom.*, I (1954), 191-231; Elisabeth D. van Buren, *Figurative Terracotta Revetments in Etruria and Latium in the VI and V Centuries B.C.* (London, 1921); Andrén, 'Osservazioni sulle terrecotte architettoniche etrusco-italiche', *Opus. Rom.*, VIII (1974), 1-16. The latter includes discussion of important new Archaic terracottas from Murlo (Poggio Civitate) near Siena and Acquarossa near Viterbo. For the Murlo friezes see further M. Cool Root, 'An Etruscan Horse Race from Poggio Civitate', *A.J.A.*, LXXVII (1973), 121-37, with bibliography; and for the monumental acroteria (human and animal figures): *Poggio Civitate: il santuario arcaico* (Florence, 1970), plates 6-20. For Acquarossa: Notes 38 and 53. The terracottas from the two temples at Pyrgi are published in 'Pyrgi', *N.S.* (1970), Supplement II.

36. 6. Piazza d'Armi, Veii: Stefani, *Mon. Ant.*, XL (1944), 228 ff.; Andrén, *Architectural Terracottas*, 8 ff.; *idem, Origine*, 24, figure 2; Ward-Perkins, *P.B.S.R.*, XVI (1961), 25 ff. Volsinii: R. Bloch, *Mél. Rome*, LXII (1950), 74 ff.; G. Maetzke, *St. Etr.*, XXIV (1955-6), 252; Andrén, *Origine*, 24 ff. The temple, however, is hardly earlier than the third century B.C.; cf. G. Colonna, *St. Etr.*, XXXIII (1965), 200, note 19.

7. Satricum: Andrén, *Architectural Terracottas*, 453-7. We now can compare also the smaller Temple (B) at Pyrgi [28] (see below, Note 14).

37. 8. Models: R. A. Staccioli, *Modelli di edifici etrusco-italici*, I: *Modelli votivi*; Andrén, *Architectural Terracottas*, XXIV-XXXIV, and *Origine*. Discussions of temple remains: Agnes Kirsopp Lake, 'The Archeological Evidence for the "Tuscan Temple"', *M.A.A.R.*, XII (1935), 89 ff.; Luisa Banti, 'Il culto del cosiddetto "Tempio del Apollo" a Veii e il problema delle triadi etrusco-italiche', *St. Etr.*, XVII (1943), 187-224; Polacco, 80 ff.; M. Cagiano de Azevedo, 'I "Capitolia" dell'Impero Romano', *Mem. Pont.*, V (1941), 1-76; Maetzke, 'Il nuovo tempio tuscanico di Fiesole', *St. Etr.*, XXIV (1955-6), 227-53; Piera Bocci, 'Nuovi scavi del tempio di Fiesole', *St. Etr.*, XXIX (1961), 411-15.

38. 9. Andrén, *Architectural Terracottas*, XLI-XLVII; Maetzke, *St. Etr.*, *loc. cit.*, 247; F. Castagnoli, 'Peripteros sine postico', *R.M.*, LXII (1955), 139-43; A.

Boëthius, 'Veteris capitoli humilia tecta', *Acta Instituti Romani Norvegiae*, I (1962), 28, note 1. *Alae* is a modern reading for *aliae* of the MS. I am convinced that the emendation is right and use it, in any case, like Morgan as a terminus technicus for the open, colonnaded wings outside the cella walls. S. Ferri, *Studi classici e orientali*, Pisa, VI (1957), 235 ff., defends *aliae*.

10. E. Gjerstad, 'A proposito della ricostruzione del tempio arcaico di Giove Capitolino in Roma', *Acta Instituti Romani Norvegiae*, I (1962), 35 ff.

39. 11. Archaic evidence for temples with two columns: Giglioli, CXLVII; Andrén, *Architectural Terracottas*, XXVI, no. 14; XXX, no. 32; F. Pfister, 'Il santuario della Dea Marica alle foci del Garigliano', *Mon. Ant.*, XXXVII (1938), 696–704. General discussion: Andrén, *op. cit.*, XLVII ff. Late specimens: Andrén, *op. cit.*, XXXII–XXXIV, nos. 41, 47; G. Becatti, 'Un rilievo con le oche capitoline', *Bull. Comm.*, LXXI (1943–5), 31–8; Nash, *s.v.* Juno Moneta. Largo Argentina: Temple A, first period: G. Marchetti-Longhi, 'L'Area sacra del Largo Argentina', *Itinerari* (1960); Crema, 42. Teano: W. Johannowsky, 'Modelli di edifici da Teano', *B. d'Arte*, XLVII (1962), 63 f. Alatri: Andrén, *Architectural Terracottas*, 390 f., figure 36. Temples with four or more columns in the pronaus; the fourth-century temple excavated by M. Torelli between Pyrgi and Civitavecchia with a cella measuring 26 by 26 ft (8 by 8 m.), no alae, and columns only in the pronaus: *I.L.N.* (6 May 1967), 24. For Roman specimens: *Cosa*, II, 45. For the future of the Roman temples with a cella, no alae, and four or more columns in the pronaus, cf. the Maison Carrée or – among others – B. Cunliffe's reconstruction of 'The Temple of Sulis Minerva at Bath', *Antiquity*, XL (1966), 199–204.

40. 12. Vitruvius, IV, 7 (Morgan's translation): '1. The place where the temple is to be built having been divided on its length into six parts, deduct one and let the rest be given to its width. Then let the length be divided into two equal parts, of which the inner be reserved as space for the cellae, and the part next to the front left for the arrangement of the columns. 2. Next let the width be divided into ten parts. Of these, let three on the right and three on the left be given to the smaller cellae, or to the alae if there are to be alae, and the other four devoted to the middle of the temple. Let the space in front of the cellae, in the pronaus, be marked out for columns thus: the corner columns should be placed opposite the antae on the line of the outside walls; the two middle columns, set out on the line of the walls which are between the antae and the middle of the temple; and through the middle, between the antae and the front columns, a second row, arranged on the same lines.' (Cf. the reconstruction, illustration 22.) It is important for the

discussion about the height of the columns, etc., to observe that Vitruvius discusses temples with three cellas without alae (or temples with one cella and alae), while the Capitoline Temple had colonnaded wings outside its three cellas.

41. 13. Luisa Banti, *loc. cit.* (Note 8); Polacco, 94–100; U. Bianchi, 'Disegno storico del culto capitolino nell'Italia romana e nelle provincie dell'impero', *Mem. Linc.*, ser. 8, II (1950), 349. [For recent evidence of a possible triad at Murlo: T. N. Gantz, *St. Etr.*, XXXIX (1971), 3–24. For the view that the three-cella plan was not adopted in Etruria before the period of Roman influence: Bianchi Bandinelli, 'Etrusca arte', *Encicl. Art. Ant.*, III, 497.]

42. 14. Ara della Regina at Tarquinia: P. Romanelli, *N.S.* (1948), 238 ff. Acropolis temple of Ardea: Stefani, *N.S.* (1944–5), 81 ff.; Andrén, *Origine*, 29 f. Portonaccio Temple of Veii: Stefani, *N.S.* (1953), 29–112; Andrén, *op. cit.*, 26 ff. The smaller temple (B) at Pyrgi has been dated to the end of the sixth century, and the typically Etruscan (Vitruvian) Temple A to *c.* 470–60: Pallottino, *N.S.* (1970), Supplement II, 741. Pallottino, *The Etruscans*, 2nd ed., plate 51, shows the most up-to-date restored plan of both temples. For the history of the sanctuary: Diodorus, XV, 14. 3; Strabo, V, 2. 8. For the Vulci temple, see Note 18. Fundamental for the study of Etruscan and Roman architecture is *Etruscan and Republican Roman Mouldings* by Lucy T. Shoe. I insist that the Etruscan mouldings have to be understood in connexion with the common Archaic architecture of the Near East – such as the seventh-century 'Lydian' wall of the central mound at Bin Tepe near Sardes (*B.A.S.O.R.*, CLXXVII (1965), 32, figure 30, and CLXXXII (1966), 27–30) and the gradually refined Greek mouldings. All the same, I admire Miss Shoe's convincing analysis of the 'Etruscan round', as it presents itself in a highly original and dynamic shape about 700 B.C. in the rock-cut foundations of the tumuli at Caere, and retains a tactile quality even when Hellenistic taste started its overwhelming influence both in Etruria and Rome. Miss Shoe emphasizes in a brilliant way the difference between the Greek and otherwise individual later Roman progressive refinement of the mouldings and the untrammelled spirit of the Etruscans. The Etruscans, in their typical free manner, disregarded accepted rules and developed their own shapes, as the impression produced on the spectators by the structures seemed to require. This creative Etruscan architectural decoration belongs to the essential prerequisites for its Roman offspring. The powerful Etruscan boldness of conception has to be brought into special prominence even when Etruscan capitals develop Greek prototypes, as for instance in the Tomba delle Colonne Doriche at Caere (cf. Lucy Shoe, 128, XXXVII, 2, and Boëthius, 'Of Tuscan Columns',

A.J.A., LXVI (1962), 251) or in the Etruscan Aeolic capitals. On the other hand, of course, the evident basic Greek influence must be borne in mind, notwithstanding the fact that the Etruscans strongly remodelled what they borrowed. For the podia, cf. especially Lucy Shoe, *op. cit.*, 83–94.

43. 15. Tomba Ildebranda: Bianchi Bandinelli, *Sovana*, 76–86; Margarete Demus-Quatember, *Etruskische Grabarchitektur*, 39.

44. 16. Fiesole: Maetzke, *loc. cit.* (Note 8); Piera Bocci, *loc. cit.* (Note 8). For another temple with a single cella and alae: O. W. von Vacano, 'Zum Grundriss des Tempels auf dem Talamonaccio', *Hommages à Marcel Renard*, III (Brussels, 1969), 675–94. Velletri model: Andrén, *Origine*, 31 ff.

46. 17. Pyrgi: see Note 14. [It is still open to question whether the larger temple (A) had three cellas or one cella and *alae*: Colonna, *N.S.* (1970), Supplement 11, 46 f.] Marzabotto: Andrén, *Architectural Terracottas*, 313 f.; *I.L.N.* (13 October 1962), 556, figure 1. Contrada Celle at Falerii, and Belvedere at Orvieto: Andrén, *op. cit.*, 81–8, 166 f.; and *Origine*, 28. Temple at Bolsena: Bloch, *Mél. Rome*, LXII (1950), 76 ff.

18. Vulci temple: Bartoccini, 'Il tempio grande di Vulci', *Études étrusco-italiques* (Louvain, 1963), 9–12. Capitoline Temple: Dionysius, III, 69 f.; IV, 59; Livy, I, 55, 56. 1; X, 23. 12; XL, 51. 3; Pliny, XXVII, 14 ff.; XXXIII, 57; XXXV, 157; XXXVI, 185. For other references: Platner-Ashby and Nash.

47. 19. For the remains on the Capitoline Hill: Gjerstad, *Early Rome*, III, 168 ff.; *San Giovenale*, 151 ff. I repeat that Vitruvius describes a temple with three cellas and eight columns in the pronaos, while the Capitoline Temple had columns along both sides (alae) and in front of the pronaus, which thus had eighteen columns in front of the temple. For rough substructures below podia and city walls: Ward-Perkins, *P.B.S.R.*, XXIX (1961), 34 ff., and Stefani, *N.S.* (1944–5), 83, figure 3.

48. 20. Gjerstad, *Early Rome*, III, 168–77. Temple C in the Largo Argentina: Marchetti-Longhi, *Bull. Comm.*, LX (1932), 280 ff.; 'L'Area sacra del Largo Argentina', *loc. cit.* (Note 11); Crema, 42.

21. The temple of Ardea: Stefani, *N.S.* (1954), 6 ff.; Lucy Shoe, *Etruscan and Republican Roman Mouldings*, 20–2, 83–6. Altars: Shoe, *op. cit.*, 94–109; Castagnoli, 'Sulla tipologia degli altari di Lavinio', *Bull. Comm.*, LXXVII (1959–60), 145–72, and my remarks, *A.J.A.*, LXVI (1962), 253.

49. 22. For the temple of 69 B.C. see below, p. 163 f. Vitruvius's rule for the columns (IV, 7) is:

'2. Let the thickness of the columns at the bottom be one seventh of their height, their height one third of the width of the temple, and the diminution of a column at the top, one fourth of its thickness at the bottom.

'3. The height of their bases should be one half of that thickness. The plinth of their bases should be circular, and in height one half of the height of the bases, the torus above it and congee being of the same height as the plinth. The height of the capital is one half the thickness of a column. The abacus has a width equivalent to the thickness of the bottom of a column. Let the height of the capital be divided into three parts, and give one to the plinth (that is, the abacus), the second to the echinus, and the third to the necking with its congee.'

Commentary: Andrén, *Architectural Terracottas*, XLIX ff. For the measurements of Greek temples: W. B. Dinsmoor, *The Architecture of Ancient Greece* (London and New York, 1950), 337 ff. Dr P. Åström has checked the height of the columns of the Olympieion. Gjerstad, *Acta Instituti Romani Norvegiae*, I (1962), 35–40 points out that Vitruvius's description of the Capitoline Temple as 'low' (*humilis*) in his paragraph about the areostyle buildings (III, 3. 5) as it stands, if not a misplaced recollection of the old temple, refers to the temple of 69 B.C. Further discussion: Boëthius, 'Nota sul Tempio Capitolino e Vitruvio III, 3. 5', *Arctos*, N.S.V. (1967), 45–9. [But Vitruvius's rule concerns three-cella temples without alae (or single-cella with alae), not, as here, three-cella with alae.]

23. Gjerstad, *Early Rome*, III, 423 f., figure 266.

51. 24. Tuscan columns are presented in a masterly way by Lucy Shoe, *Etruscan and Republican Roman Mouldings*, 115 ff. Against scholars who have assumed an internal Italic or Mycenaean prehistory for Tuscan columns (Ducati, 92; Andrén, *Architectural Terracottas*, LIV f., and others; see Boëthius, *A.J.A.*, LXVI (1962), 249–54; Polacco, 55–68. The oldest Tuscan columns: Polacco, plate 6; Fiesole: *St. Etr.*, XXIX (1961), 413 f.; Vignanello: G. Q. Giglioli, *N.S.* (1916), 41–4. For Morgantina, see E. Sjöqvist, *A.J.A.*, LXII (1958), 160. It is interesting that Inigo Jones also had a special feeling for the Tuscan order as being the most primitive of the five orders and closest to the vernacular (Sir John Summerson, 'Inigo Jones', *Proc. Brit. Ac.*, L (1964), 174–6).

52. 25. Forum Boarium: Gjerstad, *Early Rome*, III, 185 f., 448, figure 281, 1–2. Vulci: Polacco, 64, plate 6. 16; Ducati, 394, figure 453 f. For Aeolic capitals, see illustration 82; Antonia Ciasca, *Il capitello detto eolico in Etruria* (Florence, 1962); Lucy T. Shoe, *A.J.A.*, LXVIII (1964), 409 f. Doric capitals: *St. Etr.*, I (1927), 167, plate 46 B; *San Giovenale*, 71.

53. 26. Norchia: Rosi, *J.R.S.*, XV (1925), 43, figure 38; Polacco, 64 f. Tomba Ildebranda: see Note 15. 'Peopled capitals': E. von Mercklin, *Antike Figuralkapitelle* (Berlin, 1962).

57. 27. Vitruvius's words about a tympanum 'either of masonry or wood' reveal that he could have had a

Late Etruscan or Republican stone-built temple in mind. Stillicidium: Andrén's commentary in *Architectural Terracottas*, LXII-LXVI; *idem*, *Eranos*, XLIII (1945), 1-22; *idem*, *Origine*, 38 ff. Morgan's translation is of course impossible for greater temples, as pointed out by Andrén, Gjerstad, *Early Rome*, III, 185, note 4, and others. Other interpretations cited: F. E. Brown, *Cosa*, II, 39; C. Fensterbusch, *Vitruv* (Darmstadt, 1964), 197. The model from Nemi: Andrén, *Architectural Terracottas*, XXXI, no. 37, and LXVIII f.; M. Moretti, *Museo di Villa Giulia* (Rome, 1962), 224. For the *stillicidium* see also Note 56. Drip-lines: temple of the lower town of Ardea, *N.S.* (1954), 10 f., 13. Capitolium of Cosa: *Cosa*, II, 86 f., 91, figure 65. Temple D at Cosa: *Cosa*, II, 33 f., 39, figure 24. Gabii: M. A. Basch, 'Las excavaciones españolas en Gabii', *Atti del VII Congresso Internazionale di Archeologia Classica*, II (1961), 243-7. For the naiskoi of Sicily (Morgantina, Sabucina near Caltanisetta): Sjöqvist, *A.J.A.*, LXVIII (1964), 146 f.; P. Orlandini, *Arch. Cl.*, XV (1963), 88, plates 27 f.

58. 28. Model from Satricum: Andrén, *Architectural Terracottas*, XXII f., figures 7-8. Model from Heraion: Drerup, *Anz.* (1964), 194, figure 6. Cosa: *Cosa*, II, 38, 92.

59. 29. Pyrgi: G. Colonna: 'Pyrgi', *N.S.* (1970), Supplement II, 48-82; *Arch. Cl.*, XXIII (1971), plate 85. Pediment with warriors: *Ny Carlsberg Glyptothek. Den Etruskiske Samling* (Copenhagen, 1966), 29, no. 168; *San Giovenale*, 57, figure 58. Talamone: Andrén, *Architectural Terracottas*, 227 ff., plates 82-3; O. W. von Vacano, 'Ricerche sul tempio di Talamone', *N.S.* (1962), 297-300.

30. Orvieto (Belvedere): Andrén, *op. cit.*, 171 ff., plates 64-7 and C: 2-3. Orvieto (Via di S. Leonardo): Andrén, 159 ff., plates 59-61 (dated by Andrén to the last quarter of the fifth century, while Luisa Banti (*Il mondo degli Etruschi*, 83) regards them as first-century classicistic art). Civita Castellana (Lo Scasato): Andrén, 125-30, plates 46-8. Civita Alba: Andrén, 298-300, plates 98-100. Tarquinia: Romanelli, *N.S.* (1948), 254 f.

60. 31. For the Greek background of Italic terracotta decoration, Åkerström, *Die arkitektonischen Terrakotten Kleinasiens* (*Acta Ath. Suec.*, XI, 1966); and, in addition, Andrén, *Architectural Terracottas*. For central Italy: Åkerström, 'Untersuchungen über die figürlichen Terrakottafriese aus Etrurien und Latium', *Opus. Rom.*, I (1954), 191 ff.; G. von Kaschnitz-Weinberg, *Das Schöpferische in der römischen Kunst*, 98 ff. Retardation: Elisabeth Jastrow, 'Abformung und Typenwandel in der antiken Tonplastik', *Opus. Arch.*, II (1941), 1-28.

32. Antefixes and protective decoration in central Italy: Andrén, *Architectural Terracottas*, CXVI-CCXLII. Antefixes of Ardea: *Arkeologiska forskningar*

och fynd utgivna med anledning av H.M. Konung Gustaf VI Adolfs sjuttiårsdag (Stockholm, 1952), 125, note 12; *Opus. Rom.*, III (1961), 50-2, plates 20-1.

61. 33. Revetment from Fratte (Marcina; Strabo, V, 4. 13): *Anz.* (1956), 447-50. (For the splendid ridgepole revetment from Pyrgi, see Note 29.) Capitoline Temple: Pliny, XXVIII, 16; XXXV, 157; Plutarch, *Publicola*, XIII ff.; Livy, X, 23. 12, and Platner-Ashby, *s.v.* Spiral ornaments from Forum Boarium: Gjerstad, *Early Rome*, III, 187, 448, figure 280, 1-6. Spirals above the pediment: coin of M. Volteius: H. A. Grueber, *Coins of the Roman Republic in the British Museum*, I (London, 1910), 388, plate 42. 1, *circa* 78 B.C. It is in all other details different from the Capitoline Temple of 509 B.C. It seems to me unlikely that all the tympana were decorated in this way. Probably the spiral ornaments adorned only the apex.

34. Portonaccio Temple of Veii: Stefani, *N.S.* (1953), 50, III; Pallottino, 'Il grande acroterio femminile di Veio', *Arch. Cl.*, II (1950), 122-79. [Cf. now the acroteria from Murlo: Note 5.] Other sculpture on ridge-poles: sarcophagus from Cerveteri (Procoio di Ceri), Moretti (*op. cit.*, Note 27), 83, figure 58; Vagn Poulsen, *San Giovenale*, figures 387-9; Giglioli, CXXXV, 2, CLVIII, 4 (examples from Chiusi). For Sicily and Magna Graecia: Andrén, *Architectural Terracottas*, CVII (with references). Elisabeth D. Van Buren, *Archaic Fictile Revetments in Sicily and Magna Graecia* (London, 1923), figures 71, 73.

62. 35. [Arezzo simas dated to *c.* 480 by Maetzke (*B. d'Arte*, XXXIV (1949), 251 ff.).] To be added to Andrén's commentary on terracotta decoration is the fine appreciation of the classicistic style by L. Richardson in *Cosa*, II, 281-4.

63. 36. Plates of bronze: L. Pareti, *La Tomba Regolini-Galassi del Museo Gregoriano Etrusco* (Città del Vaticano, 1947), 239-44, no. 217; 289 f., no. 238; plate 32; Vagn Poulsen, *San Giovenale*, figures 342-4, 368 f. Aedicula erected by Numa: Serv. ad Aen., I, 8. Bronze gates of the Servian Wall: G. Säflund, *Le mura di Roma repubblicana*, 199. Porta Raudusculana: Varro, *Lingua Latina*, V, 163; Valerius Maximus, *Memorabilia*, V, 6. 3. The gate of Collatia: Ovid, *Fasti*, II, 785. The aedicula of Concordia in the Forum: Pliny, XXXIII, 19. Bronze revetments from Nemi and Palestrina: Andrén, *Architectural Terracottas*, CXXVI, 378 f. and 383 f.; Moretti, *Museo di Villa Giulia* (*op. cit.*, Note 27), 223, figure 164. Oriental, Archaic Greek, and Hellenistic background: Palace of Alcinous, *Odyssey*, VII, 86; what Herodotus (I, 179) relates about Babylon and Polybius (X, 27. 10 ff.) about Ecbatana, and Livy's description (XLI, 20. 9) of the Temple of Jupiter Capitolinus of Antiochus IV in Antioch, which had walls wholly covered by gilded plates.

37. Gjerstad, 'Die Ursprungsgeschichte der römis-

chen Kaiserfora', *Opus. Arch.*, 111 (1944), 40 ff. Quite different Archaic Greek planning: Birgitta Bergquist, *The Archaic Greek Temenos*, Acta Ath. Suec., XIII (1967). E. Dyggve, *Lindos*, 111. *Fouilles de l'Acropole 1902–1914 et 1952*, 516–18. Von Kaschnitz-Weinberg (*op. cit.*, Note 31), 55 f., 70. Boëthius, *The Golden House of Nero*, 40 f.

38. Orientation of altars: Vitruvius, IV, 9; Castagnoli, *Bull. Comm.*, LXXVII (1959–60), 155 f. For the altar of the Capitolium of Cosa: *Cosa*, 11, figure 71. Orientation of temples: Vitruvius, IV, 5; Thulin, *Die Ritualbücher*, 45; Enking, *St. Etr.*, XXV (1957), 541–4; Weinstock, 'Templum', *R.M.*, XLVII (1932), 95–121; Pallottino, 'Deorum sedes', *Studi in onore di A. Calderini e R. Paribeni*, 111 (1956), 223–34. [Important new evidence for the planning of sanctuaries has been found at Poggio Civitate (Murlo) near Siena. Excavations have revealed a large square building (*c.* 61 by 61 m.) of sixth-century date enclosing an open courtyard with colonnades on three sides, with a small rectangular *templum* (?) at the west side of the courtyard. The *templum* and the two entrances to the courtyard are off-centre, so there is no emphasis on axial symmetry. But the complex shows considerable sophistication of design, and invites comparison with Republican fora. See K. M. Phillips, *A.J.A.*, LXXVI (1972), 249 ff., with plan; and R. A. Staccioli, *Mélanges offerts à Jacques Heurgon*, 11 (Rome, 1976), 961–72, who discusses the possible functions (other than religious). Rather similar is a building recently excavated in 'Zone F' of the acropolis of Acquarossa near Viterbo [52]. In its final phase (second half of the sixth century) it consisted of two wings forming an irregular L-shape (*c.* 25 x 40 m.), with colonnades facing on to an open courtyard. According to the excavator it may have served as the religious or administrative centre of the settlement, or perhaps combined both functions. See E. Wetter, M. Moretti, C. E. Östenberg, *Med Kungen på Acquarossa* (Malmö, 1972); *Gli Etruschi: nuove ricerche e scoperte*, Stockholm exhibition catalogue (Viterbo, 1972); F. de Ruyt, 'Une cité étrusque d'époque archaïque à Acquarossa', *L'Antiquité Classique*, XLII (1973), 584–6; C. E. Östenberg, *Case etrusche di Acquarossa*. The complexes at both Murlo and Acquarossa have yielded great quantities of architectural terracottas (see Note 5).]

64. 39. Urartu: W. Kleiss, 'Zur Rekonstruktion des urartäischen Tempels', *Istanbuler Mitteilungen*, XIII–XIV (1963–4), 1–14. The reconstruction of Kleiss is refuted by Riemann, *Gymnasium*, LXXII (1965), 334.

65. 40. Etruscan rules: Thulin, *Die Ritualbücher*, 3–10, 30–41. Roma Quadrata: Chapter 2, Note 3.

41. Veii: Ward-Perkins: *P.B.S.R.*, XXIX (1961), 25–32; Stefani, *N.S.* (1922), 379–404. Vetulonia: Falchi, *N.S.* (1895), 272–7. San Giovenale: *San Giovenale*,

289 ff. Cf. Tarquinia: Romanelli, *N.S.* (1948), 218–23; and Rusellae: Note 3.

68. 42. Walls: Lugli, *Tecnica edilizia*, 9–153; Blake (1947), 70 ff. Walls of Populonia: De Agostino, *St. Etr.*, XXX (1962), 275–82. Veii: Ward-Perkins, *P.B.S.R.*, XXIX (1961), 32–9. Luni: *San Giovenale*, 320–4. For Rome: Dionysius, IX, 68. 3; Strabo, V, 3. 7.) Capena: G. D. B. Jones, *P.B.S.R.*, XXX (1962), 138–41. [An Etruscan town wall recently discovered at Ghiaccio Forte, between Lake Bolsena and Rusellae, may also have been hastily erected during the period of Roman expansion. Here the lower courses consisted of heavy facing stones with rubble rock fill; the upper part may have been of mud-brick. See M. A. del Chiaro, *Etruscan Ghiaccio Forte* (California, 1976); *A.J.A.*, LXXVIII (1974), 385 ff.] Rusellae: Naumann, *R.M.*, LXVI (1959), 3 ff.; Hiller, *R.M.*, LXIX (1962), 59 ff.; see also Note 3.

69. 43. The quotations are from Hyginus Gromaticus, *Constitutio Limitum*: Thulin, *Die Ritualbücher*, 31 f. For the Roman surveyors' debt to the Etruscans see also: O. Dilke, *The Roman Land Surveyors* (Newton Abbot, 1971), 32–4.

44. It now seems evident that about 600 and even before the Greeks adopted regular town planning in new towns that had no obstacles to a regular plan: Smyrna (seventh century; J. M. Cook, *The Greeks in Ionia and the East* (London, 1962), 70–4) and in south Italy and Sicily, Selinus, Akragas, Paestum, Metapontum; see the summary by A. G. Woodhead, *The Greeks in the West* (London, 1962), 121–3; Castagnoli, *Arch. Cl.*, XV (1963), 180–97.

For a concise survey of ancient town-planning see now J. B. Ward-Perkins, *Cities of Ancient Greece and Italy*. See also Castagnoli, *Ippodamo*; Boëthius, *The Golden House of Nero*, 33–54, 187; Ward-Perkins, 'The Early Development of Roman Town-Planning', *Acta Congressus Madvigiani*, IV (Copenhagen, 1958), 109–29; A. von Gerkan, *Griechische Städteanlagen*, 42–61. Urartian Zernaki Tepe affords us a grid plan in the Near East of the eighth century, no doubt a link between towns, which inspired the Greeks, and traditions from the Assyrian and Babylonian cities: Burney and Lawson, *Anatolian Studies*, X (1960), 185–8; C. Nylander, 'Remarks on the Urartian Acropolis at Zernaki Tepe', *Orientalia Suecana*, XIV–XV (1965–6), 141–54.

45. Orvieto: M. Bizzarri, 'La necropoli orvietana di Crocefisso del Tufo', *St. Etr.*, XXXIV (1966), 3 ff., with plan. Caere: *Mon. Ant.*, XLII (1955), plates 1 ff. Marzabotto: Mansuelli, 'Marzabotto, dix années de fouilles et de recherches', *Mél. Rome, Antiquité*, LXXXIV (1972), 111 ff.; *I.L.N.* (13 October 1962), 556–9. [Evidence from the latest excavations suggests that the street grid was begun in the early fifth century

and was preceded by a pre-urban phase of the late sixth.] For *strigae* and *scamna*: Castagnoli, *Ippodamo*, 50 and 100. French excavations at Casalecchio north of Marzabotto reveal another regular town: Pairault, *Mél. Rome, Antiquité*, LXXXIV (1972), 145 ff. Spina: N. Alfieri, P. E. Arias, M. Hirmer, *Spina* (Florence, 1958); J. Heurgon, *La vie quotidienne chez les étrusques*, 170 ff.

74. 46. Castagnoli, *Ippodamo*, 44-9; Heurgon, *Recherches sur l'histoire, la religion et la civilisation de Capoue préromaine* (Paris, 1942); Velleius Paterculus, I, 7, cites Cato, dating Capua to 471 B.C., probably alluding to an expansion of the town for Samnite immigrants, but see Pallottino, *La Parola del Passato*, XI (1956), 81-8. The Etruscans in Campania: H. H. Scullard, *The Etruscan Cities and Rome*, 171 ff.; Boëthius in *Symbolae philologicae O. A. Danielsson dicatae* (1932). Fratte (Marcina) and the Sorrento peninsula: Pliny, III, 70; P. C. Sestieri, *N.S.* (1952), 163; B. Neutsch, *Anz.* (1956), 351 ff. Etruscan graffiti from Pompeii and Fratte: A. Maiuri, *Saggi di varia antichità* (Venice, 1954), 245-51.

47. Plan of Pompeii: Castagnoli, *Ippodamo*, 26-32; von Gerkan, 'Der Stadtplan von Pompeii', *Gesammelte Aufsätze*, 144-58. Walls of Pompeii: Maiuri, *Mon. Ant.*, XXXIII (1930), 114 ff.; *N.S.* (1943), 275 ff.; Lugli, *Tecnica edilizia*, 295-9.

48. Tomba delle Bighe: Giglioli, CXV, 2. For actors and theatres see below, p. 198, and Sibylle Haynes, 'Ludiones Etruriae', *Festschrift für Harald Keller*, 13-21.

75. 49. Heurgon, *La vie quotidienne chez les étrusques*, 50 f., no doubt understands Diodorus V, 40. 4 rightly; Diodorus (that is, Poseidonius) speaks about the luxury of the Etruscans and their attending artisan slaves (musicians, dancers and so on), their costly attire and 'demeures particulières de toute sorte: c'est d'ailleurs aussi le fait de la plupart des hommes libres'. It is self-evident that Diodorus here is not speaking of atria and domus but of convenient dwellings of the free lower classes and the especially qualified slaves of the aristocratic households. Heurgon, *op. cit.*, 79-94, maintains a different view regarding the free lower classes of Etruscans (with full bibliography). For the agricultural centre near San Giovenale (Sambuco): *San Giovenale*, 313-20.

76. 50. For Vetulonia see Note 41. Marzabotto: Note 45. San Giovenale: *San Giovenale*, 299 ff.

77. 51. Megaron at Veii: *N.S.* (1922), 379 ff., figures 2 and 3.

79. 52. Sub-Apennine huts with benches of pebbles: Chapter 1, Note 4. House at Morgantina: Sjöqvist, *A.J.A.*, LXVIII (1964), 145. Tomb of the Thatched Roof: Mengarelli, *St. Etr.*, I (1927), 158 f., plate 23; Ricci, *Mon. Ant.*, XLII (1955), 343 ff.; Boëthius, *Palladio*, XV (1965), 3-6; *Opus. Rom.*, VI (1968), 9-19.

81. 53. [To be added to the evidence for domestic architecture are the remains of sixth-century houses recently recovered at Acquarossa near Viterbo. These have a three-fold importance: (1) They show a variety of types of plan, some of which correspond fairly closely to contemporary rock-cut tombs at Cerveteri. (2) None of those excavated so far resembles the atrium-houses described by Vitruvius. (3) Many were richly covered with decorative architectural terracottas which previously had been associated only with temples and sanctuaries. Especially remarkable are the painted terracottas with white designs on the red ground [71]. For the latter: C. Wikander, *Opus. Rom.*, XI (1976), 53-61; for the houses in general: Note 38. For mention of remains of Etruscan houses recently excavated at Graviscae, the ancient port of Tarquinia: Torelli, *N.S.* (1971), 196 ff.] For the more ambitious tombs: Margarete Demus-Quatember, *Etruskische Grabarchitektur*, 31, 33, and figure 5; Åkerström, *Etruskische Gräber*, 30, figure 4. Most important are the tomb-plans in M. Moretti, *Nuovi monumenti della pittura etrusca* (Milan, 1966).

82. 54. Coffered ceiling of Tomba della Scimmia: R. Bianchi Bandinelli, *Clusium: le pitture delle tombe arcaiche (Monumenti della pittura antica scoperti in Italia)* (Rome, 1939), 6, figures 9 and 10. Tomba del Cardinale: Ducati, 378, figure 418. Tomb at Ardea [74]: Boëthius, *Arkeologiska studier tillägnade H.K.H. Kronprins Gustaf Adolf* (1932), 262-72. Faded remains of paintings at Cerveteri: Moretti, *Mon. Ant.*, XLII (1955), 1049 ff., plates 2 and 4; and at San Giovenale (Porzarago Tomb 9): E. and K. Berggren, *San Giovenale: Results of Excavations*, I, 5 (Stockholm, 1972), 61 ff. Tomb-paintings in general: F. Poulsen, *Etruscan Tomb-Paintings* (Oxford, 1922); M. Pallottino, *Etruscan Painting* (Geneva, 1952); Ross Holloway, 'Conventions of Etruscan Painting in the Tomb of Hunting and Fishing at Tarquinia', *A.J.A.*, LXIX (1965), 341-7; M. Moretti, *op. cit.* (Note 53).

85. 55. Ornate façades: G. Rosi, 'Sepulchral Architecture as illustrated by the Rock Façades of Central Italy', *J.R.S.*, XV (1925), 1-59; XVII (1927), 59-96; Bianchi Bandinelli, *Sovana*; E. Colonna di Paolo and G. Colonna, *Castel d'Asso* (a monumental work with excellent illustrations). Protecting roofs above entrance: Rosi, *loc. cit.* (1925), 24; Åkerström, *Etruskische Gräber*, 73 ff.; Margarete Demus-Quatember, *Etruskische Grabarchitektur*, 37 f., figure 25. Elegant hillside houses: Rosi, *loc. cit.* (1925), 38-42. Doors: the voussoir arches of the later centuries have to be distinguished from rock-cut arches and corbel vaults with a keystone: Blake (1947), 195-7. Chiusi urn: Staccioli, *Arch. Cl.*, XIX (1967), 293 ff. Tomba Campana: Luisa Banti, *St. Etr.*, XXXVIII (1970), 42 f., figure 6.

86. 56. [Models of houses at tomb-entrances: a stone

model from Castel d'Asso (sixth-fifth century) is note-worthy for its very wide eaves (*stillicidium*): Colonna di Paolo, *op. cit.* (Note 55), 68-9, plates 458-60.] Gabled roofs: Boëthius, 'The Old Etruscan Towns', *Classical, Mediaeval and Renaissance Studies in Honor of B. Ullman* (1964), 9. Gabled tombs at Populonia: Luisa Banti, *Il mondo degli Etruschi*, 96, plate 8; and at Tarquinia: Giglioli, cxi-cxiii, cxv, ccii. Terracotta models of gabled temples: Note 8.

57. E. Wistrand, *Vitruviusstudier* (Göteborg, 1933), 12 ff., and *Eranos*, XXXVII (1939), 39 f.

58. Flat roofs: Boëthius, *loc. cit.* (Note 56), 9; Ducati, 378, figure 418; San Giovenale: *N.S.* (1960), 29, 38, 61; *San Giovenale*, figures 16, 60, 61 etc.; Margarete Demus-Quatember, *Etruskische Grabarchitektur*, plate 13.

89. 59. Houses of Marzabotto: Mansuelli, *R.M.*, LXX (1963), 44 ff. Tomba del Tablino at Caere: *N.S.* (1955), 106-13. Tomba dei Capitelli: *St. Etr.*, I (1927), plate 45. Tomba dei Vasi Greci: *loc. cit.*, plates 30 f. A. Boëthius, *San Giovenale*, 64 ff. (for the *cava aedium tuscanica*), and plates 69-71 (for the Tomb of the Princess at San Giuliano).

90. 60. The development of the *cava aedium tuscanica*: Maiuri, *N.S.* (1930), 381 ff.; (1942), 404 ff.; (1944-5), 130 ff.; Polacco, 117. Origin: Gjerstad, *The Swedish Cyprus Expedition*, IV, 2 (Stockholm, 1948), 232 ff.; [for a more recent discussion: J. W. Graham, 'The Greek House and the Roman House', *The Phoenix*, XX (1966), 6 ff.].

93. 61. Atria displuviata: Tomba della Mercareccia [89]: Ducati, 379, figure 419. Model from Chiusi: Ducati, 381; Giglioli, cccxxxvi, 3. Peristyle at Ostia: R. Meiggs, *Roman Ostia* (Oxford, 1960), 252. Tuscan columns: see Note 24. Columns of other orders are commonly shown on late ash-urns: Clelia Laviosa, *Scultura tardo-etrusca di Volterra* (Florence, 1964), nos. 6, 12, 16, 18; Giglioli, cccxcix, 4 ff. Tomb of the Volumnii: von Gerkan, 'Das Grab der Volumnier bei Perugia', *Gesammelte Aufsätze*, 338-51. For military decorations see city gates such as the so-called 'Gate of Augustus' at Perugia (Blake (1947), plate 13, 3), and the Tomba Giglioli at Tarquinia [93]: M. Moretti, *op. cit.* (Note 53), 307-16.

94. 62. For the barrel-vaulted tombs of the last centuries B.C. see now Oleson, *St. Etr.*, XLIV (1976), 69-85. Tomba del Granduca (Paccianese) at Chiusi: Åkerström, *Etruskische Gräber*, 172; Giglioli, cccxcv, 2; cf. Ducati, 398, figures 458 ff. The so-called Tomba di Pitagora at Cortona imitates a barrel vault by crescent-shaped gables carrying longitudinal stone slabs: Åkerström, *op. cit.*, 175 f.; Ducati, 73, figures 68 ff.; F. Coarelli (ed.), *Le città etrusche*, 53, upper figure. Velia: *Encicl. Art. Ant.*, VII, 1113, figure 1240. Lindos: E. Dyggve, *Lindos*, III (1960), 256 f., 289, 529 f. Etruscan urn in the Worcester Museum:

Worcester Art Museum Annual, V (1946), 15 ff. City gates (Volterra): Blake (1947), 199; Lugli, *Tecnica edilizia*, 338 ff.

63. Wooden roofs: Lehmann, 'The Dome of Heaven', *Art Bulletin*, XXVII (1945), 20. Cf. Vitruvius's description of vaulted ceilings of framework (V, 10. 3) and wooden vaults of baths of the Imperial Age in Gaul, A. Grenier, *Manuel d'archéologie gallo-romaine*, IV (Paris, 1960), 455 f.

64. The particularism of the Etruscans is especially well brought out by Luisa Banti in *Il mondo degli etruschi*.

65. Clelia Laviosa, 'Rusellae', *St. Etr.*, XXVIII (1960), 294 ff., plates 67b, 68. Populonia: A. Minto, *N.S.* (1924), 21, figure 7; De Agostino, *St. Etr.*, XXX (1962), 282. Ostia: *J.R.S.*, II (1961), 202. Etruscan roads in general, in addition to older authors (especially Dennis, Ashby, and Tomassetti): Ward-Perkins's and M. W. Frederiksen's studies of roads in south Etruria and the Ager Faliscus, *P.B.S.R.*, XXIII (1955), 44-72, plates 14-21; XXV (1957), 67-208, plates 17-47; *J.R.S.*, XLVI (1957), 139-43; Ward-Perkins, 'Etruscan Engineering: Road Building, Water-Supply and Drainage', *Hommages à Albert Grenier, Collection Latomus*, LVIII (1962), 1636-43, and E. Wetter, *San Giovenale*, 169 ff. Bridges, abutments: *op. cit.*, figures 279, 280; Frederiksen, *J.R.S.*, LV (1965), 290.

95. 66. For Asia Minor: Margarete Demus-Quatember, *Etruskische Grabarchitektur*, 63-76. Most important for the connexion with the Lydian mounds are the monumental chamber tombs of the Bin Tepe cemetery of Sardes. The central of the three great mounds which dominate the skyline of Bin Tepe seems undoubtedly to be the tomb of Gyges (seventh-century B.C. king of Lydia), with its group of twelve 'Gugu' signs: *A.J.A.*, LXIX (1965), 148, plate 38, figures 10, 11, and the reports: *B.A.S.O.R.*, CLXXVII (1965), 27-34; CLXXXII (1966), 27-30. Cyrene: A. Rowe, *Cyrenaican Expedition of the University of Manchester 1952* (Manchester, 1956), 4-11. Cyprus: V. Karageorghis, *Excavations in the Necropolis of Salamis*, I (Nicosia, 1967), 25 ff.

96. 67. Åkerström, *Etruskische Gräber*, 23 ff., 43 ff., discusses the earliest chamber tombs. Fundamental for the tombs at Caere (Cerveteri): R. Vighi, G. Ricci, M. Moretti, 'Caere', *Mon. Ant.*, XLII (1955); also *N.S.* (1955), 46-113. Door slabs at Tarquinia: Luisa Banti, *Il mondo degli Etruschi*, 308, plate 40.

68. Regolini-Galassi Tomb: L. Pareti, *La Tomba Regolini-Galassi*, 86 ff., plate 1. La Cocumella di Caiolo (San Giuliano): *San Giovenale*, 311 f. Orvieto: Bizzarri, *loc. cit.* (Note 45). Meloni del Sodo; Åkerström, *op. cit.*, 175-9; Margarete Demus-Quatember, *Etruskische Grabarchitektur*, 25, figures 8-9. The chamber tombs with a slit have been called 'Egyptian

tombs': Åkerström, *op. cit.*, 44, 54 f., 90 f.; at San Giovenale: Östenberg, *San Giovenale: Results of Excavations*, I, 9 (Stockholm, 1972), 4–10 (Types 3b and 4b).

98. 69. Tholos tombs in general: Ducati, 63 ff.; Margarete Demus-Quatember, *Etruskische Grabarchitektur*, 17–20. La Montagnola di Quinto Fiorentino: Caputo, *B. d'Arte*, XLVII (1962), 115–52; F. Coarelli (ed.), *Le città etrusche*, 35–8. Tomb of Casal Marittimo (reconstructed in Florence Archaeological Museum): Minto, *St. Etr.*, IV (1930), 58 ff. Cf. rock-cut tholos tomb at Riello near Viterbo: Ducati, 67, figure 55. Cf. also the corbelled architecture in Sardinia and Early Iron Age Italy: above, illustrations 5 and 8. Roman tumuli: Chapter 6, pp. 213 f.

99. 70. Populonia: Åkerström, *Etruskische Gräber*, 139–59. Tomba della Pietrera, Vetulonia: Pincelli, *St. Etr.*, XVII (1943), 47 ff., plate 6; F. Coarelli, *op. cit.*, 104–5, 109. Cisterns at Rome: Gjerstad, *Early Rome*, III, 88–110, 124 ff. Tullianum: Platner-Ashby, Nash, *s.v.*

71. Porsenna's tomb: Pliny, XXXVI, 91–3; F. Messerschmidt, 'Das Grabmal des Porsenna', *Das neue Bild der Antike*, II (1942), 53 ff. Connection with Columna Minucia: G. Becatti, *La colonna coclide istoriata* (Rome, 1960), 34–6. Tomb near Ariccia (known by various names): Crema, 247, figures 273–4; Messerschmidt, *op. cit.*, figure 1. For Ross Holloway's explanation of the Late Republican and Augustan romantic revival of old types of tombs see below, Chapter 6, Note 96. Vulci tomb (Tumulo della Cucumella): A. Hus, *Vulci étrusque et étrusco-romaine* (Paris, 1971), 73–5; G. Dennis, *Cities and Cemeteries of Etruria*, 452 ff.

100. 72. For the valleys lined with ornate tombs: Note 55 ('ornate façades'); see also Gargana, 'La necropoli rupestre di S. Giuliano', *Mon. Ant.*, XXXIII (1929), 297 ff. Tomba Inghirami: Giglioli, cccxcv, 1. Cf. the chambers around the central hall in the tomb of the Volumnii family [72]; and the six chambers of the Tomb of the Inscriptions at Vulci: Bartoccini, *Atti del VII Congresso Internazionale di Archeologia Classica*, II (1961), 278 f. For the Roman equivalent: Morpurgo, 'Un sepolcréto precristiano in Anzio', *Rend. Pont.*, XXII (1946–7), 153–66.

73. Åkerström, *Etruskische Gräber*, 73 ff.; Margarete Demus-Quatember, *Etruskische Grabarchitektur*, 36–8; see especially E. Colonna di Paolo and G. Colonna, *Castel d'Asso*.

101. 74. Criticism of the Etruscans also by Athenaeus, XII, 517 ff. Analysis of this criticism: Heurgon, *La vie quotidienne chez les étrusques*, 46–51; Boëthius, *San Giovenale*, 9 ff.; 117. Tomba François at Vulci, see *San Giovenale*, 102, note 41 (with bibliography).

75. Dionysius, I, 29. 2; Plutarch, *Camillus*, XXII, 2 (Heraclides Ponticus).

CHAPTER 4

104. 1. Fundamental are Platner-Ashby; Nash; *Fontes*; F. Castagnoli, *Topografia e urbanistica di Roma antica* (Bologna, 1969). Walls of Rome: Lugli, *Tecnica edilizia*, 170, 187, 250 f. Remains of earliest walls: G. Säflund, *Le mura di Roma repubblicana*; P. Quoniam, 'À propos du mur dit de Servius Tullius', *Mél. Rome*, LIX (1947), 41–64; E. Gjerstad, *Opus. Rom.*, I (1954), 50–65; *Early Rome*, III, 27–44; *op. cit.*, IV, 349–57. Criticism of Gjerstad's views: A. von Gerkan, *Rh. M.*, C (1957), 82–97; CIV (1961), 132–48; Romanelli, *Gnomon*, XXXVI (1964), 817 f. The aggeres: Ardea: Boëthius, *Opus. Rom.*, IV (1962), 29 ff.; Antium: Lugli, *op. cit.*, 270 f.; Satricum: Castagnoli, *L'Universo*, XLIII, 3 (1963), 505–18. Walls on the Palatine: Blake (1947), 116 f.; Romanelli, *Mon. Ant.*, XLVI (1963), 214, figures 6–8. Walls of Rusellae and Veii: Chapter 3, Note 42.

Date of the foundation of Rome: for the works by Gjerstad and for criticisms of his historical conclusions, see Chapter 2, Note 1. See also A. Momigliano, 'An Interim Report on the Origins of Rome', *J.R.S.*, LIII (1963), 95 ff.; Romanelli, 'Certezze e ipotesi sulle origini di Roma', *Studi Romani*, XIII (1965), 156 ff.; R. Bloch, *Tite-Live et les premiers siècles de Rome*; G. A. Mansuelli, *Etruria and Early Rome*; H. H. Scullard, *The Etruscan Cities and Rome*, 243 ff.; 'Les origines de la république romaine', *Entretiens sur l'Antiquité Classique, XIII. Fondation Hardt* (Geneva, 1967).

106. 2. Etruscan influence: Livy, I, 8. 3; Strabo, V, 2. 2; Diodorus, V, 40; Dionysius, III, 61–2. Fasces: *St. Etr.*, XXVIII (1960), 459–61. Limitatio: C. O. Thulin, *Die Ritualbücher*, 26–30; Festus, Pauli excerpta, Lindsay (ed.) 505: 'Termino sacra faciebant, quod in ejus tutela fines agrorum esse putabant.' Shoes: Serv. ad Aen., VIII, 458. 'Archaic Greek' alphabet, for instance Dionysius, II, 54. 2; IV, 26. 5. The Duenos inscription and Etruscan graffiti: Gjerstad, *Early Rome*, III, 160–5, 214. Etruscan seventh-century inscription found at the church of S. Omobono, Rome: *Palatino*, VIII (1964), 32 f.

3. Early houses in Rome (Archaic period and later): Gjerstad, VI, 112 f., 121, figures 43–4 (for restored elevation of a house with two storeys); B. Felleti Maj, *N.S.* (1952), 284 ff.; Colini, *Mem. Pont.*, IX, 2 (1966), 11–13. Via Sacra: recent excavations by Frank Brown below the Regia have revealed part of the Early Iron Age village, cult places, and remains of temples (see Chapter 2, Note 9). Architectural terracottas in Rome and Latium: Åkerström, 'Untersuchungen über die figürlichen Terrakottafriese aus Etrurien und Latium', *Opus. Rom.*, I (1954), 191–230; Gjerstad, *op. cit.*, III, 185, 189, 423, 448 ff.; Andrén, *Architectural Terracottas*, 324–477.

108. 4. Etruscan origin of atrium: Varro, *Lingua Latina*, v, 161. Pliny's atrium: *Epist.*, v, 6. 15. Atria at Ostia: *Scavi di Ostia*, I, 107 ff.; R. Meiggs, *Ostia*, 252 f. Atrium-house at Saepinum: V. Cianfarani, *Guida delle antichità di Sepino* (Milan, 1958), 45. Regia: Chapter 2, Note 9. Tabernae: oldest remains: Sandberg, *Eranos*, XXXIV (1936), 82–103. Further references to the old forensic tabernae: Dionysius, III, 67. 4; Livy, IX, 40. 16; XXVI, 27. 2–4. Forum of Pompeii: Crema, 36; Maiuri, *N.S.* (1941), 371 ff. Tabernae at Ostia: *Scavi di Ostia*, I, 98. Fortified refuges: Dionysius, V, 22. 1; VIII, 16. 5.

110. 5. For early subterranean sewers, see Livy, I, 38. 6, 56. 2; V, 55. 5; Dionysius, III, 67. 5. For the present Cloaca Maxima: Nash, *s.v.*; and below, Chapter 6, Note 88.

6. The author, taking into account Frontinus, maintains that the Romans learned to build castra when they captured Pyrrhus's camp after the battle of Beneventum. Livy, XXXV, 14. 8, says that Hannibal admired Pyrrhus's camps while Plutarch (*Pyrrhus*, XVI) tells us that Pyrrhus admired the Roman camps. The oldest Roman castrum known at present is the permanent fourth-century castrum fortress of Ostia [123], but what the Romans learnt from Pyrrhus may have been temporary camp fashions for ambulatory campaigns.

111. 7. For the historical and cultural context: H. H. Scullard, *The Etruscan Cities and Rome*, 247–66. For the plan of the temple and the height and decoration of the building see my discussion of the Etruscan temples (Chapter 3, Note 22). For Vulca: Pliny, XXXV, 157. For the calendar connected with the Capitoline Temple of 509: K. Hanell, *Das altrömische eponyme Amt*, 99 ff. and Gjerstad, 'Notes on the Early Roman Calendar', *Acta Archaeologica*, XXXII (1961), 193–214; [for a different view: Agnes Kirsopp Michels, *The Calendar of the Roman Republic* (Princeton, 1967)].

112. 8. For public meetings on the Capitol see also Livy, XXV, 3, and Velleius Paterculus, II, 3. 2. For statues on the Capitol, for instance: Cicero's third Catiline oration, 19–20. For the favisae: Varro quoted by Gellius, *Noctes atticae*, II, 10. For the archaic phase of the Temple of Castor and Pollux see Tenney Frank, *M.A.A.R.*, V (1925), 79–90; Blake (1947), 121; Nash, *s.v.* Archaic terracottas probably from the temples of Castor and Pollux and Saturn: *Rend. Linc.*, XVI (1961), 59, plate III.

113. 9. For the monuments around the Rostra see especially Pliny, XVIII, 15; XXXIV, 20 ff. As places for them Pliny points out: 'in foro', 20, 24, 30; 'in comitio', 21, 26; 'in rostris', 23, 24 ('oculatissimo loco'), which also confirms the unity of the Forum and the Comitium. Columna Maenia: E. Welin, *Studien zur*

Topographie des Forum Romanum, 130–74; Platner-Ashby, *s.v.*

CHAPTER 5

121. 1. For a general survey of the polygonal walls, see G. Lugli, *Tecnica edilizia*, 55 f., and 'Conclusioni sulla cronologia dell'opera poligonale in Italia', *Studi minori di topografia antica*, 27–32, and Blake (1947), 92–104. For discussion of Lugli's date, A. von Gerkan, *G.G.A.*, CCXII (1958), 181 f. Samnite walls: G. Colonna, 'Saepinum', *Arch. Cl.*, XIV (1962), 80–99. Cosa: *Cosa*, I. Pyrgi and Minturnae [113]: F. Castagnoli, *Ippodamo*, 86–8. Alba Fucens (older and later walls): *Atti del VII Congresso internazionale di archeologia classica*, II (1961), 287; *Rend. Linc.*, ser. 8, XIII (1958), 97–8.

122. 2. For the use of the tufas see Lugli, *Tecnica edilizia*; Blake (1947); T. Frank, *Roman Buildings of the Republic* (*P.A.A.R.*, III) (Rome, 1924); Gjerstad, *Early Rome*, III, 174. The final date of the Servian Wall established already by Frank and corroborated by G. Säflund, *Le mura di Roma repubblicana*; Blake (1947), 124; Lugli, *op. cit.*, 258 ff. On the walls see further von Gerkan, *Gesammelte Aufsätze*, 108–38. For vivid discussion concerning the question of whether the Tiber was left open and the Forum Boarium district was defended by walls running down to the river from the Capitoline and Aventine Hills (as I believe) or if – at least originally – a wall connected the Capitoline, the Palatine, and the Aventine: H. Lyngby, *Beiträge zur Topographie des Forum Boarium Gebietes in Rom* (*Acta Rom. Suec.*, in 8°, VII, 1954), with bibliography. Cf. *Opus. Rom.*, VIII (1974), 33 ff. For the acropolis wall of Ardea: A. Boëthius, *Opus. Rom.*, IV (1962), 29–43.

123. 3. Terracottas from Ostia: P. Mingazzini, *Rend. Pont.*, XXIII–XXIV (1947–9), 75–83. For another dating, A. Andrén, *Architectural Terracottas*, 369; *Scavi di Ostia*, I, 75, plate XXII. New discoveries of terracottas and pre-castrum pottery: Meiggs, *Roman Ostia*, 2nd ed., 379. For the gates: *Cosa*, I, 41 ff.; Lugli, *Tecnica edilizia*, 113 f. For the date and historical circumstances of Falerii Novi (Santa Maria di Falleri): Lugli, *op. cit.*, 271; M. W. Frederiksen and J. B. Ward-Perkins, *P.B.S.R.*, XXV (1957), 155–62; Zonaras, VIII, 18; Polybius, I, 65; Livy, *Epitome*, XX; Valerius Maximus, VI, 5. 1; Eutropius, II, 28.

4. For arches: Blake (1947), 123, 192 ff.; Crema, 9–12; Lugli, *Tecnica edilizia*, 36, 661 f., and 'Considerazioni sull'origine dell'arco a conci radiali', *Studi minori di topografia antica*, 97–138. The bridge on the Via Amerina: Frederiksen and Ward-Perkins, *art. cit.*, 99; P. Gazzola, *Ponti romani*, II (Florence, 1963),

29. Ponte del Diavolo: A. Rava, *Atti del III Convegno nazionale di storia dell'architettura 1938* (1940), 263-6.
126. 5. Town planning and castra: generally, Castagnoli, *Ippodamo*. For Norba see G. Schmiedt and Castagnoli, *L'antica città di Norba, documentazione aerofotometrica* (Florence, 1957). On the castra and their relation to town-planning, Castagnoli, *Ippodamo*, 85-103; Boëthius, *The Golden House of Nero*, 49-53; Crema, 33-5; Ward-Perkins, *Town Planning Review*, XXVI (1955-6), 145 ff., and *Acta Congressus Madvigiani*, IV (Copenhagen, 1958), 118-21. Cf. *Cities of Ancient Greece and Italy*, 28. For the castrum-forts, Castagnoli, *op. cit.*, 85-94; Maria Merolla, 'Allifae', *Arch. Cl.*, XVI (1964), 36-48. On Nicaea, Strabo, XII, 4. 7; V. Tscherikower, *Die hellenistischen Städtegründungen von Alexander dem Grossen bis auf die Römerzeit* (Leipzig, 1927), 135. A small square fortress excavated by Danish archaeologists on Failaka in the Emirate of Kuwait may be compared [122]. It seems clear that it was built by Alexander, and - even if it mainly served as defence for Greek temples - it belongs to the fortifications by which Alexander strengthened his position, settling in them Greek mercenaries, who were willing to live there (Arrian, *Anabasis*, VII, 21). E. Albrectsen, 'An Outpost of Alexander's Empire: the Recently Excavated Fortress on Failaka', *I.L.N.* (27 August 1960), 351-3. K. Jeppesen, 'Et Kongebud til Ikaros', *Kuml* (1960), with a sketch of the settlement on p. 154 and English summary on p. 188. [The account of the military camps given in the text in fact combines information from Polybius with that given by writers of the Imperial age.]
128. 6. Rubble work and barrel vaults of Cosa: *Cosa*, I, 59 ff., 88. Pompeii: Lugli, *Tecnica edilizia*, 379-85, and on the Porticus Metelli (built in 147 B.C.), 451, plate CVIII, 2. The history of concrete before the Roman age: Lugli, *Tecnica edilizia*, 375 ff., and 'L'opus caementicium in Vitruvio', *Studi minori di topografia antica* (1965), 33-40; Crema, 12 ff. For Greek concrete: *Corinth*, III, 1: *Acrocorinth* (1930), 39-42. Cf. Strabo on the jetties of the harbour of Puteoli, V, 4. 6. In the second century the Romans began to build the podia of their temples of concrete - to start with, rather poor and grey: the temples of Concord (121 B.C.) and Castor and Pollux (117 B.C.) on the Forum Romanum. On the podium of the Temple of Magna Mater, Blake (1947), 330 (dates to 110 B.C.).
129. 7. Crema, 61; Lugli, *Tecnica edilizia*, 11 f., 35, 450 f., *et passim*, plates CVII, 1-3; CVIII, 1. For a date about 100 B.C.: Blake (1947), 249, 251; and with arguments deserving unprejudiced consideration: von Gerkan, *Scritti in onore di G. Libertini* (1958), 153 f.; *G.G.A.*, CCXII (1958), 189 f.; *Gesammelte Aufsätze*, 121; critical remarks on the commentary of *Forma*

Urbis by Gerkan, *G.G.A.*, CCXIV (1962), 135-8. Von Gerkan denies both the possibility of dating the incertum of the great hall by the Tiber as early as 193-174 and the identification of this hall with the Porticus Aemilia. The fact that the hall shows no remains of earlier walls is thus irrelevant for him.
130. 8. The Via Appia: Lugli, *Tecnica edilizia*, especially 158 f., plate XVI, 2-3, and for later ashlar constructions *op. cit.*, plate XLVII, 3. Paved roads: Livy, X, 47. 4 (part of the Via Appia 292 B.C.), and XLI, 27 (streets in the town 174 B.C.); *Epitome*, XX (Via Flaminia). Aqua Appia: Esther Van Deman, *The Building of the Roman Aqueducts*, 23-8; T. Ashby, *The Aqueducts of Ancient Rome*, 49-54.
133. 9. G. Marchetti-Longhi, *L'area sacra del Largo Argentina* (*Itinerari*) (1959), 34-41, 49; Crema, 42 f. F. Krauss and R. Herbig, *Der korinthisch-dorische Tempel am Forum von Paestum* (Berlin, 1939). E. von Mercklin, *Antike Figuralkapitelle*, 66. Together with this should be remembered the pre-Roman Temple of Apollo at Pompeii with high podium and a peristyle with Ionian columns: Crema, 45; an interesting analysis is given by G. von Kaschnitz-Weinberg, *Die Grundlagen der republikanischen Baukunst*, 67 f., together with a most suggestive survey of the hellenistic-Roman temples. Corinthian and Doric style combined: Vitruvius, IV, 1. 2. Ionic and Doric style: Jeppesen, *Paradeigmata* (*Jutland Archaeological Society Publications*, IV) (Aarhus, 1958); review by von Gerkan, *G.G.A.*, CCXIV (1960-2), 1-15; Jeppesen, *Acta Archaeologica*, XXXII (1961), 226 f.
10. For a general description, sacred sites, places for jurisdiction, etc., see E. Welin, *Studien zur Topographie des Forum Romanum*, Platner-Ashby, and Nash. For the Maeniana: Boëthius, *Eranos*, XLIII (1945), 94-101. The Columna Maenia (above, p. 113) was a column near the Rostra erected in honour of Caius Maenius, consul in 338 B.C. Pliny, VII, 212; XXXIV, 20; Cicero, *Div. in Caecil.*, 16. 50. With this reference to the Columna Maenia Asconius wrongly connects a later Maenius, who in 184 B.C. sold the domus of the Maenii at the Comitium but reserved a stand for spectators of the gladiatorial games above one column in front of the house. In some comedy or jest in Rome this column of the late descendant of the great Maenius, who sold the old house of the family, was called Columna Maenia. We don't know if this nickname became popular or not in Rome. Welin, *op. cit.*, 130 ff. Forensis dignitas: Varro, *De vita populi romani*, II, quoted by Nonius, 532.
134. 11. Comitium: E. Sjöqvist, 'Pnyx and the Comitium', *Studies Presented to David Moore Robinson*, I (St Louis, 1951), 400-11; L. Richardson, 'Cosa and Rome', *Archaeology*, X (1957), 49-55 (cf. J. A. Hanson, *Roman Theater-Temples*, 37-9). For Agrigentum see

A. D. Trendall, *Archaeology in South Italy and Sicily* (Archaeological Reports for 1963-4 published by the Council of the Society for the Promotion of Hellenic Studies and the Managing Committee of the British School of Archaeology at Athens, 1964), 42, figure 13.

12. Boëthius, *The Golden House of Nero*, 129-88 (with bibliography). Lugli, 'Il valore topografico e giuridico dell'insula in Roma antica', *Studi minori di topografia antica*, 81-96. For another opinion about the word 'insula': von Gerkan, *Gesammelte Aufsätze*, 301. At Herculaneum a tenement house with upper storey around a central court has been excavated, but the type of house such as the Casa a Graticcio seems to be developed from the peristyle houses of the Greek towns and thus to be basically different from the Roman insulae, built upon tabernae. For the Casa a Graticcio: A. Maiuri, *Ercolano, i nuovi scavi* (Rome, 1958), 407-20. There is no reason to assume that the tenement houses mentioned by Livy were of this type. Though it seems evident to me that insula in towns of the Imperial Age (like Ostia) means tenement house, it may be added that the word in older towns (like Pompeii) might have been used for quarter. For the domus at Cosa, see V. J. Bruno, 'A Town House at Cosa', *Archaeology*, XXIII (1970), 233-41.

13. Pomponius Mela, II, 7; Strabo, XVI, 2. 13 and 23. For Carthage, see Appian, *Historia romana*, VIII, 128, and G. and Colette Picard, *La vie quotidienne à Carthage* (Paris, 1958), 49 f.

135. 14. The Circus Flaminius was built along the Tiber from the Pons Fabricius towards the Monte dei Cenci: G. Gatti, 'Dove erano situati il teatro di Balbo e il Circo Flaminio', *Capitolium*, XXXV, 7 (1960), 3-12; *Palatino*, V (1961), 17-20. Nash, *s.v.* For a different interpretation, T. P. Wiseman in *P.B.S.R.*, XLII (1974), 3-26. For constructions of spectators' galleries of wood: Pliny, XXXVI, 116-20; Suetonius, *Nero*, 12; Vitruvius, V, 5. 7. As in the Greek theatres, sloping hillsides could be adapted or earthen embankments constructed, as around the stadium of Olympia. The theatre of 155 B.C.: Livy, *Epitome*, XLVIII; Valerius Maximus, II, 4. 2; Tertullian, *Apologeticus*, 6; *De spectaculis*, 10; Appian, *Bellum civile*, I, 4. 28.

15. Crema, 126, figure 116; P. Nicorescu, *Ephemeris Dacoromana*, I (1923), 1-56; Nash, II, 352 ff. The Tomb of the Salvii at Ferento (Ferentium, Ferentis): A. Degrassi, *Rend. Pont.*, XXXIV (1961-2), 59-77. For the date of the Barbatus sarcophagus: H. Kähler, *Rom und seine Welt*, *Erläuterungen* (Munich, 1960), 110 ff. Cf. T. Dohrn, *R.M.*, LXIX (1962), 88.

CHAPTER 6

139. 1. For the early use of marble and the aedes of Jupiter Stator built by Metellus: Velleius Paterculus, I, 11. 5; cf. Note 23 below. Round Temple: D. E. Strong and J. B. Ward-Perkins, 'The Round Temple in the Forum Boarium', *P.B.S.R.*, XXVIII (1960), 7-32; cf. now F. Rakob and W.-D. Heilmeyer, *Der Rundtempel am Tiber in Rom* (Mainz, 1973) (date about 100 B.C. and discount evidence of earlier temple). For the marble columns from Athens in the rebuilt Capitoline Temple of 69 B.C. see A. Boëthius, 'Nota sul tempio Capitolino e Vitruvio III, 3. 5', *Arctos*, N.S. V (1967), 45-9. [Challenged by F. E. Brown, who points out that the columns were brought, according to Pliny, 'Capitolinis aedibus', which cannot mean 'for *the* Capitoline Temple': *Art Bulletin*, LIV (1972), 343.]

2. For the use of tufa and travertine see Blake (1947), 29 ff.; G. Lugli, *Tecnica edilizia*, 302-26. For the use of travertine only for capitals, bases, inscriptions, etc., from about 130, see *ibid.*, 327 f., and Blake (1947), 44-8 *et passim*. For the rubble see *Cosa*, 11. The late terracotta revetments from all Central Italy are described in A. Andrén's *Architectural Terracottas* and thoroughly restudied in *Cosa*, II, 151-300.

3. For the *luxuria*: Pliny, XXXVI, 3-8; 114; Augustine, *De civitate Dei*, III, 21; H. Drerup, *Zum Ausstattungsluxus in der römischen Architektur* (1957).

140. 4. For quasi-reticulate and reticulate: Lugli, *op. cit.*, 501-5; Blake (1947), 227-75.

5. Vitruvius, II, 8. 17. Morgan's translation is unsatisfactory. Vitruvius speaks of piers of stone, a structure of burnt brick (protecting the top of the walls), and walls of concrete (*parietes caementiciae*). What Vitruvius means by *structurae testaceae* can be seen in II, 8. 18 and in the turrets of second-century villa terraces at Cosa (below, pp. 190-2), which are built of coarse rubble with interposed protecting layers of roof tiles with fringes [176]. Another instance can be found in the Late Republican tombs along the Via Appia outside Terracina: *Forma Italiae*, I, 1.1. Lugli, *Anxur-Tarracina* (Rome, 1926), Zona VI, no. 8, 12, figures 2, 3, 6.

144. 6. For the tenement house in Terracina, *ibid.*, Zona III, no. 6, figure 17. The Palatine: Boëthius, *Opus. Arch.*, I (1935), 176-8. The excavations below the Neronian portico south of the Via Sacra can be found in Lugli, *Monumenti minori del Foro Romano*, 139-64, 171. For the balcony round the Terme del Foro see A. Maiuri, *Atti del I Congresso nazionale di studi romani*, I (1929), 164.

145. 7. Stabian baths: Crema, 17, figure 15. Domical vaults: Tabularium, Crema, 17, 58. Temple of Hercules Victor at Tivoli: Crema, 57 f., figure 55. The nymphaeum at Formia: Crema, 125, figure 114.

8. See Maiuri, *N.S.* (1942), 319; *N.S.* (1941), 371–86. The position of the Temple of Apollo on the western side of the forum, and an oblique wall built along the short north side before the dominating temple was constructed, show that the place in earlier times did not have the later rectangular shape and orientation. On the history of the Pompeian forum see now Eschebach, *Die städtebauliche Entwicklung des antiken Pompeji, passim.*

9. For the hellenistic piazzas: J. B. Ward-Perkins and M. H. Ballance, 'The Caesareum at Cyrene', *P.B.S.R.*, XXVI (1958), 137–94; E. Sjöqvist, 'Kaisareion', *Opus. Rom.*, I (1954), 86 ff.; Boëthius, *The Golden House of Nero*, 68 f. The origins of the Imperial fora are discussed by E. Gjerstad, *Opus. Arch.*, III (1944), 40 ff.

146. 10. E. Dyggve, *Lindos*, III (1960), *passim*; the importance for Roman architecture especially discussed on pp. 517 ff. Martin, *L'urbanisme dans la Grèce antique* (Paris, 1956), has especially well analysed the unaxial Greek architecture, showing its striking difference in comparison with hellenistic axiality. F. Fasolo and G. Gullini have in a most convincing way defined the new character acquired by hellenistic architecture in Italy in their monumental work *Il Santuario della Fortuna Primigenia a Palestrina*. See also H. Kähler, *Das Fortunaheiligtum von Palestrina Praeneste*, and *Wesenszüge der römischen Kunst* (Saarbrücken, 1958), 17 f.

148. 11. Cosa: *Cosa*, I, 72, figure 66; L. Richardson, 'Cosa and Rome', *Archaeology*, X (1957), 49–55. Forum of Pompeii: Maiuri, *N.S.* (1941), 371 ff.; (1942), 319 f. The Temple of Hercules at Alba Fucens: F. de Visscher, J. Mertens, J. Ch. Balty, 'Le Sanctuaire d'Hercule et ses portiques à Alba Fucens', *Mon. Ant.*, XLVI (1963), 334–96. For the temple and the Hercules statue: de Visscher, *Heracles Epitrapezios* (Paris, 1962). For another interpretation of the complex see H. Lauter, 'Heiligtum oder Markt?', *Anz.* (1971), 55–62. For Brixia: M. Mirabella Roberti, 'Il Capitolium repubblicano di Brescia', *Atti del VII Congresso internazionale di archeologia classica*, II (1961), 347–73. In Flavian times a Capitolium replaced the four Late Republican temples, Crema, figures 316, 323. P. C. Sestieri, *Paestum (Itinerari)* (1953), 19–22. [The account of the Pompeian forum given in the text diverges from the excavation findings, which suggested that the tabernae remained till the time of Tiberius: *N.S.* (1941), 385.]

149. 12. For the tabernae see Vitruvius, V, 1. 2: 'round about in the colonnades put the bankers' offices; and have balconies on the upper floor properly arranged so as to be convenient; and to bring in some public revenue'. In paragraph 3 Vitruvius adds that 'the columns of the upper tier should be one-fourth smaller than those of the lower'. The wide intercolumniations no doubt required 'series of wooden beams laid upon

the columns' instead of architraves of stone, as described by Vitruvius, III, 3. 5. For Lucus Feroniae see R. Bartoccini, *Atti del VII Congresso internazionale di archeologia classica*, II (1961), 249–56; G. D. B. Jones, *P.B.S.R.*, XXX (1962), 191–5.

For the combination basilica-tabernae cf. *Opus. Arch.*, I (1935), 189–95; G. Fuchs, *R.M.*, LXIII (1956), 17 f.; and N. Sandberg, *Eranos*, XXXIV (1936), 82 ff. For the basilicas: Livy, XL, 51. 4–5; XLIV, 16.1. Cato's statement about the paving of the Forum: Pliny, XIX, 24. Fornices: Crema, 100; Platner-Ashby and Nash, *s.v.* Comitium: Cicero, *Laelius*, 25, 96; Plutarch, *C. Gracchus*, 5, 3. Caesar's Rostra: Dio Cassius, XLIII, 49. 1–2.

13. For discussion and bibliography see Crema, 61–7. Cf. now K. Ohr, *Die Basilika in Pompeji* (dissertation, Karlsruhe, 1973). Vitruvius (V, 1. 4–5) describes a basilica which is probably similar to the basilicas of the Forum Romanum in his day, and in V, 1. 6–10, a basilica which he supervised in Colonia Julia Fanestris (Fano). He further (VI, 3. 9) describes in private houses so-called Egyptian oeci with an arrangement similar to the basilicas, and mentions basilicas in VI, 5. 2.

150. 14. For Cato's Basilica Porcia see especially Livy, XXXIX, 44, 7, and Aurelius Victor, *Viri illustres*, 47, 5. The basilica, which Plautus mentions (*Curculio*, 472), may have been the oldest building below the Basilica Aemilia; see the remains on the plan of G. Carettoni, *N.S.* (1948), 111. Cf. Fuchs, *art. cit.*, 25, note 40; and G. E. Duckworth, in *Ut pictura poesis: Studia latina Petro Johanni Enk oblata* (Leiden, 1955), 58–65.

15. The basilica of Ardea is published in *Bollettino dell'Associazione internazionale di studi mediterranei*, III, 3 (August–September 1932), 3 ff.; V, 1–2 (April–July 1934), 7–21, plates II–III. Boëthius, in *Apophoreta Gotoburgensia Vilelmo Lundström oblata* (1936), 353 f. The old sacrifices: Strabo, V, 3. 5. The basilica of Ardea measures 150 by 78 feet (45.80 by 23.80 m.). For the water cistern it should be remembered that old temples in central Italy usually had a well, cistern, or tank close at hand; see *Cosa*, II, 108, note 77.

151. 16. For the public use of the basilicas in Late Republican times: E. Welin, *Studien zur Topographie des Forum Romanum (Acta Rom. Suec.*, in 8°, VI) (1953), 111 ff. The basilica of Cosa: *Cosa*, I, 75–8; F. E. Brown, *Roman Architecture*, 22 f., plates 27–8. The length of the basilica on the outside is 117 feet (35.52 m.). Brown reconstructs the basilicas of Cosa and Ardea with colonnaded fronts (*op. cit.*, plates 27 and 29).

17. To me Fuchs' identification of the column bases F 1, 3, 2 on Carrettoni's plan and the Aemilia of 179 B.C. seems convincing (*loc. cit.*, Note 12). This building was later repaired in 80–78 B.C., when, according to Pliny, XXXV, 13, the consul M. Aemilius Lepidus

put up portrait shields on it, and also in 55–54 B.C. (Cicero, *Ad Atticum*, IV, 17, 7; Plutarch, *Caesar*, 29). Until now no remains have clarified how the northern, rear side of the Basilica Aemilia was built. The coin of 59 B.C. has been interpreted in two different ways. Fuchs contends that it depicts the northern, long side and that the northern aisle of the basilica was open towards market-places behind the basilica, like a colonnaded portico; in this case, the portrait shields would have decorated the façade of this northern side of the building. I agree with other scholars, who assume that the basilica, as in the Imperial Age, had a wall outside the northern aisle, and explain the coin as representing one side of the interior of the nave with its two-storeyed aisles. They assign the shields to this interior. The wording of Pliny makes it clear that the shields belonged to the basilica and not to the portico with the tabernae towards the Forum.

152. 18. Maiuri, *Ercolano*, 284–90. For the Egyptian, Corinthian, and tetrastyle oeci, which are all related to the basilicas, see also Crema, 115 f., figures 106–8. [It is possible to argue, contrary to the statement in the text, that Vitruvius's basilica at Fanum *was* lit by clerestories above two-storeyed aisles (v. 1. 6–7).]

18a. Ohr, *op. cit.* (see Note 13).

155. 19. Tabularium: for bibliography and photographs see Nash, II, 402–8.

157. 20. See Boëthius–Ward-Perkins, 195. The standard works for the Late Republican temples are: R. Delbrück, *Hellenistiche Bauten in Latium, Das Capitolium von Signia*, and *Die drei Tempel am Forum Holitorium*; and Lucy Shoe, *Etruscan and Republican Roman Mouldings* (M.A.A.R., XXVIII) (1965); see further Lugli, I *monumenti antichi di Roma e suburbio* with Supplemento and *Itinerario di Roma antica*. For further references: Crema, 41–9.

Temple A on the Largo Argentina: G. Marchetti-Longhi, *L'area sacra del Largo Argentina (Itinerari)*, 47–55; Nash, I, 136 ff. (*s.v.* Area sacra del Largo Argentina). The temples on the Forum Holitorium: Lugli, I *monumenti antichi di Roma e suburbio*, I, 352–65, and *Itinerario di Roma antica*, 287–94.

158. 21. Andrén, *Architectural Terracottas, passim*. For stylistic analysis of the revetments see above all *Cosa*, II, 137, 165, 183, 225, and *passim*. Pedimental groups: Giglioli, CCCXVII, CCCXVIII, CCCXXI, CCCXXXV; *Cosa*, II, 312 ff. For late Greek pedimental sculpture: Phyllis Williams Lehmann, *The Pedimental Sculptures of the Hieron in Samothrace* (New York, 1962); *Samothrace*, III. *The Hieron*, I (London, 1969), 253–328.

159. 22. Cf. Boëthius, 'Of Tuscan Columns', *A.J.A.*, LXVI (1962), 249–54 (p. 252, note 22) and above, pp. 49–52. For Cosa: *Cosa*, II, 43, 102 f. The tufa columns of the Capitolium (about 150) are the earliest stone columns found at Cosa. The Doric capital of Temple

D, second phase (100–75 B.C.), *Cosa*, II, 111 f. For the temple on the Via delle Botteghe Oscure in Rome see Nash, I, 202 f., and for a possible identification F. Coarelli, *Palatino*, XII (1968), 365–73. For the revival of the so-called Aeolic capitals, once so popular in Archaic architecture, see Antonia Ciasca, *Il capitello detto eolico in Etruria* (Florence, 1962).

162. 23. Temples with two columns prostyle: above pp. 38–9; W. Johannowsky, 'Modelli di edifici da Teano', *B. d'Arte*, XLVII (1962), 63–9. For Cori: Brandizzi Vittucci, *Cora*, 77–96. For Ostia: *Scavi di Ostia*, I, 105 f. Jupiter Stator: *Forma Urbis*, plate XXIX. For literature on the temples cited see the works by Delbrück (cited above, Note 20); A. de Franciscis, 'Templum Dianae Tifatinae', *Archivio storico di Terra di Lavoro*, I (Caserta, 1956), 301–58. M. Almagro Basch, 'Las excavaciones españolas en Gabii', *Atti del VII Congresso internazionale di archeologia classica*, II (1961), 237–48. J. A. Hanson, *Roman Theater-Temples*, 29–39. For the date of the temples of Gabii, Cagliari, and the other Late Republican temples, see further Crema, 42, 49. He suggests a date at the end of the third century for Gabii and the beginning of the third century for Cagliari. Comparing the temples of Cosa, the mouldings of the podia, etc., I maintain that these dates and others more ancient which have been suggested are too early. [For a new theory about the plan of the temple of Jupiter Stator, P. Gros, 'Hermodoros et Vitruve', *Mél. Rome*, LXXXV (1973), 137–61.]

163. 24. For Temple B on the Largo Argentina: Marchetti Longhi, *L'area sacra del Largo Argentina (Itinerari)*, 55–62; Nash, I, 136, 142 f. [The temple is now convincingly recognized as that of Fortuna Huiusce Diei, erected *c.* 100 B.C.: see Coarelli, *loc. cit.*]

25. For the Capitolia see *Cosa*, II, 49 ff.; Agnes Kirsopp Lake, *M.A.A.R.*, XII (1935), 101–13; J. Johnson, *Excavations at Minturnae*, I (Philadelphia, 1935), 18–41. The Roman colony was founded in 296 as a castrum-fort (above, p. 125) with an aedes Jovis (Livy, XXXVI, 37); the forum with its Capitolium was built west of the castrum-fort in the second century (Johnson, *op. cit.*, 5). See further especially Luisa Banti, *St. Etr.*, XVII (1943), 187–224; M. Cagiano de Azevedo, *Mem. Pont.*, V (1940), 1–76; U. Bianchi, *Mem. Linc.*, ser. 8, II (1950), 349 ff.; Polacco, 80 ff.; and Crema, 37–9 (with bibliography).

164. 26. The Capitoline Temple: Gjerstad's description, *Early Rome*, III, 168–90, and the *Acta* of the Institutum Romanum Norvegiae, I (1962), 35–40, with criticism of the interpretation of Vitruvius, III, 3. 5 in my article 'Veteris Capitoli humilia tecta', *ibid.*, 27–33. Cf. above, pp. 37–8, Notes 9–10.

The text of Vitruvius, III, 3. 5 is | *baryce* | *barycephalae humiles latae*, but as Professor E. Wistrand has pointed out, *baryce* is most likely a dittography.

For Tacitus, *Historiae*, III, 71, see Wistrand, *Eranos*,
XL (1942), 169, and Boëthius, *The Golden House of
Nero*, 60-1, notes 57 and 59. The suggestion about
memorial coins representing a gable of a temple in
conventional form has been made by F. Castagnoli,
Arch. Cl., V (1953), 104-5. The temple was heightened
after the fire in A.D. 69 (Tacitus, *Historiae*, IV, 53).
[For vindication of Vitruvius's statement about the
temple of 69 B.C., cf. F. E. Brown, *Art Bulletin*, LIV
(1972), 343, and Note 1 above.]

27. A. M. Colini, 'Aedes Veiovis inter Arcem et
Capitolium', *Bull. Comm.*, LXX (1942), 1-55. Bibliography, Nash, II, 490. For Vitruvius's rather misleading remarks (IV, 8. 4) and the Imperial Age:
Crema, 47. The Pantheon of Agrippa in its original
form had the same kind of plan as the Temples of
Veiovis and Concord: Kähler, 'Das Pantheon in Rom',
in *Meilensteine der europäischen Kunst* (Munich, 1965),
47 f., 55 f.; cf. K. De Fine Licht, *The Rotunda in Rome*
(Copenhagen, 1968), 172 ff.

165. 28. For these temples see J. A. Hanson, *Roman
Theater-Temples*, 29-39. Crema, 49, suggests that the
temple of Diana Tifatina also had some similar
arrangement in front. For Morgantina see *A.J.A.*,
LXVI (1962), plate 29. 2.

29. P. Mingazzini, *N.S.* (1949), 213 ff.; *Studi Sardi*,
X-XI (1950-1), 161 ff.; Hanson, *op. cit.*, 32 f. Cf. G.
Pesce, *Sardegna punica* (Cagliari, 1961), 63-5.

169. 30. C. Carducci, *Tibur* (Istituto di Studi Romani,
1940), 64-75. Fasolo and Gullini, *Il Santuario della
Fortuna Primigenia a Palestrina*, 353 ff., 424-33.
Hanson, *op. cit.*, 31 f. See now Giuliani, *Tibur*, I, 164-
201.

170. 31. Strabo, V, 3. 11. Appian, *Bellum Civile*, I, 94,
says that Praeneste was very rich and that Sulla gave
it over to plunder. In contrast to that he mentions that
'no plunder was gained' from Norba after its destruc-
tion shortly afterwards. The only possible conclusion
seems to me to be that both the lower and the upper
sanctuaries were built on the site of older shrines as a
kind of simultaneous memorial of the victory and
sacrifice of atonement. Fasolo and Gullini in their
monumental work, cited in Note 30 above, try in a
most interesting way to prove that the upper part of
the sanctuary was built in the middle of the second
century B.C. (cf. later *Arch. Cl.*, VI (1954), 133-46). In
my opinion Lugli has entirely disproved this in *Rend.
Linc.*, ser. 8, IX (1954), 51-87, *Arch. Cl.*, VI (1954),
305-11, and *Palladio*, N.S. IV (1954), 178. See also his
Tecnica edilizia. Especially important observations
are added by Kähler, *Das Fortunaheiligtum von Palestrina Praeneste*; see also *Gnomon*, XXX (1958), 366-
83, Helga von Heintze, *Gymnasium*, LXIII (1956),
526-44, and G. Jacopi, *Il Santuario della Fortuna
Primigenia (Itinerari)* (1963), bibliography, 23 f. [A.
Degrassi, *Mem. Linc.*, ser. 8, XIV (1969-70), has now

presented strong epigraphic evidence in favour of a
second-century date for the upper sanctuary. Cf. S.
Mazzarino, *Il pensiero storico classico*, II, 2 (Bari,
1968), 318-20. Generally on the sanctuary and its
problems, G. Gullini, 'La datazione e l'inquadramento stilistico del Santuario della Fortuna Primigenia a Palestrina', in H. Temporini (ed.), *Aufstieg
und Niedergang der römischen Welt*, I, 4 (Berlin and
New York, 1973), 746-99.]

32. This is the reconstruction by Fasolo and Gullini,
op. cit., and the conclusion of their painstaking discussion (pp. 32 ff.).

173. 33. This is G. Becatti's explanation of the term,
Scavi di Ostia, IV, 254-9. Cf. *J.R.S.*, LIII (1963),
231 f. Pliny, XXXVI, 184-9; Varro, *De re rustica*, III,
1. 10: 'villam . . . pavimentis nobilibus lithostrotis
spectandam'. Other explanations, refuted by Becatti:
Marion Blake, *M.A.A.R.*, VIII (1930), 50 ff.; Maiuri,
La Villa dei Misteri, 209 ff.; Fasolo and Gullini, *op.
cit.*, 307 ff. [See now Gullini, *art. cit.*, 752 ff., arguing
convincingly that 'lithostron' is a general term for
tessera mosaic floors, especially those with all-over
representational compositions. The two Palestrina
mosaics are almost universally dated to the time of
Sulla.]

174. 34. 'locus saeptus religiose', in Cicero's words,
loc. cit. The identification with the small enclosed
shrine on the fourth terrace was first suggested by
Mingazzini, *Arch. Cl.*, VI (1954), 295-301, and later
Kähler, *op. cit.*, accepts and develops Mingazzini's
assumption. [But see Gullini, *art. cit.*, 751.]

35. In identifying the round temple with the Temple
of Fortuna I follow Kähler, *op. cit.* [But against
Kähler's restoration of the round building as a peripteral tholos visible above the semicircular portico see
Gullini, *art. cit.*, 748-50. The interpretation of the
semicircular stairs as a kind of theatre is also controversial.]

176. 36. Lugli, in *Forma Italiae*, I, I. 1, 154-78. Fasolo
and Gullini, *op. cit.*, 362 f., 415-21. They date the
great wall to the time of the war against Hannibal (pp.
326-8), and suggest that the urgent need of a defence
against Hannibal caused construction in great haste
with the new building material, concrete, of coarsest
quality. Cf. Gullini, *art. cit.*, 782-4.

37. V. Cianfarani, *Santuari nel Sannio* (Pescara,
1960), 7-16, plates 4-5. For Morgantina see *A.J.A.*,
LXVI (1962), plate 29. 2.

177. 38. Lugli, *Tecnica edilizia*, 127-31, 326, plates VI,
1; XLVIII, 3. A. Bartoli, *B. d'Arte*, XXXIV (1949),
293-306. Gullini, *Arch. Cl.*, VI (1954), 185-216. C. C.
van Essen, *Arch. Cl.*, XIII (1961), 145-51. V. Celani,
Ferentino (1965). Gullini argues for a date in the first
half of the second century: *loc. cit.*, and *art. cit.* in Note
31 above, 780-2.

39. For Bavai, Arles, Reims, Narbonne, and Aosta

see R. A. Staccioli, *Rend. Linc.*, ser. 8, IX (1954), 645 ff.; *Arch. Cl.*, VI (1954), 284 ff.; Lugli, *Atti del X Congresso di storia dell'architettura* (1959), 189–95. On cryptoporticoes in general, *Les cryptoportiques dans l'architecture romaine* (Paris, 1973).

179. 40. Porta di Casamari (S. Maria) at Ferentinum: Lugli, *Tecnica edilizia*, 326, plate LXX, 2.

41. G. Säflund, *Le mura di Roma repubblicana*, 22–6. Another arch of the same type on the Quirinal, *op. cit.*, 89–91. Lugli, *Tecnica edilizia*, plate LXVI, 1–2.

180. 42. For the walls and terrace of Alba Fucens: Mertens, 'Alba Fucens, urbanisme et centuriation', *Atti del VII Congresso Internazionale di Archeologia Classica*, II (1961), 283–93, with bibliography, and *Rend. Linc.*, ser. 8, XIII (1958), 97–9; de Visscher, 'Alba Fucens 1957–1958', *Académie Royale de Belgique, Bulletin de la Classe des Lettres*, etc., ser. 5, XLIV (1958), 512 ff., and 'Alba Fucens: a Roman Colony', *Archaeology*, XII (1959), 123–32; Mertens, 'Problèmes et méthodes de la recherche dans une ville republicaine: l'exemple d'Alba Fucens', *Studi Romagnoli*, XIII (1962), 133–41.

181. 43. Lugli, *Anxur-Tarracina (Forma Italie, I, 1. 1)* (Rome, 1926), 67–9, figures 13–14, and *Tecnica edilizia*, 147 f.

44. Fundi: Lugli, *Tecnica edilizia*, 152–4, plates VI, 3; CXXI, 1. Cora: *op. cit.*, 134–7, 425; Brandizzi Vittucci, *Cora*, 37–45.

45. Lugli, *Tecnica edilizia*, 295–9, 475–6, figure 99; cf. *Mon. Ant.*, XXXIII (1930), 114 ff.; *N.S.* (1943), 275 ff.

46. G. Calza and Becatti, *Ostia (Itinerari)* (1961), 7–9. R. Meiggs, *Roman Ostia*, 34 ff. Lugli, *Tecnica edilizia*, 419, 477, 494 f., plate CXII, 3. *Scavi di Ostia*, I, 79–88.

183. 47. For regular Late Republican towns: Castagnoli, *Ippodamo*, 81 ff., and especially Surrentum (Sorrento), 90 f.; Alife, 93. *Strigae* and *scamna* are terms used for camps and land surveying: Hyginus Gromaticus, *De munitionibus castrorum*, I, 6, 7, 14, 15.

48. *Atrium testudinatum*: Crema, 105, 108; above, p. 86. Casa dello Scheletro: Maiuri, *Ercolano*, 265 ff., and *Ercolana (Itinerari)*, 7th ed. (1970), 33 f. For the architectural term *atrium* and its different meanings see Welin, *Studien zur Topographie des Forum Romanum*, 179 ff. and *passim*.

185. 49. Crema, 105 f. Casa del Tramezzo di Legno: Maiuri, *Ercolano, i nuovi scavi*, 207 ff.

50. Ostia: *Scavi di Ostia*, I, 107 ff.; Meiggs, *Roman Ostia*, 253.

186. 51. G. Fiorelli first observed that the oldest atria at Pompeii did not have impluvia: *Gli scavi di Pompei dal 1861 al 1872* (Naples, 1873), XII, 78 ff. This has been confirmed by Maiuri's excavation in the Casa del Chirurgo, *N.S.* (1930), 391 f. See also Crema, 105, 108.

52. Saepinum: *Anz.* (1959), 232. Palm tree: Livy, XLIII, 13. 6. An excellent analysis of the history of an atrium house is given by L. Richardson, Jr, in 'The Casa dei Dioscuri and its Painters', *M.A.A.R.*, XXIII (1955), 96–110. For the investigations of the German Archaeological Institute in the early levels of the Casa del Fauno at Pompeii, see A. W. Van Buren, 'News Letter from Rome', *A.J.A.*, LXVII (1963), 402 f. Cf. recent American investigations in the Casa del Sallustio: *A.J.A.*, LXXV (1971), 206 f.

53. For atrium-houses at Pompeii the best surveys are still Overbeck and Mau, *Pompeji in seinen Gebäuden, Alterthümern und Kunstwerken*, 244–376; Mau, *Pompeji in Leben und Kunst*, 2nd ed., 250 ff. For Herculaneum, Maiuri, *Ercolano, i nuovi scavi*, 197 ff. For Ostia see Note 50 above.

187. 54. Tetrastyle atria: Casa del Fauno; Casa delle Nozze d'Argento; Casa del Labirinto. Corinthian atria: Casa di Epidio Rufo; Casa dei Dioscuri; the Fullonica VI 8, 21.

55. Meiggs, *Roman Ostia*, 252.

56. The main treatment of this subject remains P. Grimal, *Les jardins romains*. Cf. Crema, 105. The importance of the new prolonged axiality and views has been analysed with fine comprehension by H. Drerup, *R.M.*, LXVI (1959), 147 ff., and in 'Die römische Villa', *Marburger Winckelmann-Programm* (1959), 1–24.

188. 57. Boëthius, *Opus. Arch.*, I (1935), 182–9; *The Golden House of Nero*, 137, figure 78. *Forma Urbis*, plate LIII. Meiggs, *Roman Ostia*, 123 f.

58. Maiuri, *Ercolano, i nuovi scavi*, 284–90. Crema, 116, figure 106.

59. Crema, 116, figure 109. Richardson, *op. cit.*, 63–5, note 370, claims that room 48 in the Casa dei Dioscuri is the only Cyzicene oecus so far (1955) discovered in Pompeii.

60. F. Noack and K. Lehmann-Hartleben, *Baugeschichtliche Untersuchungen am Stadtrand von Pompeji* (Berlin, 1936). Crema, 112, figure 101. For the coastal villas see e.g. V. Spinazzola, *Pompei*, II (Rome, 1953), 859, figure 861.

189. 61. Casa dei Grifi: G. E. Rizzo, *Le pitture della 'Casa dei Grifi' (Monumenti della pittura antica scoperti in Italia*, 3, 1) (Rome, 1936). Crema, 21 (figures 18, 19), 117. For other views on the dating R. J. Ling, *P.B.S.R.*, XL (1972), 25, 28; H. Mielsch, *Römische Stuckreliefs (R.M. Ergänzungsheft*, XXI) (Heidelberg, 1967), 16 f. The houses on the south side of the Palatine: Carettoni, 'Una nuova casa repubblicana sul Palatino', *Rend. Pont.*, XXIX (1956–7), 51–62; 'I problemi della zona augustea del Palatino', *Rend. Pont.*, XXXIX (1966–7), 55–75. See now *N.S.* (1967), 287 ff. Suetonius, *Augustus*, 45; Dio, LVII, 11.

62. The first of the so-called Pompeian Styles was introduced to Italy from the hellenistic world in the

third century B.C. (or even earlier): cf. V. J. Bruno, 'Antecedents of the Pompeian First Style', *A.J.A.*, LXIII (1969), 305-17. For the history of the First and Second Styles see above all Beyen, *Die pompejanische Wanddekoration*, I and II, 1. For the great wall paintings see also Maiuri, *La Villa dei Misteri*; Phyllis Williams Lehmann, *Roman Wall Paintings from Boscoreale*. Odyssey landscapes: P. H. von Blancken-hagen, 'The Odyssey Frieze', *R.M.*, LXX (1963), 100-46; A. Gallina, *Le pitture con paesaggi dell'Odissea dall'Esquilino* (Rome, 1964). For the theory that early Second Style paintings reflected contemporary architecture, J. Engemann, *Architekturdarstellungen des frühen zweiten Stils* (*R.M. Ergänzungsheft*, XII) (Heidelberg, 1967). For the sectile pavements, lithostroton, and mosaics see above, Note 33.

190. 63. G. Pesce, *Il 'Palazzo delle Colonne' in Tolemaide di Cirenaica* (*Monografie di archeologia libica*, II, Rome, 1950); H. Lauter, 'Ptolemais in Libyen', *J.D.A.I.*, LXXXVI (1971), 149-78. For another view of the date see Boëthius-Ward-Perkins, 462-4. Delos: D. S. Robertson, *A Handbook of Greek and Roman Architecture*, 2nd ed. (Cambridge, 1943), 300-2; *Exploration archéologique de Délos*, VIII (Paris, 1922-4).

64. On villas see Crema, 120-2, with bibliography. Luxury villas: D. Mustilli, 'La villa pseudourbana ercolanese', *Rend. Nap.*, N.S. XXXI (1956), 77-97. Cf. Drerup, 'Die römische Villa' (see Note 56). On farms the main ancient sources are Cato, *De agricultura*, Varro, *De re rustica*, especially I, 13, Vitruvius, VI, 6, Columella, I, 6. The typical villas with courtyards are discussed by M. Rostovtzeff, *The Social and Economic History of the Roman Empire*, 2nd ed. (Oxford, 1957), 63, 551-3, 564 f.; Mau, *Pompeji in Leben und Kunst*, 2nd ed., 382-8, and others. For the simple villa see the Villa Sambuco (second century B.C.) near San Giovenale, cf. *San Giovenale*, 313-20. Two rustic villas, Posto and San Rocco, have been excavated by P. H. von Blanckenhagen in collaboration with Ward-Perkins near Francolise: *P.B.S.R.*, XXXIII (1965), 55-69. Cf. Boëthius-Ward-Perkins, figure 124. They date from the last two centuries B.C. and exhibit courtyards (in contrast to the Villa Sambuco), wells, an oil-separating cistern, slave quarters, etc., but were rebuilt in the third quarter of the first century. Compare also E. Berggren, 'A New Approach to the Closing Centuries of Etruscan History', *Arctos*, V (1967), 29-43. For the smaller farms: G. D. B. Jones, *P.B.S.R.*, XXXI (1963), 147-58.

191. 65. Lugli, *Tecnica edilizia*, 452 f., plate CXXVI, 1. D. Levi, *St. Etr.*, I (1927), 479. Crema, 121, figure 110. Castagnoli, *M.A.A.R.*, XXIV (1956), 164.

192. 66. Maiuri, *Villa dei Misteri*, 37 ff., 99 ff.

67. For the Villa dei Papyri, I am convinced by Mustilli (cited in Note 64 above), but see also Maiuri, *Ercolano* (*Itinerari*), 7th ed. (1970), 77-82. The Late

Republican villa below Hadrian's villa was discovered by Lugli, *Studi minori di topografia antica*, 384-403 (*Bull. Comm.*, LV (1927), 139-204).

194. 68. Fundamental is K. M. Swoboda, *Römische und romanische Paläste*, 2nd ed. (Vienna, 1924), 29 ff. See further L. d'Orsi, *Gli scavi di Stabia*, 2nd ed. (Stabia, 1961), plate XXXI, and Boëthius, *The Golden House of Nero*, 100 f.

195. 69. Lugli, 'Nymphaea sive musaea', *Studi minori di topografia antica*, 169-81 (*Atti del IV Congresso nazionale di studi romani*, I (1938), 155-68). For the use of the words 'nymphaeum' and 'musaeum': Mingazzini, *Arch. Cl.*, VII (1955), 156-62, uses the word 'musaeum' for natural grottoes with later extensions and 'nymphaeum' only for monumental, public fountains. Cf. Neuerburg, *L'architettura delle fontane e dei ninfei nell'Italia antica*, 27-9. Crema, 122-5. The grottoes from Locri are published by P. E. Arias, *Palladio*, V (1941), 193-206. Bovillae: Neuerburg, 159 f. Doric Nymphaeum: Neuerburg, 157 f.; cf. *Journal of the Society of Architectural Historians*, XXII (1963), 123, figures 5 and 6. Villa di S. Antonio, Tibur: Neuerburg, 249 f.; cf. Lugli, *Tecnica edilizia*, plate CXXII, 1. The nymphaea of the 'Villa di Cicerone', Neuerburg, 145-7. Subterranean halls ('aestivi recessus' or 'specus'): P. Mingazzini, *Festschrift Eugen v. Mercklin* (1964), 96 ff. (classifies as 'musaea'). One 'recessus' of this kind was perhaps originally the subterranean hall of the lower town of Ardea, though used in early medieval times as a church: A. Ferrua, *Rend. Pont.*, XXXVII (1964-5), 283-306. [For the S. Antonio nymphaeum see now, with a new reconstruction and interpretation, Giuliani, *Tibur*, I, 300 ff. Formia: C. F. Giuliani and M. Guaitoli, 'Il ninfeo minore della villa detta di Cicerone a Formia', *R.M.*, LXXIX (1972), 191-219. On the use of the term 'nymphaeum' see further S. Settis, 'Esedra e ninfeo nella terminologia architettonica del mondo romano', in H. Temporini (ed.), *Aufstieg und Niedergang der römischen Welt*, I, 4 (Berlin and New York, 1973), 661-745.]

70. *Scavi di Ostia*, I, 117 f.

70a. See Boëthius-Ward-Perkins, 298 f.

197. 71. For the baths and palaestrae: Crema, 68-75; Staccioli, *Arch. Cl.*, X (1958), 273-8; XIII (1961), 92 ff.; Rosanna Maccanico, *Arch. Cl.*, XV (1963), 32 ff.; J. Delorme, *Les palestres* (*Exploration archéologique de Délos*, XXV) (1961), 145; *Gymnasion, étude sur les monuments consacrés à l'éducation en Grèce* (*Bibliothèque des Écoles Françaises d'Athènes et de Rome*, CXCVI) (Paris, 1960). For Orata: Pliny, IX, 168 f.; Cicero as quoted by Nonius, 194; Valerius Maximus, IX, 1. Greek hypocausts: Olympia (about 100 B.C.): *IV. Bericht über die Ausgrabungen in Olympia* (Berlin, 1944), 51-6, 79 f.; Gortys (Arcadia, third century B.C.): *B.C.H.*, LXXVII (1953), 263 ff., LXXIX (1955), 331 ff. R. Ginouvès, *L'établissement thermal de Gortys*

d'Arcadie (*Études péloponnésiennes*, 11) (Paris, 1959), *passim*; Gela: D. Adamesteanu and P. Orlandini, *N.S.* (1960), 181–202 (probable hypocaust, early third century). For thermae and balneolae of Imperial Rome see the summaries of the *Curiosum Urbis Romae Regionum XIIII* (Nordh, *Libellus de regionibus urbis Romae*). For the peristyle behind Pompey's theatre, Hanson, *Roman Theater-Temples*, 53 ff. [On the development of the Stabian Baths see now the researches of H. Eschebach: *Die städtebauliche Entwicklung des antiken Pompeji*, 41–5; *R.M.*, LXXX (1973), 235–42 (argues that the frigidarium was originally a laconicum); B. Andreae and H. Kyrieleis (eds.), *Neue Forschungen in Pompeji* (Recklinghausen, 1975), 179–92.]

198. 72. General survey and bibliography: Crema, 99 f. The site of the Circus Flaminius: Chapter 5, Note 14 above. Capua: A. De Franciscis, 'Commento a due nuove "tituli magistrorum Campanorum"', in *Studi in onore di A. Calderini e R. Paribeni* (Milan, 1956), III, 353–8. Gioiosa Ionica: S. Ferri, *N.S.* (1926), 332 ff.

73. For the history of the Roman theatres and their interrelations with hellenistic and South Italian Greek theatres: Margarete Bieber, *The History of the Greek and Roman Theater*, 167 ff.; A. Neppi Modona, *Gli edifici teatrali greci e romani*, 71 ff.; Crema, 75–95. A recent contribution to our knowledge about the Etruscan players: see Chapter 3, Note 48.

202. 74. For the history of the theatre of Pompeii: Margarete Bieber, *op. cit.*, 170–3; Crema, 89 ff.; Maiuri, *N.S.* (1951), 126 ff. Scaenae frons: the terracotta relief from the Santangelo Collection in the National Museum of Naples, see Crema, 76, 87, figure 80, and Margarete Bieber, *op. cit.*, 129 ff. where also the vase paintings representing Italian popular comedies are illustrated and analysed. Siparia and aulaea: Crema, 81 f., Margarete Bieber, *op. cit.*, 179 f. Aulaea from Pergamon: Donatus, *Excerpta de comoedia*, 8. 8 (p. 30 in the Teubner edition of *Aelii Donati quod fertur Commentum Terenti*, 1). Seats: Plautus, *Amphitruo*, 65–8; *Miles gloriosus*, 81–3; *Poenulus*, 5, 17–20, 1224; *Truculentus*, 968. The summary of Livy's book XLVIII ('and for some time thereafter the people stood to see the theatrical performances') cannot be exact. The same confusion between permanent theatres and seats for the spectators by Valerius Maximus, 11, 4. 2. For the reform of 194 B.C. see Livy, XXXIV, 44. 5; 54.

75. Convincing is Hanson's discussion in *Roman Theater-Temples*, 9–26. For the theatre of 154 B.C.: Livy, *Epitome*, XLVIII; Valerius Maximus, 11, 4. 2; Velleius Paterculus, I, 15. 3; Appian, *Bellum civile*, I, 28; Augustine, *De civitate Dei*, 11, 5; Hanson, *op. cit.*, 24 f.; Margarete Bieber, *op. cit.*, 168; Crema, 85–6. Pietrabbondante: Cianfarani, *Santuari nel Sannio* (1960), plate I; *Encicl. Art. Ant.*, VI (1965), 161 f.

203. 76. Pliny's main description of the theatres of Scaurus and Curio: XXXVI, 114–17. Statues: XXXIV, 36. Marble walls: XXXVI, 50. Glass mosaics: XXXVI, 189. Columns: XXXVI, 5–7, where Pliny also expatiates on the distribution of columns, etc., to the domus. Six columns of marble from Hymettus transferred to Crassus's house from the theatre of his aedileship, Pliny, XVII, 6. The paintings referred to in Pliny, XXXV, 127, may have been exhibited in Scaurus's theatre. See also Crema, 86, and H. Drerup, *Zum Ausstattungsluxus in der römischen Architektur* (Münster, 1957), 16 f. For the crocodiles see Pliny, VIII, 96.

204. 77. Crema, 98 f. (with bibliography).

205. 78. For the Late Republican rearrangement of the theatre of Pompeii, cf. the references in Note 74 above. See also G. Traversari, *Gli spettacoli in acqua nel teatro tardo-antico* (Rome, 1960), 68 ff.; *Dioniso*, XV (1952), 308 ff.

79. For the recent discussion of the small theatre of Pompeii, see Crema, 92 f. On the wooden roofs of Rome cf. the Diribitorium, Dio, LV, 8; Pliny, XVI, 201, and XXXVI, 102. For the theatre of Alba Fucens: *Archaeology*, XII (1959), 128 f.; *Anz.* (1959), 210 f. Other theatres probably having Late Republican first periods are: Faesulae (Fiesole), Crema, 93; Ferentum, P. Romanelli, *Dioniso*, I (1929), 260 ff.; Gubbio, P. Moschella, *Dioniso*, VII (1939), 3 ff. Add Cales and Teano: W. Johannowsky, *B. d'Arte*, XLVI (1961), 263; XLVIII (1963), 152–9.

80. *Forma Urbis*, plate XXXII, pp. 103–6. See Plutarch, *Pompey*, 42, 52; Tacitus, *Ann.*, III, 72 (fire), XIV, 20; Dio, XXXIX, 38; LXII, 8; Pliny, VII, 34; Ammianus Marcellinus, XVI, 10. 14. See also Hanson, *op. cit.*, 43–55; Margarete Bieber, *op. cit.*, 181–2; Neppi Modona, *op. cit.*, 77–9; Crema, 93–5. Cf. Platner-Ashby and Nash, *s.v.*

206. 81. Plutarch, *Caesar*, 66. For the discussion about the place where Caesar was murdered (the 'curia Pompei') see Hanson, *op. cit.*, 48, note 28, and Marchetti Longhi, *Rend. Pont.*, ser. 3, XII (1936), 267–79.

82. For the entire discussion about the Temple of Venus see Hanson, *op. cit.*, 44 ff.; cf. Tertullian, *De spectaculis*, X, 5; Gellius, X, I. 6-7. For the other shrines on the top of the theatre: Suetonius, *Claudius*, 21, I, and *C.I.L.*, I², p. 324 (Fasti Amiternini and Allifani, under Aug. 12).

83. Cf. pp. 133–4 and Chapter 5, Note 11 above. See further Kähler, *Das Fortunaheiligtum von Praeneste* (quoted in Note 10), 219–28.

207. 84. For the early importation of provisions by river boats on the Tiber or by merchantmen from the Etruscan coast, Sicily, and south Italy, see Livy, IV, 52. 6 (412 B.C.); V, 13. 1 (399 B.C. - the Tiber became unnavigable, but the price of corn, owing to the supply which had been brought in before, did not go up). See also Dionysius, VII, 1. 1–3 and 2. 1 (about 490 B.C. -

a great quantity of provisions from Sicily), and XII, 1 (Maelius brought many merchantmen laden with corn from Tuscany, Cumae, and other parts of Italy by river boat via Ostia). Among other testimonies about river boats on the Tiber is Dionysius, X, 14. 1–2. For the Horrea Galbae see Platner-Ashby and Nash, s.v. The granaries of Syracuse are mentioned in Livy, XXIV, 21. 11–12. For hellenistic markets, cf. Pergamon, Magnesia, and, especially, Dura Europos, *Dura*, IX; cf. Ward-Perkins, 'The Roman West and the Parthian East', *Proc. Brit. Ac.*, 11 (1965), 186, plates LI–LII. For the caravanserais, cf. that of Kassope in Epirus, see *J.H.S.*, LXXIII (1953), 120 f. See now, on the origins of the horrea type, Rickman, *Roman Granaries and Store Buildings*, 148–55.

85. For the Magazzini Repubblicani see *Scavi di Ostia*, I, 112, 190 f. and figure 41; Meiggs, *Roman Ostia*, 130. Horrea on the Via del Sabazeo: Meiggs, *op. cit.*, 124. On transport to Rome: J. Le Gall, *Le Tibre, fleuve de Rome dans l'antiquité* (Paris, 1953), *passim*; L. Casson, 'Harbour and River Boats of Ancient Rome', *J.R.S.*, LV (1965), 31–9. [For the area east of the castrum and north of the decumanus at Ostia see now Meiggs, *Roman Ostia*, 2nd ed. (1973), 579 f.]

208. 86. See Boëthius and N. Carlgren, *Acta Archaeologica*, III (1932), 181 ff.; Gullini, *Arch. Cl.*, VI (1954), 202 ff. (on Ferentinum); and Carducci, *Tibur* (Istituto di Studi Romani, 1940), 60 f. For Caesarea Maritima see *I.L.N.* (2 November 1963), 728–31. For Tivoli see now Giuliani, *Tibur*, I, 218–22.

87. Arches also appear above colonnades in the late Republic, for instance in buildings and paintings at Pompeii: Engemann, *op. cit.* (see Note 62), 58 ff., plates 18–20, 22. For the bridges see Crema, 12; Platner-Ashby and Nash, *ss.vv.* Ponte di Nona: Blake (1947), 211 f.; cf. L. Quilici, *Collatia (Forma Italiae*, I, X) (Rome, 1974), 373–81, especially 375 and figure 809. For the construction of the bridges: T. Frank, *Roman Buildings*, 139.

88. On the Cloaca Maxima see Frank, *op. cit.*, 74, 142; Blake (1947), 38, 159–61, 198; Lugli, *Tecnica edilizia*, 257, 308, 357; Nash, s.v.; Crema, 12.

209. 89. The Roman economy in the use of more valuable material is especially clear when travertine was used. Reticulate was sometimes strengthened by alternating layers of travertine blocks, evidently making the network façade more sturdy. Burnt brick was also used in the same way in walls both of concrete and of sun-dried bricks. See pp. 190–1 and 212–13. Aqua Marcia: T. Ashby, *The Aqueducts of Ancient Rome*, 88–158; Esther Van Deman, *The Building of the Roman Aqueducts*, 67–146; Lugli, *Tecnica edilizia*, *passim*; Frank, *op. cit.*, 137–9.

90. For the tombs of the Scipiones and the Sempronii see Nash, II, 352 ff., and Crema, 126; among

other contributions see especially P. Nicorescu, 'La Tomba degli Scipioni', *Ephemeris Dacoromana*, 1 (1923), 1–56. See also p. 135 above. For the historical painting from the tomb on the Esquiline see also *Bull. Comm.* (1889), 340 ff., and F. Coarelli, 'Frammento di affresco dall'Esquilino con scena storica', in *Affreschi romani dalle raccolte dell'Antiquarium Comunale* (Rome, 1976), 13–21 (with bibliography).

211. 91. Calza, *La necropoli del porto di Roma nell' Isola Sacra* (Rome, 1940), 44, figures 9, 10. Early tomb apartments resembling the catacombs: Lucia Morpurgo, 'Un sepolcreto precristiano di Anzio', *Rend. Pont.*, ser. 3, XXII (1946–7), 155–66. Maria Floriani Squarciapino, *Scavi di Ostia*, III, 1, 63–113. Lugli, 'Scavo di un sepolcreto romano presso la basilica di S. Paolo', *N.S.* (1919), 285–354, *passim*. F. Magi, 'Ritrovamenti archeologici nell'area dell'autoparco vaticano', *Triplice omaggio a Sua Santità Pio XII*, 11 (Città del Vaticano, 1958), 92. For *bustum* and *ustrinum*: Festus, s.v. Bustum.

92. Together with these monuments, which show that the riversides could be used in the same way as the surroundings of the roads, is to be remembered that in Imperial times common burials were aligned along the Tiber. They have been found south and north of the districts around the Forum Boarium and the branches of the city walls which very likely already in the fourth century were built from the Capitoline Hill and the Aventine to the Tiber to protect the settlement on the Forum Boarium, which already belonged to Early Rome. Le Gall, *Le Tibre, fleuve de Rome dans l'antiquité*, 188 f.

212. 93. For the tombs of Bibulus and Servius Sulpicius Galba see Crema, 129 f., Nash, II, 319 f., 370, with bibliography. For tombs of Pompeii and Sicily: Crema, 128 ff.; A. de Franciscis-R. Pane, *Mausolei romani in Campania* (Naples, 1957), figure 22, and P. Marconi, *Agrigento* (Florence, 1929), 123–7. For sepulchral monuments in Asia Minor: W. B. Dinsmoor, *The Architecture of Ancient Greece* (London and New York, 1950), 255–61, 328–30.

213. 94. For the sepulchral monuments of Terracina see Lugli, *Anxur Tarracina (Forma Italiae*, I, 1. 1), 184, 186, nos. 8 and 12, figures 2, 3, 6.

95. Tholos tomb at Cumae: Crema, 17, 125, figure 14.

214. 96. See Crema, 130 f., 243, figures 118, 260, and B. Götze, *Ein römisches Rundgrab in Falerii* (Stuttgart, 1939) (denies derivation of Roman round tombs from Etruscan tumuli). Ross Holloway's idea (*A.J.A.*, LXX (1966), 171–3) that the tombs of the princes of Troy should have been the model for Roman round tombs of the Augustan Age seems narrow-viewed, even if we take into consideration the romantic revival of other famous, foreign types of tombs, such as the Pyramid of Cestius (cf. Horace, *Odes*, III, 30) and the tholos

tomb at Cumae (see above, p. 213) in Late Republican and Augustan times. Ross Holloway has obviously forgotten that Etruscan ancestry was à la mode in Augustan Rome (Horace, *Odes*, III, 29. 1; cf. I, 1. 1). He further overlooks the obvious imitations of Etruscan tumuli on the Via Appia, cited in the text. Dionysius (I, 64. 1) and Vergil (*Aen.*, XI, 849 f.) further attest that there were old mounds in Latium, which appealed to the Romans. There was, of course, no unbroken tradition whatever between the archaic Etruscan and Latin tumuli and their sophisticated return to vogue, but it seems self-evident to me that it was the ancient Etruscan and Latin monuments which inspired the late Romans and became the models for such archaistic tombs as the mounds of the Via Appia, as well as for the distinguished tumuli, which were provided with high sculptured substructures in hellenistic style, like the tombs of Augustus, of Caecilia Metella on the Via Appia, of Munatius Plancus at Gaeta, or the Torrione di Micara at Tusculum (with its burnt brick on the inside; Vitruvius, II, 8. 4). These round Roman tombs no doubt created a fashion in and around the Empire, a trend which we can follow from the mound called the 'Tombeau de la Chrétienne' in Mauretania

to Belgium. This does not, of course, prevent people from speculating widely and connecting the tomb of Augustus with the tombs of the 'epic past', that is, of his Trojan forefathers and their greatest enemy, Achilles. It seems less far-fetched, however, to bring to mind Aeneas' or Anchises' small mound near Lavinium, 'round which have been set out in regular rows trees that are well worth seeing', to quote Dionysius (*loc. cit.*). [The Tumulo dei Curiazi seems, at least in its original form, to go back to the fourth century or earlier, since the Via Appia apparently swerves to avoid it.]

97. See Strabo, V, 2. 5, and Pliny, XXXVI, 14. Blake (1947), 53; Lugli, *Tecnica edilizia*, 327–9.

215. 98. For the inner propylaea of Eleusis: Dinsmoor, *op. cit.* (Note 93), 286–7; G. E. Mylonas, *Eleusis and the Eleusinian Mysteries* (Princeton, 1961), 156–60, *et passim*. See Cagiano de Azevedo, 'I "Capitolia" dell'impero romano', *Mem. Pont.*, ser. 3, V, 1 (1940), 1–76, especially 43 ff., 67. The odeion in the Athenian Agora: H. A. Thompson and R. E. Wycherley, *The Agora of Athens* (*The Athenian Agora*, XIV) (Princeton, 1972), 111–14, and Boëthius–Ward-Perkins, 379–81.

SELECT GLOSSARY

In the glossary which follows Greek terms are given in their Latin form, where such is attested, or else in the English form in common use. The extent of anglicization, especially as regards plurals, is a matter of taste. The classical plurals are here added in brackets to those words that are most likely to be met in this form.

Fuller glossaries will be found in W. B. Dinsmoor, *The Architecture of Ancient Greece* (London and New York, 1950), and in D. S. Robertson, *A Handbook of Greek and Roman Architecture*, 2nd ed. (Cambridge, 1943). For the names of the various types of building construction used in Rome and Central Italy, see further G. Lugli, *La Tecnica edilizia romana con particolare riguardo a Roma e Lazio*, 2 vols (Rome, 1957), 48–50.

abacus. The upper member of a capital.

acropolis. Citadel (Latin, *arx*).

acroterium (-a). Ornamental finial(s) at the apex or outer angles of a pediment.

aedicula (-ae). Diminutive of *aedes*, a temple; whence a small columnar or pilastered tabernacle used ornamentally.

Aeolic capital. Palmiform capital evolved by the Greeks of north-western Asia Minor.

agger. Rampart.

agora. The Greek equivalent of the Roman forum.

ala (-ae). Outer passage(s) flanking the side walls of the cella (or cellas) of an Etruscan temple (Vitruvius, IV. 7. 2, *aliae* in MS). Wings extending to right and left at the far end of an atrium. See illustration 85.

amphitheatre. Oval building with seating facing inwards on to a central arena for gladiatorial or similar spectacles.

anta (-ae). Pilasters forming the ends of the lateral walls of a temple cella. When the façade consists of columns set between two antae the columns are said to be *in antis*.

antefix. Decorative termination of the row of covering tiles (*imbrices*) laid over the joints between two rows of flat tiles (*tegulae*) of a roof.

Apennine Culture. The principal Bronze Age culture of peninsular Italy (from about 1500 B.C.).

apodyterium (-a). The changing room of a bath-building.

Archaic. Term in conventional use to denote art and architecture from the seventh century B.C. to the Classical period.

architrave. The horizontal element, of stone or timber, spanning the interval between two columns or piers.

areostyle. With columns widely spaced, as regularly in Etruscan temples. As distinct from eustyle (mediumly spaced) and pycnostyle (closely spaced).

arx. Citadel (Greek, *acropolis*). In Rome the name of the northern part of the Capitoline Hill.

ashlar. Regular masonry of squared stones laid in horizontal courses with vertical joints.

asser (-es). Common rafter. See illustration 43.

atrium. See illustrations 85, 91. The central hall of a Roman house of Etruscan type. In the later centuries B.C. the central part of the roof sloped inwards to a central opening (*compluvium*) to channel rainwater into the basin beneath (*impluvium*). See also *cavum aedium*.

Attic base. Type of bell-shaped column-base often used in the Ionic order.

aulaeum. The curtain of a theatre, raised from a slot in front of the stage. See p. 200.

balneum, balineum, balneolum (-ae). Bath-building, public or private, of ordinary size, as distinct from the great public baths (*thermae*).

basilica. In strict architectural usage an elongated rectangular building with an internal ambulatory enclosing a taller central area, or else with a central nave and lateral aisles, in either case lit by a clerestory; often provided with one or more apses or tribunes. Originally a roofed extension of the forum for the use of the public, from the Late Republic onwards it was used for a variety of official purposes, notably judicial. During the Empire the term came to be used of any hall that was basilican in plan, irrespective of its purpose; and also of any large covered hall, irrespective of its plan.

basis villae. The platform of a Roman villa.

bucchero. Shiny black pottery used by the Etruscans.

bucranium (-a). Decorative motif in the form of an ox-skull, shown frontally.

bustum (-a). Enclosure for the performance of cremation and the conservation of ash-urns.

caldarium (-a). The hot room of a Roman bath.

cantherius. Spar under roof, rafter (see illustration 43).

capital. The upper member of a classical column or pilaster.

capitolium (-a). Temple of the Capitoline triad (Jupiter, Juno, and Minerva).

cappellaccio. The local tufa stone of the hills of Rome; used monumentally in the sixth century B.C., later only for constructions of secondary importance.

carceres. The starting gate of a hippodrome or circus.

cardo. Part of the terminology of the Roman surveyors (*agrimensores*). The planning of the countryside and, wherever possible, of the associated towns was based ideally on the intersection at right angles of two main streets, the *cardo* (north–south) and the *decumanus* (east–west). Hence, by extension, in modern usage, the two main streets of a town, whether they comply with the rules of surveying or not.

castrum. Military camp, theoretically rectangular though in practice commonly square or trapezoidal in plan. The layouts normally conform to one of two main types, one with two main streets (*via quintana* and *via principalis*) running parallel to the long sides, the other (characteristic of permanent fortresses) with two main streets (usually known as *cardo* and *decumanus*) intersecting at right angles.

cavea. The auditorium of a theatre or amphitheatre.

cavum (-a) aedium (cavaedium). The Vitruvian term for the hall in Late Republican and Early Imperial houses represented at Pompeii, Herculaneum, and Ostia. See also *atrium*. Vitruvius (VI. 3) distinguishes five main types: *tuscanicum*, which Varro ascribed to the Etruscans; *tetrastyle*, with columns at each angle of the compluvium; *Corinthian*, with intermediate columns also; *displuviatum*, with roof sloping downwards and outwards on all four sides; and *testudinatum*, without a compluvium.

cella. The central chamber or sanctuary of a temple.

cenaculum. Dining-room; later an upper storey.

centuriatio. See *limitatio*.

chalcidicum. Monumental porch constituting the façade of a building.

cippus. Small stone tomb-marker.

circus (Greek, *hippodromos*). Long narrow arena, curved at one end (exceptionally at both ends), for chariot racing.

Classical. Term in conventional use to denote the art and architecture of the fifth and fourth centuries B.C.

clerestory. Upper row of windows lighting the nave of a basilica, above the inner colonnades.

cloaca. Drain, sewer.

comitium. Enclosed place of political assembly, notably that at the north-western corner of the Forum Romanum.

compluvium. The open portion of the roof of a Roman atrium, above the impluvium.

conclave (-ia). Room, chamber.

consuetudo Italica. Vitruvius's term for Late Republican Roman usage.

corbel. Stone bracket supporting a projecting feature. Also *corbelled*, describing a system of vaulting by means of overlapping courses of stone. See illustration 95.

Corinthian order. A sub-form of the Ionic order, whose most distinctive feature is a bell-shaped capital with carved leaf-decoration. See illustrations 132 and 154.

cornice. Projecting element, designed to throw rain water from the face of a building. The upper member of a classical entablature, subdivided into bed-moulding, corona, and sima.

crypta. Subterranean gallery.

cryptoportico. Underground vaulted corridor, usually with oblique lighting through the vault.

cubiculum. Bed chamber.

cuneus (-i). Wedge-shaped block of seating, between radiating passages, in a theatre or amphitheatre.

curia. The meeting-place of the Roman Senate. Whence, the assembly place of any municipal council.

cyclopean masonry. Masonry of massive blocks. Originally that of Mycenaean Greece, but often used also of the polygonal limestone walls of Central Italy, from about 400 B.C.

dado. The lower part of a wall when treated decoratively as a continuous plinth or wainscot.

decumanus. See *cardo*.

dentillated. With dentils, i.e. decorative rectangular blocks in the bed-mould of an Ionic cornice; derived from the ends of the joists carrying a flat roof.

displuviate. See *cavum aedium*.

dolium (-a). Large earthenware jar.

domical. Dome-shaped, or (of rectangular vaults) with four surfaces converging upwards and inwards as in a dome.

domus (-us). House, the well-to-do residence of a single family as distinct both from the huts or tenements of the poor and, under the Empire, from the apartment houses (*insulae*) of middle-class usage.

Doric order. The order evolved in the Doric and western region of Greece, characterized by columns without bases and with simple cushion-capitals, and by the triglyph frieze. See illustration 152.

dromos. Horizontal or sloping passage forming the entrance to a subterranean chamber-tomb.

echinus. The convex moulding which supports the abacus of a Doric capital. The moulding, carved with egg-and-dart, placed under the cushion of an Ionic capital.

engaged. Of columns projecting from, but forming an

integral part of, the wall against which they stand. 'Semi-engaged' when only the entablature is engaged and the columns are free-standing.

entablature. The horizontal superstructure carried by a colonnade, or the equivalent superstructure over a wall.

exedra (-ae). Open bay or recess, often set behind the peristyle in a house.

fastigium. Gable, pediment.

fauces. The entrance passage of a house, leading from the street to the atrium.

fibula. Ancient type of safety pin, often ornamental.

fornix (-ces). Term used for the earliest triumphal arches.

forum (-a). An open square or piazza for public affairs. Market-place.

fossa. Ditch or trench, especially that outside a city wall.

fossa grave. Trenched inhumation burial.

frieze. The middle member of an entablature, often enriched with relief sculpture. Any horizontal band so carved.

frigidarium. The cold room of a Roman bath.

gutta (-ae). Small, peglike motif beneath the triglyphs and mutules of a Doric entablature.

gymnasium. Greek sports and cultural centre incorporating such features as a palaestra, running-track, bathrooms, changing-rooms, lecture-halls, and libraries.

Hellenistic. Belonging to the Greek culture of the period between Alexander the Great (d. 323 B.C.) and the first century B.C.

hexastyle. Consisting of six columns.

hippodrome. See *circus*.

horreum (-a). Building for storage. Granary.

hortus (-i). Garden. Park.

ianua. The outer door of a house.

imbrex. Roof-tile, semicircular or triangular in section, covering the joint between the flanges of two rows of flat roof-tiles (*tegulae*).

impasto. A type of pottery common in the early Iron Age in Etruria.

impluvium. Shallow pool in the atrium of a Roman house, to catch the rain falling through the compluvium.

impost. Upper course of wall from which arch or vault springs.

insula. Tenement or apartment house, as distinct from a private house (*domus*). Also, in conventional modern usage, a city block.

Ionic order. The order evolved in Ionian Greece,

characterized by columns with bases and volute capitals and by richly carved mouldings. See illustration 151.

laconicum (-a). The hot dry room of a Roman bath.

limitatio. The laying-out of field-boundaries (*limites*).

loculus (-i). Niche in a tomb.

maenianum. Balcony.

megalography. Form of painting with life-size or near-life-size figures.

megaron. The principal hall of a Mycenaean palace and, later, of a Greek house. More generally, a large rectangular chamber entered through a porch.

meta (-ae). Turning-point for the chariots in a Roman circus.

metope. The panel, plain or sculptured, between the triglyphs of a Doric entablature.

modillion. Horizontal corbel supporting the upper part of a Corinthian cornice.

musaeum. A grotto like a *nymphaeum*, but originally sacred to the Muses.

mutule. A projecting slab on the soffit of a Doric cornice. Also one of the horizontal beams projecting below the pediment of an Etruscan temple. See illustration 43.

naiskos. Diminutive of *naos*. A small shrine.

necropolis. Cemetery.

nuraghe (-i). Sardinian tower-like fortress (see illustration 5), used from the fifteenth century B.C. until Roman times.

nymphaeum (-a). Originally a cave with running water, dedicated to the Nymphs. Whence, any artificial fountain grotto (*musaeum, specus aestivus*) or, by extension, any public fountain.

odeum (Greek, *odeion*). Small roofed theatre, for concerts and lectures.

oecus (Greek, *oikos*). The main room of a Greek house, successor of the Mycenaean megaron. In Roman houses a banqueting room, of which Vitruvius (VI. 3. 8-10) distinguishes four kinds: Tetrastyle, Corinthian, Egyptian, and Cyzicene.

opus caementicium (structura caementicia). Roman concrete masonry of undressed stones (*caementa*) laid in a mortar of lime, sand, and, in Rome and Campania, pozzolana (q.v.).

opus incertum. The facing of irregularly shaped small blocks used with opus caementicium from the second century B.C. (cf. illustration 124) and developed from the irregular rubble facing of the previous century, as at Cosa.

opus reticulatum. The successor to opus incertum (earliest known example the Theatre of Pompey,

55 B.C.), with a facing consisting of a network of small squared blocks laid in neat diagonal lines. From the Latin *reticulum*, a fine net.

opus sectile. Paving or wall decoration made of shaped tiles of coloured marble.

opus signinum. Floor of concrete varied by irregular splinters of terracotta, stone, and marble. Used conventionally also of any Roman waterproof concrete made with crushed brick.

orchestra. Originally the circular 'dancing floor' of a Greek theatre; whence the corresponding semi-circular space in front of the stage (*proscaenium*) of a Roman theatre.

ostium. Front door.

palaestra. Exercise ground in the thermae or in a gymnasium.

parodos. Lateral entrance to the orchestra of a theatre.

pediment. The triangular gabled end of a ridged roof.

pendentive. Concave triangle of spherical section, constituting the transition from a square or polygonal building to a dome of circular plan.

peperino. Volcanic tufa stone from the Alban Hills, south-east of Rome.

peripteral. Having a continuous outer ring of columns.

peristyle. The inner, colonnaded garden court of a Pompeian (or hellenistic) house. Also used to describe the external colonnade of a peripteral building.

pisé. Stiff clay used as a building material, laid within a shuttering of boards and regularly faced with stucco.

podium (-a). Platform, used most commonly of temples or columnar façades; normally with mouldings at top and bottom.

pozzo. Cremation tomb with a vertical circular shaft.

pozzolana (Latin, *pulvis puteolanus*). The volcanic ash of Central Italy, so named from Puteoli (Pozzuoli), where its properties were first recognized; the material which gave Roman concrete its strength and hydraulic properties.

praecinctio. Horizontal passageway between the successive tiers of seats of a theatre or amphitheatre.

prodomus. See *pronaus*. Generally any sort of porch.

pronaus (Greek, *pronaos*). Porch in front of the cella of a temple.

propylaeum (-a). Entrance building(s) to the enclosure of a temple or other monumental building. Also *propylon*, strictly a simpler version of the same.

proscaenium. The stage of a theatre, in front of the stage-building (*scaena*). See p. 200.

prostyle. Having a projecting columnar façade.

pseudoperipteral. As peripteral, but with some of the columns engaged instead of free-standing.

pulpitum. The stage of a Roman theatre.

puteal. Stone well-head.

quadriportico. Enclosed courtyard with porticoes on all four sides.

quasi-reticulate (work). Type of wall-facing intermediate between opus incertum and opus reticulatum.

reticulate (work). See *opus reticulatum*.

revetment. Superficial facing (e.g. of terracotta or marble) applied to a beam or to a wall built of some other material. See illustration 43.

ridge pole. Beam along the ridge of a roof.

rostra. The speakers' tribune of the comitium of the Forum Romanum, so called because it was ornamented with the prows (*rostra*) of the ships captured at Antium in 338 B.C. By extension, any speakers' platform.

sacrarium. Chapel.

sarcophagus. Stone or terracotta coffin.

scaena (Greek, *skene*). Stage-building of a Roman theatre. The façade of it (*scaenae frons*) formed the backdrop of the stage.

scamnum (-a). Rectangular house- or barrack-block, laid out with its short side facing the main street of a town or camp. The opposite of *striga*.

scandula (-ae). Wooden roof-shingle.

semi-column. Half-column, of an engaged order or composite pier.

sima. Crowning moulding (originally the gutter) of a cornice. See illustration 43.

siparium. Minor curtain in a theatre. See p. 200.

specus. Cave. The channel of an aqueduct.

spina. The long, narrow dividing wall down the centre of a circus.

springer. Part of arch or vault where curve begins.

stadium. A running track, six hundred Greek feet long.

stillicidium. The lowest part of the eaves of a building, from which the rainwater drips.

stoa. Name given to a Greek type of building which consists basically of a colonnade, closed at the back, often with shops or offices in the back half, and sometimes two-storeyed.

striga (-ae). As *scamnum*, but with its long side parallel to the main street.

taberna (-ae). Rectangular chamber opening directly off the street and used as shop, workshop, or habitation for the lower classes.

tablinum. The central room at the far end of an atrium, originally the main bedroom; record room.

tabularium. Archive building.

tegula (-ae). Roofing tile.

temenos. Sacred enclosure or precinct.

templum (-a). Originally the place marked out by an augur for the purpose of taking auspices. Whence any consecrated place or sanctuary. Also a purlin in a wooden roof. See illustration 43.

tepidarium (-a). The warm room of a Roman bath.

Terramare. Conventional term for the culture of the Bronze Age villages of the second half of the second millennium B.C. in the south-central Po valley.

testudinate. Having a ridge roof, i.e. (with reference to the atrium) without a compluvium.

tetrastyle. With four columns, e.g. of a façade, of an aedicula, or of an atrium with columns at the four corners of the impluvium.

thermae. Large public baths, as distinct from *balnea*.

tholos (-oi). Vaulted circular tomb. Any circular building.

tignum. Wooden beam or joist.

torus. Rounded convex moulding; as (twice) in the typical Attic column base.

travertine. Silvery-grey calcareous building stone quarried near Tivoli and extensively used in Late Republican and Early Imperial Rome.

tribunal. Raised platform (or box in the theatre) for magistrates.

triclinium (-a). Originally a dining-room, so-called from the conventional arrangement of three banqueting couches (*klinai*) around three sides of a square.

triglyph. Projecting member separating the metopes of a Doric frieze and divided into three strips by two vertical grooves.

tufa (more correctly 'tuff'). The principal local building stone of Latium and Campania, a concreted volcanic dust. The many qualities include cappellaccio, peperino, and the stones of Monte Verde, Grotta Rossa, Grotta Oscura, and Gabii.

Tuscan order. The plain shafts with bases and capitals (see pp. 49–50) which are occasionally found in early Etruscan contexts (e.g. tombs of the sixth century B.C.) are evidently those included by Vitruvius in his description (I V. 7. 2 f.) of the Tuscan style; but the Etruscans seem in fact to have preferred the Aeolic and other Greek capitals. The Tuscan order as generally understood was probably created by the Etruscans in Italy. We can follow it from the sixth century B.C. to Republican and Imperial architecture.

Tuscanicae dispositiones. Vitruvius's term for the Etruscan style of temple architecture. See pp. 33–4.

tympanum. The vertical wall-face of a pediment.

ustrinum. Place for burning corpses.

velum (-a). The awning stretched above a forum, a theatre, or an amphitheatre to protect the public from the sun.

vestibulum. Vestibule; especially of the entrance from the street to the fauces of a house.

Villanovan culture. The principal Iron Age culture of central Italy.

volute. The spiral scroll of an Ionic capital.

vomitorium (-a). Entrance on to the *cavea* of a theatre or amphitheatre.

voussoir. Wedge-shaped stone forming one of the units of an arch.

BIBLIOGRAPHY

I. GENERAL WORKS

ANDERSON, W. J., and SPIERS, R. P. *Architecture of Greece and Rome*, II, *The Architecture of Ancient Rome*, revised and rewritten by T. Ashby. London, 1927.
BOËTHIUS, A. *Roman and Greek Town Architecture* (*Göteborgs Högskolas Årsskrift*, LIV). Gothenburg, 1948.
BROWN, F. E. *Roman Architecture*. New York, 1961.
COZZO, G. *Ingegneria romana*. Rome, 1928.
CREMA, L. *L'Architettura romana* (*Enciclopedia classica*, III, vol. 12, 1). Turin, 1959. Quoted as: Crema.
CREMA, L. 'L'Architettura romana nell'età della Repubblica', in H. Temporini (ed.), *Aufstieg und Niedergang der römischen Welt*, I, 4, 633-60. Berlin and New York, 1973.
DURM, J. *Die Baukunst der Etrusker. Die Baukunst der Römer* (*Handbuch der Architektur*, II, vol. 2). Stuttgart, 1905. Quoted as: Durm, *Baukunst*.
FENSTERBUSCH, C. *Vitruv zehn Bücher über Architektur*. Darmstadt, 1964.
FRANK, T. *Roman Buildings of the Republic* (*P.A.A.R.*, III). Rome, 1924.
KASCHNITZ-WEINBERG, G. VON. *Römische Kunst*, III. *Die Grundlagen der republikanischen Baukunst*. Hamburg, 1962.
MORGAN, M. H. *Vitruvius. The Ten Books on Architecture*. Cambridge (Mass.), 1914.
PATRONI, G. *Architettura preistorica generale ed italica. Architettura etrusca*. Bergamo, 1941.
POLACCO, L. *Tuscanicae dispositiones*. Padua, 1952.
PLOMMER, W. H. *Ancient and Classical Architecture*. London, 1956.
ROBERTSON, D. S. *A Handbook of Greek and Roman Architecture*. 2nd ed. Cambridge, 1943.
VITRUVIUS. *De Architectura* (ed. F. Krohn). Leipzig, 1912.

2. ROMAN TOWN PLANNING

CASTAGNOLI, F. *Ippodamo di Mileto e l'urbanistica a pianta ortogonale*. Rome, 1956. English translation: *Orthogonal Town Planning in Antiquity*. Cambridge (Mass.) and London, 1971.

GERKAN, A. VON. *Griechische Städteanlagen*, chapter IV. Berlin-Leipzig, 1924.
HAVERFIELD, F. *Ancient Town Planning*. Oxford, 1913.
LEHMANN, K. 'Städtebau Italiens und des römischen Reiches', *P.W.*, III-A, 2016ff.
WARD-PERKINS, J. B. 'Early Roman Towns in Italy', *Town Planning Review*, XXVI (1955), 127-54.
WARD-PERKINS, J. B. *Cities of Ancient Greece and Italy*. London, 1974.

3. ROME AND ITALY

BLAKE, M. *Ancient Roman Construction in Italy from the Prehistoric Period to Augustus*. Washington, 1947. Quoted as: Blake (1947).
BOËTHIUS, A. *The Golden House of Nero*. Ann Arbor, 1960.
CASTAGNOLI, F. *Topografia e urbanistica di Roma antica*. Bologna, 1969.
GJERSTAD, E. *Early Rome*, I-VI. Lund, 1953-73.
LUGLI, G. *Fontes ad topographiam veteris urbis Romae pertinentes*. Rome, 1952- (in progress).
LUGLI, G. *La Tecnica edilizia romana con particolare riguardo a Roma e Lazio*. 2 vols. Rome, 1957. Quoted as: Lugli, *Tecnica edilizia*.
LUGLI, G. *Monumenti minori del Foro Romano*. Rome, 1947.
LUGLI, G. *Studi minori di topografia antica*. Rome, 1965.
LUGLI, G. *I Monumenti antichi di Roma e suburbio*. 3 vols. Rome, 1930-8. Suppl., 1940.
LUGLI, G. *Roma antica: il centro monumentale*. Rome, 1946.
LUGLI, G. *Itinerario di Roma antica*. Milan, 1970.
NASH, E. *Pictorial Dictionary of Ancient Rome*. 2nd ed. 2 vols. London, 1968. Quoted as: Nash.
PLATNER, S. B., and ASHBY, T. *A Topographical Dictionary of Ancient Rome*. London, 1929. Quoted as: Platner-Ashby.
RICHTER, O. *Topographie der Stadt Rom* (I. von Müller (ed.), *Handbuch der klassischen Altertumswissenschaft* III, 3. 2). Munich, 1901.
SHOE, L. T. *Etruscan and Republican Roman Mouldings* (*M.A.A.R.*, XXVIII). Rome, 1965.

4. INDIVIDUAL TYPES OF BUILDING

Many of the books and articles listed deal with Republican buildings only incidentally to their Imperial development.

ÅKERSTRÖM, Å. *Studien über die etruskischen Gräber.* Lund, 1934. Quoted as: Åkerström, *Etruskische Gräber.*

ALTMANN, W. *Die italischen Rundbauten.* Berlin, 1906.

ANDRÉN, A. *Architectural Terracottas from Etrusco-Italic Temples.* Lund, 1939–40.

ANDRÉN, A. 'Origine e formazione dell'architettura templare etrusco-italica', *Rend. Pont.*, XXXII (1959–60), 21–59. Quoted as: Andrén, *Origine.*

ASHBY, T. *The Aqueducts of Ancient Rome*, ed. I. A. Richmond. Oxford, 1935.

BIEBER, M. *The History of the Greek and Roman Theater.* 2nd ed. Princeton, 1961.

BROWN, D. F. *Temples as Coin Types (American Numismatic Notes and Monographs*, XC). New York, 1940.

Cryptoportiques dans l'architecture romaine, Les (Colloques internationaux du Centre National de la Recherche Scientifique, 545). Paris, 1973.

DEMUS-QUATEMBER, M. *Etruskische Grabarchitektur: Typologie und Ursprungsfragen.* Baden-Baden, 1958.

GAZZOLA, P. *Ponti romani.* Florence, 1963.

HANSON, J. A. *Roman Theater-temples.* Princeton, 1959.

KÄHLER, H. 'Triumphbogen (Ehrenbogen)', *P.W.*, VII a, 373 ff.

KIRSOPP LAKE, A. 'The Archaeological Evidence for the "Tuscan Temple"', *M.A.A.R.*, XII (1935), 89–149.

MANSUELLI, G. A. 'El Arco honorifico en el desarrollo de la arquitectura romana', *Archivo español de arqueologia*, XXVII (1954), 93–178.

NEPPI MODONA, A. *Gli Edifici teatrali greci e romani.* Florence, 1961.

NEUERBERG, N. *L'Architettura delle fontane e dei ninfei nell'Italia antica.* Naples, 1965.

RICKMAN, G. E. *Roman Granaries and Store Buildings.* Cambridge, 1971.

SETTIS, S. '"Esedra" e "ninfeo" nella terminologia architettonica del mondo romano', in H. Temporini (ed.), *Aufstieg und Niedergang der römischen Welt*, I:4, 661–745. Berlin and New York, 1973.

SWOBODA, K. M. *Römische und romanische Paläste.* Vienna, 1924.

VAN DEMAN, E. B. *The Building of the Roman Aqueducts.* Washington, 1934.

See also the articles in *Encicl. Art. Ant.* under the following headings: 'Arcus', 'Anfiteatro', 'Basilica', 'Circo e Ippodromo', 'Magazzino (horreum)', 'Monumento funerario', 'Palestra', 'Teatro e Odeon', 'Terme'.

CHAPTERS 1–2

BARFIELD, L. *Northern Italy (Ancient Peoples and Places).* London, 1971.

BERNABÒ BREA, L. *Sicily before the Greeks (Ancient Peoples and Places).* London, 1957.

Civiltà del ferro (Studi pubblicati nella ricorrenza centenaria della scoperta di Villanova). Bologna, 1960.

Civiltà del Lazio primitivo (ed. G. Colonna). Palazzo delle Esposizioni. Rome, 1976.

DUHN, F. VON. *Italische Gräberkunde* (umgearbeitet und ergänzt von F. Messerschmidt), I–II. Heidelberg, 1924–39.

EVANS, J. D. *Malta (Ancient Peoples and Places).* London, 1959.

EVANS, J. D. *The Prehistoric Antiquities of the Maltese Islands.* London, 1971.

FURUMARK, A. *Det äldsta Italien.* Uppsala, 1947.

GIEROW, P. G. *The Iron Age Culture of Latium*, I–II. Lund, 1964–6.

GUIDO, M. *Sardinia (Ancient Peoples and Places).* London, 1963.

HAWKES, C. F. C. *The Prehistoric Foundations of Europe to the Mycenaean Age.* London, 1940.

HENCKEN, H. *Tarquinia, Villanovans and Early Etruscans.* Cambridge (Mass.), 1968.

LAVIOSA-ZAMBOTTI, P. *Il Mediterraneo, l'Europa, e l'Italia durante la preistoria.* Turin, 1954.

LILLIU, G. *La Civiltà dei sardi dal neolitico all'età dei nuraghi.* 2nd ed. Turin, 1967.

MANSUELLI, G. A., and SCARANI, R. *L'Emilia prima dei Romani.* Milan, 1961.

MONTELIUS, O. *La Civilisation primitive en Italie.* 2 vols. Stockholm, 1895–1910.

ÖSTENBERG, C. E. *Luni sul Mignone e problemi della preistoria d'Italia.* Lund, 1967.

PALLOTTINO, M. 'Le Origini storiche dei popoli italici', in *Relazioni del X Congresso Internazionale di Scienze Storiche. Storia dell' antichità*, II. Florence, 1955.

PEET, T. E. *The Stone and Bronze Ages in Italy and Sicily.* Oxford, 1909.

PERONI, R. *Archeologia della Puglia preistorica.* Rome, 1967.

PERONI, R. *L'Età del bronzo nella penisola italiana*, I: *l'antica età del bronzo.* Florence, 1971.

Popoli e civiltà dell'Italia antica, I–III. Rome, 1974. (I, 2: A. M. Radmilli, *Dal paleolitico all'età del bronzo*; II, I: B. d'Agostino, *La Civiltà del ferro nell'Italia meridionale*; II, 4: G. Colonna, *Preistoria di Roma e del Lazio*; III, 2: E. Contu, *La Sardegna dell'età nuragica*).

PUGLISI, S. M. *La Civiltà appenninica: origine delle comunità pastorali in Italia*. Florence, 1959.

RADMILLI, A. M. *La Preistoria d'Italia alla luce delle ultime scoperte*. Florence, 1963.

RANDALL-MACIVER, D. *Villanovans and Early Etruscans*. Oxford, 1924.

RANDALL-MACIVER, D. *The Iron Age in Italy*. Oxford, 1927.

SÄFLUND, G. *Le Terremare delle province di Modena, Reggio Emilia, Parma, Piacenza*. Lund, 1939.

TRUMP, D. *Central and Southern Italy before Rome (Ancient Peoples and Places)*. London, 1966.

CHAPTER 3

BANTI, L. *Il Mondo degli etruschi*. Rome, 1960. English translation: *The Etruscan Cities and their Culture*. London, 1973.

BIANCHI BANDINELLI, R. *Sovana*. Florence, 1929.

BLOCH, R. *Etruscan Art*. London, 1959.

BLOCH, R. *The Etruscans (Ancient Peoples and Places)*. London, 1958.

'Caere: scavi di R. Mengarelli', *Mon. Ant.*, XLII (1955).

CIASCA, A. *Il Capitello detto eolico in Etruria*. Florence, 1962.

COARELLI, F. (ed.) *Le Città etrusche*. Milan, 1973. English translation: *Etruscan Cities*. London, 1975.

COLONNA DI PAOLO, E., and COLONNA, G. *Castel d'Asso*. Rome, 1970.

DENNIS, G. *The Cities and Cemeteries of Etruria*. 3rd ed. London, 1883.

DUCATI, P. *Storia dell'arte etrusca*. Florence, 1927. Quoted as: Ducati.

Etruscan Culture. Land and People (Archaeological research and studies conducted in San Giovenale and its environs by members of the Swedish Institute in Rome). New York and Malmö, 1962. Quoted as: *San Giovenale*.

FROVA, A. *L'Arte etrusca*. Milan, 1957.

GIGLIOLI, G. Q. *L'Arte etrusca*. Milan, 1935. Quoted as: Giglioli.

HEURGON, J. *La Vie quotidienne chez les étrusques*. Paris, 1961. English translation: *Daily Life of the Etruscans*. London, 1964.

MANSUELLI, G. A. *Etruria and Early Rome*. London, 1966.

MORETTI, M. *Museo Nazionale di Villa Giulia*. Rome, 1962.

MORETTI, M. *Nuovi monumenti della pittura etrusca*. Milan, 1966.

MORETTI, M., and MAETZKE, G. *The Art of the Etruscans*. London, 1970.

NOGARA, B. *Gli Etruschi e la loro civiltà*. Milan, 1933.

ÖSTENBERG, C. E. *Case etrusche di Acquarossa*. Rome, 1975.

PALLOTTINO, M. *Etruscan Painting*. Geneva, 1952.

PALLOTTINO, M. *Civiltà artistica etrusco-italica*. Florence, 1971.

PALLOTTINO, M. *Etruscologia*. 6th ed. Milan, 1973. English translation (revised and enlarged): *The Etruscans*. 2nd ed. London, 1975.

PARETI, L. *La Tomba Regolini-Galassi del Museo Gregoriano Etrusco*. Città del Vaticano, 1947.

POULSEN, F. *Etruscan Tomb-Paintings*. Oxford, 1922.

'Pyrgi: scavi del santuario etrusco (1959–67)', *N.S.* (1970), Supplement II.

RICHARDSON, E. H. *The Etruscans: their Art and Civilization*. Chicago and London, 1964.

RICHTER, G. M. A. *Ancient Italy. A Study of the Interrelations of its Peoples as shown in their Arts*. Ann Arbor, 1955.

RIIS, P. J. *An Introduction to Etruscan Art*. Copenhagen, 1953.

San Giovenale. See *Etruscan Culture. Land and People*.

San Giovenale: Results of Excavations (conducted by the Swedish Institute of Classical Studies at Rome and the Soprintendenza alle Antichità dell'Etruria Meridionale), I. (*Acta Rom. Suec.*, XXVI, I). Lund and Stockholm, 1969–72.

SCULLARD, H. H. *The Etruscan Cities and Rome*. London, 1967.

STACCIOLI, R. A. *Modelli di edifici etrusco-italici, I: modelli votivi*. Florence, 1968.

Studi sulla città antica (Atti del Convegno sulla Città Etrusca e Italica Preromana). Bologna, 1970.

THULIN, C. O. *Die Ritualbücher und zur Geschichte und Organisation der Haruspices (Die etruskische Disciplin, III) (Göteborgs Högskolas Årsskrift, XV)*. 1909.

VAN BUREN, E. D. *Figurative Terracotta Revetments in Etruria and Latium in the VI and V Centuries B.C.* London, 1921.

CHAPTERS 4–5

BLOCH, R. *The Origins of Rome (Ancient Peoples and Places)*. London, 1960.

BLOCH, R. *Tite-Live et les premiers siècles de Rome (Collection d'études anciennes)*. Paris, 1965.

BROWN, F. E. *Cosa I, History and Topography (M.A.A.R., XX)*. Rome, 1951.

BROWN, F. E., RICHARDSON, E. H., and RICHARDSON, L., JR. *Cosa II, The Temples of the Arx (M.A.A.R., XXVI)*. Rome, 1960.

Cosa. See Brown, F. E., Richardson, E. H., and Richardson, L., Jr.

HANELL, K. *Das altrömische eponyme Amt* (*Acta Rom. Suec.*, in 8°, 11). 1946.

MEIGGS, R. *Roman Ostia.* Oxford, 1960. 2nd ed., 1973.

RYBERG, I. S. *An Archaeological Record of Rome from the Seventh to the Second Century B.C.* Philadelphia, 1940.

SÄFLUND, G. *Le Mura di Roma repubblicana* (*Acta Rom. Suec.*, in 4°, 1). 1932.

Scavi di Ostia. See Chapter 6.

WELIN, E. *Studien zur Topographie des Forum Romanum* (*Acta Rom. Suec.*, in 8°, VI). 1953.

CHAPTER 6

BEYEN, H. G. *Pompejanische Wanddekoration vom zweiten bis zum vierten Stil*, I, 11.1. The Hague, 1938 and 1960.

BOËTHIUS, A. 'Roman Architecture from its Classicistic to its Late Imperial Phase', *Acta Universitatis Gotoburgensis*, XLVII (1941).

BOËTHIUS, A. 'Vitruvius and the Roman Architecture of his Age', *Dragma Martino P. Nilsson dedicatum* (*Acta Rom. Suec.*, in 8°, I (1939), 114–43).

BRANDIZZI VITTUCCI, P. *Cora* (*Forma Italiae*, I, V). Rome, 1968.

DELBRÜCK, R. *Das Capitolium von Signia.* Rome, 1903.

DELBRÜCK, R. *Die drei Tempel am Forum Holitorium.* Rome, 1903.

DELBRÜCK, R. *Hellenistische Bauten in Latium*, I–II. Strassburg, 1907–12.

ESCHEBACH, H. *Die städtebauliche Entwicklung des antiken Pompeji* (*R.M. Ergänzungsheft*, XVII). Heidelberg, 1970.

FASOLO, F., and GULLINI, G. *Il Santuario della Fortuna Primigenia a Palestrina.* Rome, 1953.

GIULIANI, C. F. *Tibur*, I (*Forma Italiae*, I, VII). Rome, 1970.

GRIMAL, P. *Les Jardins romains à la fin de la république et aux deux premiers siècles de l'empire* (*Bibliothèque des Écoles Françaises d'Athènes et de Rome*, CLV). Paris, 1943.

GULLINI, G. 'La Datazione e l'inquadramento stilistico del Santuario della Fortuna Primigenia a Palestrina', in H. Temporini (ed.), *Aufstieg und Niedergang der römischen Welt*, I: 4, 746–99. Berlin and New York, 1973.

KÄHLER, H. *Das Fortunaheiligtum von Palestrina Praeneste* (*Annales Universitatis Saraviensis, Philosophie-Lettres*, VII, 3/4, pp. 189–240). Saarbrücken, 1958.

LUGLI, G. *Ager Pomptinus*, I. *Anxur-Tarracina* (*Forma Italiae*, I, I). Rome, 1926.

MAIURI, A. *Alla ricerca di Pompei preromana.* Naples, 1973.

MAIURI, A. *Ercolano. I nuovi scavi (1927–1958).* Rome, 1958.

MAIURI, A. *La Villa dei Misteri.* Rome, 1931.

MAU, A. *Pompeji in Leben und Kunst.* 2nd ed. Leipzig, 1908.

OHR, K. *Die Basilika in Pompeji.* Dissertation, Karlsruhe, 1973.

OVERBECK, J., and MAU, A. *Pompeji in seinen Gebäuden, Alterthümern und Kunstwerken.* 4th ed. Leipzig, 1884.

Scavi di Ostia. I. G. Calza and G. Becatti, *Topografia generale.* Rome, 1953. III. 1. Maria Floriani Squarciapino and others, *Le Necropoli.* Rome, 1958. IV. G. Becatti, *Mosaici e pavimenti marmorei.* Rome, 1961.

TAMM, B. *Auditorium and Palatium.* Stockholm, 1963.

LIST OF ILLUSTRATIONS

Where not otherwise indicated, copyright in photographs belongs to the museum in which objects are located, by whose courtesy they are reproduced.

The line drawings in the text were executed by Sheila Gibson and the map was drawn by Donald Bell-Scott.

INDEX

References to the notes are given to the page on which the note occurs, followed by the number of the chapter and the number of the note; thus, $240(6)^{96}$ indicates page 240, chapter 6, note 96. Notes are indexed only when they contain information other than bibliographical, to which there is no obvious reference from the text. Classical authors are indexed only if they are referred to in the text.

THE PELICAN HISTORY OF ART

COMPLETE LIST OF TITLES

* Also published in an integrated edition.
† Published only in an integrated edition.
‡ Not yet published.

ARCHITECTURE IN BRITAIN: 1530–1830* *John Summerson, 6th ed., 1977*

SCULPTURE IN BRITAIN: 1530–1830 *Margaret Whinney, 1st ed., 1964*

PAINTING IN BRITAIN: 1530–1790* *Ellis Waterhouse, 4th ed., 1978*

PAINTING IN BRITAIN: 1770–1890‡ *Michael Kitson and R. Ormond*

ARCHITECTURE: NINETEENTH AND TWENTIETH CENTURIES* *Henry-Russell Hitchcock, 4th ed., 1977*

PAINTING AND SCULPTURE IN EUROPE: 1780–1880* *Fritz Novotny, 3rd ed., 1978*

PAINTING AND SCULPTURE IN EUROPE: 1880–1940* *George Heard Hamilton, 2nd ed., 1972, reprinted 1978*

AMERICAN ART *John Wilmerding, 1st ed., 1976*

* Also published in an integrated edition.
‡ Not yet published.

THE ART AND ARCHITECTURE OF ANCIENT AMERICA *George Kubler, 2nd ed., 1975*

THE ART AND ARCHITECTURE OF RUSSIA *George Heard Hamilton, 2nd ed., 1975*

THE ART AND ARCHITECTURE OF ANCIENT EGYPT *W. Stevenson Smith, 2nd ed., 1965*

THE ART AND ARCHITECTURE OF INDIA: HINDU, BUDDHIST, JAIN* *Benjamin Rowland, 4th ed., 1977*

THE ART AND ARCHITECTURE OF ISLAM‡ *Richard Ettinghausen and Oleg Grabar*

THE ART AND ARCHITECTURE OF THE ANCIENT ORIENT* *Henri Frankfort, 4th ed., 1970, reprinted 1977*

THE ART AND ARCHITECTURE OF JAPAN* *Robert Treat Paine and Alexander Soper, 2nd ed., 1975*

THE ART AND ARCHITECTURE OF CHINA* *Laurence Sickman and Alexander Soper, 3rd ed., 1971*

TRIBAL ART‡ *Roy Sieber, Jean Guiart, Frederick Dockstader, and Solange Thierry*